The 70s Music Compendium

By Dave Kinzer

The 70s Music Compendium

Copyright 2019 Dave Kinzer

ISBN-13: 9781690045007

First Edition

To contact the author, email him at davekinzerbooks@gmail.com and visit his website: www.davekinzer.com.

INTRODUCTION

After I finished my first two compendiums (the 80s and 60s), I knew the 70s had to be next. Unfortunately, I was dreading the project. There were 5,344 songs that made the Billboard Hot 100 chart, and in my mind, I imagined that approximately 5,000 of them were lame. I just wasn't looking forward to listening to hundreds of light rock and easy listening songs.

I'm much more a classic rock guy. And somehow I guess I forgot just how many terrific classic rock songs there are from that era. It's hard to go wrong with Led Zeppelin, Heart, The Who, Queen, The Eagles, Boston, etc. The pop songs weren't so bad either. John Denver, Stevie Wonder, The Jackson 5, Elton John, Gilbert O'Sullivan, and of course, ABBA… tons of great music.

And what about Disco? The best of the disco hits have definitely stood the test of time. The Bee Gees, Donna Summer, Gloria Gaynor, Kool & The Gang, Earth, Wind, and Fire… good stuff.

The cool thing about the 1970s music scene, is that it was incredibly diverse. Don't like disco? That's fine, check out the R&B songs. R&B not your thing? No problem, take a listen to the pop songs. If you don't like 70s pop, you've still got classic rock, country-pop crossovers, instrumental hits, 50s and 60s remakes, etc. And light rock… I guess.

Still can't find anything you like? Huh. You might be reading the wrong book.

But for the rest of you… take a look, take a listen. I hope you enjoy this compendium. Thanks for reading!

Dave Kinzer

P.S. Drop me a line if you have a question or comment at davekinzerbooks@gmail.com. Check out my website at www.davekinzer.com.

A word about spelling…

If you're like me, you hate having to put up with spelling mistakes in newspapers, magazines, and books. How hard can it be to use spell-check, right? Well, for a book like this, it's tedious enough making sure I spelled names like Lynyrd Skynyrd, Linda Ronstadt, Engelbert Humperdinck, and The Rubinoos correctly. Then you throw in artists like Ray Charles' backup group, "The Raeletts", who sometimes spelled it as "The Raelets", and at other times, "The Raelettes". So which is it? And why did they think that adding and subtracting an "e" or a "t" would matter? Dionne Warwick is another artist who sometimes added an "e" to her name to make it "Warwicke".

Then you take a look at certain songs that were spelled a little…creatively. "Welfare Cadilac", "Parrty", "Amerikan Music", "Nutrocker", "Up in Heah", and "Stillsane" are all spelled correctly. Or rather, they are spelled incorrectly, but that is how the artist(s) wanted them spelled.

And trust me, there are many more examples of strange spellings of both artists and songs.

So if you see a musician or song title spelled incorrectly, before you disparage my name or this book in an online review, check to see if it really *is* spelled incorrectly. Maybe it's supposed to be spelled wrong. Which would mean that I spelled it right by spelling it wrong. Errr… you know what I mean.

One more thing...

For the purposes of this book, a song is only considered to have been a "hit" if it peaked on Billboard's Hot 100 chart between 1970-1979. If a song didn't appear on the Hot 100, then it won't be included in any list, no matter how great that song is. What if a song debuted in December of 1969, but was also popular in 1970? I always look at what year the song hit its peak position. So a song that peaked on the charts in December of 1969 but hung around on the charts into January of 1970 will not appear in this book. Likewise for the end of the decade: a song that peaks on the Hot 100 in December of 1979 will appear in this book, even if it remained popular well into 1980.

TABLE OF CONTENTS	PAGE

GENRES

LIVE SONGS

YEAR	SONG	ARTIST	HOT 100
1970	Get Ready	Rare Earth	#4
1970	The Letter	Joe Cocker w/Leon Russell	#7
1970	The Wonder of You	Elvis Presley	#9
1970	Cry Me a River	Joe Cocker	#11
1970	Summertime Blues	The Who	#27
1970	Make It Easy on Yourself	Dionne Warwick	#37
1970	Sunday Morning Coming Down	Johnny Cash	#46
1970	Black Hands White Cotton	The Caboose	#79
1970	Compared to What	Les McCann & Eddie Harris	#85
1970	Country Preacher	Cannonball Adderley	#86
1971	Never My Love	The 5th Dimension	#12
1971	Mean Mistreater	Grand Funk Railroad	#47
1971	Gimme Some Lovin'-Pt. 1	Traffic	#68
1971	C'mon	Poco	#69
1971	I Don't Need No Doctor	Humble Pie	#73
1971	Hill Where the Lord Hides	Chuck Mangione	#76
1971	Jumpin' Jack Flash	Johnny Winter	#89
1972	My Ding-A-Ling	Chuck Berry	#1
1972	Conquistador	Procol Harum	#16
1972	Don't Do It	The Band	#34
1972	Together Let's Find Love	The 5th Dimension	#37
1972	Sweet Inspiration/Where You Lead	Barbra Streisand	#37
1972	For Emily, Whenever I May Find Her	Simon & Garfunkel	#53
1972	What'd I Say	Rare Earth	#61
1972	An American Trilogy	Elvis Presley	#66
1972	Nutrocker	Emerson, Lake & Palmer	#70
1972	I Can't Turn You Loose	Edgar Winter's White Trash	#81
1972	Wholy Holy	Aretha Franklin	#81
1972	Evil Ways	Carlos Santana & Buddy Miles	#84
1972	One Way Out	Allman Brothers Band	#86
1972	Down on Me	Janis Joplin	#91
1972	Sing a Song/Make Your Own Kind of Music	Barbra Streisand	#94
1972	Runnin' Back to Saskatoon	The Guess Who	#96
1973	Steamroller Blues	Elvis Presley	#17

LIVE SONGS (cont'd)

1973	Reelin' & Rockin'	Chuck Berry	#27
1973	"Cherry Cherry" from Hot August Night	Neil Diamond	#31
1973	Oh La De Da	The Staple Singers	#33
1973	Give Your Baby a Standing Ovation	The Dells	#34
1973	"Having a Party" Medley	The Ovations	#56
1973	Everybody's Had the Blues	Merle Haggard	#62
1973	What About Me	Anne Murray	#64
1973	Friend of Mine	Bill Withers	#80
1973	Didn't We	Barbra Streisand	#82
1973	Queen of the Roller Derby	Leon Russell	#89
1974	Bennie and the Jets	Elton John	#1
1974	Give It to the People	The Righteous Brothers	#20
1974	Distant Lover	Marvin Gaye	#28
1974	Ballero	War	#33
1974	Daddy What If	Bobby Bare	#41
1974	Most Likely You Go Your Way (And I'll Go Mine)	Bob Dylan/The Band	#66
1974	Scratch	The Crusaders	#81
1975	Thank God I'm a Country Boy	John Denver	#1
1975	The Way We Were/Try to Remember	Gladys Knight & The Pips	#11
1975	Sweet Surrender	John Denver	#13
1975	I'll Play for You	Seals & Crofts	#18
1975	Big Yellow Taxi	Joni Mitchell	#24
1975	Me and Mrs. Jones	Ron Banks/Dramatics	#47
1975	Sunshine Part II	O'Jays	#48
1975	The Biggest Parakeets in Town	Jud Strunk	#50
1975	Wooden Heart	Bobby Vinton	#58
1976	Show Me the Way	Peter Frampton	#6
1976	Junk Food Junkie	Larry Groce	#9
1976	Do You Feel Like We Do	Peter Frampton	#10
1976	Baby, I Love Your Way	Peter Frampton	#12
1976	Rock and Roll All Nite	Kiss	#12
1976	Good Hearted Woman	Waylon Jennings & Willie Nelson	#25
1976	Brand New Love Affair	Jigsaw	#66
1976	Nutbush City Limits	Bob Seger	#69
1977	My Way	Elvis Presley	#22
1977	Daybreak	Barry Manilow	#23
1977	Edge of the Universe	Bee Gees	#26
1977	I Just Want to Make Love to You	Foghat	#33
1977	Free Bird	Lynyrd Skynyrd	#38
1977	Watch Closely Now	Kris Kristofferson	#52
1977	Grandmother's Song	Steve Martin	#72

	LIVE SONGS (cont'd)		
1977	Fly By Night/In the Mood	Rush	#88
1977	Ridin' the Storm Out	REO Speedwagon	#94
1978	On Broadway	George Benson	#7
1978	Stay	Jackson Browne	#20
1978	Shout It Out Loud	Kiss	#54
1978	Yank Me, Crank Me	Ted Nugent	#58
1979	I Want You to Want Me	Cheap Trick	#7
1979	Soul Man	Blues Brothers	#14
1979	Ain't That a Shame	Cheap Trick	#35
1979	Rubber Biscuit	Blues Brothers	#37
1979	Boom Boom (Out Go the Lights)	Pat Travers	#56
1979	Lonely Wind	Kansas	#60
1979	Cruel Shoes	Steve Martin	#91

NOVELTY SONGS

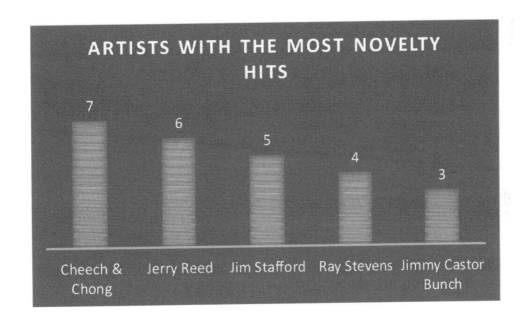

YEAR	SONG	ARTIST	HOT 100
1970	Gimme Dat Ding	The Pipkins	#9
1970	Rubber Duckie	Ernie (Jim Henson)	#16
1970	Tennessee Bird Walk	Jack Blanchard & Misty Morgan	#23
1970	My Wife, the Dancer	Eddie & Dutch	#52
1970	Welfare Cadilac	Guy Drake	#63
1970	Humphrey the Camel	Jack Blanchard & Misty Morgan	#78
1970	Thank God and Greyhound	Roy Clark	#90

NOVELTY SONGS (cont'd)

1970	Monster Mash	Bobby Pickett	#91
1971	Amos Moses	Jerry Reed	#8
1971	When You're Hot, You're Hot	Jerry Reed	#9
1971	Chick-A-Boom (Don't Ya Jes' Love It)	Daddy Dewdrop	#9
1971	Saturday Morning Confusion	Bobby Russell	#28
1971	Bridget the Midget (The Queen of the Blues)	Ray Stevens	#50
1971	The Court Room	Clarence Carter	#61
1971	Do You Know What Time It Is?	P-Nut Gallery	#62
1972	My Ding-A-Ling	Chuck Berry	#1
1972	Troglodyte (Cave Man)	Jimmy Castor Bunch	#6
1972	Coconut	Nilsson	#8
1972	Convention '72	The Delegates	#8
1972	Hot Rod Lincoln	Commander Cody	#9
1972	Chantilly Lace	Jerry Lee Lewis	#43
1972	Those Were the Days	Carroll O'Connor & Jean Stapleton	#43
1972	In Heaven There Is No Beer	Clean Living	#49
1972	Alabama Wild Man	Jerry Reed	#62
1972	Another Puff	Jerry Reed	#65
1972	Amerikan Music	Steve Alaimo	#79
1972	Deteriorata	National Lampoon	#91
1972	Buzzy Brown	Tim Davis	#91
1973	The Cover of "Rolling Stone"	Dr. Hook	#6
1973	Uneasy Rider	Charlie Daniels	#9
1973	Funky Worm	Ohio Players	#15
1973	Basketball Jones featuring Tyrone Shoelaces	Cheech & Chong	#15
1973	Dead Skunk	Loudon Wainwright III	#16
1973	Super Fly Meets Shaft	John & Ernest	#31
1973	Watergate	Dickie Goodman	#42
1973	Lord, Mr. Ford	Jerry Reed	#68
1973	Roland the Roadie and Gertrude the Groupie	Dr. Hook	#83
1973	They're Coming to Take Me Away, Ha-Haa!	Napoleon XIV	#87
1973	Dueling Tubas	Martin Mull	#92
1973	Smoke! Smoke! Smoke! (That Cigarette)	Commander Cody	#94
1973	The Red Back Spider	Brownsville Station	#96
1974	The Streak	Ray Stevens	#1
1974	Wildwood Weed	Jim Stafford	#7
1974	Earache My Eye	Cheech & Chong (Featuring Alice Bowie)	#9
1974	My Girl Bill	Jim Stafford	#12
1974	Sister Mary Elephant (Shudd-Up!)	Cheech & Chong	#24
1974	Daddy What If	Bobby Bare	#41
1974	Old Home Filler-Up An' Keep On-A-Truckin' Café	C.W. McCall	#54

NOVELTY SONGS (cont'd)

1974	Black Lassie (Featuring Johnny Stash)	Cheech & Chong	#55
1974	Evil Boll-Weevil	Grand Canyon	#72
1974	Moonlight Special	Ray Stevens	#73
1974	Makin' the Best of a Bad Situation	Dick Feller	#85
1974	Don't Eat the Yellow Snow	Frank Zappa	#86
1974	The Crude Oil Blues	Jerry Reed	#91
1975	Mr. Jaws	Dickie Goodman	#4
1975	The Bertha Butt Boogie (Part 1)	Jimmy Castor Bunch	#16
1975	Black Superman – "Muhammad Ali"	Johnny Wakelin	#21
1975	Your Bulldog Drinks Champagne	Jim Stafford	#24
1975	Shaving Cream	Benny Bell	#30
1975	I Got Stoned and I Missed It	Jim Stafford	#37
1975	Wolf Creek Pass	B.T. Express	#40
1975	(How I Spent My Summer Vacation) Or A Day at the Beach with Pedro & Man – Parts I & II	Cheech & Chong	#54
1975	Hoppy, Gene and Me	Roy Rogers	#65
1975	King Kong – Pt. 1	Jimmy Castor Bunch	#69
1975	The Funky Gibbon	The Goodies	#79
1975	The Millionaire	Dr. Hook	#95
1976	Disco Duck (Part 1)	Rick Dees	#1
1976	Convoy	C.W. McCall	#1
1976	Junk Food Junkie	Larry Groce	#9
1976	The White Knight	Cledus Maggard	#19
1976	One Piece at a Time	Johnny Cash	#29
1976	Hit the Road	Stampeders	#40
1976	Framed	Cheech & Chong	#41
1976	Yes, Yes, Yes	Bill Cosby	#46
1976	Hey Shirley (This Is Squirrely)	Shirley & Squirrely	#48
1976	Bigfoot	Bro Smith	#57
1976	Eh! Cumpari	Gaylord & Holiday	#72
1976	Kentucky Moonrunner	Cledus Maggard	#85
1976	The Fonz Song	The Heyettes	#91
1977	Telephone Man	Meri Wilson	#18
1977	In the Mood	Henhouse Five Plus Too (Ray Stevens)	#40
1977	Dis-Gorilla (Part 1)	Rick Dees	#56
1977	The Martian Boogie	Brownsville Station	#59
1977	C.B. Savage	Rod Hart	#67
1977	Up Your Nose	Gabriel Kaplan	#91
1977	Six Packs a Day	Billy Lemmons	#93
1977	Turn Loose of My Leg	Jim Stafford	#98
1977	Discomania	The Lovers	#100
1978	Short People	Randy Newman	#2

NOVELTY SONGS (cont'd)			
1978	King Tut	Steve Martin and The Toot Uncommons	#17
1978	Cheeseburger in Paradise	Jimmy Buffett	#32
1978	Themes from "The Wizard of Oz"	Meco	#35
1978	Paradise by the Dashboard Light	Meat Loaf	#39
1978	Bloat on Featuring the Bloaters	Cheech & Chong	#41
1979	Rubber Biscuit	Blues Brothers	#37
1979	Dancin' Fool	Frank Zappa	#45
1979	The Football Card	Glenn Sutton	#46
1979	I Need Your Help Barry Manilow	Ray Stevens	#49
1979	Do You Think I'm Disco?	Steve Dahl	#58
1979	The Topical Song	The Barron Knights	#70
1979	Animal House	Stephen Bishop	#73

COUNTRY SONGS

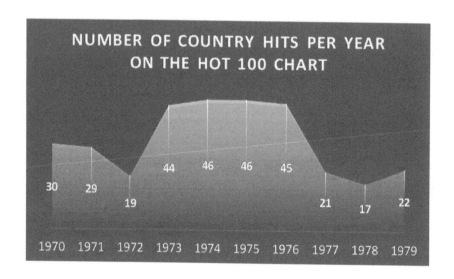

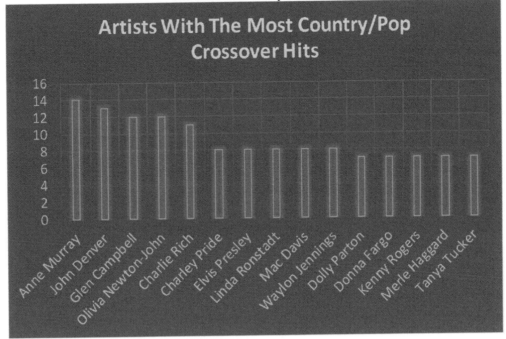

YEAR	SONG	ARTIST	COUNTRY CHART	HOT 100
1970	Everything Is Beautiful	Ray Stevens	#39	#1
1970	Snowbird	Anne Murray	#10	#8
1970	You Don't Have to Say You Love Me	Elvis Presley	#56	#11
1970	Tennessee Bird Walk	Jack Blanchard & Misty Morgan	#1	#23
1970	If I Were a Carpenter	Johnny Cash & June Carter	#2	#36
1970	Okie from Muskogee	Merle Haggard	#1	#41
1970	My Woman, My Woman, My Wife	Marty Robbins	#1	#42
1970	My Elusive Dreams	Bobby Vinton	#27	#46
1970	Sunday Morning Coming Down	Johnny Cash	#1	#46
1970	Morning	Jim Ed Brown	#4	#47
1970	Everything a Man Could Ever Need	Glen Campbell	#5	#52
1970	Whoever Finds This, I Love You	Mac Davis	#43	#53
1970	Hello Darlin'	Conway Twitty	#1	#60
1970	Is Anybody Goin' to San Antone	Charley Pride	#1	#70
1970	I Can't Believe That You've Stopped Loving Me	Charley Pride	#1	#71
1970	Can You Feel It	Bobby Goldsboro	#71	#75
1970	Mornin' Mornin'	Bobby Goldsboro	#56	#78
1970	Six White Horses	Tommy Cash	#4	#79
1970	Fifteen Years Ago	Conway Twitty	#1	#81
1970	Coal Miner's Daughter	Loretta Lynn	#1	#83
1970	July 12, 1939	Charlie Rich	#47	#85
1970	It's Just a Matter of Time	Sonny James	#1	#87
1970	Wonder Could I Live There Anymore	Charley Pride	#1	#87
1970	Thank God and Greyhound	Roy Clark	#6	#90

COUNTRY SONGS (cont'd)				
1970	Run, Woman, Run	Tammy Wynette	#1	#92
1970	The Fightin' Side of Me	Merle Haggard	#1	#92
1970	Then She's a Lover	Roy Clark	#31	#94
1970	The Taker	Waylon Jennings	#5	#94
1970	He Loves Me All the Way	Tammy Wynette	#1	#97
1970	I'll See Him Through	Tammy Wynette	#2	#100
1971	Take Me Home, Country Roads	John Denver	#50	#2
1971	Rose Garden	Lynn Anderson	#1	#3
1971	Help Me Make It Through the Night	Sammi Smith	#1	#8
1971	Watching Scotty Grow	Bobby Goldsboro	#7	#11
1971	Easy Loving	Freddie Hart	#1	#17
1971	I Really Don't Want to Know	Elvis Presley	#23	#21
1971	The Year That Clayton Delaney Died	Tom T. Hall	#1	#42
1971	He's so Fine	Jody Miller	#5	#53
1971	Flesh and Blood	Johnny Cash	#1	#54
1971	After the Fire Is Gone	Conway Twitty & Loretta Lynn	#1	#56
1971	Man in Black	Johnny Cash	#3	#58
1971	Bed of Rose's	The Statler Brothers	#9	#58
1971	The Last Time I Saw Her	Glen Campbell	#21	#61
1971	How Can I Unlove You	Lynn Anderson	#1	#63
1971	Turn Your Radio On	Ray Stevens	#17	#63
1971	You're My Man	Lynn Anderson	#1	#63
1971	I'd Rather Be Sorry	Ray Price	#2	#70
1971	Oh, Singer	Jeannie C. Riley	#4	#74
1971	I'd Rather Love You	Charley Pride	#1	#79
1971	And I Love You So	Bobby Goldsboro	#48	#83
1971	Sing High – Sing Low	Anne Murray	#53	#83
1971	Soldier's Last Letter	Merle Haggard	#3	#90
1971	Baby, I'm Yours	Jody Miller	#5	#91
1971	She's All I Got	Johnny Paycheck	#2	#91
1971	Bright Lights, Big City	Sonny James	#1	#91
1971	Empty Arms	Sonny James	#1	#93
1971	I Wanna Be Free	Loretta Lynn	#3	#94
1971	I'm Just Me	Charley Pride	#1	#94
1971	Good Enough to Be Your Wife	Jeannie C. Riley	#7	#97
1972	Garden Party	Rick Nelson	#44	#6
1972	The Happiest Girl in the Whole U.S.A.	Donna Fargo	#1	#11
1972	Kiss an Angel Good Mornin'	Charley Pride	#1	#21
1972	If You Leave Me Tonight I'll Cry	Jerry Wallace	#1	#28
1972	Me and Bobby McGee	Jerry Lee Lewis	#1	#40
1972	Until It's Time for You to Go	Elvis Presley	#68	#40

COUNTRY SONGS (cont'd)

1972	To Get to You	Jerry Wallace	#12	#48
1972	Carolyn	Merle Haggard	#1	#58
1972	I Will Never Pass This Way Again	Glen Campbell	#45	#61
1972	Josie	Kris Kristofferson	#70	#63
1972	Cotton Jenny	Anne Murray	#11	#71
1972	Cry	Lynn Anderson	#3	#71
1972	Delta Dawn	Tanya Tucker	#6	#72
1972	Kate	Johnny Cash	#2	#75
1972	I've Got to Have You	Sammi Smith	#13	#77
1972	Bedtime Story	Tammy Wynette	#1	#86
1972	It's Four in the Morning	Faron Young	#1	#92
1972	All His Children	Charley Pride w/Henry Mancini	#2	#92
1972	Me and Jesus	Tom T. Hall	#8	#98
1973	The Night the Lights Went Out in Georgia	Vicki Lawrence	#36	#1
1973	The Most Beautiful Girl	Charlie Rich	#1	#1
1973	Paper Roses	Marie Osmond	#1	#5
1973	Danny's Song	Anne Murray	#10	#7
1973	Uneasy Rider	Charlie Daniels	#67	#9
1973	Daisy a Day	Jud Strunk	#33	#14
1973	Behind Closed Doors	Charlie Rich	#1	#15
1973	Why Me	Kris Kristofferson	#1	#16
1973	You've Never Been This Far Before	Conway Twitty	#1	#22
1973	Satin Sheets	Jeanne Pruett	#1	#28
1973	If We Make It Through December	Merle Haggard	#1	#28
1973	Teddy Bear Song	Barbara Fairchild	#1	#32
1973	Soul Song	Joe Stampley	#1	#37
1973	Drinking Wine Spo-Dee O'Dee	Jerry Lee Lewis	#20	#41
1973	Superman	Donna Fargo	#1	#41
1973	I Knew Jesus (Before He was a Star)	Glen Campbell	#48	#45
1973	Country Sunshine	Dottie West	#2	#49
1973	A Song I'd Like to Sing	Kris Kristofferson & Rita Coolidge	#92	#49
1973	Little Girl Gone	Donna Fargo	#2	#57
1973	Everybody's Had the Blues	Merle Haggard	#1	#62
1973	What About Me	Anne Murray	#20	#64
1973	The Lord Knows I'm Drinking	Cal Smith	#1	#64
1973	Lord, Mr. Ford	Jerry Reed	#1	#68
1973	Please, Daddy	John Denver	#69	#69
1973	Ridin' My Thumb to Mexico	Johnny Rodriguez	#1	#70
1973	Nobody Wins	Brenda Lee	#5	#70
1973	Send a Little Love My Way	Anne Murray	#79	#72
1973	Kids Say the Darndest Things	Tammy Wynette	#1	#72

		COUNTRY SONGS (cont'd)		
1973	Dream Me Home	Mac Davis	#47	#73
1973	Top of the World	Lynn Anderson	#2	#74
1973	Blood Red and Goin' Down	Tanya Tucker	#1	#74
1973	One Last Time	Glen Campbell	#33	#78
1973	Roll in My Sweet Baby's Arms	Hank Wilson (Leon Russell)	#57	#78
1973	Slippin' Away	Jean Shepard	#4	#81
1973	You're the Best Thing That Ever Happened to Me	Ray Price	#1	#82
1973	You Always Come Back (To Hurting Me)	Johnny Rodriguez	#1	#86
1973	What's Your Mama's Name	Tanya Tucker	#1	#86
1973	Sunshine	Mickey Newbury	#53	#87
1973	Your Side of the Bed	Mac Davis	#36	#88
1973	Come Live with Me	Roy Clark	#1	#89
1973	You Were Always There	Donna Fargo	#1	#93
1973	She's Got to Be a Saint	Ray Price	#1	#93
1973	Kid Stuff	Barbara Fairchild	#2	#95
1973	If It's All Right with You	Dottie West	#28	#97
1974	Annie's Song	John Denver	#9	#1
1974	I Honestly Love You	Olivia Newton-John	#6	#1
1974	Spiders & Snakes	Jim Stafford	#66	#3
1974	If You Love Me (Let Me Know)	Olivia Newton-John	#2	#5
1974	Back Home Again	John Denver	#1	#5
1974	Let Me Be There	Olivia Newton-John	#7	#6
1974	Wildwood Weed	Jim Stafford	#57	#7
1974	Stop and Smell the Roses	Mac Davis	#40	#9
1974	A Very Special Love Song	Charlie Rich	#1	#11
1974	My Girl Bill	Jim Stafford	#64	#12
1974	Love Song	Anne Murray	#5	#12
1974	I Love	Tom T. Hall	#1	#12
1974	Fairytale	The Pointer Sisters	#37	#13
1974	Rub It In	Billy "Crash" Craddock	#1	#16
1974	There Won't Be Anymore	Charlie Rich	#1	#18
1974	I Love My Friend	Charlie Rich	#1	#24
1974	Come Monday	Jimmy Buffett	#58	#30
1974	You Can Have Her	Sam Neely	#49	#34
1974	One Day at a Time	Marilyn Sellars	#19	#37
1974	I've Got a Thing About You Baby	Elvis Presley	#4	#39
1974	No Charge	Melba Montgomery	#1	#39
1974	Daddy What If	Bobby Bare	#2	#41
1974	It Could Have Been Me	Sami Jo	#61	#46
1974	Would You Lay with Me	Tanya Tucker	#1	#46
1974	She Called Me Baby	Charlie Rich	#1	#47

COUNTRY SONGS (cont'd)

1974	I Don't See Me in Your Eyes Anymore	Charlie Rich	#1	#47
1974	Room Full of Roses	Mickey Gilley	#1	#50
1974	When the Morning Comes	Hoyt Axton	#10	#54
1974	You Can't Be a Beacon (If Your Light Don't Shine)	Donna Fargo	#1	#57
1974	Jolene	Dolly Parton	#1	#60
1974	That Song Is Driving Me Crazy	Tom T. Hall	#2	#63
1974	Silver Threads and Golden Needles	Linda Ronstadt	#20	#67
1974	Houston (I'm Comin' to See You)	Glen Campbell	#20	#68
1974	Early Morning Love	Sammy Johns	#79	#68
1974	Mississippi Cotton Picking Delta Town	Charley Pride	#3	#70
1974	I'm a Ramblin' Man	Waylon Jennings	#1	#75
1974	Somewhere Between Love and Tomorrow	Roy Clark	#2	#81
1974	Delta Dirt	Larry Gatlin	#14	#84
1974	Makin' the Best of a Bad Situation	Dick Feller	#11	#85
1974	Something	Johnny Rodriguez	#6	#85
1974	Loving Arms	Kris Kristofferson & Rita Coolidge	#98	#86
1974	U.S. of A	Donna Fargo	#9	#86
1974	The Man That Turned My Mama On	Tanya Tucker	#4	#86
1974	The Americans (A Canadian's Opinion)	Tex Ritter	#35	#90
1974	The Crude Oil Blues	Jerry Reed	#13	#91
1974	Please Don't Tell Me How the Story Ends	Ronnie Milsap	#1	#95
1975	Rhinestone Cowboy	Glen Campbell	#1	#1
1975	Before the Next Teardrop Falls	Freddy Fender	#1	#1
1975	(Hey Won't You Play) Another Somebody Done Somebody Wrong Song	B.J. Thomas	#1	#1
1975	Have You Never Been Mellow	Olivia Newton-John	#3	#1
1975	Thank God I'm a Country Boy	John Denver	#1	#1
1975	I'm Sorry	John Denver	#1	#1
1975	Please Mr. Please	Olivia Newton-John	#5	#3
1975	I'm Not Lisa	Jessi Colter	#1	#4
1975	Misty	Ray Stevens	#3	#14
1975	Third Rate Romance	Amazing Rhythm Aces	#11	#14
1975	Rock N' Roll (I Gave You the Best Years of My Life)	Mac Davis	#29	#15
1975	Sally G	Paul McCartney & Wings	#51	#17
1975	Every Time You Touch Me (I Get High)	Charlie Rich	#3	#19
1975	My Boy	Elvis Presley	#14	#20
1975	Blue Eyes Crying in the Rain	Willie Nelson	#1	#21
1975	Ride 'Em Cowboy	Paul Davis	#47	#23
1975	Rainy Day People	Gordon Lightfoot	#47	#26
1975	Ruby, Baby	Billy "Crash" Craddock	#1	#33
1975	T-R-O-U-B-L-E	Elvis Presley	#11	#35

COUNTRY SONGS (cont'd)

1975	Lizzie and the Rainman	Tanya Tucker	#1	#37
1975	Who's Sorry Now	Marie Osmond	#29	#40
1975	Wolf Creek Pass	B.T. Express	#12	#40
1975	Since I Met You Baby	Freddy Fender	#10	#45
1975	It Doesn't Matter Anymore	Linda Ronstadt	#54	#47
1975	My Elusive Dreams	Charlie Rich	#3	#49
1975	Burnin' Thing	Mac Davis	#31	#53
1975	(If You Add) All the Love in the World	Mac Davis	#69	#54
1975	Devil in the Bottle	T.G. Sheppard	#1	#54
1975	Sneaky Snake	Tom T. Hall	#69	#55
1975	What's Happened to Blue Eyes	Jessi Colter	#5	#57
1975	If I Could Only Win Your Love	Emmylou Harris	#4	#58
1975	Blind Man in the Bleachers	Kenny Starr	#2	#58
1975	Are You Sure Hank Done It This Way	Waylon Jennings	#1	#60
1975	Linda on My Mind	Conway Twitty	#1	#61
1975	Love Is a Rose	Linda Ronstadt	#5	#63
1975	Help Me Make It (To My Rockin' Chair)	B.J. Thomas	#37	#64
1975	Reconsider Me	Narvel Felts	#2	#67
1975	Indian Love Call	Ray Stevens	#38	#68
1975	The Pill	Loretta Lynn	#5	#70
1975	Blanket on the Ground	Billie Jo Spears	#1	#78
1975	I'll Still Love You	Jim Weatherly	#9	#87
1975	I'll Go to My Grave Loving You	The Statler Brothers	#3	#93
1975	What a Man My Man Is	Lynn Anderson	#1	#93
1975	Tryin' to Beat the Morning Home	T.G. Sheppard	#1	#95
1975	It Do Feel Good	Donna Fargo	#7	#98
1975	Sunday Sunrise	Anne Murray	#49	#98
1976	Afternoon Delight	Starland Vocal Band	#94	#1
1976	Let Your Love Flow	Bellamy Brothers	#21	#1
1976	The Wreck of the Edmund Fitzgerald	Gordon Lightfoot	#50	#2
1976	That'll Be the Day	Linda Ronstadt	#27	#11
1976	Country Boy (You Got Your Feet in L.A.)	Glen Campbell	#3	#11
1976	Fly Away	John Denver	#12	#13
1976	Come on Over	Olivia Newton-John	#5	#23
1976	Tracks of My Tears	Linda Ronstadt	#11	#25
1976	Good Hearted Woman	Waylon Jennings & Willie Nelson	#1	#25
1976	Paloma Blanca	George Baker Selection	#33	#26
1976	Don't Pull Your Love/Then You Can Tell Me Goodbye	Glen Campbell	#4	#27
1976	Hurt	Elvis Presley	#6	#28
1976	Looking for Space	John Denver	#30	#29
1976	Let It Shine	Olivia Newton-John	#5	#30

COUNTRY SONGS (cont'd)

1976	You'll Lose a Good Thing	Freddy Fender	#1	#32
1976	Don't Stop Believin'	Olivia Newton-John	#14	#33
1976	Like a Sad Song	John Denver	#34	#36
1976	Teddy Bear	Red Sovine	#1	#40
1976	The End Is Not in Sight (The Cowboy Tune)	Amazing Rhythm Aces	#12	#42
1976	Hey Shirley (This Is Squirrely)	Shirley & Squirrely	#28	#48
1976	Easy as Pie	Billy "Crash" Craddock	#2	#54
1976	If Not You	Dr. Hook	#26	#55
1976	Every Face Tells a Story	Olivia Newton-John	#21	#55
1976	Vaya Con Dios	Freddy Fender	#7	#59
1976	It Makes Me Giggle	John Denver	#70	#60
1976	Baby Boy	Mary Kay Place	#3	#60
1976	Don't Cry Joni	Conway Twitty w/Joni Lee	#4	#63
1976	Remember Me	Willie Nelson	#2	#67
1976	Since I Fell for You	Charlie Rich	#10	#71
1976	I'll Get Over You	Crystal Gayle	#1	#71
1976	Amazing Grace (Used to Be Her Favorite Song)	Amazing Rhythm Aces	#9	#72
1976	There Won't Be No Country Music (There Won't Be No Rock 'N' Roll)	C.W. McCall	#19	#73
1976	Rocky Mountain Music	Eddie Rabbitt	#5	#76
1976	Forever Lovers	Mac Davis	#17	#76
1976	Here's Some Love	Tanya Tucker	#1	#82
1976	'Til I Can Make It on My Own	Tammy Wynette	#1	#84
1976	Kentucky Moonrunner	Cledus Maggard	#42	#85
1976	Things	Anne Murray	#22	#89
1976	The Call	Anne Murray	#19	#91
1976	I'm So Lonesome I Could Cry	Terry Bradshaw	#17	#91
1976	Texas	Charlie Daniels Band	#36	#91
1976	Young Love	Ray Stevens	#48	#93
1976	Love Lifted Me	Kenny Rogers	#19	#97
1976	Can't You See	Waylon Jennings	#4	#97
1976	Solitary Man	T.G. Sheppard	#14	#100
1977	Southern Nights	Glen Campbell	#1	#1
1977	Blue Bayou	Linda Ronstadt	#2	#3
1977	It's so Easy	Linda Ronstadt	#81	#5
1977	Lucille	Kenny Rogers	#1	#5
1977	Right Time of the Night	Jennifer Warnes	#17	#6
1977	After the Lovin'	Engelbert Humperdinck	#40	#8
1977	The King Is Gone	Ronnie McDowell	#13	#13
1977	Heard It in a Love Song	Marshall Tucker Band	#51	#14
1977	It Was Almost Like a Song	Ronnie Milsap	#1	#16
1977	Luckenbach, Texas (Back to the Basics of Love)	Waylon Jennings	#1	#25

COUNTRY SONGS (cont'd)				
1977	Daytime Friends	Kenny Rogers	#1	#28
1977	Moody Blue	Elvis Presley	#1	#31
1977	Sunflower	Glen Campbell	#4	#39
1977	9,999,999 Tears	Dickey Lee	#3	#52
1977	From Graceland to the Promised Land	Merle Haggard	#4	#58
1977	Baby, You Look Good to Me Tonight	John Denver	#65	#22
1977	Heaven's Just a Sin Away	The Kendalls	#1	#69
1977	Brooklyn	Cody Jameson	#64	#74
1977	I Can't Help Myself	Eddie Rabbitt	#2	#77
1977	Light of a Clear Blue Morning	Dolly Parton	#11	#87
1977	Goodbye My Friend	Engelbert Humperdinck	#93	#97
1978	You Needed Me	Anne Murray	#4	#1
1978	Here You Come Again	Dolly Parton	#1	#3
1978	Poor Poor Pitiful Me	Linda Ronstadt	#46	#31
1978	Love or Something Like It	Kenny Rogers	#1	#32
1978	Heartbreaker	Dolly Parton	#1	#37
1978	Can You Fool	Glen Campbell	#16	#38
1978	Mammas Don't Let Your Babies Grow Up to Be Cowboys	Waylon Jennings & Willie Nelson	#1	#42
1978	Sweet, Sweet Smile	Carpenters	#8	#44
1978	How Can I Leave You Again	John Denver	#22	#44
1978	Sweet Music Man	Kenny Rogers	#9	#44
1978	You Don't Love Me Anymore	Eddie Rabbitt	#1	#53
1978	It Amazes Me	John Denver	#72	#59
1978	Only One Love in My Life	Ronnie Milsap	#1	#63
1978	What a Difference You've Made in My Life	Ronnie Milsap	#1	#80
1978	I Love You, I Love You, I Love You	Ronnie McDowell	#5	#81
1978	Georgia on My Mind	Willie Nelson	#1	#84
1978	Woman to Woman	Barbara Mandrell	#4	#92
1979	A Little More Love	Olivia Newton-John	#94	#3
1979	The Devil Went Down to Georgia	Charlie Daniels Band	#1	#3
1979	She Believes in Me	Kenny Rogers	#1	#5
1979	Deeper Than the Night	Olivia Newton-John	#87	#11
1979	I Just Fall in Love Again	Anne Murray	#1	#12
1979	Broken Hearted Me	Anne Murray	#1	#12
1979	Suspicions	Eddie Rabbitt	#1	#13
1979	The Gambler	Kenny Rogers	#1	#16
1979	Crazy Love	Poco	#95	#17
1979	Do It or Die	Atlanta Rhythm Section	#92	#19
1979	I Know a Heartache When I See One	Jennifer Warnes	#10	#19
1979	Heart of the Night	Poco	#96	#20
1979	Baby I'm Burnin'	Dolly Parton	#48	#25

	COUNTRY SONGS (cont'd)			
1979	Shadows in the Moonlight	Anne Murray	#1	#25
1979	Every Which Way but Loose	Eddie Rabbitt	#1	#30
1979	(If Loving You Is Wrong) I Don't Want to Be Right	Barbara Mandrell	#1	#31
1979	If I Said You Have a Beautiful Body Would You Hold It Against Me	The Bellamy Brothers	#1	#39
1979	Amanda	Waylon Jennings	#1	#54
1979	You're the Only One	Dolly Parton	#1	#59
1979	Sweet Summer Lovin'	Dolly Parton	#7	#77
1979	Dancin' 'Round and 'Round	Olivia Newton-John	#29	#82
1979	Fooled By a Feeling	Barbara Mandrell	#4	#89

BLUES

YEAR	SONG	ARTIST	HOT 100
1970	The Thrill Is Gone	B.B. King	#15
1970	Let's Work Together (Part 1)	Wilbert Harrison	#32
1970	Chains and Things	B.B. King	#45
1970	Hummingbird	B.B. King	#48
1970	Laughin' and Clownin'	Ray Charles	#98
1971	Ask Me No Questions	B.B. King	#40
1971	Don't Make Me Pay for Your Mistakes	Z.Z. Hill	#62
1971	Ghetto Woman	B.B. King	#68
1971	Slipped, Tripped and Fell in Love	Clarence Carter	#84
1971	Help the Poor	B.B. King	#90
1971	That Evil Child	B.B. King	#97
1971	I'm Sorry	Bobby Bland	#97
1972	Trouble in My Home	Joe Simon	#50
1972	That's What Love Will Make You Do	Little Milton	#59
1972	Everybody Knows About My Good Thing Pt. 1	Little Johnny Taylor	#60
1972	I Love You More Than You'll Ever Know	Donny Hathaway	#60
1972	Do What You Set Out to Do	Bobby Bland	#64
1972	I Got Some Help I Don't Need	B.B. King	#92
1972	Sweet Sixteen	B.B. King	#93
1973	Steamroller Blues	Elvis Presley	#17
1974	This Time I'm Gone for Good	Bobby Blue Bland	#42
1974	Goin' Down Slow	Bobby Blue Bland	#69
1975	Wasted Days and Wasted Nights	Freddy Fender	#8

Jazz

YEAR	SONG	ARTIST	HOT 100
1970	Breaking Up Is Hard to Do	Lenny Welch	#34
1970	Black Fox	Freddy Robinson	#56
1970	Compared to What	Les McCann & Eddie Harris	#85
1971	Handbags and Gladrags	Chase	#84
1971	Way Back Home	The Jazz Crusaders	#90
1972	Pain (Part 1)	Ohio Players	#64
1974	Bad, Bad Leroy Brown	Frank Sinatra	#83
1975	Sun Goddess	Ramsey Lewis & Earth, Wind & Fire	#44
1976	Breaking Up Is Hard to Do	Neil Sedaka	#8
1976	This Masquerade	George Benson	#10
1976	Popsicle Toes	Michael Franks	#43

CHRISTMAS SONGS

YEAR	SONG	ARTIST	HOT 100
1973	If We Make It Through December	Merle Haggard	#28
1973	It Doesn't Have to Be That Way	Jim Croce	#64
1973	Please, Daddy	John Denver	#69
1974	When a Child Is Born	Michael Holm	#53
1974	Christmas Dream	Perry Como	#92
1975	Christmas for Cowboys	John Denver	#58
1975	I Believe in Father Christmas	Greg Lake	#95
1975	The Little Drummer Boy	Moonlion	#95
1978	Please Come Home for Christmas	Eagles	#18
1978	Mary's Boy Child/Oh My Lord	Boney M	#85

INSTRUMENTAL SONGS

Instrumental songs popped up on Billboard's Hot 100 chart somewhat regularly until the latter half of the 1970s. This decline in popularity continued into the eighties, where only 36 instrumental hits charted in the entire decade.

*Songs marked with an asterisk have some singing. Usually, it is a part so minor, that the song is still considered to be an instrumental.

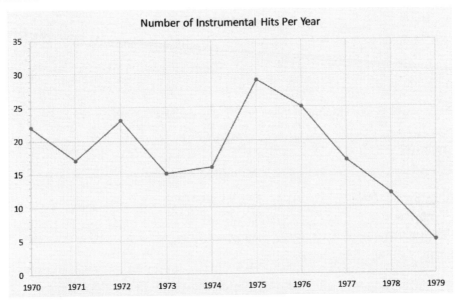

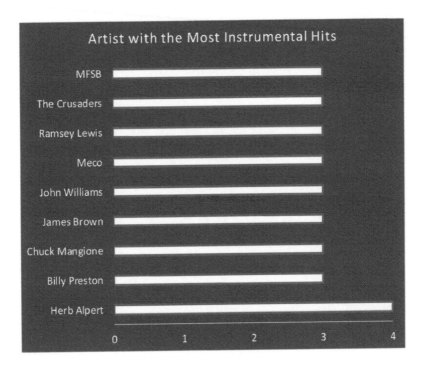

YEAR	SONG	ARTIST	HOT 100	FEATURED INSTRUMENT
1970	Midnight Cowboy*	Ferrante & Teicher	#10	Piano
1970	Overture from Tommy (A Rock Opera)	Assembled Multitude	#16	Orchestra
1970	Ain't It Funky Now (Part 1)*	James Brown	#24	Trumpet/Organ
1970	Viva Tirado – Part 1	El Chicano	#28	Organ
1970	Airport Love Theme (Gwen and Vern)	Vincent Bell	#31	Orchestra/Piano
1970	Wigwam*	Bob Dylan	#41	Orchestra
1970	Chicken Strut*	The Meters	#50	Guitar
1970	Oh Well – Pt. 1*	Fleetwood Mac	#55	Guitar
1970	Look-Ka Py Py*	The Meters	#56	Organ
1970	Black Fox	Freddy Robinson	#56	Guitar
1970	Song from M*A*S*H	Al DeLory	#70	Piano
1970	Jerusalem*	Herb Alpert & The Tijuana Brass	#74	Horns
1970	Something	Booker T. & The M.G.'s	#76	Piano/Guitar
1970	Stoned Cowboy	Fantasy	#77	Guitar
1970	Woodstock	The Assembled Multitude	#79	Orchestra
1970	The Gang's Back Again*	Kool & The Gang	#85	Horns
1970	Country Preacher	Cannonball Adderley	#86	Saxophone
1970	Groovin' with Mr. Bloe	Cool Heat	#89	Harmonica
1970	Theme Music for the Film "2001" A Space Odyssey from "Also Sprach Zarathustra"	Berlin Philharmonic	#90	Orchestra
1970	Funky Chicken (Part 1)*	Willie Henderson w/The Soul Explosions	#91	Saxophone
1970	Lady Lay Lay*	Ferrante & Teicher	#99	Piano
1970	Listen Here	Brian Auger/The Trinity	#100	Piano/Guitar
1971	Theme from Love Story*	Henry Mancini	#13	Piano
1971	Theme from "Summer of '42"	Peter Nero	#21	Piano
1971	Double Barrel*	Dave & Ansil Collins	#22	Piano
1971	Cool Aid	Paul Humphrey	#29	Guitar/Organ
1971	Theme from Love Story	Francis Lai	#31	Piano
1971	Booty Butt*	Ray Charles Orchestra	#36	Piano/Sax/Guitar
1971	K-Jee	The Nite-Liters	#39	Horns
1971	Melting Pot	Booker T. & The M.G.'s	#45	Organ
1971	Whole Lotta Love*	C.C.S.	#58	Guitar/Horns
1971	Whole Lotta Love	King Curtis	#64	Sax/Horns
1971	Hill Where the Lord Hides	Chuck Mangione	#76	Horns
1971	It's the Real Thing – Pt. 1*	The Electric Express	#81	Sax
1971	Spinning Wheel (Pt. 1)	James Brown	#90	Organ/Sax
1971	Way Back Home	The Jazz Crusaders	#90	Sax
1971	Help the Poor	B.B. King	#90	
1971	Mandrill*	Mandrill	#94	Horns

	INSTRUMENTAL SONGS (cont'd)			
1971	Medley from "Superstar" (A Rock Opera)	The Assembled Multitude	#95	Orchestra
1972	Outa-Space	Billy Preston	#2	Organ/Guitar
1972	Scorpio	Dennis Scorpio	#6	Bass Guitar
1972	Joy	Apollo 100	#6	Organ
1972	Rock and Roll Part 2*	Gary Glitter	#7	Guitar
1972	Jungle Fever*	The Chackachas	#8	
1972	Popcorn	Hot Butter	#9	
1972	Amazing Grace	Royal Scots Dragoon Guards	#11	Bagpipes
1972	Taurus*	Dennis Coffey	#18	Guitar
1972	Theme from "The Men"*	Isaac Hayes	#38	Horns
1972	Honky Tonk – Part 1*	James Brown	#44	Sax
1972	Walk in the Night*	Jr. Walker/The All Stars	#46	Sax
1972	Let's Stay Together*	Isaac Hayes	#48	Sax
1972	Afro-Strut	The Nite-Liters	#49	Horns
1972	Way Back Home*	Jr. Walker/The All Stars	#52	Sax
1972	Put It Where You Want It	The Crusaders	#52	Sax
1972	Brian's Song*	Michel LeGrand	#56	Piano
1972	Mr. Penguin – Pt. 1*	Lunar Funk	#63	Organ
1972	Love Theme from "The Godfather"*	Carlo Savina	#66	Orchestra
1972	Gimme Some More*	The JB's	#67	
1972	Nutrocker	Emerson, Lake & Palmer	#70	Clavinet
1972	Getting It On	Dennis Coffey	#93	Guitar
1972	Mendelssohn's 4th (Second Movement)	Apollo 100	#94	Orchestra
1972	Pass the Peas*	The JB's	#95	Trumpet
1973	Frankenstein	Edgar Winter Group	#1	Guitar
1973	Dueling Banjos	Eric Weissberg & Steve Mandell	#2	Banjo/Guitar
1973	Also Sprach Zarathustra (2001)	Deodato	#2	Piano
1973	Space Race	Billy Preston	#4	Horns
1973	Hocus Pocus*	Focus	#9	Guitar
1973	Soul Makossa*	Manu Dibango	#35	
1973	Sister James*	Nino Tempo & 5th Ave. Sax	#53	Sax
1973	Bongo Rock	The Incredible Bongo Band	#57	Bongos
1973	Last Tango in Paris	Herb Alpert & The Tijuana Brass	#77	Trumpet
1973	Hang Loose*	Mandrill	#83	Horns
1973	Cosmic Sea*	The Mystic Moods	#83	Orchestra
1973	Don't Let It Get You Down	The Crusaders	#86	Sax
1973	Sylvia*	Focus	#89	Guitar
1973	Dueling Tubas	Martin Mull	#92	Tubas
1973	Kufanya Mapenzi (Making Love)	Ramsey Lewis	#93	Keyboards
1974	TSOP (The Sound of Philadelphia)*	MFSB/Three Degrees	#1	Orchestra

INSTRUMENTAL SONGS (cont'd)

1974	Love's Theme	Love Unlimited Orchestra	#1	Orchestra
1974	The Entertainer	Marvin Hamlisch	#3	Woodwinds/Piano
1974	Tubular Bells	Mike Oldfield	#7	Keyboards
1974	Machine Gun	The Commodores	#22	Keyboards
1974	Ballero	War	#33	Flute
1974	Chameleon	Herbie Hancock	#42	Sax
1974	Dance with the Devil*	Cozy Powell	#49	Drums
1974	Rhapsody in White	Barry White	#63	Strings
1974	Jessica	Allman Brothers Band	#65	Guitar/Piano
1974	Pepper Box*	The Peppers	#76	Keyboards
1974	Scratch	The Crusaders	#81	Sax
1974	Fox Hunt	Herb Alpert & The TJB	#84	Trumpet
1974	Daybreaker	Electric Light Orchestra	#87	Keyboards
1974	Feel Like Making Love	Bob James	#88	Electric piano
1974	Georgia Porcupine	George Fischoff	#93	Piano
1975	Fly, Robin, Fly*	Silver Convention	#1	Strings
1975	Pick Up the Pieces*	Average White Band	#1	Sax
1975	The Hustle*	Van McCoy & The Soul City Symphony	#1	Orchestra
1975	Express*	B.T. Express	#4	
1975	The Rockford Files	Mike Post	#10	Keyboards
1975	Dynomite – Part 1*	Bazuka	#10	Horns
1975	Brazil*	The Ritchie Family	#11	Orchestra
1975	Struttin'	Billy Preston	#22	Synthesizer
1975	Satin Soul	The Love Unlimited Orchestra	#22	Orchestra
1975	Autobahn*	Kraftwerk	#25	Synthesizer
1975	Main Title (Theme from "Jaws")	John Williams	#32	Orchestra
1975	Sexy	MFSB	#42	Orchestra
1975	El Bimbo*	Bimbo Jet	#43	Keyboards
1975	Sun Goddess*	Ramsey Lewis & Earth, Wind & Fire	#44	Keyboards
1975	Hot Dawgit*	Ramsey Lewis & Earth, Wind & Fire	#50	Keyboards
1975	Mister Magic	Grover Washington, Jr.	#54	
1975	Caribbean Festival*	Kool & The Gang	#55	
1975	Manhattan Spiritual	Mike Post	#56	
1975	Summer of '42	Biddu Orchestra	#57	Orchestra
1975	Sneakin' Up Behind You*	The Brecker Brothers	#58	Sax
1975	Philadelphia*	B.B. King	#64	Guitar
1975	Salsoul Hustle	Salsoul Orchestra	#76	Strings
1975	Shotgun Shuffle*	The Sunshine Band	#88	Horns
1975	Life and Death in G & A*	Love Childs Afro Cuban Blues Band	#90	
1975	The Zip*	MFSB	#91	Orchestra
1975	The Little Drummer Boy	Moonlion	#95	Orchestra

INSTRUMENTAL SONGS (cont'd)

1975	Chase the Clouds Away	Chuck Mangione	#96	Flute
1975	Honey Trippin'	The Mystic Moods	#98	Strings
1975	Chinese Kung Fu*	Banzaii	#98	Keyboards
1976	Theme from S.W.A.T.	Rhythm Heritage	#1	Orchestra
1976	Nadia's Theme (The Young and The Restless)	Barry DeVorzon & Perry Botkin, Jr.	#8	Piano
1976	Movin'*	Brass Construction	#14	Horns
1976	Tangerine*	The Salsoul Orchestra	#18	Orchestra
1976	Flight '76	Walter Murphy	#44	Orchestra
1976	Hard Work*	John Handy	#46	Sax
1976	My Sweet Summer Suite	The Love Unlimited Orchestra	#48	Orchestra
1976	Street Talk*	B.C.G. (B.C. Generation)	#56	Orchestra
1976	BLT	Lee Oskar	#59	Harmonica
1976	Lipstick	Michel Polnareff	#61	Orchestra
1976	Let's Get It Together*	El Coco	#61	Horns
1976	The Jam*	Graham Central Station	#63	Organ
1976	Breezin'	George Benson	#63	Guitar
1976	I Could Have Danced All Night*	Biddu Orchestra	#72	Orchestra
1976	Scotch on the Rocks	Band of the Black Watch	#75	Bagpipes
1976	Uptown & Country	Tom Scott	#80	Organ
1976	Peter Gunn*	Deodato	#84	Sax
1976	Rattlesnake*	Ohio Players	#90	Guitar
1976	Makes You Blind*	The Glitter Band	#91	Guitar/Sax
1976	Disco Sax*	Houston Person	#91	Sax
1976	Bad Luck	The Atlanta Disco Band	#94	Guitar
1976	Grasshopper	Spin	#95	Horns
1976	Wow	Andre Gagnon	#95	Piano
1976	Night Walk	Van McCoy	#96	Orchestra
1976	Tubular Bells	Champs' Boys Orchestra	#98	Orchestra
1977	Star Wars Theme/Cantina Band	Meco	#1	Orchestra
1977	Gonna Fly Now*	Bill Conti	#1	Horns
1977	Star Wars Theme (Main Title)	John Williams	#10	Orchestra
1977	Disco Lucy (I Love Lucy Theme)	Wilton Place Street Band	#24	Orchestra
1977	Gonna Fly Now (Theme from Rocky)	Maynard Ferguson	#28	Horns
1977	Love in 'C' Minor – Pt. 1*	Cerrone	#36	Orchestra
1977	Spring Rain*	Silvetti	#39	
1977	In the Mood	Henhouse Five Plus Too (Ray Stevens)	#40	
1977	Dancin'*	Crown Heights Affair	#42	Horns
1977	O-H-I-O*	Ohio Players	#45	Horns
1977	Theme from Charlie's Angels	Henry Mancini	#45	Orchestra
1977	Love in 'C' Minor*	Heart & Soul Orchestra	#46	Orchestra
1977	Ha Cha Cha (Funktion)*	Brass Construction	#51	Orchestra

	INSTRUMENTAL SONGS (cont'd)			
1977	Theme from King Kong (Pt. 1)	Love Unlimited Orchestra	#68	
1977	Bless the Beasts and Children*	Barry DeVorzon & Perry Botkin, Jr.	#82	Orchestra
1977	Theme from "Rocky" (Gonna Fly Now)*	Rhythm Heritage	#94	Orchestra
1977	For Elise*	The Philharmonics	#100	Orchestra
1978	Feels So Good	Chuck Mangione	#4	Flugelhorn
1978	Theme from "Close Encounters of the Third Kind"	John Williams	#13	Orchestra
1978	Theme from "Close Encounters of the Third Kind"	Meco	#25	Orchestra
1978	Themes from "The Wizard of Oz"*	Meco	#35	
1978	Let's All Chant*	Michael Zager Band	#36	Bass
1978	Cocomotion*	El Coco	#44	Strings
1978	Le Spank*	Le Pamplemousse	#58	Keyboards
1978	Trans-Europe Express*	Kraftwerk	#67	Keyboards
1978	Was Dog a Doughnut	Cat Stevens	#70	Keyboards
1978	Home Bound	Ted Nugent	#70	Guitar
1978	Disco Rufus*	Stargard	#88	Keyboards
1978	Shaker Song	Spyro Gyra	#90	Saxophone
1979	Rise	Herb Alpert	#1	Trumpet
1979	Music Box Dancer*	Frank Mills	#3	Piano
1979	Morning Dance	Spyro Gyra	#24	Sax, Steel Drums
1979	Chase	Giorgio Moroder	#33	Keyboards
1979	Peter Piper	Frank Mills	#48	Piano

RELIGIOUS SONGS

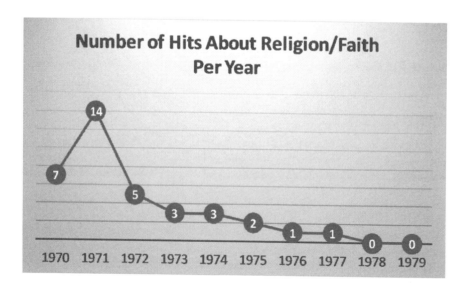

YEAR	SONG	ARTIST	HOT 100
1970	My Sweet Lord	George Harrison	#1

RELIGIOUS SONGS (cont'd)

1970	Spirit in the Sky	Norman Greenbaum	#3
1970	Oh Happy Day	Glen Campbell	#40
1970	My Woman, My Woman, My Wife	Marty Robbins	#42
1970	Free the People	Delaney & Bonnie & Friends	#75
1970	I Heard the Voice of Jesus	Turley Richards	#99
1970	Move Me, O Wondrous Music	Ray Charles Singers	#99
1971	Put Your Hand in the Hand	Ocean	#2
1971	Amazing Grace	Judy Collins	#15
1971	Mighty Clouds of Joy	B.J. Thomas	#34
1971	Life	Elvis Presley	#53
1971	Church Street Soul Revival	Tommy James	#62
1971	Turn Your Radio On	Ray Stevens	#63
1971	Think His Name	Johnny Rivers	#65
1971	Come Back Home	Bobby Goldsboro	#69
1971	Deep Enough for Me	Ocean	#73
1971	Top Forty	Sha Na Na	#84
1971	My Sweet Lord	Billy Preston	#90
1971	Take My Hand	Kenny Rogers & The First Edition	#91
1971	We're All Goin' Home	Bobby Bloom	#93
1971	Love Me	The Rascals	#95
1972	Morning Has Broken	Cat Stevens	#6
1972	Amazing Grace	Royal Scots Dragoon Guards	#11
1972	Day by Day	Godspell	#13
1972	Jubilation	Paul Anka	#65
1972	Me and Jesus	Tom T. Hall	#98
1973	Love Jones	Brighter Side of Darkness	#16
1973	I Knew Jesus (Before He was a Star)	Glen Campbell	#45
1973	He	Today's People	#90
1974	The Lord's Prayer	Sister Janet Mead	#4
1974	One Day at a Time	Marilyn Sellars	#37
1974	You Can't Be a Beacon (If Your Light Don't Shine)	Donna Fargo	#57
1975	Operator	The Manhattan Transfer	#22
1975	No Charge	Shirley Caesar	#91
1976	Love Lifted Me	Kenny Rogers	#97
1977	From Graceland to the Promised Land	Merle Haggard	#58

MEDLEYS

A medley is a song that consists of parts of at least two songs. All the parts are put together to form a new song, called a medley. Usually, the medley will use the catchiest parts of the other songs, like the chorus.

YEAR	SONG	ARTIST	HOT 100
1970	Traces/Memories Medley	The Lettermen	#47
1970	A Change is Gonna Come & People Gotta Be Free	The 5th Dimension	#60
1970	You Keep Me Hangin' On/Hurt so Bad	Jackie DeShannon	#96
1971	What the World Needs Now Is Love/Abraham, Martin and John	Tom Clay	#8
1971	My Part/Make It Funky (Part 3)	James Brown	#68
1971	I Don't Know How to Love Him/Everything's Alright	The Kimberlys	#99
1972	An American Trilogy	Mickey Newbury	#26
1972	American City Suite	Cashman & West	#27
1972	Sweet Inspiration/Where You Lead	Barbra Streisand	#37
1972	An American Trilogy	Elvis Presley	#66
1972	Runaway/Happy Together	Dawn featuring Tony Orlando	#79
1972	Sing a Song/Make Your Own Kind of Music	Barbra Streisand	#94
1973	Pinball Wizard/See Me, Feel Me	The New Seekers	#29
1973	"Having a Party" Medley	The Ovations	#56
1975	The Way We Were/Try to Remember	Gladys Knight & The Pips	#11
1975	Hush/I'm Alive	Blue Swede	#61
1975	I Won't Last a Day Without You/Let Me Be the One	Al Wilson	#70
1976	The Best Disco in Town	The Ritchie Family	#17
1976	Don't Pull Your Love/Then You Can Tell Me Goodbye	Glen Campbell	#27
1976	Chain Gang Medley	Jim Croce	#63
1977	Uptown Festival (Part 1)	Shalamar	#25
1977	Whispering/Cherchez La Femme/Se Si Bon	Dr. Buzzard's Original Savannah Band	#27
1977	"Roots" Medley	Quincy Jones	#57
1977	Fly By Night/In the Mood	Rush	#88
1977	Discomania	The Lovers	#100
1978	We Will Rock You/We are the Champions	Queen	#4
1978	Themes from "The Wizard of Oz"	Meco	#35
1978	Sgt. Pepper's Lonely Hearts Club Band/With a Little Help From My Friends	The Beatles	#70
1978	Africanism/Gimme Some Lovin'	Kongas	#84
1979	Free Me from My Freedom/Tie Me to a Tree (Handcuff Me)	Bonnie Pointer	#58
1979	Light My Fire/137 Disco Heaven	Amii Stewart	#69

AMERICAN PATRIOTIC SONGS

YEAR	SONG	ARTIST	HOT 100
1970	America, Communicate with Me	Ray Stevens	#45
1970	The Declaration	The 5th Dimension	#64
1970	The Fightin' Side of Me	Merle Haggard	#92
1970	Where Have All Our Heroes Gone	Bill Anderson	#93
1972	An American Trilogy	Elvis Presley	#66
1974	Americans	Byron MacGregor	#4
1974	My Country	Jud Strunk	#59
1974	U.S. of A	Donna Fargo	#86

BREAK-IN SONGS

Break-in songs are just kind of odd. A break-in song is one that consists of parts of a bunch of different songs, but they are different from medleys. Usually, a medley will have parts of only 2-4 different songs, and each section will be an entire verse or chorus. Break-in songs will commonly join ten or more songs together. Each excerpt usually lasts only two or three seconds. These parts are joined together by spoken dialogue that is usually telling some silly story.

Dickie Goodman continued his reign from the sixties as the most successful break-in artist.

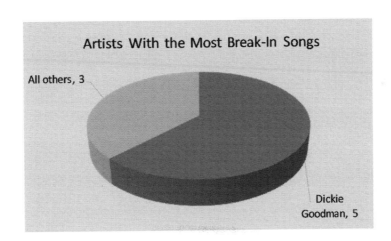

YEAR	SONG	ARTIST	HOT 100
1972	Convention '72	The Delegates	#8
1973	Super Fly Meets Shaft	John & Ernest	#31
1973	Watergate	Dickie Goodman	#42
1974	Energy Crisis '74	Dickie Goodman	#33
1974	Evil Boll-Weevil	Grand Canyon	#72
1974	Mr. President	Dickie Goodman	#73
1975	Mr. Jaws	Dickie Goodman	#4
1977	Kong	Dickie Goodman	#48

REGGAE SONGS

YEAR	SONG	ARTIST	HOT 100
1973	Stir It Up	Johnny Nash	#12
1976	Roots, Rock, Reggae	Bob Marley	#51
1978	(You Got to Walk And) Don't Look Back	Peter Tosh with Mick Jagger	#81

COMEDY SONGS

YEAR	SONG	ARTIST	HOT 100
1971	Ajax Liquor Store	Hudson & Landry	#43
1972	Ajax Airlines	Hudson & Landry	#68
1975	The Biggest Parakeets in Town	Jud Strunk	#50
1977	Grandmother's Song	Steve Martin	#72
1979	Cruel Shoes	Steve Martin	#91

SONGS FROM TV SHOWS

YEAR	SONG	ARTIST	HOT 100	TV SHOW
1970	Gimme Dat Ding	The Pipkins	#9	"Oliver & The Overlord"
1970	Rubber Duckie	Jim Henson	#16	"The Muppets"
1970	Long Lonesome Highway	Michael Parks	#20	"Then Came Bronson"
1970	Song from M*A*S*H	Al DeLory	#70	"M*A*S*H"
1971	Me and My Arrow	Nilsson	#34	"The Point"
1972	Theme from "The Men"	Isaac Hayes	#38	"The Men"
1972	If You Leave Me Tonight I'll Cry	Jerry Wallace	#38	"Rod Serling's Night Gallery"
1972	Those Were the Days	Carroll O'Connor & Jean Stapleton	#43	"All in the Family"
1973	Sing	Carpenters	#3	"Sesame Street"
1973	Steamroller Blues	Elvis Presley	#17	"Aloha from Hawaii via Satellite"
1974	TSOP (The Sound of Philadelphia)	MFSB	#1	"Soul Train"
1974	TSOP (The Sound of Philadelphia)	The Three Degrees	#1	"Soul Train"
1974	(We're Gonna) Rock Around the Clock	Bill Haley and His Comets	#39	"Happy Days"
1975	The Rockford Files	Mike Post	#10	"The Rockford Files"
1975	Keep Your Eye on the Sparrow	Merry Clayton	#45	"Baretta"

	SONGS FROM TV SHOWS (cont'd)			
1975	Chico and the Man	José Feliciano	#96	"Chico and the Man"
1976	Welcome Back	John Sebastian	#1	"Welcome Back Kotter"
1976	Theme from S.W.A.T.	Rhythm Heritage	#1	"S.W.A.T."
1976	Happy Days	Pratt & McClain	#5	"Happy Days"
1976	Nadia's Theme (The Young and the Restless)	Barry DeVorzon & Perry Botkin, Jr.	#8	"Bless the Beasts and Children"
1976	Baretta's Theme ("Keep Your Eye on the Sparrow")	Rhythm Heritage	#20	"S.W.A.T."
1976	Making Our Dreams Come True	Cyndi Grecco	#25	"LaVerne & Shirley"
1976	Mary Hartman, Mary Hartman	The Deadly Nightshade	#79	"Mary Hartman, Mary Hartman"
1976	Peter Gunn	Deodata	#84	"Peter Gunn"
1977	Disco Lucy (I Love Lucy Theme)	Wilton Place Street Band	#24	"I Love Lucy"
1977	"Roots" Medley	Quincy Jones	#57	"Roots"
1977	Shakey Ground	Phoebe Snow	#70	"Shaky Ground"
1978	Who Are You	The Who	#14	"CSI: Crime Scene Investigation"
1978	Thank You for Being a Friend	Andrew Gold	#25	"The Golden Girls"
1979	My Life	Billy Joel	#3	"Bosom Buddies"
1979	Different Worlds	Maureen McGovern	#18	"Different Worlds"

SONGS FROM MOVIES AND MUSICALS

YEAR	SONG	ARTIST	HOT 100	MOVIE/MUSICAL
1970	Come and Get It	Badfinger	#7	"The Magic Christian"
1970	Man of Constant Sorrow	Ginger Baker's Air Force	#85	"O Brother, Where Art Thou?"
1970	Let It Be	The Beatles	#1	"Let It Be"
1970	The Long and Winding Road	The Beatles	#1	"Let It Be"
1970	Airport Love Theme (Gwen and Vern)	Vincent Bell	#31	"Airport"
1970	Theme Music for the Film "2001" A Space Odyssey from Also Sprach Zarathustra	Berlin Philharmonic	#90	"2001 A Space Odyssey"
1970	(How 'Bout a Little Hand For) The Boys in the Band	The Boys in the Band	#48	"The Phynx"
1970	Where Are You Going	Jerry Butler	#95	"Joe"
1970	Everything a Man Could Ever Need	Glen Campbell	#52	"Norwood"
1970	Song from M*A*S*H*	Al DeLory	#70	"M*A*S*H*"
1970	(If You Let Me Make Love to You Then) Why Can't I Touch You?	Ronnie Dyson	#8	"Salvation"
1970	Superstar	Murray Head	#74	"Jesus Christ Superstar"
1970	Que Sera, Sera (Whatever Will Be, Will Be)	Mary Hopkin	#77	"The Man Who Knew Too Much"
1970	Feelings	Barry Mann	#93	"Getting Straight"
1970	Can't Help Falling in Love	Al Martino	#51	"Blue Hawaii"

SONGS FROM MOVIES AND MUSICALS (cont'd)

1970	See Me, Feel Me	The Who	#12	"Tommy"
1970	Overture from Tommy (A Rock Opera)	Assembled Multitude	#16	"Tommy"
1971	Medley from "Superstar" (A Rock Opera)	The Assembled Multitude	#95	"Jesus Christ Superstar"
1971	For All We Know	Carpenters	#3	"Lovers and Other Strangers"
1971	Flesh and Blood	Johnny Cash	#54	"I Walk the Line" (1970)
1971	One Tin Soldier, The Legend of Billy Jack	Coven	#26	"Billy Jack"
1971	Burning Bridges	Mike Curb Congregation	#34	"Kelly's Heroes"
1971	I Don't Know How to Love Him	Yvonne Elliman	#28	"Jesus Christ Superstar"
1971	Everything's Alright	Yvonne Elliman	#92	"Jesus Christ Superstar"
1971	Light Sings	The 5th Dimension	#44	"The Me Nobody Knows"
1971	Theme from Shaft	Isaac Hayes	#7	"Shaft"
1971	Superstar	Murray Head	#14	"Jesus Christ Superstar"
1971	Dolly Dagger	Jimi Hendrix	#74	"Rainbow Bridge"
1971	Friends	Elton John	#34	"Friends"
1971	I Don't Know How to Love Him/ Everything's Alright	The Kimberlys	#99	"Jesus Christ Superstar"
1971	Theme from Love Story	Francis Lai and His Orchestra	#31	"Love Story"
1971	Theme from Love Story	Henry Mancini and His Orchestra	#13	"Love Story"
1971	Theme from "Summer of '42"	Peter Nero	#21	"Summer of '42"
1971	I Don't Know How to Love Him	Helen Reddy	#13	"Jesus Christ Superstar"
1971	Someone Who Cares	Kenny Rogers & The First Edition	#51	"Fools"
1971	(Where Do I Begin) Love Story	Andy Williams	#9	"Love Story"
1972	Diamonds Are Forever	Shirley Bassey	#57	"Diamonds Are Forever"
1972	Love's Street and Fool's Road	Solomon Burke	#89	"Cool Breeze"
1972	I Only Have Eyes for You	Jerry Butler	#85	"Dames"
1972	Bless the Beasts and Children	Carpenters	#67	"Bless the Beasts and Children"
1972	The Candy Man	Mike Curb Congregation	#1	"Willy Wonka and The Chocolate Factory"
1972	The Candy Man	Sammy Davis Jr.	#1	"Willy Wonka and The Chocolate Factory"
1972	The First Time Ever I Saw Your Face	Roberta Flack	#1	"Play Misty for Me"
1972	Too Beautiful to Last	Engelbert Humperdinck	#86	"Nicholas and Alexandra"
1972	Ben	Michael Jackson	#1	"Ben"
1972	Money Runner	Quincy Jones	#57	""$""
1972	Brian's Song	Michel LeGrand	#56	"Brian's Song"
1972	Freddie's Dead (Theme from "Superfly")	Curtis Mayfield	#4	"Superfly"
1972	Slaughter	Billy Preston	#50	"Slaughter"
1972	All His Children	Charley Pride	#92	"Sometimes a Great Notion"
1972	Love Theme from "The Godfather"	Carlo Savina	#66	"The Godfather"
1972	I Guess I'll Miss the Man	The Supremes	#85	"Pippin"

SONGS FROM MOVIES AND MUSICALS (cont'd)

1972	Love Theme from "The Godfather" (Speak Softly Love)	Andy Williams	#34	"The Godfather"
1973	Last Tango in Paris	Herb Alpert and The Tijuana Brass	#77	"Last Tango in Paris"
1973	Smoke Gets in Your Eyes	Blue Haze	#27	"Roberta"
1973	Down and Out in New York City	James Brown	#50	"Black Caesar"
1973	Sexy, Sexy, Sexy	James Brown	#50	"Slaughter's Big Rip-Off"
1973	I Got a Name	Jim Croce	#10	"The Last American Hero"
1973	Happy	Bobby Darin	#67	"Lady Sings the Blues"
1973	Also Sprach Zarathustra (2001)	Deodato	#2	"2001: A Space Odyssey"
1973	Beyond the Blue Horizon	Neil Diamond	#34	"Jonathan Livingston Seagull"
1973	Knockin' on Heaven's Door	Bob Dylan	#12	"Pat Garrett and Billy the Kid"
1973	Living Together, Growing Together	The 5th Dimension	#32	"Lost Horizon"
1973	Are You Man Enough	Four Tops	#15	"Shaft in Africa"
1973	Trouble Man	Marvin Gaye	#7	"Trouble Man"
1973	Brother's Gonna Work It Out	Willie Hutch	#67	"The Mack"
1973	Slick	Willie Hutch	#65	"The Mack"
1973	Hurts So Good	Millie Jackson	#24	"Cleopatra Jones"
1973	Superfly	Curtis Mayfield	#8	"Superfly"
1973	Live and Let Die	Paul McCartney (Wings)	#2	"Live and Let Die"
1973	The Morning After	Maureen McGovern	#1	"The Poseidon Adventure"
1973	Send a Little Love My Way	Anne Murray	#72	"Oklahoma Crude"
1973	Pinball Wizard/See Me, Feel Me	The New Seekers	#29	"Tommy"
1973	Lost Horizon	Shawn Phillips	#2	"Lost Horizon"
1973	Separate Ways	Elvis Presley	#20	"Elvis on Tour"
1973	Good Morning Heartache	Diana Ross	#34	"Lady Sings the Blues"
1973	Theme from Cleopatra Jones	Joe Simon	#18	"Cleopatra Jones"
1973	Dueling Banjos	Eric Weissberg & Steve Mandell	#2	"Deliverance"
1973	Across 110th Street	Bobby Womack	#56	"Across 110th Street"
1974	Beyond the Blue Horizon	Lou Christie	#80	"Monte Carlo"
1974	One Tin Soldier, The Legend of Billy Jack	Coven	#73	"Billy Jack"
1974	Skybird	Neil Diamond	#75	"Jonathan Livingston Seagull"
1974	The Entertainer	Marvin Hamlisch	#3	"The Sting"
1974	On and On	Gladys Knight & The Pips	#5	"Claudine"
1974	Daybreak	Nilsson	#39	"Son of Dracula"
1974	Tubular Bells	Mike Oldfield	#7	"The Exorcist"
1974	The Way We Were	Barbra Streisand	#1	"The Way We Were"
1974	Ma! (He's Making Eyes at Me)	Lena Zavaroni	#91	"The Midnight Rounders"
1975	Summer of '42	Biddu Orchestra	#57	"Summer of '42"
1975	Send in the Clowns	Judy Collins	#36	"A Little Night Music"
1975	Ease on Down the Road	Consumer Rapport	#42	"The Wiz"

SONGS FROM MOVIES AND MUSICALS (cont'd)

1975	I Only Have Eyes for You	Art Garfunkel	#18	"Dames"
1975	Sky High	Jigsaw	#3	"The Dragon Flies"
1975	We May Never Love Like This Again	Maureen McGovern	#83	"The Towering Inferno"
1975	Main Title (Theme from "Jaws")	John Williams	#32	"Jaws"
1976	Mamma Mia	ABBA	#32	"Mamma Mia"
1976	I Could Have Danced All Night	Biddu Orchestra	#72	"My Fair Lady"
1976	I'm Easy	Keith Carradine	#17	"Nashville"
1976	Tubular Bells	The Champs' Boys Orchestra	#98	"The Exorcist"
1976	Nadia's Theme (The Young and the Restless)	Barry DeVorzon & Perry Botkin, Jr.	#8	"Bless the Beasts and Children"
1976	The Homecoming	Hagood Hardy	#41	"The Waltons"
1976	So Sad the Song	Gladys Knight & The Pips	#47	"Pipe Dreams"
1976	Lipstick	Michel Polnareff	#61	"Lipstick"
1976	Theme from Mahogany (Do You Know Where You're Going To)	Diana Ross	#1	"Mahogany"
1976	Norma Jean Wants to Be a Movie Star	Sundown Company	#84	"Goodbye Norma Jean"
1977	Magical Mystery Tour	Ambrosia	#39	"All This and World War II"
1977	How Deep Is Your Love	Bee Gees	#1	"Saturday Night Fever"
1977	The Greatest Love of All	George Benson	#24	"The Greatest"
1977	You Light Up My Life	Debby Boone	#1	"You Light Up My Life"
1977	You Light Up My Life	Kacey Cisyk	#80	"You Light Up My Life"
1977	Send in the Clowns	Judy Collins	#19	"A Little Night Music"
1977	Gonna Fly Now	Bill Conti	#1	"Rocky"
1977	Theme from "Rocky" (Gonna Fly Now)	Current	#94	"Rocky"
1977	You Take My Heart Away	James Darren	#52	"Rocky"
1977	Bless the Beasts and Children	Barry DeVorzon & Perry Botkin, Jr.	#82	"Bless the Beasts and Children"
1977	Gonna Fly Now (Theme from "Rocky")	Maynard Ferguson	#28	"Rocky"
1977	Watch Closely Now	Kris Kristofferson	#52	"A Star Is Born"
1977	Theme from Rocky (Gonna Fly Now)	Rhythm Heritage	#94	"Rocky"
1977	Car Wash	Rose Royce	#1	"Car Wash"
1977	I Wanna Get Next to You	Rose Royce	#10	"Car Wash"
1977	I'm Going Down	Rose Royce	#70	"Car Wash"
1977	My Fair Share	Seals & Crofts	#10	"One on One"
1977	Nobody Does It Better	Carly Simon	#2	"The Spy Who Loved Me"
1977	Love Theme from "A Star Is Born" (Evergreen)	Barbra Streisand	#1	"A Star Is Born"
1977	Star Wars (Main Title)	John Williams	#10	"Star Wars"
1978	Come Together	Aerosmith	#23	"Sgt. Pepper's Lonely Hearts Club Band"
1978	Stayin' Alive	Bee Gees	#1	"Saturday Night Fever"
1978	Night Fever	Bee Gees	#1	"Saturday Night Fever"

SONGS FROM MOVIES AND MUSICALS (cont'd)

1978	Louie, Louie	Blues Brothers	#89	"National Lampoon's Animal House"
1978	Almost Summer	Celebration featuring Mike Love	#28	"Almost Summer"
1978	If My Friends Could See Me Now	Linda Clifford	#54	"Sweet Charity"
1978	Got to Get You Into My Life	Earth, Wind & Fire	#9	"Sgt. Pepper's Lonely Hearts Club Band"
1978	If I Can't Have You	Yvonne Elliman	#1	"Saturday Night Fever"
1978	If Ever I See You Again	Roberta Flack	#24	"If Ever I See You Again"
1978	Goodbye Girl	David Gates	#15	"Goodbye Girl"
1978	Ease on Down the Road	Michael Jackson	#41	"The Wiz"
1978	Almost Like Being in Love	Michael Johnson	#32	"Brigadoon"
1978	Boogie Shoes	KC and The Sunshine Band	#35	"Saturday Night Fever"
1978	Thank God It's Friday	Love and Kisses	#22	"Thank God It's Friday"
1978	Copacabana (At the Copa)	Barry Manilow	#8	"Foul Play"
1978	Ready to Take a Chance Again	Barry Manilow	#11	"Foul Play"
1978	Get Back	Billy Preston	#86	"Sgt. Pepper's Lonely Hearts Club Band"
1978	Ease on Down the Road	Diana Ross	#41	"The Wiz"
1978	Theme Song from "Which Way Is Up"	Stargard	#21	"Which Way Is Up"
1978	FM (No Static at All)	Steely Dan	#22	"FM"
1978	Love Theme from "Eyes of Laura Mars" (Prisoner)	Barbra Streisand	#21	"Eyes of Laura Mars"
1978	Last Dance	Donna Summer	#3	"Thank God It's Friday"
1978	Over the Rainbow	Gary Tanner	#69	"The Wizard of Oz"
1978	More Than a Woman	Tavares	#32	"Saturday Night Fever"
1978	You're the One That I Want	John Travolta & Olivia Newton-John	#1	"Grease"
1978	Summer Nights	John Travolta & Olivia Newton-John	#5	"Grease"
1978	Greased Lightnin'	John Travolta	#47	"Grease"
1978	Chattanooga Choo Choo	Tuxedo Junction	#32	"Sun Valley Serenade"
1978	Grease	Frankie Valli	#1	"Grease"
1978	Life's Been Good	Joe Walsh	#12	"FM"
1978	Theme from "Close Encounters of the Third Kind"	John Williams	#13	"Close Encounters of the Third Kind"
1978	Hopelessly Devoted to You	Olivia Newton-John	#3	"Grease"
1979	California Dreamin'	America	#56	"California Dreaming"
1979	Easy to Be Hard	Cheryl Barnes	#64	"Hair"
1979	Animal House	Stephen Bishop	#73	"Animal House"
1979	Moment By Moment	Yvonne Elliman	#59	"Moment By Moment"
1979	Rock II Disco	Maynard Ferguson	#82	"Rocky"
1979	Rainbow Connection	Jim Henson	#25	"The Muppet Movie"
1979	Good Friend	Mary MacGregor	#39	"Meatballs"
1979	Theme from Ice Castles (Through the Eyes of Love)	Melissa Manchester	#76	"Ice Castles"

	SONGS FROM MOVIES AND MUSICALS (cont'd)			
1979	Can You Read My Mind	Maureen McGovern	#52	"Superman"
1979	Get a Move On	Eddie Money	#46	"Americathon"
1979	Chase	Giorgio Moroder	#33	"Midnight Express"
1979	Makin' It	David Naughton	#5	"Meatballs"
1979	Every Which Way But Loose	Eddie Rabbitt	#30	"Every Which Way But Loose"
1979	You Take My Breath Away	Rex Smith	#10	"Sooner or Later"
1979	The Main Event/Fight	Barbra Streisand	#3	"The Main Event"
1979	For You and I	10cc	#85	"Moment By Moment"
1979	Long Live Rock	The Who	#54	"The Kids Are Alright"
1979	5:15	The Who	#45	"Quadrophenia"
1979	Theme from "Superman" (Main Title)	John Williams	#81	"Superman"
1979	Pinball, That's All	Billy Wray	#96	"Tilt"

SONGS FROM COMMERCIALS/JINGLES

YEAR	SONG	ARTIST	HOT 100	COMMERCIAL/JINGLE
1970	We've Only Just Begun	Carpenters	#2	Crocker Bank of California
1970	She Lets Her Hair Down in the Morning (Early in the Morning)	The Tokens	#61	Breck Shampoo
1971	California on My Mind	Cashman & West	#96	Kodak
1972	I'd Like to Teach the World to Sing (In Perfect Harmony)	The Hillside Singers	#13	Coca-Cola
1972	We're Together	The Hillside Singers	#100	McDonalds
1972	I'd Like to Teach the World to Sing (In Perfect Harmony)	The New Seekers	#7	Coca-Cola
1972	When You Say Love	Sonny & Cher	#32	Budweiser
1973	That's Why You Remember	Kenny Karen	#82	Faygo (soda)
1973	Country Sunshine	Dottie West	#49	Coca-Cola
1976	Times of Your Life	Paul Anka	#7	Kodak

TRUCK DRIVER SONGS

YEAR	SONG	ARTIST	HOT 100
1974	Old Home Filler-Up An' Keep On-A-Truckin' Café	C.W. McCall	#54
1975	Wolf Creek Pass	C.W. McCall	#40
1976	Convoy	C.W. McCall	#1
1976	The White Knight	Cledus Maggard and The Citizen's Band	#19
1976	Teddy Bear	Red Sovine	#40
1976	Kentucky Moonrunner	Cledus Maggard and The Citizen's Band	#85
1977	C.B. Savage	Rod Hart	#67

TRIBUTE SONGS

YEAR	SONG	ARTIST	HOT 100	SUBJECT OF TRIBUTE
1970	Cole, Cooke & Redding	Wilson Pickett	#91	Nat "King" Cole, Sam Cooke, & Otis Redding
1971	What the World Needs Now Is Love/Abraham, Martin and John	Tom Clay	#8	Abraham Lincoln, Martin Luther King, Jr., John F. Kennedy, and Robert Kennedy
1972	Vincent	Don McLean	#12	Vincent van Gogh
1972	Amerikan Music	Steve Alaimo	#79	Many early Rock and Roll stars
1975	Philadelphia Freedom	Elton John	#1	Billie Jean King
1975	Free Bird	Lynyrd Skynyrd	#19	Duane Allman of The Allman Brothers Band
1975	Wonderful Baby	Don McLean	#93	Fred Astaire
1975	Hoppy, Gene and Me	Roy Rogers	#65	Hopalong Cassidy, Gene Autry and Roy Rogers
1975	The Immigrant	Neil Sedaka	#22	John Lennon
1977	Sir Duke	Stevie Wonder	#1	Duke Ellington, Count Basie, Glen Miller, Louis Armstrong
1977	The King Is Gone	Ronnie McDowell	#13	Elvis Presley
1977	Free Bird	Lynyrd Skynyrd	#38	Duane Allman of The Allman Brothers Band
1977	Platinum Heroes	Bruce Foster	#63	The Beatles
1979	Pops, We Love You (A Tribute to Father)	Diana Ross, Marvin Gaye, Smokey Robinson & Stevie Wonder	#59	Berry Gordy Sr.

STORY SONGS

YEAR	SONG	ARTIST	HOT 100
1970	One Tin Soldier	The Original Caste	#34
1970	Got to See if I Can't Get Mommy (To Come Back Home)	Jerry Butler	#62
1971	Gypsys, Tramps & Thieves	Cher	#1
1971	Amos Moses	Jerry Reed	#8
1971	Chick-A-Boom (Don't Ya Jes' Love It)	Daddy Dewdrop	#9
1971	Timothy	The Buoys	#17
1971	Stagger Lee	Tommy Roe	#25
1971	One Tin Soldier (The Legend of Billy Jack)	Coven	#26
1971	The Court Room	Clarence Carter	#61
1972	You Don't Mess Around with Jim	Jim Croce	#8
1972	Hot Rod Lincoln	Commander Cody	#9
1972	Taxi	Harry Chapin	#24

	STORY SONGS (cont'd)		
1972	Buzzy Brown	Tim Davis	#91
1973	Bad, Bad Leroy Brown	Jim Croce	#1
1973	The Night the Lights Went Out in Georgia	Vicki Lawrence	#1
1973	Uneasy Rider	Charlie Daniels	#9
1973	Swamp Witch	Jim Stafford	#39
1974	Billy, Don't Be a Hero	Bo Donaldson & The Heywoods	#1
1974	Dark Lady	Cher	#1
1974	Last Kiss	Wednesday	#34
1974	Old Home Filler-Up An' Keep On-A-Truckin' Café	C.W. McCall	#54
1974	The Lone Ranger	Oscar Brown Jr.	#69
1974	Battle of New Orleans	Nitty Gritty Dirt Band	#72
1974	Bad, Bad Leroy Brown	Frank Sinatra	#83
1974	Don't Eat the Yellow Snow	Frank Zappa	#86
1974	Last Kiss	J. Frank Wilson & The Cavaliers	#92
1974	Tell Laura I Love Her	Johnny T. Angel	#94
1974	Billy – Don't Be a Hero	Paper Lace	#96
1975	Lyin' Eyes	The Eagles	#2
1975	Wildfire	Michael Murphey	#3
1975	Run Joey Run	David Geddes	#4
1975	The Last Game of the Season (A Blind Man in the Bleachers)	David Geddes	#18
1975	Your Bulldog Drinks Champagne	Jim Stafford	#24
1975	Judy Mae	Boomer Castleman	#33
1975	Lizzie and the Rainman	Tanya Tucker	#37
1975	Blind Man in the Bleachers	Kenny Starr	#58
1975	Alvin Stone (The Birth & Death of a Gangster)	Fantastic Four	#74
1976	The Wreck of the Edmund Fitzgerald	Gordon Lightfoot	#2
1976	Take the Money and Run	Steve Miller	#11
1976	The White Knight	Cledus Maggard	#19
1976	One Piece at a Time	Johnny Cash	#29
1976	Hurricane (Part 1)	Bob Dylan	#33
1976	Teddy Bear	Red Sovine	#40
1976	Without Your Love (Mr. Jordan)	Charlie Ross	#42
1976	Teddy Bear's Last Ride	Diana Williams	#66
1976	Jasper	Jim Stafford	#69
1976	Kentucky Moonrunner	Cledus Maggard	#85
1976	Better Place to Be (Parts 1 & 2)	Harry Chapin	#86
1977	The Killing of Georgie (Part 1 and 2)	Rod Stewart	#30
1977	C.B. Savage	Rod Hart	#67
1977	Ma Baker	Boney M	#96
1979	The Devil Went Down to Georgia	Charlie Daniels Band	#3
1979	Cruel Shoes	Steve Martin	#91

SONGS ABOUT LOVE/TOGETHERNESS

YEAR	SONG	ARTIST	HOT 100
1970	Share the Land	The Guess Who	#10
1970	United We Stand	Brotherhood of Man	#13
1970	A Song of Joy (Himno a la Elegria)	Miguel Ríos	#14
1970	Wonderful World, Beautiful People	Jimmy Cliff	#25
1970	Let's Work Together	Canned Heat	#26
1970	Save the Country	The 5th Dimension	#27
1970	Let's Work Together (Part 1)	Wilbert Harrison	#32
1970	Ungena Za Ulimwengu (Unite the World)	The Temptations	#33
1970	Let's Give Adam and Eve Another Chance	Gary Puckett & The Union Gap	#41
1970	The Onion Song	Marvin Gaye & Tammi Terrell	#50
1970	Think About Your Children	Mary Hopkin	#87
1971	What the World Needs Now Is Love/Abraham, Martin and John	Tom Clay	#8
1972	If We Only Have Love	Dionne Warwick	#84
1973	Believe in Humanity	Carole King	#28
1973	Living Together, Growing Together	The 5th Dimension	#32
1976	Wake Up Everybody (Part 1)	Harold Melvin	#12
1976	Shower the People	James Taylor	#22
1976	Love and Understanding (Come Together)	Kool & The Gang	#77
1979	Love Is the Answer	England Dan & John Ford Coley	#10

SONGS ABOUT DANCES

This list includes songs about a particular dance, as opposed to songs about dancing. Songs about dances were quite popular in the 60s. Chubby Checker alone had more hits about dances in the 60s then everyone had in the 70s! For some reason though, their appeal wore off in the 70s.

YEAR	SONG	ARTIST	HOT 100
1970	Do the Funky Chicken	Rufus Thomas	#28
1972	Do the Funky Penguin (Part 1)	Rufus Thomas	#44
1974	The Loco-Motion	Grand Funk	#1
1975	The Bertha Butt Boogie (Part 1)	Jimmy Castor Bunch	#16
1975	Attitude Dancing	Carly Simon	#21
1975	I Wanna Dance Wit' Choo (Doo Dat Dance), Part 1	Disco Tex & His Sex-O-Lettes	#23
1975	Dance the Kung Fu	Carl Douglas	#48
1975	The Funky Gibbon	The Goodies	#79

SONGS WITH DEATHS

Over 200 people died in the songs of the 1970s! This is pretty tame compared to the 60s, where over 4,000 people died, but still. The songs are arranged in order, from the songs with the most deaths to the songs with the fewest deaths.

YEAR	SONG	ARTIST	HOT 100	# DEATHS
1974	The Night Chicago Died	Paper Lace	#1	100+
1976	The Wreck of the Edmund Fitzgerald	Gordon Lightfoot	#2	29
1977	Ma Baker	Boney M	#96	6
1970	Ohio	Crosby, Stills, Nash & Young	#14	4
1970	Six White Horses	Tommy Cash	#79	3
1973	The Night the Lights Went Out in Georgia	Vicki Lawrence	#1	3
1976	Hurricane (Part 1)	Bob Dylan	#33	3
1970	Patches	Clarence Carter	#4	2
1970	My Woman, My Woman, My Wife	Marty Robbins	#42	2
1973	Keep on Singing	Austin Roberts	#50	2
1973	Blood Red and Goin' Down	Tanya Tucker	#74	2
1974	Dark Lady	Cher	#1	2
1974	I Shot the Sheriff	Eric Clapton	#1	2
1975	Judy Mae	Boomer Castleman	#33	2
1976	Ode to Billie Joe	Bobbie Gentry	#54	2
1976	Forever Lovers	Mac Davis	#76	2
1970	Fancy	Bobbie Gentry	#31	1
1970	Jennifer Tomkins	Street People	#36	1
1970	Mongoose	Elephant's Memory	#50	1
1970	Got to See if I Can't Get Mommy (To Come Back Home)	Jerry Butler	#62	1
1970	Rock Island Line	Johnny Cash	#93	1
1971	The Night They Drove Old Dixie Down	Joan Baez	#3	1
1971	Amos Moses	Jerry Reed	#8	1
1971	Timothy	The Buoys	#17	1
1971	The Year That Clayton Delaney Died	Tom T. Hall	#42	1
1971	Bed of Rose's	The Statler Brothers	#58	1
1971	Soldier's Last Letter	Merle Haggard	#90	1
1971	Banks of the Ohio	Olivia Newton-John	#94	1
1972	No Sad Song	Helen Reddy	#61	1
1972	Buzzy Brown	Tim Davis	#91	1
1973	Swamp Witch	Jim Stafford	#39	1
1973	What's Your Mama's Name	Tanya Tucker	#86	1

	SONGS WITH DEATHS (cont'd)			
1974	Billy, Don't Be a Hero	Bo Donaldson & The Heywoods	#1	1
1974	Keep on Singing	Helen Reddy	#15	1
1974	Last Kiss	Wednesday	#34	1
1974	Last Kiss	J. Frank Wilson & The Cavaliers	#92	1
1974	Tell Laura I Love Her	Johnny T. Angel	#94	1
1974	Billy – Don't Be a Hero	Paper Lace	#96	1
1975	Wildfire	Michael Murphey	#3	1
1975	Run Joey Run	David Geddes	#4	1
1975	Emma	Hot Chocolate	#8	1
1975	Rocky	Austin Roberts	#9	1
1975	The Last Game of the Season (A Blind Man in the Bleachers)	David Geddes	#18	1
1975	Saturday Night Special	Lynyrd Skynyrd	#27	1
1975	Blind Man in the Bleachers	Kenny Starr	#58	1
1975	Alvin Stone (The Birth & Death of a Gangster)	Fantastic Four	#74	1
1976	Teddy Bear's Last Ride	Diana Williams	#66	1
1976	Johnny Cool	Steve Gibbons Band	#72	1
1976	Norma Jean Wants to Be a Movie Star	Sundown Company	#84	1
1977	The Killing of Georgie (Part 1 and 2)	Rod Stewart	#30	1
1978	Werewolves of London	Warren Zevon	#21	1
1978	Portrait (He Knew)	Kansas	#64	1
1979	Ghost Dancer	Addrisi Brothers	#45	1
1970	One Tin Soldier	The Original Caste	#34	?
1971	One Tin Soldier (The Legend of Billy Jack)	Coven	#26	?

COVERS

A cover song is a new recording of a song by someone other than the original recording artist. For this category, I am listing only covers of songs that previously landed on any of the main Billboard charts. Billboard started these charts ("Best Sellers in Stores", "Most Played by Disc Jockeys", and "Most Played in Jukeboxes") in 1955. The Hot 100 chart began in 1958. As a result, any cover of a song that appeared on a chart before 1955 will not be listed.

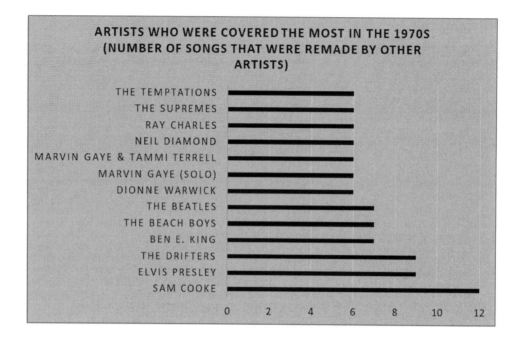

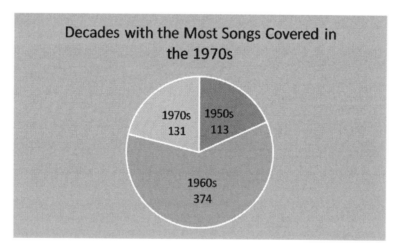

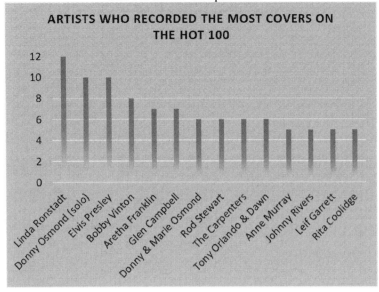

Artists must enjoy doing their own versions of previous hits- there were over 600 covers in the 70s alone. They don't often perform as well on the charts as the original hit, however. Almost 75% of covers recorded in the 70s peaked at a lower position on the Hot 100 than the original hit.

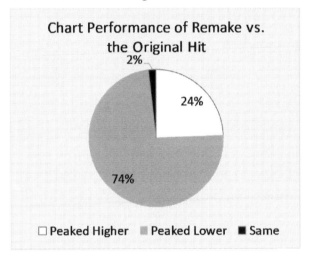

1950s COVERS

YEAR	COVER	COVER ARTIST	COVER'S CHART POSITION	ORIGINAL HIT'S YEAR	ORIGINAL ARTIST	ORIGINAL'S CHART POSITION
1973	Ain't Got No Home	The Band	#73	1957	Clarence Henry	#20
1979	Ain't That a Shame	Cheap Trick	#35	1955	Fats Domino	#10
1970	All I Have to Do Is Dream	Bobbie Gentry & Glen Campbell	#27	1958	Everly Brothers	#1
1975	All I Have to Do Is Dream	Nitty Gritty Dirt Band	#66	1958	Everly Brothers	#1
1974	All Shook Up	Suzi Quatro	#85	1957	Elvis Presley	#1
1974	Are You Lonesome Tonight	Donny Osmond	#14	1959	Jaye P. Morgan	#65

	**1950s COVERS (cont'd)**
1976	Baby Face	The Wing and a Prayer Fife and Drum Corps.	#14	1958	Little Richard	#41
1978	Back in the U.S.A.	Linda Ronstadt	#16	1959	Chuck Berry	#37
1974	Battle of New Orleans	Nitty Gritty Dirt Band	#72	1959	Johnny Horton	#1
1973	Blue Suede Shoes	Johnny Rivers	#38	1956	Carl Perkins	#2
1973	Bongo Rock	The Incredible Bongo Band	#57	1959	Preston Epps	#14
1972	Chantilly Lace	Jerry Lee Lewis	#43	1958	The Big Bopper	#6
1975	Children's Marching Song	Purple Reign	#48	1959	Cyril Stapleton	#13
1975	Children's Marching Song	Purple Reign	#48	1959	Mitch Miller	#16
1973	Come Softly to Me	The New Seekers	#95	1959	The Fleetwoods	#1
1972	Cry	Lynn Anderson	#71	1959	Knightsbridge Strings	#53
1970	Cry Me a River	Joe Cocker	#11	1955	Julie London	#9
1972	Dedicated to the One I Love	The Temprees	#93	1959	The Shirelles	#83
1976	Deep Purple	Donny & Marie Osmond	#14	1957	Billy Ward	#20
1978	Devoted to You	Carly Simon & James Taylor	#36	1958	The Everly Brothers	#10
1973	Do You Want to Dance	Bette Midler	#17	1958	Bobby Freeman	#5
1978	Do You Want to Dance	The Ramones	#86	1958	Bobby Freeman	#5
1975	Don't Let Go	Commander Cody	#56	1958	Roy Hamilton	#13
1971	Empty Arms	Sonny James	#93	1957	Teresa Brewer	#13
1972	Every Day of My Life	Bobby Vinton	#24	1956	McGuire Sisters	#37
1973	Fever	Rita Coolidge	#76	1956	Little Willie John	#24
1974	Fool Such as I	Bob Dylan	#55	1959	Elvis Presley	#2
1975	For Your Love	Christopher Paul & Shawn	#91	1958	Ed Townsend	#13
1972	For Your Precious Love	Linda Jones	#74	1958	Jerry Butler & The Impressions	#11
1972	Gone	Joey Heatherton	#24	1957	Ferlin Husky	#4
1972	Guess Who	B.B. King	#62	1959	Jesse Belvin	#31
1971	Heartbreak Hotel	Frijid Pink	#72	1956	Elvis Presley	#1
1973	Hearts of Stone	Blue Ridge Rangers	#37	1955	Fontane Sisters	#1
1977	Here Comes Summer	Wildfire	#49	1959	Jerry Keller	#14
1973	Hey Little Girl	Foster Sylvers	#92	1959	Dee Clark	#20
1972	Honky Tonk	James Brown	#44	1956	Bill Doggett (Parts 1 & 2)	#2
1972	Hushabye	Robert John	#99	1959	The Mystics	#20
1976	I Could Have Danced All Night	Biddu Orchestra	#72	1956	Sylvia Syms	#20

1950s COVERS (cont'd)

1971	I Hear You Knocking	Dave Edmunds	#4	1955	Gale Storm	#2
1972	I Only Have Eyes for You	Jerry Butler	#85	1959	The Flamingos	#11
1975	I Only Have Eyes for You	Art Garfunkel	#18	1959	The Flamingos	#11
1972	I'm Movin' On	John Kay	#52	1959	Ray Charles	#40
1974	I've Had It	Fanny	#79	1959	Bell Notes	#6
1970	If I Didn't Care	The Moments	#44	1959	Connie Francis	#22
1974	In the Mood	Bette Midler	#51	1959	Ernie Fields	#4
1974	In the Mood	Henhouse Five Plus Too (Ray Stevens)	#40	1959	Ernie Fields	#4
1975	Indian Love Call	Ray Stevens	#68	1958	Ernie Freeman	#59
1975	It Doesn't Matter Anymore	Linda Ronstadt	#47	1959	Buddy Holly	#13
1970	It's All in the Game	The Four Tops	#24	1958	Tommy Edwards	#1
1970	It's Just a Matter of Time	Sonny James	#87	1959	Brook Benton	#3
1970	It's Only Make Believe	Glen Campbell	#10	1958	Conway Twitty	#1
1974	Jim Dandy	Black Oak Arkansas	#25	1957	LaVern Baker	#17
1970	Johnny B. Goode	Johnny Winter	#92	1958	Chuck Berry	#8
1974	Kissin' Time	Kiss	#83	1959	Bobby Rydell	#11
1972	Little Bitty Pretty One	The Jackson 5	#13	1957	Thurston Harris	#6
1975	Little Drummer Boy	Moonlion	#95	1958	Harry Simeone Chorale	#13
1971	Lonely Teardrops	Brian Hyland	#54	1959	Jackie Wilson	#7
1976	Lonely Teardrops	Narvel Felts	#62	1959	Jackie Wilson	#7
1970	Long Lonely Nights	The Dells	#74	1957	Lee Andrews and The Hearts	#45
1970	Long Lonely Nights	The Dells	#74	1957	Clyde McPhatter	#49
1972	Love Potion Number Nine	The Coasters	#76	1959	The Clovers	#23
1975	Lover's Question	Loggins & Messina	#89	1959	Clyde McPhatter	#6
1975	Manhattan Spiritual	Mike Post	#56	1959	Reg Owen	#10
1978	Mary's Boy Child	Boney M (medley)	#85	1956	Harry Belafonte	#12
1970	Maybe	Three Degrees	#29	1958	The Chantels	#15
1975	Misty	Ray Stevens	#14	1959	Johnny Mathis	#12
1976	Moonlight Serenade	Bobby Vinton	#97	1959	The Rivieras	#47
1975	Morning Side of the Mountain	Donny & Marie Osmond	#8	1959	Tommy Edwards	#27
1970	No Arms Can Ever Hold You	Bobby Vinton	#93	1955	Georgie Shaw	#23
1970	No Arms Can Ever Hold You	Bobby Vinton	#93	1955	Pat Boone	#26

1950s COVERS (cont'd)

1970	No Arms Can Ever Hold You	Bobby Vinton	#93	1955	The Gaylords	#67
1976	Only Sixteen	Dr. Hook	#6	1959	Sam Cooke	#28
1975	Only You (And You Alone)	Ringo Starr	#6	1955	The Platters	#5
1978	Peggy Sue	The Beach Boys	#59	1957	Buddy Holly	#3
1976	Peter Gunn	Deodato	#84	1959	Ray Anthony	#8
1970	Primrose Lane	O.C. Smith	#86	1959	Jerry Wallace	#8
1978	Put Your Head on My Shoulder	Leif Garrett	#58	1959	Paul Anka	#2
1970	Que Sera, Sera (Whatever Will Be, Will Be)	Mary Hopkin	#77	1956	Doris Day	#2
1978	Raining in My Heart	Leo Sayer	#47	1959	Buddy Holly	#88
1976	Rock and Roll Music	The Beach Boys	#5	1957	Chuck Berry	#8
1974	Rock Around the Clock	Bill Haley	#39	1955	Bill Haley and His Comets	#1
1970	Rock Island Line	Johnny Cash	#93	1956	Lonnie Donegan	#8
1973	Rockin' Pneumonia and the Boogie Woogie Flu	Johnny Rivers	#6	1957	Huey Smith & The Clowns	#52
1972	Rockin' Robin	Michael Jackson	#2	1958	Bobby Day	#2
1973	Roll Over Beethoven	Electric Light Orchestra	#42	1956	Chuck Berry	#29
1971	Sea Cruise	Johnny Rivers	#84	1959	Frankie Ford	#14
1979	Since I Don't Have You	Art Garfunkel	#53	1959	The Skyliners	#12
1975	Since I Met You Baby	Freddy Fender	#45	1956	Ivory Joe Hunter	#12
1976	Sixteen Tons	Don Harrison Band	#47	1955	"Tennessee" Ernie Ford	#1
1973	Smoke Gets in Your Eyes	Blue Haze	#27	1958	Richard Barrett	#94
1971	Stagger Lee	Tommy Roe	#25	1959	Lloyd Price	#1
1970	Summertime Blues	The Who	#27	1958	Eddie Cochran	#8
1970	Suzie-Q	José Feliciano	#84	1957	Dale Hawkins	#27
1976	That'll Be the Day	Linda Ronstadt	#11	1957	The Crickets	#1
1973	Think	James Brown	#77	1957	The "5" Royales	#66
1971	Till	Tom Jones	#41	1957	Percy Faith and His Orchestra	#63
1973	Tweedlee Dee	Little Jimmy Osmond	#59	1955	LaVern Baker	#14
1973	Twelfth of Never	Donny Osmond	#8	1957	Johnny Mathis	#9
1975	Volare (Nel Blu Dipinto Di Blu)	Al Martino	#33	1958	Domenico Modugno	#1
1975	Volare (Nel Blu Dipinto Di Blu)	Al Martino	#33	1958	Dean Martin	#12
1975	What a Diff'rence a Day Makes	Esther Phillips	#20	1959	Dinah Washington	#8

	1950s COVERS (cont'd)					
1972	What am I Living For	Ray Charles	#54	1958	Chuck Willis	#9
1972	What'd I Say	Rare Earth	#61	1959	Ray Charles	#6
1975	Who's Sorry Now	Marie Osmond	#40	1958	Connie Francis	#4
1972	Why	Donny Osmond	#13	1959	Frankie Avalon	#1
1974	Willie and the Hand Jive	Eric Clapton	#26	1958	Johnny Otis Show	#9
1970	Without Love (There Is Nothing)	Tom Jones	#5	1957	Clyde McPhatter	#19
1970	Wonder of You	Elvis Presley	#9	1959	Ray Peterson	#25
1971	You Send Me	Ponderosa Twins + One	#78	1957	Sam Cooke	#1
1972	You Were Made for Me	Luther Ingram	#93	1958	Sam Cooke	#27
1976	Young Blood	Bad Company	#20	1957	The Coasters	#8
1973	Young Love	Donny Osmond	#25	1957	Sonny James	#1
1976	Young Love	Ray Stevens	#93	1957	Sonny James	#1

1960s COVERS

YEAR	COVER	COVER ARTIST	COVER'S CHART POSITION	ORIGINAL HIT'S YEAR	ORIGINAL ARTIST	ORIGINAL'S CHART POSITION
1971	Abraham, Martin and John	Tom Clay (medley)	#8	1968	Dion	#4
1970	Ain't No Mountain High Enough	Diana Ross	#1	1967	Marvin Gaye & Tammi Terrell	#19
1972	Ain't Nobody Home	B.B. King	#46	1966	Howard Tate	#63
1974	Ain't Nothing Like the Real Thing	Aretha Franklin	#47	1968	Marvin Gaye & Tammi Terrell	#8
1977	Ain't Nothing Like the Real Thing	Donny & Marie Osmond	#21	1968	Marvin Gaye & Tammi Terrell	#8
1972	Ain't That Peculiar	Fanny	#85	1965	Marvin Gaye	#8
1975	Ain't That Peculiar	Diamond Reo	#44	1965	Marvin Gaye	#8
1974	Ain't Too Proud to Beg	Rolling Stones	#17	1966	Temptations	#13
1971	All My Trials	Ray Stevens	#71	1964	Dick & DeeDee	#89
1977	All Strung Out	John Travolta	#34	1966	Nino Tempo & April Stevens	#26
1974	Another Saturday Night	Cat Stevens	#6	1963	Sam Cooke	#10
1972	Baby Don't You Do It	The Band	#34	1964	Marvin Gaye	#27
1970	Baby I Love You	Little Milton	#82	1966	Jimmy Holiday	#98
1970	Baby I Need Your Loving	O.C. Smith	#52	1964	Four Tops	#11
1979	Baby I Need Your Loving	Eric Carmen	#62	1964	Four Tops	#11
1971	Baby, I'm Yours	Jody Miller	#91	1965	Barbara Lewis	#11
1978	Back in My Arms	Genya Ravan	#92	1965	The Supremes	#1
1970	Be My Baby	Andy Kim	#17	1963	The Ronettes	#2

	1960s Covers (cont'd)					
1971	Be My Baby	Cissy Houston	#92	1963	The Ronettes	#2
1970	The Bells	The Originals	#12	1960	James Brown	#68
1971	Birds of a Feather	The Raiders	#23	1969	Joe South	#96
1977	Blue Bayou	Linda Ronstadt	#3	1963	Roy Orbison	#29
1970	Breaking Up Is Hard to Do	Lenny Welch	#34	1962	Neil Sedaka	#1
1972	Breaking Up Is Hard to Do	The Partridge Family	#28	1962	Neil Sedaka	#1
1971	Bright Lights Big City	Sonny James	#91	1961	Jimmy Reed	#58
1970	Bring It on Home to Me	Lou Rawls	#96	1962	Sam Cooke	#13
1972	Brown Eyed Girl	El Chicano	#45	1967	Van Morrison	#10
1973	But I Do	Bobby Vinton	#82	1961	Clarence Henry	#4
1971	By the Time I Get to Phoenix	Glen Campbell/Anne Murray (medley)	#81	1967	Glen Campbell	#26
1979	California Dreamin'	America	#56	1966	The Mamas & The Papas	#4
1970	California Soul	Marvin Gaye & Tammi Terrell	#56	1969	The 5th Dimension	#25
1971	Can I Get a Witness	Lee Michaels	#39	1963	Marvin Gaye	#22
1976	Can You Do It	Grand Funk Railroad	#45	1964	The Contours	#41
1970	Can't Help Falling in Love	Al Martino	#51	1962	Elvis Presley	#2
1970	Can't Help Falling in Love	Andy Williams	#88	1962	Elvis Presley	#2
1976	Chain Gang	Jim Croce (medley)	#63	1960	Sam Cooke	#2
1970	Change Is Gonna Come	The 5th Dimension	#60	1965	Sam Cooke	#31
1978	Chattanooga Choo Choo	Tuxedo Junction	#32	1960	Ernie Fields	#54
1971	Cherish	David Cassidy	#9	1966	The Association	#1
1976	C'mon Marianne	Donny Osmond	#38	1967	The 4 Seasons	#9
1970	Come Together	Ike & Tina Turner	#57	1969	The Beatles	#1
1978	Come Together	Aerosmith	#23	1969	The Beatles	#1
1971	Cry Baby	Janis Joplin	#42	1963	Garnet Mimms & The Enchanters	#4
1976	Cry to Me	Freddie Scott	#70	1962	Solomon Burke	#44
1970	Cupid	Johnny Nash	#39	1961	Sam Cooke	#17
1976	Cupid	Tony Orlando & Dawn	#22	1961	Sam Cooke	#17
1972	Da Doo Ron Ron	Ian Matthews	#96	1963	The Crystals	#3
1977	Da Doo Ron Ron	Shaun Cassidy	#1	1963	The Crystals	#3
1973	Daddy's Home	Jermaine Jackson	#9	1961	Shep & The Limelites	#2
1978	Darlin'	Paul Davis w/Susan Collins	#51	1968	The Beach Boys	#19
1970	Day Is Done	Brooklyn Bridge	#98	1969	Peter, Paul & Mary	#21
1975	Day Tripper	Anne Murray	#59	1966	The Beatles	#5

		1960s Covers (cont'd)					
1976	Devil with a Blue Dress On	Pratt & McClain	#71	1966	Mitch Ryder & The Detroit Wheels (medley)	#4
1973	Didn't We	Barbra Streisand	#82	1969	Richard Harris	#63
1978	Do You Believe in Magic	Shaun Cassidy	#31	1965	The Lovin' Spoonful	#9
1970	Don't It Make You Want to Go Home	Brook Benton	#45	1969	Joe South & The Believers	#41
1978	Don't Let Me Be Misunderstood	Santa Esmeralda w/Leroy Gomez	#15	1965	The Animals	#15
1970	Don't Make Me Over	Brenda & The Tabulations	#77	1963	Dionne Warwick	#21
1970	Don't Play That Song	Aretha Franklin w/The Dixie Flyers	#11	1962	Ben E. King	#11
1970	Don't Worry Baby	The Tokens	#95	1964	The Beach Boys	#24
1977	Don't Worry Baby	B.J. Thomas	#17	1964	The Beach Boys	#24
1971	Dream Baby (How Long Must I Dream)	Glen Campbell	#31	1962	Roy Orbison	#4
1975	Dream Merchant	New Birth	#36	1959	Jerry Butler	#38
1975	Drive My Car	Gary Toms Empire	#69	1966	Bob Kuban	#93
1979	Easy to Be Hard	Cheryl Barnes	#64	1969	Three Dog Night	#4
1970	End of Our Road	Marvin Gaye	#40	1968	Gladys Knight & The Pips	#15
1970	Eve of Destruction	The Turtles	#100	1965	Barry McGuire	#1
1974	Everlasting Love	Carl Carlton	#6	1967	Robert Knight	#13
1975	Every Day I Have to Cry Some	Arthur Alexander	#45	1963	Steve Alaimo	#46
1971	Feeling Alright	Grand Funk Railroad	#54	1969	Joe Cocker	#69
1975	Forever Came Today	The Jackson 5	#60	1968	The Supremes	#28
1979	Four Strong Winds	Neil Young	#61	1964	Bobby Bare	#60
1976	Funny How Time Slips Away	Dorothy Moore	#58	1962	Jimmy Elledge	#22
1978	Georgia on My Mind	Willie Nelson	#84	1960	Ray Charles	#1
1978	Get Back	Billy Preston	#86	1969	The Beatles	#1
1971	Gimme Some Lovin'	Traffic, Etc.	#68	1967	The Spencer Davis Group	#7
1972	Giving Up	Donny Hathaway	#81	1964	Gladys Knight & The Pips	#38
1971	Glory of Love	The Dells	#92	1961	The Roommates	#49
1971	Go Away Little Girl	Donny Osmond	#1	1963	Steve Lawrence	#1
1978	God Only Knows	Marilyn Scott	#61	1966	The Beach Boys	#39
1970	Gonna Give Her All the Love I've Got	Marvin Gaye	#67	1967	Jimmy Ruffin	#29
1976	Good Vibrations	Todd Rundgren	#34	1966	The Beach Boys	#1
1970	Gypsy Woman	Brian Hyland	#3	1961	The Impressions	#20
1977	Handy Man	James Taylor	#4	1960	Jimmy Jones	#2
1970	Hang on Sloopy	The Lettermen	#93	1964	The Vibrations (My Girl Sloopy)	#26

					1960s Covers (cont'd)	
1975	Hang on Sloopy	Rick Derringer	#94	1964	The Vibrations (My Girl Sloopy)	#26
1972	Happy Together	Dawn feat. Tony Orlando (medley)	#79	1967	The Turtles	#1
1973	Having a Party	The Ovations (medley)	#56	1962	Sam Cooke	#17
1971	He (She) Called Me Baby	Candi Staton	#52	1969	Ella Washington	#77
1974	He (She) Called Me Baby	Charlie Rich	#47	1969	Ella Washington	#77
1975	He Don't Love You (Like I Love You)	Tony Orlando & Dawn	#1	1960	Jerry Butler	#7
1971	He's So Fine	Jody Miller	#53	1963	The Chiffons	#1
1978	He's So Fine	Kristy & Jimmy McNichol	#70	1978	The Chiffons	#1
1978	He's So Fine	Jane Olivor	#77	1978	The Chiffons	#1
1975	Heat Wave	Linda Ronstadt	#5	1963	Martha & The Vandellas	#4
1979	Heaven Must Have Sent You	Bonnie Pointer	#11	1966	The Elgins	#50
1973	Hello It's Me	Todd Rundgren	#5	1969	Nazz	#71
1973	Hello Stranger	Fire and Rain	#100	1963	Barbara Lewis	#3
1977	Hello Stranger	Yvonne Elliman	#15	1963	Barbara Lewis	#3
1975	Help Me, Rhonda	Johnny Rivers	#22	1965	The Beach Boys	#1
1974	Help Yourself	The Undisputed Truth	#63	1968	Tom Jones	#35
1977	Hey! Baby	Ringo Starr	#74	1962	Bruce Channel	#1
1972	Hey, Girl	Donny Osmond	#9	1963	Freddie Scott	#10
1970	Hey There Lonely Girl (Boy)	Eddie Holman	#2	1963	Ruby & The Romantics	#27
1976	Hit the Road Jack	The Stampeders	#40	1961	Ray Charles	#1
1971	Holly Holy	Jr. Walker	#75	1969	Neil Diamond	#6
1974	Hooked on a Feeling	Blue Swede	#1	1969	B.J. Thomas	#5
1972	Hot Rod Lincoln	Commander Cody	#9	1960	Charlie Ryan and The Timberline Riders	#33
1970	House of the Rising Sun	Frijid Pink	#7	1964	The Animals	#1
1978	House of the Rising Sun	Santa Esmeralda	#78	1964	The Animals	#1
1972	How Can I Be Sure	David Cassidy	#25	1967	Young Rascals	#4
1975	How High the Moon	Gloria Gaynor	#75	1960	Ella Fitzgerald	#76
1975	How Sweet It Is (To Be Loved By You)	James Taylor	#5	1965	Marvin Gaye	#6
1975	Hurt	The Manhattans	#97	1961	Timi Yuro	#4
1976	Hurt	Elvis Presley	#28	1961	Timi Yuro	#4
1970	Hurt So Bad	Jackie DeShannon (medley)	#96	1965	Little Anthony & The Imperials	#10
1975	Hush	Blue Swede (medley)	#61	1967	Billy Joe Royal	#52

	1960s Covers (cont'd)					
1978	I Ain't Gonna Eat Out My Heart Anymore	Angel	#44	1966	Young Rascals	#52
1971	I Can't Get Next to You	Al Green	#60	1969	The Temptations	#1
1972	I Can't Help Myself	Donnie Elbert	#22	1965	Four Tops	#1
1972	I Can't Turn You Loose	Edgar Winter's White Trash	#81	1968	The Chambers Brothers	#37
1971	I Cried	James Brown	#50	1963	Tammy Montgomery	#99
1979	I Do Love You	GQ	#20	1965	Billy Stewart	#26
1975	I Don't Know Why	The Rolling Stones	#42	1969	Stevie Wonder	#39
1971	I Don't Need No Doctor	Humble Pie	#73	1966	Ray Charles	#72
1972	I Don't Need No Doctor	New Riders of the Purple Sage	#81	1966	Ray Charles	#72
1970	I Don't Want to Cry	Ronnie Dyson	#50	1961	Chuck Jackson	#36
1971	I Feel So Bad	Ray Charles	#68	1961	Elvis Presley	#5
1975	I Fought the Law	Sam Neely	#54	1966	Bobby Fuller Four	#9
1975	I Go to Pieces	Cotton, Lloyd & Christian	#66	1965	Peter & Gordon	#9
1976	I Heard It Through the Grapevine	Creedence Clearwater Revival	#43	1967	Gladys Knight & The Pips	#2
1970	I Just Don't Know What to Do with Myself	Gary Puckett	#61	1966	Dionne Warwick	#26
1970	(I Know) I'm Losing You	Rare Earth	#7	1966	The Temptations	#8
1971	(I Know) I'm Losing You	Rod Stewart w/Faces	#24	1966	The Temptations	#8
1975	I Like It Like That	Loggins & Messina	#84	1961	Chris Kenner	#2
1976	I Only Want to Be with You	Bay City Rollers	#12	1964	Dusty Springfield	#12
1971	I Pity the Fool	Ann Peebles	#85	1961	Bobby Bland	#45
1971	I Really Don't Want to Know	Elvis Presley	#21	1960	Tommy Edwards	#18
1971	I Say a Little Prayer	Glen Campbell/Anne Murray (medley)	#81	1967	Dionne Warwick	#4
1970	I Stand Accused	Isaac Hayes	#42	1964	Jerry Butler	#61
1977	I Think We're Alone Now	The Rubinoos	#45	1967	Tommy James & The Shondells	#4
1970	I Want to Do (Do Everything for You)	The Raeletts	#96	1965	Joe Tex	#23
1970	I Want to Take You Higher	Ike & Tina Turner	#34	1969	Sly & The Family Stone	#60
1970	I (Who Have Nothing)	Tom Jones	#14	1963	Ben E. King	#29
1970	I (Who Have Nothing)	Liquid Smoke	#82	1963	Ben E. King	#29
1979	I (Who Have Nothing)	Sylvester	#40	1963	Ben E. King	#29
1970	I'll Never Fall in Love Again	Dionne Warwick	#6	1969	Burt Bacharach	#93
1971	I'm a Believer	Neil Diamond	#51	1966	The Monkees	#1

1960s Covers (cont'd)

1971	I'm a Man	Chicago	#49	1967	Spencer Davis Group	#10
1975	I'm a Woman	Maria Muldaur	#12	1963	Peggy Lee	#54
1974	I'm in Love	Aretha Franklin	#19	1967	Wilson Pickett	#45
1974	I'm Leaving It Up to You	Donny & Marie Osmond	#4	1963	Dale & Grace	#1
1976	I'm So Lonesome I Could Cry	Terry Bradshaw	#91	1962	Johnny Tillotson	#89
1971	I'm So Proud	Main Ingredient	#49	1964	The Impressions	#14
1973	I'm Sorry	Joey Heatherton	#87	1960	Brenda Lee	#1
1970	If I Were a Carpenter	Johnny Cash & June Carter	#36	1966	Bobby Darin	#8
1972	If I Were a Carpenter	Bob Seger	#76	1966	Bobby Darin	#8
1974	If I Were a Carpenter	Leon Russell	#73	1966	Bobby Darin	#8
1974	If You Go Away	Terry Jacks	#68	1967	Damita Jo	#68
1972	Iko Iko	Dr. John	#71	1965	The Dixie Cups	#20
1972	In the Ghetto	Candi Staton	#48	1969	Elvis Presley	#3
1973	In the Midnight Hour	Cross Country	#30	1965	Wilson Pickett	#21
1979	In the Midnight Hour	Samantha Sang	#88	1965	Wilson Pickett	#21
1971	Indian Reservation	The Raiders	#1	1968	Don Fardon	#20
1973	It May Be Winter Outside (But in My Heart It's Spring)	Love Unlimited	#83	1967	Felice Taylor	#42
1976	It Should Have Been Me	Yvonne Fair	#85	1968	Gladys Knight & The Pips	#40
1971	It's for You	Springwell	#60	1964	Cilla Black	#79
1971	It's Only Love	Elvis Presley	#51	1960	B.J. Thomas	#45
1978	It's the Same Old Thing	KC and The Sunshine Band	#35	1965	The Four Tops	#5
1972	Jambalaya (On the Bayou)	The Nitty Gritty Dirt Band	#84	1960	Bobby Comstock	#90
1973	Jambalaya (On the Bayou)	Blue Ridge Rangers	#16	1960	Bobby Comstock	#90
1971	Jumpin' Jack Flash	Johnny Winter	#89	1968	The Rolling Stones	#3
1975	(Just Like) Romeo & Juliet	Sha Na Na	#55	1964	The Reflections	#6
1974	Just One Look	Anne Murray	#86	1963	Doris Troy	#10
1979	Just One Look	Linda Ronstadt	#44	1963	Doris Troy	#10
1979	Knock on Wood	Amii Stewart	#1	1966	Eddie Floyd	#28
1974	Last Kiss	Wednesday	#34	1964	J. Frank Wilson	#2
1970	Lay Lady Lay	Ferrante & Teicher	#99	1969	Bob Dylan	#7
1972	Lay Lady Lay	The Isley Brothers	#71	1969	Bob Dylan	#7
1975	Life and Death in G & A	Love Childs Afro Cuban Blues Band	#90	1969	Abaco Dream	#74
1979	Light My Fire	Amii Stewart (medley)	#69	1967	The Doors	#1

			1960s Covers (cont'd)			
1972	The Lion Sleeps Tonight	Robert John	#3	1961	The Tokens	#1
1970	Listen Here	Brian Auger & The Trinity	#100	1968	Eddie Harris	#45
1970	Little Bit of Soap	Paul Davis	#52	1961	Jarmels	#12
1979	Little Bit of Soap	Nigel Olsson	#34	1961	Jarmels	#12
1977	Little Darling, I Need You	The Doobie Brothers	#48	1966	Marvin Gaye	#47
1974	The Loco-Motion	Grand Funk	#1	1962	Little Eva	#1
1971	Look of Love	Isaac Hayes	#79	1967	Dusty Springfield	#22
1972	Lookin' for a Love	J. Geils Band	#39	1962	The Valentinos	#72
1974	Lookin' for a Love	Bobby Womack	#10	1962	The Valentinos	#72
1973	Looking Through the Eyes of Love	The Partridge Family	#39	1965	Gene Pitney	#28
1978	Louie Louie	John Belushi	#89	1963	The Kingsmen	#2
1971	Love Makes the World Go Round	Odds & Ends	#83	1966	Deon Jackson	#11
1971	Love Makes the World Go Round	Kiki Dee	#87	1966	Deon Jackson	#11
1971	Love's Made a Fool of You	Cochise	#96	1966	The Bobby Fuller Four	#26
1971	MacArthur Park	The Four Tops	#38	1968	Richard Harris	#2
1978	MacArthur Park	Donna Summer	#1	1968	Richard Harris	#2
1970	Make It Easy on Yourself	Dionne Warwick	#37	1962	Jerry Butler	#20
1975	Make the World Go Away	Donny & Marie Osmond	#44	1963	Timi Yuro	#24
1970	Memories	The Lettermen (medley)	#47	1969	Elvis Presley	#35
1973	Million to One	Donny Osmond	#23	1960	Jimmy Charles	#5
1976	Misty Blue	Dorothy Moore	#3	1967	Eddy Arnold	#57
1974	Mockingbird	Carly Simon & James Taylor	#5	1963	Inez Foxx w/Charlie Foxx	#7
1973	Mother-In-Law	Clarence Carter	#80	1961	Ernie K-Doe	#1
1971	Mr. Bojangles	Nitty Gritty Dirt Band	#9	1968	Jerry Jeff Walker	#77
1977	My Cherie Amour	Soul Train Gang	#92	1969	Stevie Wonder	#4
1970	My Elusive Dreams	Bobby Vinton	#46	1967	David Houston & Tammy Wynette	#89
1975	My Elusive Dreams	Charlie Rich	#49	1967	David Houston & Tammy Wynette	#89
1972	My Guy	Petula Clark	#70	1964	Mary Wells	#1
1970	My Way	Brook Benton	#72	1969	Frank Sinatra	#27
1977	My Way	Elvis Presley	#22	1969	Frank Sinatra	#27
1977	Needles and Pins	Smokie	#68	1963	Jackie DeShannon	#84
1971	Never My Love	The 5th Dimension	#12	1967	The Association	#2
1974	Never My Love	Blue Swede	#7	1967	The Association	#2
1977	Never My Love	The Addrisi Brothers	#80	1967	The Association	#2

	1960s Covers (cont'd)					
1971	No Good to Cry	Poppy Family	#84	1967	The Wildweeds	#88
1979	Not Fade Away	Tanya Tucker	#70	1964	The Rolling Stones	#48
1972	Nutrocker	Emerson, Lake & Palmer	#70	1962	B. Bumble & The Stingers	#23
1976	Ob-La-Di, Ob-La-Da	The Beatles	#49	1969	Arthur Conley	#51
1970	Oh Happy Day	Glen Campbell	#40	1969	Edwin Hawkins' Singers	#4
1973	Oh No Not My Baby	Rod Stewart	#59	1965	Maxine Brown	#24
1973	Oh No Not My Baby	Merry Clayton	#72	1965	Maxine Brown	#24
1978	On Broadway	George Benson	#7	1963	The Drifters	#9
1976	One Fine Day	Julie Budd	#93	1963	The Chiffons	#5
1979	One Fine Day	Rita Coolidge	#66	1963	The Chiffons	#5
1972	One Night Affair	Jerry Butler	#52	1969	The O'Jays	#68
1977	Only Love Can Break a Heart	Bobby Vinton	#99	1962	Gene Pitney	#2
1979	Ooh Baby Baby	Linda Ronstadt	#7	1965	The Miracles	#16
1971	Ooh Poo Pah Doo	Ike & Tina Turner	#60	1960	Jessie Hill	#28
1975	Our Day Will Come	Frankie Valli	#11	1963	Ruby & The Romantics	#1
1978	Over the Rainbow	Gary Tanner	#69	1960	The Demensions	#16
1973	Paper Roses	Marie Osmond	#5	1960	Anita Bryant	#5
1970	Part Time Love	Ann Peebles	#45	1963	Little Johnny Taylor	#19
1970	People Got to Be Free	The 5th Dimension	#60	1968	The Rascals	#1
1973	Pinball Wizard	The New Seekers (medley)	#29	1969	The Who	#19
1978	Please Come Home for Christmas	The Eagles	#18	1961	Charles Brown	#76
1975	Please Mr. Postman	The Carpenters	#1	1961	The Marvelettes	#1
1974	Promised Land	Elvis Presley	#14	1965	Chuck Berry	#41
1971	Proud Mary	Ike & Tina Turner	#4	1969	Creedence Clearwater Revival	#2
1975	Proud One	The Osmonds	#22	1966	Frankie Valli	#68
1972	Puppy Love	Donny Osmond	#3	1960	Paul Anka	#2
1971	Reach Out I'll Be There	Diana Ross	#29	1966	The Four Tops	#1
1975	Reach Out I'll Be There	Gloria Gaynor	#60	1966	The Four Tops	#1
1975	Reconsider Me	Narvel Felts	#67	1969	Johnny Adams	#28
1977	Red Hot	Robert Gordon w/Link Wray	#83	1966	Sam the Sham & The Pharoahs	#82
1970	Red Red Wine	Vic Dana	#72	1968	Neil Diamond	#62
1973	Reelin' and Rockin'	Chuck Berry (live)	#27	1965	Dave Clark Five	#23
1979	Remember (Walkin' in the Sand)	Louise Goffin	#43	1964	The Shangri-Las	#5
1976	Rescue Me	Melissa Manchester	#78	1965	Fontella Bass	#4
1971	River Deep-Mountain High	Supremes & Four Tops	#14	1966	Ike & Tina Turner	#88

			1960s Covers (cont'd)			
1975	Ruby Baby	Billy "Crash" Craddock	#33	1963	Dion	#2
1971	Ruby Tuesday	Melanie	#52	1967	The Rolling Stones	#1
1978	Runaround Sue	Leif Garrett	#13	1961	Dion	#1
1972	Runaway	Dawn feat. Tony Orlando (medley)	#79	1961	Del Shannon	#1
1975	Runaway	Charlie Kulis	#46	1961	Del Shannon	#1
1977	Runaway	Bonnie Raitt	#57	1961	Del Shannon	#1
1974	Save the Last Dance for Me	The DeFranco Family	#18	1960	The Drifters	#1
1972	Sealed with a Kiss	Bobby Vinton	#19	1962	Brian Hyland	#3
1975	Secret Love	Freddy Fender	#20	1966	Richard "Groove" Holmes	#99
1970	She (He) Cried	The Lettermen	#73	1962	Jay & The Americans	#5
1971	She's a Very Lovely Woman	José Feliciano	#70	1967	Merry-Go-Round	#94
1977	She's Not There	Santana	#27	1964	The Zombies	#2
1977	Shoop Shoop Song (It's in His Kiss)	Kate Taylor	#49	1964	Betty Everett	#6
1976	Shop Around	Captain & Tennille	#4	1961	The Miracles	#2
1974	Silver Threads and Golden Needles	Linda Ronstadt	#67	1962	The Springfields	#20
1972	Simple Song of Freedom	Buckwheat	#84	1969	Tim Hardin	#50
1972	Since I Fell for You	Laura Lee	#76	1963	Lenny Welch	#4
1976	Since I Fell for You	Charlie Rich	#71	1963	Lenny Welch	#4
1977	Since I Fell for You	Hodges, James and Smith (medley)	#96	1963	Lenny Welch	#4
1979	(Sittin' On) The Dock of the Bay	Sammy Hagar	#65	1968	Otis Redding	#1
1976	Sixteen Reasons	Laverne & Shirley	#65	1960	Connie Stevens	#3
1976	Solitary Man	T.G. Sheppard	#100	1966	Neil Diamond	#55
1977	Some Enchanted Evening	Jane Olivor	#91	1965	Jay & The Americans	#13
1975	Some Kind of Wonderful	Grand Funk	#3	1967	Soul Brothers Six	#91
1977	Something About You	LeBlanc & Carr	#48	1965	The Four Tops	#19
1979	Soul Man	Blues Brothers	#14	1967	Sam & Dave	#2
1970	Soulshake	Delaney & Bonnie	#43	1969	Peggy Scott & Jo Jo Benson	#37
1971	Sound of Silence	Peaches & Herb	#100	1966	Simon & Garfunkel	#1
1971	Spanish Harlem	Aretha Franklin	#2	1961	Ben E. King	#10
1971	Spinning Wheel	James Brown	#90	1969	Blood, Sweat & Tears	#2
1979	Spooky	Atlanta Rhythm Section	#17	1967	Mike Sharpe	#57
1970	Stand By Me	David & Jimmy Ruffin	#61	1961	Ben E. King	#4

	1960s Covers (cont'd)					
1975	Stand By Me	John Lennon	#20	1961	Ben E. King	#4
1970	Stand By Your Man	Candi Staton	#24	1969	Tammy Wynette	#19
1978	Stay Awhile	Continental Miniatures	#90	1964	Dusty Springfield	#38
1970	Steal Away	Johnnie Taylor	#37	1964	Jimmy Hughes	#17
1971	Stop! In the Name of Love	Margie Joseph	#96	1965	The Supremes	#1
1979	Stormy	Santana	#32	1968	Classics IV	#5
1970	Sugar, Sugar	Wilson Pickett	#25	1969	The Archies	#1
1972	Sunday Kind of Love	Lenny Welch	#96	1962	Jan & Dean	#95
1970	Sunday Morning Coming Down	Johnny Cash	#46	1969	Ray Stevens	#81
1977	Surfin' U.S.A.	Leif Garrett	#20	1963	The Beach Boys	#3
1971	Suspicious Minds	Dee Dee Warwick	#80	1969	Elvis Presley	#1
1972	Sweet Caroline (Good Times Never Seemed So Good)	Bobby Womack	#51	1969	Neil Diamond	#4
1972	Sweet Inspiration	Barbra Streisand (medley)	#37	1968	The Sweet Inspirations	#18
1979	Sweets for My Sweet	Tony Orlando	#54	1961	The Drifters	#16
1975	Take Me in Your Arms (Rock Me)	The Doobie Brothers	#11	1965	Kim Weston	#50
1974	Teen Angel	Wednesday	#79	1960	Mark Dinning	#1
1976	Tell It Like It Is	Andy Williams	#72	1967	Aaron Neville	#2
1974	Tell Laura I Love Her	Johnny T. Angel	#94	1960	Ray Peterson	#7
1976	Then You Can Tell Me Goodbye	Glen Campbell (medley)	#27	1967	The Casinos	#6
1979	Then You Can Tell Me Goodbye	Toby Beau	#57	1967	The Casinos	#6
1976	There's a Kind of Hush (All Over the World)	The Carpenters	#12	1967	Herman's Hermits	#4
1970	(There's) Always Something There to Remind Me	R.B. Greaves	#27	1964	Lou Johnson	#49
1976	Things	Anne Murray	#89	1962	Bobby Darin	#3
1970	This Bitter Earth	The Satisfactions	#96	1960	Dinah Washington	#24
1976	This Old Heart of Mine	Rod Stewart	#83	1966	The Isley Brothers	#12
1970	Ticket to Ride	The Carpenters	#54	1965	The Beatles	#1
1970	Tobacco Road	Jamul	#93	1964	Nashville Teens	#14
1973	Tossin' and Turnin'	Bunny Sigler	#97	1961	Bobby Lewis	#1
1970	Traces	The Lettermen (medley)	#47	1969	Classics IV	#2
1976	Tracks of My Tears	Linda Ronstadt	#25	1965	The Miracles	#16
1975	Try to Remember	Gladys Knight & The Pips (medley)	#11	1965	Ed Ames	#73
1972	Turn on Your Love Light	Jerry Lee Lewis	#95	1962	Bobby Bland	#28
1973	Twistin' the Night Away	Rod Stewart	#59	1962	Sam Cooke	#9

	1960s Covers (cont'd)					
1978	Um, Um, Um, Um, Um, Um	Johnny Rivers	#41	1964	Major Lance	#5
1978	Under the Boardwalk	Billy Joe Royal	#82	1964	The Drifters	#4
1970	Up on the Roof	Laura Nyro	#92	1963	The Drifters	#5
1979	Up on the Roof	James Taylor	#28	1963	The Drifters	#5
1972	Vaya con Dios	Dawn feat. Tony Orlando	#95	1964	The Drifters	#43
1976	Vaya con Dios	Freddy Fender	#59	1964	The Drifters	#43
1975	Walk on By	Gloria Gaynor	#98	1964	Dionne Warwick	#6
1979	Walk on By	AWB	#92	1964	Dionne Warwick	#6
1977	Walk Right In	Dr. Hook	#46	1963	The Rooftop Singers	#1
1970	Walkin' in the Rain	Jay & The Americans	#19	1964	The Ronettes	#23
1978	The Wanderer	Leif Garrett	#49	1962	Dion	#2
1974	Wang Dang Doodle	Pointer Sisters	#61	1966	Ko Ko Taylor	#58
1972	Way of Love	Cher	#7	1965	Kathy Kirby	#88
1978	The Way You Do the Things You Do	Rita Coolidge	#20	1964	The Temptations	#11
1971	We Can Work It Out	Stevie Wonder	#13	1966	The Beatles	#1
1971	What the World Needs Now Is Love	Tom Clay (medley)	#8	1965	Jackie DeShannon	#7
1979	What's a Matter Baby	Ellen Foley	#92	1962	Timi Yuro	#12
1974	What's Your Name	Andy & David Williams	#92	1962	Don & Juan	#7
1973	When I Fall in Love	Donny Osmond	#55	1961	Etta Jones	#65
1971	When My Little Girl Is Smiling	Steve Alaimo	#72	1962	The Drifters	#28
1970	When We Get Married	The Intruders	#45	1961	The Dreamlovers	#10
1975	When Will I Be Loved	Linda Ronstadt	#2	1960	The Everly Brothers	#8
1975	When You're Young and in Love	Choice Four	#91	1964	Ruby & The Romantics	#48
1975	When You're Young and in Love	Ralph Carter	#95	1964	Ruby & The Romantics	#48
1971	Where Did Our Love Go	Donnie Elbert	#15	1961	The Supremes	#1
1976	Where Did Our Love Go	J. Geils Band	#68	1961	The Supremes	#1
1977	Whispering	Dr. Buzzard's Original Savannah Band (medley)	#27	1964	Nino Tempo & April Stevens	#11
1970	Whiter Shade of Pale	R.B. Greaves	#82	1967	Procol Harum	#5
1974	Wild Thing	Fancy	#74	1966	The Troggs	#1
1972	Will You Love Me Tomorrow	Roberta Flack	#76	1961	The Shirelles	#1
1973	Will You Love Me Tomorrow	Melanie	#82	1961	The Shirelles	#1
1976	Will You Love Me Tomorrow	Dana Valery	#95	1961	The Shirelles	#1
1978	Will You Love Me Tomorrow	Dave Mason	#39	1961	The Shirelles	#1

1960s Covers (cont'd)						
1978	With a Little Help from My Friends	The Beatles (medley)	#71	1968	Joe Cocker	#68
1972	With Pen in Hand	Bobby Goldsboro	#94	1968	Billy Vera	#43
1978	Wonderful World	Art Garfunkel w/James Taylor & Paul Simon	#17	1960	Sam Cooke	#12
1975	Wooden Heart	Bobby Vinton	#58	1961	Joe Dowell	#1
1974	You Can Have Her (Him)	Sam Neely	#34	1961	Roy Hamilton	#12
1970	You Don't Have to Say You Love Me	Elvis Presley	#11	1966	Dusty Springfield	#4
1975	(You Don't Know) How Glad I Am	Kiki Dee	#74	1964	Nancy Wilson	#11
1970	You Got Me Hummin''	Cold Blood	#52	1967	Sam & Dave	#77
1978	(You Got to Walk And) Don't Look Back	Peter Tosh w/Mick Jagger	#81	1966	The Temptations	#83
1970	You Keep Me Hangin' On	Jackie DeShannon (medley)	#96	1966	The Supremes	#1
1978	You Really Got Me	Van Halen	#36	1964	The Kinks	#7
1976	You'll Lose a Good Thing	Freddy Fender	#32	1962	Barbara Lynn	#8
1973	You'll Never Get to Heaven (If You Break My Heart)	The Stylistics	#23	1964	Dionne Warwick	#34
1971	You're All I Need to Get By	Aretha Franklin	#19	1968	Marvin Gaye & Tammi Terrell	#7
1975	You're All I Need to Get By	Tony Orlando & Dawn	#34	1968	Marvin Gaye & Tammi Terrell	#7
1978	You're All I Need to Get By	Johnny Mathis & Deniece Williams	#47	1968	Marvin Gaye & Tammi Terrell	#7
1978	(You're My) Soul and Inspiration	Donny & Marie Osmond	#38	1966	The Righteous Brothers	#1
1977	You're My World	Helen Reddy	#18	1964	Cilla Black	#26
1975	You're No Good	Linda Ronstadt	#1	1964	Betty Everett	#51
1974	You're Sixteen	Ringo Starr	#1	1960	Johnny Burnette	#8
1971	You've Lost That Lovin' Feelin'	Roberta Flack & Donny Hathaway	#71	1965	The Righteous Brothers	#1
1979	You've Lost That Lovin' Feelin'	Long John Baldry & Kathi MacDonald	#89	1965	The Righteous Brothers	#1
1970	You've Made Me So Very Happy	Lou Rawls	#95	1967	Brenda Holloway	#39
1972	You've Really Got a Hold on Me	Gayle McCormick	#98	1963	The Miracles	#8
1979	You've Really Got a Hold on Me	Eddie Money	#72	1963	The Miracles	#8
1977	(Your Love Keeps Lifting Me) Higher and Higher	Rita Coolidge	#2	1967	Jackie Wilson	#6

1970s COVERS

YEAR	COVER	COVER ARTIST	COVER'S CHART POSITION	ORIGINAL HIT'S YEAR	ORIGINAL ARTIST	ORIGINAL'S CHART POSITION
1974	After Midnight	Maggie Bell	#97	1970	Eric Clapton	#18
1972	After Midnight	J.J. Cale	#42	1970	Eric Clapton	#18
1972	Ain't That Loving You (For More Reasons Than One)	Isaac Hayes & David Porter	#86	1970	Luther Ingram	#45
1975	All Right Now	Lea Roberts	#92	1970	Free	#4
1973	Also Sprach Zarathustra (2001)	Deodato	#2	1970	Berlin Philharmonic	#90
1972	Amazing Grace	Royal Scots Dragoon Guards	#11	1971	Judy Collins	#15
1973	And I Love You So	Perry Como	#29	1971	Bobby Goldsboro	#83
1979	Another Night	Wilson Bros.	#94	1975	The Hollies	#71
1976	Anytime (I'll Be There)	Paul Anka	#33	1975	Frank Sinatra	#75
1978	Arms of Mary	Chilliwack	#67	1976	Sutherland Brothers and Quiver	#81
1977	Avenging Annie	Roger Daltrey	#88	1973	Andy Pratt	#78
1974	Bad, Bad Leroy Brown	Frank Sinatra	#83	1973	Jim Croce	#1
1976	Bad Luck	Atlanta Disco Band	#94	1975	Harold Melvin	#15
1979	Bang a Gong (Get It On)	T. Rex	#10	1979	Witch Queen	#68
1976	Baretta's Theme ("Keep Your Eye on the Sparrow")	Rhythm Heritage	#20	1975	Merry Clayton	#45
1974	You're the Best Thing That Ever Happened to Me	Gladys Knight & The Pips	#3	1973	Ray Price	#82
1974	You're the Best Thing That Ever Happened to Me	The Persuaders	#85	1973	Ray Price	#82
1977	Bless the Beasts and Children	Barry DeVorzon & Perry Botkin, Jr.	#82	1972	The Carpenters	#67
1971	Bridge Over Troubled Water	Aretha Franklin	#6	1970	Simon & Garfunkel	#1
1979	Bridge Over Troubled Water	Linda Clifford	#41	1970	Simon & Garfunkel	#1
1977	Can't You See	Marshall Tucker Band	#76	1976	Waylon Jennings	#97
1976	Could It Be Magic	Donna Summer	#52	1975	Barry Manilow	#6
1975	Dear Prudence	Katfish	#62	1970	The 5 Stairsteps	#66
1973	Delta Dawn	Helen Reddy	#1	1972	Tanya Tucker	#72
1977	Do Ya	Electric Light Orchestra	#24	1972	Move	#93

		1970s Covers (cont'd)					
1974	Don't Knock My Love	Diana Ross & Marvin Gaye	#46	1971	Wilson Pickett	#13
1976	Don't Pull Your Love	Glen Campbell (medley)	#27	1971	Hamilton, Joe Frank & Reynolds	#4
1971	(Don't Try to Lay No Boogie Woogie on The) "King of Rock & Roll"	John Baldry	#73	1970	Crow	#52
1978	Ease on Down the Road	Diana Ross & Michael Jackson	#41	1975	Consumer Rapport	#42
1979	Feel the Need	Leif Garrett	#57	1977	The Detroit Emeralds	#90
1977	Feelings	Walter Jackson	#93	1975	Morris Albert	#6
1977	The First Cut Is the Deepest	Rod Stewart	#21	1973	Keith Hampshire	#70
1976	Free Ride	Tavares	#52	1973	Edgar Winter Group	#14
1971	Gimme Shelter	Grand Funk Railroad	#61	1970	Merry Clayton	#73
1976	Got to Get You Into My Life	The Beatles	#7	1975	Blood, Sweat & Tears	#62
1978	Got to Get You Into My Life	Earth, Wind & Fire	#9	1978	Blood, Sweat & Tears	#9
1979	Groove Me	Fern Kinney	#54	1971	King Floyd	#6
1972	Handbags and Gladrags	Rod Stewart	#42	1971	Chase	#84
1972	Help Me Make It Through the Night	Gladys Knight & The Pips	#33	1971	Sammi Smith	#8
1977	Hold Back the Night	Graham Parker w/The Rumour	#58	1976	The Trammps	#35
1979	Hot Summer Nights	Night	#18	1978	Walter Egan	#55
1978	I Believe You	The Carpenters	#68	1977	Dorothy Moore	#27
1978	I Can't Stand the Rain	Eruption	#18	1973	Ann Peebles	#38
1974	I Won't Last a Day Without You	The Carpenters	#11	1973	Maureen McGovern	#89
1975	I Won't Last a Day Without You	Al Wilson	#70	1973	Maureen McGovern	#89
1974	I'm Coming Home	The Spinners	#18	1973	Johnny Mathis	#75
1974	I've Got a Thing About You Baby	Elvis Presley	#39	1972	Billy Lee Riley	#93
1973	If It's Alright with You	Dottie West	#97	1971	Rose Colored Glass	#95
1975	(If Loving You Is Wrong) I Don't Want to Be Right	Millie Jackson	#42	1972	Luther Ingram	#3
1979	(If Loving You Is Wrong) I Don't Want to Be Right	Barbara Mandrell	#31	1972	Luther Ingram	#3
1977	It Keeps You Runnin'	The Doobie Brothers	#37	1976	Carly Simon	#46
1973	Je T'Aime…Moi Non Plus	Sylvia & Ralfi Pagan (Soul)	#99	1970	Jane Birkin & Serge Gainsbourg	#58
1973	Jesus Is Just Alright	The Doobie Brothers	#35	1970	The Byrds	#97
1974	Just Don't Want to Be Lonely	The Main Ingredient	#10	1973	Ronnie Dyson	#60
1974	Keep on Singing	Helen Reddy	#15	1973	Austin Roberts	#50

	1970s Covers (cont'd)					
1971	Let It Be	Joan Baez	#49	1970	The Beatles	#1
1978	Let's Live Together	Cazz	#70	1976	Road Apples	#35
1975	Living for the City	Ray Charles	#91	1974	Stevie Wonder	#8
1972	Look What They've Done to My Song Ma	Ray Charles	#65	1970	The New Seekers	#14
1979	Love Ballad	George Benson	#18	1976	L.T.D.	#20
1976	Love Hurts	Nazareth	#8	1975	Jim Capaldi	#97
1978	Love Theme from "Eyes of Laura Mars" (Prisoner)	Barbra Streisand	#21	1977	L.A. Jets	#86
1974	Loving Arms	Kris Kristofferson & Rita Coolidge	#86	1973	Dobie Gray	#61
1977	Make It with You	The Whispers	#94	1970	Bread	#1
1972	Mama Told Me (Not to Come)	Wilson Pickett	#99	1970	Three Dog Night	#1
1973	Mammy Blue	Stories	#50	1971	The Pop-Tops	#57
1975	Mandy	Barry Manilow	#1	1972	Scott English (Brandy)	#91
1972	Me and Bobby McGee	Jerry Lee Lewis	#40	1971	Janis Joplin	#1
1975	Me and Mrs. Jones	The Dramatics	#47	1972	Billy Paul	#1
1974	Midnight Rider	Gregg Allman	#19	1972	Joe Cocker w/The Chris Stainton Band	#27
1976	Muskrat Love	Captain & Tennille	#4	1973	America	#67
1975	My Boy	Elvis Presley	#20	1972	Richard Harris	#41
1974	My Love	Margie Joseph	#69	1973	Paul McCartney	#1
1977	My Sweet Lady	John Denver	#32	1974	Cliff DeYoung	#17
1971	My Sweet Lord	Billy Preston	#90	1970	George Harrison	#1
1975	Never Can Say Goodbye	Gloria Gaynor	#9	1971	The Jackson 5	#2
1972	Nickel Song	Melanie	#35	1971	The New Seekers	#81
1975	No Charge	Shirley Caesar	#91	1974	Melba Montgomery	#39
1976	Nutbush City Limits	Bob Seger	#69	1973	Ike & Tina Turner	#22
1972	Oh Me Oh My (I'm a Fool for You Baby)	Aretha Franklin	#73	1970	Lulu	#22
1979	Oh Well	The Rockets	#30	1970	Fleetwood Mac	#55
1979	One Chain Don't Make No Prison	Santana	#59	1974	The Four Tops	#41
1971	One Tin Soldier (The Legend of Billy Jack)	Coven	#26	1970	Original Caste	#34
1971	Only You Know and I Know	Delaney & Bonnie	#20	1970	Dave Mason	#42
1974	Power of Love	Martha Reeves	#76	1972	Joe Simon	#11
1971	Puppet Man	Tom Jones	#26	1970	The 5th Dimension	#24
1974	Rings	Lobo	#43	1971	Cymarron	#17
1974	Rings	Reuben Howell	#86	1971	Cymarron	#86
1974	Rock 'N' Roll (I Gave You the Best Years of My Life)	Terry Jacks	#97	1973	Kevin Johnson	#73

1970s Covers (cont'd)

1975	Rock 'N' Roll (I Gave You the Best Years of My Life)	Mac Davis	#15	1973	Kevin Johnson	#73
1974	Rub It In	Billy "Crash" Craddock	#16	1971	Layng Martine	#65
1973	See Me, Feel Me	The New Seekers (medley)	#29	1970	The Who	#12
1977	Shakey Ground	Phoebe Snow	#70	1975	The Temptations	#26
1975	Showdown	Odia Coates	#71	1974	Electric Light Orchestra	#53
1977	Signed, Sealed and Delivered	Peter Frampton	#18	1970	Stevie Wonder	#3
1979	Since You Been Gone	Rainbow	#57	1978	Head East	#46
1973	Sing a Song	The Carpenters	#3	1972	Barbra Streisand (medley)	#94
1974	Something	Johnny Rodriguez	#85	1970	Booker T. & The M.G.'s	#76
1976	Somewhere in the Night	Helen Reddy	#19	1975	Batdorf & Rodney	#69
1979	Somewhere in the Night	Barry Manilow	#9	1975	Batdorf & Rodney	#69
1971	Spill the Wine	The Isley Brothers	#49	1970	Eric Burdon & War	#3
1974	Summer Breeze	Seals & Crofts	#6	1960	The Isley Brothers	#60
1979	Superman	Herbie Mann	#26	1977	Celi Bee	#41
1971	Superstar – Jesus Christ Superstar	Assembled Multitude	#95	1970	Murray Head w/The Trinidad Singers	#74
1979	Take Me to the River	Talking Heads	#26	1975	Syl Johnson	#48
1975	Theme from "Summer of '42"	Biddu Orchestra	#57	1971	Peter Nero	#21
1972	(They Long to Be) Close to You	Jerry Butler w/Brenda Lee Eager	#91	1970	The Carpenters	#1
1976	(They Long to Be) Close to You	B.T. Express	#82	1970	The Carpenters	#1
1979	This Night Won't Last Forever	Michael Johnson	#19	1978	Bill LaBounty	#65
1976	Tubular Bells	Champs' Boys Orchestra	#98	1974	Mike Oldfield	#7
1978	Tumbling Dice	Linda Ronstadt	#32	1972	The Rolling Stones	#7
1972	Until It's Time for You to Go	Elvis Presley	#40	1970	Neil Diamond	#53
1973	Until It's Time for You to Go	New Birth	#97	1970	Neil Diamond	#53
1972	Way Back Home	Jr. Walker	#52	1971	The Jazz Crusaders	#90
1975	The Way We Were	Gladys Knight & The Pips (medley)	#11	1974	Barbra Streisand	#1
1977	We're All Alone	Rita Coolidge	#7	1976	Frankie Valli	#78
1972	Wedding Song (There Is Love)	Petula Clark	#61	1971	Paul Stookey	#24
1978	Wedding Song (There Is Love)	Mary MacGregor	#81	1971	Paul Stookey	#24
1971	When You Get Right Down to It	Ronnie Dyson	#94	1970	The Delfonics	#53
1971	Whole Lotta Love	C.C.S.	#58	1970	Led Zeppelin	#4

		1970s Covers (cont'd)					
1971	Whole Lotta Love	King Curtis	#64	1970	Led Zeppelin	#4
1979	Whole Lotta Love	Wonder Band	#87	1970	Led Zeppelin	#4
1974	Wildflower	New Birth	#45	1973	Skylark	#9
1978	Woman to Woman	Barbara Mandrell	#92	1974	Shirley Brown	#22
1971	Woodstock	Matthews' Southern Comfort	#23	1970	Crosby, Stills, Nash & Young	#11
1975	Words (Are Impossible)	Margie Joseph	#91	1973	Drupi (Vado Via)	#88
1976	Words (Are Impossible)	Donny Gerrard	#87	1973	Drupi (Vado Via)	#88
1977	Yesterday's Hero	Bay City Rollers	#54	1976	John Paul Young	#42
1978	You Brought the Woman Out of Me	Hot	#71	1975	Evie Sands	#50
1978	You're a Part of Me	Gene Cotton w/Kim Carnes	#36	1975	Susan Jacks	#90
1971	You're the One	Three Degrees	#77	1970	Little Sister	#22

SONGS BY MULTIPLE ARTISTS THAT DEBUTED IN THE SAME YEAR

YEAR	SONG	ARTIST	HOT 100	ARTIST	HOT 100
1972	America	Yes	#46	Simon & Garfunkel	#97
1972	American Trilogy	Mickey Newbury	#26	Elvis Presley	#66
1970	Big Yellow Taxi	The Neighborhood	#29	Joni Mitchell	#67
1974	Billy, Don't Be a Hero	Bo Donaldson	#1	Paper Lace	#96
1978	Blame It on the Boogie	The Jacksons	#54	Mick Jackson	#61
1970	Border Song	Aretha Franklin	#37	Elton John	#92
1970	Carolina in My Mind	James Taylor	#67	Crystal Mansion	#73
1971	Chirpy Chirpy Cheep Cheep	Mac and Katie Kissoon	#20	Lally Stott	#92
1970	Cinnamon Girl	Gentrys	#52	Neil Young & Crazy Horse	#55
1973	Come Live with Me	Ray Charles	#82	Roy Clark	#89
1979	Dancin' Shoes	Nigel Olsson	#18	Faith Band	#54
1970	Down By the River	Buddy Miles	#68	Brooklyn Bridge	#91
1971	Everything's Alright	Yvonne Elliman	#92	The Kimberlys (medley)	#99
1974	Feel Like Makin' Love	Roberta Flack	#1	Bob James	#88
1970	He Ain't Heavy, He's My Brother	The Hollies	#7	Neil Diamond	#20
1976	Heart on My Sleeve	Gallagher and Lyle	#67	Bryan Ferry	#86
1974	Honey, Honey	ABBA	#27	Sweet Dreams	#68
1972	I'd Like to Teach the World to Sing (In Perfect Harmony)	The New Seekers	#7	The Hillside Singers	#13
1975	I'm on Fire	5000 Volts	#26	Jim Gilstrap	#78
1978	It's a Heartache	Bonnie Tyler	#3	Juice Newton	#86
1971	It's Impossible	Perry Como	#10	New Birth	#52
1974	La La Peace Song	Al Wilson	#30	O.C. Smith	#62

Songs By Multiple Artists… (cont'd)

1975	Last Game of the Season (A Blind Man in the Bleachers)	David Geddes	#18	Kenny Starr	#58
1972	Let's Stay Together	Al Green	#1	Isaac Hayes	#48
1970	Let's Work Together	Canned Heat	#26	Wilbert Harrison	#32
1976	Love Hangover	Diana Ross	#1	The 5th Dimension	#80
1977	Love in 'C' Minor	Heart & Soul Orchestra	#46	Cerrone	#36
1971	Love the One You're With	Stephen Stills	#14	The Isley Brothers	#18
1971	Make It Funky	James Brown	#22	James Brown (My Part)	#68
1971	Mother	John Lennon	#43	Barbra Streisand	#79
1971	Never Can Say Goodbye	The Jackson 5	#2	Isaac Hayes	#22
1973	Outlaw Man	The Eagles	#59	David Blue	#94
1972	Papa Was a Rollin' Stone	The Temptations	#1	The Undisputed Truth	#63
1971	Resurrection Shuffle	Tom Jones	#38	Ashton, Gardner & Dyke	#40
1972	Rock Me on the Water	Jackson Browne	#48	Linda Ronstadt	#85
1977	Save Me	Merrilee Rush	#54	Donna McDaniel	#90
1970	Save the Country	The 5th Dimension	#27	Thelma Houston	#74
1976	Save Your Kisses for Me	Brotherhood of Man	#27	Bobby Vinton	#75
1974	Second Avenue	Art Garfunkel	#34	Tim Moore	#58
1973	Shambala	Three Dog Night	#3	B.W. Stevenson	#66
1970	She Lets Her Hair Down (Early in the Morning)	The Tokens	#61	Gene Pitney	#89
1971	She's All I Got	Freddie North	#39	Johnny Paycheck	#91
1974	She's Gone	Tavares	#50	Daryl Hall & John Oates	#60
1977	Slow Dancin' (Swayin' to the Music)	Johnny Rivers	#10	The Funky Kings	#61
1970	Something	Shirley Bassey	#55	Booker T. & The M.G.'s	#76
1972	Son of My Father	Giorgio	#46	Chicory	#91
1973	Soul Makossa	Manu Dibango	#35	Afrique	#47
1970	Spirit in the Sky	Norman Greenbaum	#3	Dorothy Morrison	#99
1977	Star Wars Theme	Meco	#1	John Williams	#10
1970	That Same Old Feeling	The Fortunes	#62	Pickettywitch	#67
1978	Theme from "Close Encounters"	John Williams	#13	Meco	#25
1973	Top of the World	The Carpenters	#1	Lynn Anderson	#74
1971	Wild World	Cat Stevens	#11	The Gentrys	#97
1977	You Light Up My Life	Debby Boone	#1	Kacey Cisyk	#80
1979	You Stepped Into My Life	Melba Moore	#47	Wayne Newton	#90
1973	You're a Lady	Peter Skellern	#50	Dawn feat. Tony Orlando	#70
1977	You're Movin' Out Today	Bette Midler	#42	Carole Bayer Sager	#69
1971	You've Got a Friend	James Taylor	#1	Roberta Flack & Donny Hathaway	#29

This next list is a continuation of the previous list, but it consists solely of songs that were recorded by at least three artists, and debuted on the Hot 100 in the same year.

YEAR	SONG	ARTIST	HOT 100
1974	Americans	Byron MacGregor	#4
1974	Americans	Gordon Sinclair	#24
1974	Americans	Tex Ritter	#90
1970	Fire and Rain	James Taylor	#3
1970	Fire and Rain	R.B. Greaves	#82
1970	Fire and Rain	Johnny Rivers	#94
1977	Gonna Fly Now (Theme from "Rocky")	Bill Conti	#1
1977	Gonna Fly Now (Theme from "Rocky")	Maynard Ferguson	#28
1977	Gonna Fly Now (Theme from "Rocky")	Rhythm Heritage	#94
1977	Gonna Fly Now (Theme from "Rocky")	Current	#94
1971	Help Me Make It Through the Night	Sammi Smith	#8
1971	Help Me Make It Through the Night	Joe Simon	#69
1971	Help Me Make It Through the Night	O.C. Smith	#91
1971	I Don't Know How to Love Him	Helen Reddy	#13
1971	I Don't Know How to Love Him	Yvonne Elliman	#28
1971	I Don't Know How to Love Him	The Kimberlys (medley)	#99
1972	Love Theme from "The Godfather"	Andy Williams	#34
1972	Love Theme from "The Godfather"	Carlo Savina	#66
1972	Love Theme from "The Godfather"	Al Martino	#80
1971	Theme from "Love Story"	Andy Williams (Where Do I Begin)	#9
1971	Theme from "Love Story"	Henry Mancini	#13
1971	Theme from "Love Story"	Francis Lai	#31
1976	You to Me Are Everything	Real Thing	#64
1976	You to Me Are Everything	Broadway	#86
1976	You to Me Are Everything	Revelation	#98

SONGS THAT HIT THE HOT 100 TWICE (BY THE SAME ARTIST)

YEAR	SONG	ARTIST	HOT 100	NEXT YEAR SONG CHARTED	NEXT HOT 100
1971	Bell Bottom Blues	Derek & The Dominos	#91	1973 (Eric Clapton)	#78
1970	Big Yellow Taxi	Joni Mitchell	#67	1975 (live)	#24
1962	Breaking Up Is Hard to Do	Neil Sedaka	#1	1976 (slow version)	#8
1972	Changes	David Bowie	#66	1975	#41
1966	Cherry, Cherry	Neil Diamond	#6	1973 (live)	#31

		SONGS THAT HIT THE HOT 100 TWICE (BY THE SAME ARTIST) (cont'd)				
1976	Crazy on You	Heart	#35	1978	#62
1977	Disco Inferno	The Trammps	#53	1978	#11
1968	Down on Me	Big Brother & The Holding Company (Janis Joplin)	#68	1972	#91
1973	Dream On	Aerosmith	#59	1976	#6

INSTRUMENTS

The following section lists songs that feature a particular instrument. "Feature" is the key word. If a song uses a piano, for example, but it's so far in the background you can barely hear it, or it's only in the song for two seconds, then it will not be included in the list. In other words, for an instrument to be listed, it must be fairly easy to hear, and/or important to the song. For the sake of space, I did this for most instruments.

In addition, the piano, organ, and harmonica sections list songs that featured solos by those instruments. There is also a section for the longest guitar solos of the decade.

If a song has an instrument like the flute, violin, clarinet, or other similar instruments that are usually part of an orchestra, then the song will be listed under the "orchestra" section. If a song has one of these instruments without an orchestra, then it will be listed in that particular instrument's section.

ACCORDION

YEAR	SONG	ARTIST	HOT 100
1970	Look What They've Done to My Song Ma	The New Seekers	#14
1970	Paper Maché	Dionne Warwick	#43
1970	Dear Ann	George Baker Selection	#93
1971	Mr. Bojangles	Nitty Gritty Dirt Band	#9
1971	Nickel Song	The New Seekers	#81
1971	Banks of the Ohio	Olivia Newton-John	#94
1972	Vincent (Starry, Starry Night)	Don McLean	#12
1972	The City of New Orleans	Arlo Guthrie	#18
1972	How Can I Be Sure	David Cassidy	#25
1972	No Sad Song	Helen Reddy	#61
1972	Love Theme from "The Godfather"	Carlo Savina	#66
1972	That's What Friends are For	B.J. Thomas	#74
1972	Speak Softly Love	Al Martino	#80
1972	Vahevala	Loggins & Messina	#84
1973	Hocus Pocus	Focus	#9
1974	Piano Man	Billy Joel	#25
1974	On a Night Like This	Bob Dylan/The Band	#44

ACCORDION (cont'd)			
1974	Worse Comes to Worst	Billy Joel	#80
1974	Christmas Dream	Perry Como	#92
1975	Before the Next Teardrop Falls	Freddy Fender	#1
1975	Lonely People	America	#5
1975	Blue Eyes Crying in the Rain	Willie Nelson	#21
1975	Beer Barrel Polka	Bobby Vinton	#33
1975	Wooden Heart	Bobby Vinton	#58
1976	Sorry Seems to Be the Hardest Word	Elton John	#6
1976	Squeeze Box	The Who	#16
1976	Hurricane (Part 1)	Bob Dylan	#33
1976	Heart on My Sleeve	Gallagher and Lyle	#67
1977	C'est La Vie	Greg Lake	#91
1977	Pirate	Cher	#93

BANJO

YEAR	SONG	ARTIST	HOT 100
1970	In the Summertime	Mungo Jerry	#3
1970	Everybody's Out of Town	B.J. Thomas	#26
1970	Morning Much Better	Ten Wheel Drive	#74
1970	Coal Miner's Daughter	Loretta Lynn	#83
1970	Heighdy-Ho Princess	Neon Philharmonic	#94
1971	Take Me Home, Country Roads	John Denver	#2
1971	Sweet City Woman	Stampeders	#8
1971	The Drum	Bobby Sherman	#29
1971	Battle Hymn of Lt. Calley	C Company	#37
1971	Pushbike Song	The Mixtures	#44
1971	Some of Shelly's Blues	Nitty Gritty Dirt Band	#64
1971	Mare, Take Me Home	Matthews' Southern Comfort	#96
1972	A Cowboy's Work Is Never Done	Sonny & Cher	#8
1972	Honky Cat	Elton John	#8
1972	Listen to the Music	The Doobie Brothers	#11
1972	Take It Easy	Eagles	#12
1972	Speak to the Sky	Rick Springfield	#14
1972	Old Man	Neil Young	#31
1972	Long Haired Lover from Liverpool	Little Jimmy Osmond w/The Mike Curb Congregation	#38
1972	Down By the River	Albert Hammond	#91
1973	Uneasy Rider	Charlie Daniels	#9
1973	Daisy a Day	Jud Strunk	#14

	BANJO (cont'd)		
1973	Dead Skunk	Loudon Wainwright III	#16
1973	Harry Hippie	Bobby Womack	#31
1973	Don't Cross the River	America	#35
1973	Superman	Donna Fargo	#41
1973	Little Girl Gone	Donna Fargo	#57
1973	Send a Little Love My Way	Anne Murray	#72
1973	Roll in My Sweet Baby's Arms	Hank Wilson (Leon Russell)	#78
1973	California Saga (On My Way to Sunny Californ-i-a)	The Beach Boys	#84
1974	The Show Must Go On	Three Dog Night	#4
1974	Last Time I Saw Him	Diana Ross	#14
1974	Old Home Filler-Up An' Keep On-A-Truckin' Café	C.W. McCall	#54
1974	Travelin' Prayer	Billy Joel	#77
1975	Long Tall Glasses (I Can Dance)	Leo Sayer	#9
1975	Sweet Surrender	John Denver	#13
1975	Misty	Ray Stevens	#14
1975	Carolina in the Pines	Michael Murphey	#21
1975	The Entertainer	Billy Joel	#34
1975	The Biggest Parakeets in Town	Jud Strunk	#50
1975	Sneaky Snake	Tom T. Hall	#55
1975	If I Could Only Win Your Love	Emmylou Harris	#58
1975	Love Is a Rose	Linda Ronstadt	#63
1975	(All I Have to Do Is) Dream	Nitty Gritty Dirt Band	#66
1976	Convoy	C.W. McCall	#1
1976	Say You Love Me	Fleetwood Mac	#11
1976	Squeeze Box	The Who	#16
1976	The White Knight	Cledus Maggard	#19
1976	Last Child	Aerosmith	#21
1976	Let It Shine	Olivia Newton-John	#30
1976	Banapple Gas	Cat Stevens	#41
1976	Baby Boy	Mary Kay Place	#60
1976	There Won't Be No Country Music (There Won't Be No Rock 'N' Roll)	C.W. McCall	#73
1976	Rocky Mountain Music	Eddie Rabbitt	#76
1976	Kentucky Moonrunner	Cledus Maggard	#85
1977	Southern Nights	Glen Campbell	#1
1977	Dreamboat Annie	Heart	#42
1977	Sing	Tony Orlando & Dawn	#58
1977	Baby, You Look Good to Me Tonight	John Denver	#22
1977	Grandmother's Song	Steve Martin	#72
1978	Sweet, Sweet Smile	Carpenters	#44
1978	In for the Night	The Dirt Band	#86
1979	Rainbow Connection	Kermit (Jim Henson)	#25

	BANJO (cont'd)		
1979	Free Me from My Freedom/Tie Me to a Tree (Handcuff Me)	Bonnie Pointer	#58
1979	Sweet Summer Lovin'	Dolly Parton	#77
1979	Cruel Shoes	Steve Martin	#91

BARRED INSTRUMENTS

Barred instruments are xylophones, metallophones, marimbas, glockenspiels, and other similar instruments.

YEAR	SONG	ARTIST	HOT 100
1970	Hey There Lonely Girl	Eddie Holman	#2
1970	Cecilia	Simon & Garfunkel	#4
1970	Easy Come Easy Go	Bobby Sherman	#9
1970	La La La (If I Had You)	Bobby Sherman	#9
1970	Didn't I (Blow Your Mind This Time)	The Delfonics	#10
1970	Groovy Situation	Gene Chandler	#12
1970	The Bells	The Originals	#12
1970	Look What They've Done to My Song Ma	The New Seekers	#14
1970	Rubber Duckie	Ernie (Jim Henson)	#16
1970	Silver Bird	Mark Lindsay	#25
1970	Everything's Tuesday	Chairman of the Board	#38
1970	New World Coming	Mama Cass Elliot	#42
1970	My Woman, My Woman, My Wife	Marty Robbins	#42
1970	Paper Maché	Dionne Warwick	#43
1970	Ain't That Loving You (For More Reasons Than One)	Luther Ingram	#45
1970	When We Get Married	The Intruders	#45
1970	Sunday Morning Coming Down	Johnny Cash	#46
1970	Who's Gonna Take the Blame	Smokey Robinson & The Miracles	#46
1970	I've Gotta Make You Love Me	Steam	#46
1970	Sweetheart	Engelbert Humperdinck	#47
1970	Traces/Memories Medley	The Lettermen	#47
1970	I Do Take You	The Three Degrees	#48
1970	My Wife, the Dancer	Eddie & Dutch	#52
1970	Whoever Finds This, I Love You	Mac Davis	#53
1970	Stand By Me	David & Jimmy Ruffin	#61
1970	Nothing Succeeds Like Success	Bill Deal/The Rhondels	#62
1970	That Same Old Feeling	The Fortunes	#62
1970	Got to See if I Can't Get Mommy (To Come Back Home)	Jerry Butler	#62
1970	You, Me and Mexico	Edward Bear	#68
1970	Grover Henson Feels Forgotten	Bill Cosby	#70
1970	If Only I Had My Mind on Something Else	Bee Gees	#91
1970	You Keep Me Hangin' On/Hurt so Bad	Jackie DeShannon	#96

	BARRED INSTRUMENTS (cont'd)		
1970	Angelica	Oliver	#97
1971	One Bad Apple	The Osmonds	#1
1971	Go Away Little Girl	Donny Osmond	#1
1971	Never Can Say Goodbye	The Jackson 5	#2
1971	Lonely Days	Bee Gees	#3
1971	Mercy Mercy Me (The Ecology)	Marvin Gaye	#4
1971	Got to Be There	Michael Jackson	#4
1971	Never My Love	The 5th Dimension	#12
1971	Here Comes That Rainy Day Feeling Again	The Fortunes	#15
1971	I Don't Blame You at All	Smokey Robinson & The Miracles	#18
1971	The Drum	Bobby Sherman	#29
1971	The Love We Had (Stays on My Mind)	The Dells	#30
1971	1900 Yesterday	Liz Damon's Orient Express	#33
1971	Don't Change on Me	Ray Charles	#36
1971	I Won't Mention It Again	Ray Price	#42
1971	Time and Love	Barbra Streisand	#51
1971	Can't Find the Time	Rose Colored Glasses	#54
1971	(I Can Feel Those Vibrations) This Love Is Real	Jackie Wilson	#56
1971	All I Have	The Moments	#56
1971	Angel Baby	Dusk	#57
1971	Jennifer	Bobby Sherman	#60
1971	Do You Know What Time It Is?	P-Nut Gallery	#62
1971	I Wish I Were	Andy Kim	#62
1971	How Can I Unlove You	Lynn Anderson	#63
1971	I Like What You Give	Nolan (Nolan Porter)	#70
1971	When My Little Girl Is Smiling	Steve Alaimo	#72
1971	Everything Is Good About You	The Lettermen	#74
1971	One-Way Ticket	Tyrone Davis	#75
1971	Love Makes the World Go Round	Kiki Dee	#87
1971	Solo	Billie Sans	#91
1971	The Glory of Love	The Dells	#92
1971	Mandrill	Mandrill	#94
1971	You Just Can't Win (By Making the Same Mistake)	Gene Chandler & Jerry Butler	#94
1971	A Part of You	Brenda & The Tabulations	#94
1971	Love Me	The Impressions	#94
1971	I Want to Pay You Back (For Loving Me)	The Chi-Lites	#95
1971	Lucky Me	Moments	#98
1972	Back Stabbers	O'Jays	#3
1972	Everybody Plays the Fool	The Main Ingredient	#3
1972	Nice to Be with You	Gallery	#4
1972	(Last Night) I Didn't Get to Sleep at All	The 5th Dimension	#8

BARRED INSTRUMENTS (cont'd)			
1972	The Happiest Girl in the Whole U.S.A.	Donna Fargo	#11
1972	Why	Donny Osmond	#13
1972	Lookin' Through the Window	The Jackson 5	#16
1972	People Make the World Go Round	The Stylistics	#25
1972	How Can I Be Sure	David Cassidy	#25
1972	All the King's Horses	Aretha Franklin	#26
1972	Loving You Just Crossed My Mind	Sam Neely	#29
1972	Automatically Sunshine	The Supremes	#37
1972	Angel	Rod Stewart	#40
1972	My Boy	Richard Harris	#41
1972	Walk in the Night	Jr. Walker/The All Stars	#46
1972	Can't You Hear the Song?	Wayne Newton	#48
1972	Let's Stay Together	Isaac Hayes	#48
1972	Satisfaction	Smokey Robinson & The Miracles	#49
1972	Son of Shaft	The Bar-Kays	#53
1972	992 Arguments	The O'Jays	#57
1972	It Doesn't Matter	Stephen Stills	#61
1972	Victim of a Foolish Heart	Bettye Swann	#63
1972	Toast to the Fool	Dramatics	#67
1972	I've Got to Have You	Sammi Smith	#77
1972	How Could I Let You Get Away	The Spinners	#77
1972	Butterfly	Danyel Gerard	#78
1972	Vahevala	Loggins & Messina	#84
1972	I Guess I'll Miss the Man	The Supremes	#85
1972	Bedtime Story	Tammy Wynette	#86
1972	The People Tree	Sammy Davis, Jr. w/The Mike Curb Congregation	#92
1972	I Could Never Be Happy	The Emotions	#93
1972	I Thank You	Donny Hathaway & June Conquest	#94
1972	It's All Up to You	The Dells	#94
1972	Fool's Paradise	The Sylvers	#94
1973	Keep on Truckin' (Part 1)	Eddie Kendricks	#1
1973	The Night the Lights Went Out in Georgia	Vicki Lawrence	#1
1973	Touch Me in the Morning	Diana Ross	#1
1973	Playground in My Mind	Clint Holmes	#2
1973	Funny Face	Donna Fargo	#5
1973	Break Up to Make Up	The Stylistics	#5
1973	Daddy's Home	Jermaine Jackson	#9
1973	You're a Special Part of Me	Diana Ross & Marvin Gaye	#12
1973	Aubrey	Bread	#15
1973	Misdemeanor	Foster Sylvers	#22
1973	You'll Never Get to Heaven (If You Break My Heart)	The Stylistics	#23

BARRED INSTRUMENTS (cont'd)

1973	And I Love You So	Perry Como	#29
1973	Some Guys Have All the Luck	The Persuaders	#39
1973	Friends	Bette Midler	#40
1973	You've Got to Take It (If You Want It)	The Main Ingredient	#46
1973	A Song I'd Like to Sing	Kris Kristofferson & Rita Coolidge	#49
1973	Evil	Earth, Wind & Fire	#50
1973	With a Child's Heart	Michael Jackson	#50
1973	Don't Let It End ('Til You Let It Begin)	The Miracles	#56
1973	Loving Arms	Dobie Gray	#61
1973	Yesterday I Had the Blues	Harold Melvin	#63
1973	It's Forever	The Ebonys	#68
1973	Kids Say the Darndest Things	Tammy Wynette	#72
1973	You'd Better Believe It	Manhattans	#77
1973	You're in Good Hands	Jermaine Jackson	#79
1973	Didn't We	Barbra Streisand	#82
1973	Come Live with Me	Ray Charles	#82
1973	I Won't Last a Day Without You	Maureen McGovern	#89
1973	Come Live with Me	Roy Clark	#89
1973	Somebody Loves You	The Whispers	#94
1973	Saw a New Morning	The Bee Gees	#94
1973	Mr. Magic Man	Wilson Pickett	#98
1974	You Make Me Feel Brand New	The Stylistics	#2
1974	The Lord's Prayer	Sister Janet Mead	#4
1974	Be Thankful for What You Got	William DeVaughn	#4
1974	Everlasting Love	Carl Carlton	#6
1974	Never My Love	Blue Swede	#7
1974	Sideshow	Blue Magic	#8
1974	Love Me for a Reason	The Osmonds	#10
1974	Let's Put It All Together	The Stylistics	#18
1974	Touch a Hand, Make a Friend	The Staple Singers	#23
1974	Son of Sagittarius	Eddie Kendricks	#28
1974	Come Monday	Jimmy Buffett	#30
1974	Three Ring Circus	Blue Magic	#36
1974	Sugar Baby Love	The Rubettes	#37
1974	One Day at a Time	Marilyn Sellars	#37
1974	I Just Can't Get You Out of My Mind	Four Tops	#62
1974	Give Me a Reason to Be Gone	Maureen McGovern	#71
1974	Stop to Start	Blue Magic	#74
1974	My Main Man	The Staple Singers	#76
1974	Somewhere Between Love and Tomorrow	Roy Clark	#81
1974	Fox Hunt	Herb Alpert & The TJB	#84

BARRED INSTRUMENTS (cont'd)

1974	Rings	Reuben Howell	#86
1974	Don't Eat the Yellow Snow	Frank Zappa	#86
1974	The Golden Age of Rock 'N' Roll	Mott The Hoople	#96
1974	Newsy Neighbors	First Choice	#97
1975	Island Girl	Elton John	#1
1975	Before the Next Teardrop Falls	Freddy Fender	#1
1975	The Hustle	Van McCoy & The Soul City Symphony	#1
1975	Low Rider	War	#7
1975	Don't Call Us, We'll Call You	Sugarloaf	#9
1975	Look in My Eyes Pretty Woman	Tony Orlando & Dawn	#11
1975	Mornin' Beautiful	Tony Orlando & Dawn	#14
1975	To the Door of the Sun (Alle Porte Del Sole)	Al Martino	#17
1975	Secret Love	Freddy Fender	#20
1975	Born to Run	Bruce Springsteen	#23
1975	I Believe I'm Gonna Love You	Frank Sinatra	#47
1975	This Old Man	Purple Reign	#48
1975	Mexico	James Taylor	#49
1975	Baby, Hang Up the Phone	Carl Graves	#50
1975	To Each His Own	Faith, Hope & Charity	#50
1975	I Have a Dream	Donny Osmond	#50
1975	(If You Add) All the Love in the World	Mac Davis	#54
1975	We're Almost There	Michael Jackson	#54
1975	Hoppy, Gene and Me	Roy Rogers	#65
1975	Thank You Baby	The Stylistics	#70
1975	Salsoul Hustle	Salsoul Orchestra	#76
1975	When You're Young and in Love	The Choice Four	#91
1975	Hang on Sloopy	Rick Derringer	#94
1975	When You're Young and in Love	Ralph Carter	#95
1976	Kiss and Say Goodbye	Manhattans	#1
1976	Let 'Em In	Paul McCartney & Wings	#3
1976	Lonely Nights (Angel Face)	Captain & Tennille	#3
1976	Moonlight Feels Right	Starbuck	#3
1976	Sorry Seems to Be the Hardest Word	Elton John	#6
1976	Walk Away From Love	David Ruffin	#9
1976	Grow Some Funk of Your Own	Elton John	#14
1976	Heaven Must Be Missing an Angel (Part 1)	Tavares	#15
1976	Shower the People	James Taylor	#22
1976	Save Your Kisses for Me	Brotherhood of Man	#27
1976	Mamma Mia	ABBA	#32
1976	Banana Gas	Cat Stevens	#41
1976	I Got to Know	Starbuck	#43

	BARRED INSTRUMENTS (cont'd)		
1976	Heavy Love	David Ruffin	#47
1976	I Thought It Took a Little Time (But Today I Fell in Love)	Diana Ross	#47
1976	Everything's Coming Up Love	David Ruffin	#49
1976	Jealousy	Major Harris	#73
1976	Save Your Kisses for Me	Bobby Vinton	#75
1976	You Are Beautiful	The Stylistics	#78
1976	Train Called Freedom	South Shore Commission	#86
1976	You to Me Are Everything	Broadway	#86
1976	Daydreamer	C.C. & Company	#91
1976	All Roads (Lead Back to You)	Donny Most	#97
1977	Blue Bayou	Linda Ronstadt	#3
1977	My Heart Belongs to Me	Barbra Streisand	#4
1977	Margaritaville	Jimmy Buffett	#8
1977	After the Lovin'	Engelbert Humperdinck	#8
1977	Crackerbox Palace	George Harrison	#19
1977	Save It for a Rainy Day	Stephen Bishop	#22
1977	Uptown Festival (Part 1)	Shalamar	#25
1977	So You Win Again	Hot Chocolate	#31
1977	Everybody Be Dancin'	Starbuck	#38
1977	Dreamboat Annie	Heart	#42
1977	Amarillo	Neil Sedaka	#44
1977	Sunshine	Enchantment	#45
1977	If It's the Last Thing I Do	Thelma Houston	#47
1977	The Whistler	Jethro Tull	#59
1977	C.B. Savage	Rod Hart	#67
1977	Sorry	Grace Jones	#71
1977	Closer to the Heart	Rush	#76
1977	Sad Girl	Carl Graves	#83
1977	Nothing But a Breeze	Jesse Winchester	#86
1977	My Cherie Amour	Soul Train Gang	#92
1977	Goodbye My Friend	Engelbert Humperdinck	#97
1977	Ritzy Mambo	Salsoul Orchestra	#99
1978	Too Much, Too Little, Too Late	Johnny Mathis & Deniece Williams	#1
1978	How Much I Feel	Ambrosia	#3
1978	Theme from "Close Encounters of the Third Kind"	John Williams	#13
1978	Theme from "Close Encounters of the Third Kind"	Meco	#25
1978	Rivers of Babylon	Boney M	#30
1978	It's You That I Need	Enchantment	#33
1978	Themes from "The Wizard of Oz"	Meco	#35
1978	Cocomotion	El Coco	#44
1978	Dreadlock Holiday	10 CC	#44

BARRED INSTRUMENTS (cont'd)

1978	The Next Hundred Years	Al Martino	#49
1978	Put Your Head on My Shoulder	Leif Garrett	#58
1978	I Love You, I Love You, I Love You	Ronnie McDowell	#81
1978	Manana	Jimmy Buffett	#84
1978	Never Had a Love	Pablo Cruise	#87
1978	Shaker Song	Spyro Gyra	#90
1978	Dancing in Paradise	El Coco	#91
1979	Rise	Herb Alpert	#1
1979	Sad Eyes	Robert John	#1
1979	Makin' It	David Naughton	#5
1979	Half the Way	Crystal Gayle	#15
1979	Come to Me	France Joli	#15
1979	Blow Away	George Harrison	#16
1979	Love Ballad	George Benson	#18
1979	Morning Dance	Spyro Gyra	#24
1979	Video Killed the Radio Star	The Buggles	#40
1979	Keep on Dancin'	Gary's Gang	#41
1979	Dancin' Fool	Frank Zappa	#45
1979	Pow Wow	Cory Daye	#76

CASTANETS

YEAR	SONG	ARTIST	HOT 100
1979	The Logical Song	Supertramp	#6
1979	Love Pains	Yvonne Elliman	#34
1979	One Last Kiss	The J. Geils Band	#35
1979	Dance Away	Roxy Music	#44

CLARINET

YEAR	SONG	ARTIST	HOT 100
1972	Day and Night	The Wackers	#65
1973	Don't Let It End ('Til You Let It Begin)	The Miracles	#56
1974	Steppin' Out (Gonna Boogie Tonight)	Tony Orlando & Dawn	#7
1975	Low Rider	War	#7
1975	Harry Truman	Chicago	#13
1977	Don't Turn the Light Out	Cliff Richard	#57

	CLARINET (cont'd)		
1978	Shadow Dancing	Andy Gibb	#1
1979	Take the Long Way Home	Supertramp	#10

CLAVINET

YEAR	SONG	ARTIST	HOT 100
1970	War	Edwin Starr	#1
1972	Nutrocker	Emerson, Lake & Palmer	#70
1973	Superstition	Stevie Wonder	#1
1973	Nutbush City Limits	Ike & Tina Turner	#22
1973	I Found Sunshine	The Chi-Lites	#47
1973	Finder's Keepers	Chairman of the Board	#59
1973	Am I Black Enough for You	Billy Paul	#79
1974	You Haven't Done Nothin'	Stevie Wonder	#1
1974	Rock Me Gently	Andy Kim	#1
1974	Whatever Gets You Thru the Night	John Lennon	#1
1974	Dancing Machine	The Jackson 5	#2
1974	Sexy Ida (Part 1)	Ike & Tina Turner	#65
1974	Do It, Fluid	The Blackbyrds	#69
1974	City in the Sky	The Staple Singers	#79
1975	Don't Call Us, We'll Call You	Sugarloaf	#9
1975	Trampled Under Foot	Led Zeppelin	#38
1975	Changes	Loggins & Messina	#84
1976	Get Up and Boogie (That's Right)	Silver Convention	#2
1976	Open	Smokey Robinson	#81
1977	Life in the Fast Lane	Eagles	#11
1977	It Keeps You Runnin'	The Doobie Brothers	#37
1977	Welcome to Our World (Of Merry Music)	Mass Production	#68
1977	Disco 9000	Johnnie Taylor	#86
1978	Dance (Disco Heat)	Sylvester	#19
1979	High on Your Love Suite	Rick James	#72

FINGER CYMBALS

YEAR	SONG	ARTIST	HOT 100
1970	Darkness, Darkness	The Youngbloods	#86
1970	Angelica	Oliver	#97
1972	Runaway/Happy Together	Dawn featuring Tony Orlando	#79

FINGER CYMBALS (cont'd)			
1973	Killing Me Softly with His Song	Roberta Flack	#1
1974	Would You Lay with Me	Tanya Tucker	#46
1975	Lady	Styx	#6
1975	I Am Love (Parts I & II)	The Jackson 5	#15
1975	Baby That's Backatcha	Smokey Robinson	#26
1975	We May Never Love Like This Again	Maureen McGovern	#83
1979	You Can Do It	Niteflyte	#37

FLUTE

YEAR	SONG	ARTIST	HOT 100
1970	Spill the Wine	Eric Burdon & War	#3
1970	El Condor Pasa (If I Could)	Paul Simon	#18
1970	One Tin Soldier	The Original Caste	#34
1970	Temma Harbour	Mary Hopkin	#39
1970	Trying to Make a Fool Out of Me	The Delfonics	#40
1970	My Woman, My Woman, My Wife	Marty Robbins	#42
1970	I Stand Accused	Isaac Hayes	#42
1970	And the Grass Won't Pay No Mind	Mark Lindsay	#44
1970	Good Guys Only Win in the Movies	Mel and Tim	#45
1970	Sunday Morning Coming Down	Johnny Cash	#46
1970	We're All Playing in the Same Band	Bert Sommer	#48
1970	The Touch of You	Brenda & The Tabulations	#50
1970	Seems Like I Gotta Do Wrong	The Whispers	#50
1970	Until it's Time for You to Go	Neil Diamond	#53
1970	When You Get Right Down to It	The Delfonics	#53
1970	On the Beach (In the Summertime)	The 5th Dimension	#54
1970	Oh Well – Pt. 1	Fleetwood Mac	#55
1970	Something	Shirley Bassey	#55
1970	She Lets Her Hair Down (Early in the Morning)	The Tokens	#61
1970	You've Been My Inspiration	The Main Ingredient	#64
1970	Long Lonely Nights	The Dells	#74
1970	Don't Make Me Over	Brenda & The Tabulations	#77
1970	Barbara, I Love You	New Colony Six	#78
1970	The Court of the Crimson King – Part 1	King Crimson	#80
1970	Sunset Strip	Ray Stevens	#81
1970	Groovin' (Out on Life)	The Newbeats	#82
1970	Susie-Q	José Feliciano	#84
1970	I Would Be in Love (Anyway)	Frank Sinatra	#88
1970	Mill Valley	Miss Abrams	#90

	FLUTE (cont'd)		
1970	I'm Better off Without You	The Main Ingredient	#91
1970	(I Remember) Summer Morning	Vanity Fare	#98
1970	A Song that Never Comes	Mama Cass Elliot	#99
1971	Go Away Little Girl	Donny Osmond	#1
1971	Never Can Say Goodbye	The Jackson 5	#2
1971	Lonely Days	Bee Gees	#3
1971	I've Found Someone of My Own	The Free Movement	#5
1971	So Far Away	Carole King	#14
1971	Born to Wander	Rare Earth	#17
1971	Never Can Say Goodbye	Isaac Hayes	#22
1971	Loving Her Was Easier (Than Anything I'll Ever Do Again)	Kris Kristofferson	#26
1971	One Tin Soldier (The Legend of Billy Jack)	Coven	#26
1971	You've Got a Friend	Roberta Flack & Donny Hathaway	#29
1971	Spill the Wine	The Isley Brothers	#49
1971	Life	Elvis Presley	#53
1971	Whole Lotta Love	C.C.S.	#58
1971	We Were Always Sweethearts	Boz Scaggs	#61
1971	Mozart Symphony No. 40 in G Minor K.550, 1st Movement	Waldo de los Rios	#67
1971	Beautiful People	New Seekers	#67
1971	Hill Where the Lord Hides	Chuck Mangione	#76
1971	Never Dreamed You'd Leave in Summer	Stevie Wonder	#78
1971	I Say a Little Prayer/By the Time I Get to Phoenix	Glen Campbell/Anne Murray	#81
1971	Your Love Is so Doggone Good	The Whispers	#93
1971	Mandrill	Mandrill	#94
1971	Medley from "Superstar" (A Rock Opera)	The Assembled Multitude	#95
1971	You've Got to Earn It	The Staple Singers	#97
1971	Be Good to Me Baby	Luther Ingram	#97
1971	I Don't Know How to Love Him/Everything's Alright	The Kimberlys	#99
1971	What About Me	Quicksilver Messenger Service	#100
1972	Rockin' Robin	Michael Jackson	#2
1972	Freddie's Dead (Theme from "Superfly")	Curtis Mayfield	#4
1972	It Never Rains in Southern California	Albert Hammond	#5
1972	Day Dreaming	Aretha Franklin	#5
1972	It's Going to Take Some Time	Carpenters	#12
1972	I Wanna Be Where You Are	Michael Jackson	#16
1972	Lookin' Through the Window	The Jackson 5	#16
1972	Corner of the Sky	The Jackson 5	#18
1972	It's One of Those Nights (Yes Love)	The Partridge Family	#20
1972	An American Trilogy	Mickey Newbury	#26
1972	Isn't Life Strange	The Moody Blues	#29

	FLUTE (cont'd)		
1972	Loving You Just Crossed My Mind	Sam Neely	#29
1972	Alive	The Bee Gees	#34
1972	We're Free	Beverly Bremers	#40
1972	Handbags and Gladrags	Rod Stewart	#42
1972	Everything Good Is Bad	100 Proof	#45
1972	Brown Eyed Girl	El Chicano	#45
1972	The Coldest Days of My Life (Part 1)	The Chi-Lites	#47
1972	Let's Stay Together	Isaac Hayes	#48
1972	The Harder I Try (The Bluer I Get)	Free Movement	#50
1972	Duncan	Paul Simon	#52
1972	Son of Shaft	The Bar-Kays	#53
1972	Pain (Part 1)	Ohio Players	#64
1972	Love Theme from "The Godfather"	Carlo Savina	#66
1972	Colorado	Danny Holien	#66
1972	An American Trilogy	Elvis Presley	#66
1972	Toast to the Fool	Dramatics	#67
1972	Bed and Board	Barbara Mason	#70
1972	Love Potion Number Nine	Coasters	#76
1972	What a Wonderful Thing We Have	Fabulous Rhinestones	#78
1972	Taos New Mexico	R. Dean Taylor	#83
1972	If We Only Have Love	Dionne Warwick	#84
1972	Tell Me This Is a Dream	Delfonics	#86
1972	I Could Never Be Happy	The Emotions	#93
1972	One Way Sunday	Mark-Almond	#94
1972	Number Wonderful	Rock Flowers	#95
1973	The Cisco Kid	War	#2
1973	Sing	Carpenters	#3
1973	Ain't No Woman (Like the One I've Got)	Four Tops	#4
1973	Hocus Pocus	Focus	#9
1973	Keeper of the Castle	The Four Tops	#10
1973	I Believe in You (You Believe in Me)	Johnnie Taylor	#11
1973	Living in the Past	Jethro Tull	#11
1973	Stir It Up	Johnny Nash	#12
1973	You're a Special Part of Me	Diana Ross & Marvin Gaye	#12
1973	You'll Never Get to Heaven (If You Break My Heart)	The Stylistics	#23
1973	Cook with Honey	Judy Collins	#32
1973	Master of Eyes (The Deepness of Your Eyes)	Aretha Franklin	#33
1973	Looking Through the Eyes of Love	The Partridge Family	#39
1973	Down and Out in New York City	James Brown	#50
1973	My Pretending Days Are Over	The Dells	#51
1973	Tweedlee Dee	Little Jimmy Osmond	#59

	FLUTE (cont'd)		
1973	Follow Your Daughter Home	The Guess Who	#61
1973	That's Why You Remember	Kenny Karen	#82
1973	It May Be Winter Outside, (But in My Heart It's Spring)	Love Unlimited	#83
1973	Black Byrd	Donald Byrd	#88
1973	On and Off (Part 1)	Anacostia	#90
1973	Love Is All	Engelbert Humperdinck	#91
1973	Saw a New Morning	The Bee Gees	#94
1974	The Way We Were	Barbra Streisand	#1
1974	Kung Fu Fighting	Carl Douglas	#1
1974	Billy, Don't Be a Hero	Bo Donaldson & The Heywoods	#1
1974	Annie's Song	John Denver	#1
1974	Love's Theme	Love Unlimited Orchestra	#1
1974	Sunshine on My Shoulders	John Denver	#1
1974	Until You Come Back to Me (That's What I'm Gonna Do)	Aretha Franklin	#3
1974	Best Thing That Ever Happened to Me	Gladys Knight & The Pips	#3
1974	Distant Lover	Marvin Gaye	#28
1974	Ballero	War	#33
1974	Daybreak	Nilsson	#39
1974	Funky President (People It's Bad)	James Brown	#44
1974	It Could Have Been Me	Sami Jo	#46
1974	In the Bottle	Brother to Brother	#46
1974	Homely Girl	The Chi-Lites	#54
1974	Midnight Flower	Four Tops	#55
1974	Black Lassie (Featuring Johnny Stash)	Cheech & Chong	#55
1974	Virgin Man	Smokey Robinson	#56
1974	Too Late	Tavares	#59
1974	Sleepin'	Diana Ross	#70
1974	Watching the River Run	Loggins & Messina	#71
1974	Put a Little Love Away	The Emotions	#73
1974	Skybird	Neil Diamond	#75
1974	Under the Influence of Love	Love Unlimited	#76
1974	Loving Arms	Kris Kristofferson & Rita Coolidge	#86
1974	Ain't No Love in the Heart of the City	Bobby Bland	#91
1974	I Wish It Was Me You Loved	The Dells	#94
1975	Bad Blood	Neil Sedaka	#1
1975	Philadelphia Freedom	Elton John	#1
1975	Please Mr. Please	Olivia Newton-John	#3
1975	Express	B.T. Express	#4
1975	Walking in Rhythm	The Blackbyrds	#6
1975	Rockin' Chair	Gwen McCrae	#9

		FLUTE (cont'd)		
1975	Nightingale	Carole King	#9
1975	Brazil	The Ritchie Family	#11
1975	Bungle in the Jungle	Jethro Tull	#12
1975	Sweet Surrender	John Denver	#13
1975	Something Better to Do	Olivia Newton-John	#13
1975	Mornin' Beautiful	Tony Orlando & Dawn	#14
1975	Hijack	Herbie Mann	#14
1975	Rock N' Roll (I Gave You the Best Years of My Life)	Mac Davis	#15
1975	Shoeshine Boy	Eddie Kendricks	#18
1975	Baby That's Backatcha	Smokey Robinson	#26
1975	Peace Pipe	B.T. Express	#31
1975	Glasshouse	The Temptations	#37
1975	Fire on the Mountain	Marshall Tucker Band	#38
1975	I Dreamed Last Night	Justin Hayward & John Lodge	#47
1975	Sunshine Part II	O'Jays	#48
1975	Get the Cream off the Top	Eddie Kendricks	#50
1975	I Have a Dream	Donny Osmond	#50
1975	Hollywood Hot	The Eleventh Hour	#55
1975	My Little Lady	Bloodstone	#57
1975	Hey There Little Firefly (Part 1)	Firefly	#67
1975	Flyin' High	The Blackbyrds	#70
1975	This Ol' Cowboy	Marshall Tucker Band	#78
1975	Waterfall	Carly Simon w/James Taylor	#78
1975	Minstrel in the Gallery	Jethro Tull	#79
1975	Come An' Get Yourself Some	Leon Haywood	#83
1975	Chase the Clouds Away	Chuck Mangione	#96
1975	Honey Trippin'	The Mystic Moods	#98
1976	Let 'Em In	Paul McCartney & Wings	#3
1976	Lowdown	Boz Scaggs	#3
1976	Times of Your Life	Paul Anka	#7
1976	Beth	Kiss	#7
1976	You are the Woman	Firefall	#9
1976	Turn the Beat Around	Vickie Sue Robinson	#10
1976	Tryin' to Get the Feeling Again	Barry Manilow	#10
1976	Never Gonna Fall in Love Again	Eric Carmen	#11
1976	A Little Bit More	Dr. Hook	#11
1976	Fly Away	John Denver	#13
1976	Tangerine	The Salsoul Orchestra	#18
1976	Baretta's Theme ("Keep Your Eye on the Sparrow")	Rhythm Heritage	#20
1976	Looking for Space	John Denver	#29
1976	Still Crazy After All These Years	Paul Simon	#40

	FLUTE (cont'd)		
1976	The Homecoming	Hagood Hardy	#41
1976	Don't Think…Feel	Neil Diamond	#43
1976	Mr. Melody	Natalie Cole	#49
1976	Let's Be Young Tonight	Jermaine Jackson	#55
1976	Lipstick	Michel Polnareff	#61
1976	Locomotive Breath	Jethro Tull	#62
1976	Breezin'	George Benson	#63
1976	Party	Van McCoy	#69
1976	The Lonely One	Special Delivery	#75
1976	Close to You	B.T. Express	#82
1976	Rock Creek Park	The Blackbyrds	#93
1977	You Don't Have to Be a Star (To Be in My Show)	Marilyn McCoo & Billy Davis, Jr.	#1
1977	Dazz	Brick	#3
1977	My Heart Belongs to Me	Barbra Streisand	#4
1977	You and Me	Alice Cooper	#9
1977	Heard It in a Love Song	Marshall Tucker Band	#14
1977	Dusic	Brick	#18
1977	Another Star	Stevie Wonder	#32
1977	Cinderella	Firefall	#34
1977	All You Get from Love Is a Love Song	Carpenters	#35
1977	You're Throwing a Good Love Away	Spinners	#43
1977	If It's the Last Thing I Do	Thelma Houston	#47
1977	"Roots" Medley	Quincy Jones	#57
1977	The Whistler	Jethro Tull	#59
1977	I Believe in Love	Kenny Loggins	#66
1977	See You When I Git There	Lou Rawls	#66
1977	Sorry	Grace Jones	#71
1977	Can't You See	Marshall Tucker Band	#75
1977	Land of Make Believe	Chuck Mangione w/Esther Saterfield	#86
1977	Save Me	Donna McDaniel	#90
1977	Love to the World	L.T.D.	#91
1977	C'est La Vie	Greg Lake	#91
1977	Moondance	Van Morrison	#92
1977	Dance Little Lady Dance	Danny White	#100
1978	Last Dance	Donna Summer	#3
1978	Dance, Dance, Dance (Yowsah, Yowsah, Yowsah)	Chic	#6
1978	Strange Way	Firefall	#11
1978	Ready to Take a Chance Again	Barry Manilow	#11
1978	Falling	LeBlanc & Carr	#13
1978	She's Always a Woman	Billy Joel	#17

FLUTE (cont'd)			
1978	Ffun	Con Funk Shun	#23
1978	Lady Love	Lou Rawls	#24
1978	Close the Door	Teddy Pendergrass	#25
1978	More Than a Woman	Tavares	#32
1978	Forever Autumn	Justin Hayward	#47
1978	I Want to Live	John Denver	#55
1978	I Believe You	Carpenters	#68
1978	Dancin' Fever	Claudja Barry	#72
1978	Let's Get Crazy Tonight	Rupert Holmes	#72
1978	Dream Lover	Marshall Tucker Band	#75
1978	Daylight and Darkness	Smokey Robinson	#75
1978	Love Me Right	Denise LaSalle	#80
1978	Don't Let It Show	Alan Parsons Project	#92
1979	Reunited	Peaches & Herb	#1
1979	You Decorated My Life	Kenny Rogers	#7
1979	Tusk	Fleetwood Mac	#8
1979	Lotta Love	Nicolette Larson	#8
1979	Suspicions	Eddie Rabbitt	#13
1979	I Don't Know if It's Right	Evelyn "Champagne" King	#23
1979	Superman	Herbie Mann	#26
1979	Good Friend	Mary MacGregor	#39
1979	Turn Off the Lights	Teddy Pendergrass	#48
1979	Can You Read My Mind	Maureen McGovern	#52
1979	Pops, We Love You (A Tribute to Father)	Diana Ross, Marvin Gaye, Smokey Robinson & Stevie Wonder	#59
1979	Theme from Ice Castles (Through the Eyes of Love)	Melissa Manchester	#76
1979	Sweet Summer Lovin'	Dolly Parton	#77
1979	This Is It	Dan Hartman	#91

GUITAR (SLIDE)

YEAR	SONG	ARTIST	HOT 100
1970	My Sweet Lord	George Harrison	#1
1970	Teach Your Children	Crosby, Stills, Nash & Young	#16
1970	Joanne	Michael Nesmith	#21
1970	Mississippi	John Phillips	#32
1970	She Belongs to Me	Rick Nelson	#33
1970	My Elusive Dreams	Bobby Vinton	#46
1970	Sunday Morning Coming Down	Johnny Cash	#46
1970	Morning	Jim Ed Brown	#47

GUITAR (SLIDE) (cont'd)

1970	Easy to Be Free	Rick Nelson	#48
1970	Hello Darlin'	Conway Twitty	#60
1970	Is Anybody Goin' to San Antone	Charley Pride	#70
1970	I Can't Believe That You've Stopped Loving Me	Charley Pride	#71
1970	Fifteen Years Ago	Conway Twitty	#81
1970	Coal Miner's Daughter	Loretta Lynn	#83
1970	Wonder Could I Live There Anymore	Charley Pride	#87
1970	Sweet Sweetheart	Bobby Vee	#88
1970	Run, Woman, Run	Tammy Wynette	#92
1970	He Loves Me All the Way	Tammy Wynette	#97
1970	I'll See Him Through	Tammy Wynette	#100
1971	Take Me Home, Country Roads	John Denver	#2
1971	Here Comes the Sun	Richie Havens	#16
1971	Easy Loving	Freddie Hart	#17
1971	Woodstock	Matthews' Southern Comfort	#23
1971	If Not for You	Olivia Newton-John	#25
1971	Wild Night	Van Morrison	#28
1971	Nothing to Hide	Tommy James	#41
1971	The Year That Clayton Delaney Died	Tom T. Hall	#42
1971	Silver Moon	Michael Nesmith	#42
1971	Change Partners	Stephen Stills	#43
1971	Friends with You	John Denver	#47
1971	After the Fire Is Gone	Conway Twitty & Loretta Lynn	#56
1971	How Can I Unlove You	Lynn Anderson	#63
1971	You're My Man	Lynn Anderson	#63
1971	I'd Rather Love You	Charley Pride	#79
1971	Sing High – Sing Low	Anne Murray	#83
1971	Top Forty	Sha Na Na	#84
1971	She's All I Got	Johnny Paycheck	#91
1971	I Wanna Be Free	Loretta Lynn	#94
1971	I'm Just Me	Charley Pride	#94
1971	Good Enough to Be Your Wife	Jeannie C. Riley	#97
1971	I'm Gonna Be a Country Girl Again	Buffy Sainte-Marie	#98
1972	Heart of Gold	Neil Young	#1
1972	The Lion Sleeps Tonight	Robert John	#3
1972	Nice to Be with You	Gallery	#4
1972	Sylvia's Mother	Dr. Hook	#5
1972	Never Been to Spain	Three Dog Night	#5
1972	Garden Party	Rick Nelson	#6
1972	Kiss an Angel Good Mornin'	Charley Pride	#21
1972	Old Man	Neil Young	#31

	GUITAR (SLIDE) (cont'd)		
1972	Tiny Dancer	Elton John	#41
1972	No	Bulldog	#44
1972	What am I Living For	Ray Charles	#54
1972	Josie	Kris Kristofferson	#63
1972	Cotton Jenny	Anne Murray	#71
1972	Cry	Lynn Anderson	#71
1972	Rock Me on the Water	Linda Ronstadt	#85
1972	Bedtime Story	Tammy Wynette	#86
1972	Buzzy Brown	Tim Davis	#91
1972	It's Four in the Morning	Faron Young	#92
1972	All His Children	Charley Pride w/Henry Mancini	#92
1972	Shake Off the Demon	Brewer & Shipley	#98
1972	Southbound Train	Graham Nash & David Crosby	#99
1973	Top of the World	Carpenters	#1
1973	The Most Beautiful Girl	Charlie Rich	#1
1973	Give Me Love – (Give Me Peace on Earth)	George Harrison	#1
1973	Paper Roses	Marie Osmond	#5
1973	Funny Face	Donna Fargo	#5
1973	Danny's Song	Anne Murray	#7
1973	Rocky Mountain High	John Denver	#9
1973	Behind Closed Doors	Charlie Rich	#15
1973	Jambalaya (On the Bayou)	The Blue Ridge Rangers	#16
1973	You've Never Been This Far Before	Conway Twitty	#22
1973	Big City Miss Ruth Ann	Gallery	#23
1973	Satin Sheets	Jeanne Pruett	#28
1973	Soul Song	Joe Stampley	#37
1973	Hearts of Stone	Blue Ridge Rangers	#37
1973	Superman	Donna Fargo	#41
1973	Country Sunshine	Dottie West	#49
1973	Little Girl Gone	Donna Fargo	#57
1973	Everybody's Had the Blues	Merle Haggard	#62
1973	The Lord Knows I'm Drinking	Cal Smith	#64
1973	Palace Guard	Rick Nelson	#65
1973	Please, Daddy	John Denver	#69
1973	Ridin' My Thumb to Mexico	Johnny Rodriguez	#70
1973	Slippin' Away	Jean Shepard	#81
1973	California Saga (On My Way to Sunny Californ-i-a)	The Beach Boys	#84
1973	You Always Come Back (To Hurting Me)	Johnny Rodriguez	#86
1973	What's Your Mama's Name	Tanya Tucker	#86
1973	Sunshine	Mickey Newbury	#87
1973	Come Live with Me	Roy Clark	#89

GUITAR (SLIDE) (cont'd)			
1973	You Were Always There	Donna Fargo	#93
1973	Smoke! Smoke! Smoke! (That Cigarette)	Commander Cody	#94
1973	Kid Stuff	Barbara Fairchild	#95
1973	Working Class Hero	Tommy Roe	#97
1973	If It's All Right with You	Dottie West	#97
1974	The Streak	Ray Stevens	#1
1974	If You Love Me (Let Me Know)	Olivia Newton-John	#5
1974	Love Song	Anne Murray	#12
1974	Fairytale	The Pointer Sisters	#13
1974	Rub It In	Billy "Crash" Craddock	#16
1974	I Love My Friend	Charlie Rich	#24
1974	Come Monday	Jimmy Buffett	#30
1974	Workin' at the Car Wash Blues	Jim Croce	#32
1974	One Day at a Time	Marilyn Sellars	#37
1974	No Charge	Melba Montgomery	#39
1974	Daddy What If	Bobby Bare	#41
1974	Room Full of Roses	Mickey Gilley	#50
1974	Love Has No Pride	Linda Ronstadt	#51
1974	When the Morning Comes	Hoyt Axton	#54
1974	You Can't Be a Beacon (If Your Light Don't Shine)	Donna Fargo	#57
1974	Silver Threads and Golden Needles	Linda Ronstadt	#67
1974	Mississippi Cotton Picking Delta Town	Charley Pride	#70
1974	Beyond the Blue Horizon	Lou Christie	#80
1974	Somewhere Between Love and Tomorrow	Roy Clark	#81
1974	U.S. of A	Donna Fargo	#86
1974	Please Don't Tell Me How the Story Ends	Ronnie Milsap	#95
1975	He Don't Love You (Like I Love You)	Tony Orlando & Dawn	#1
1975	Best of My Love	The Eagles	#1
1975	Dance with Me	Orleans	#6
1975	Long Tall Glasses (I Can Dance)	Leo Sayer	#9
1975	Misty	Ray Stevens	#14
1975	Sally G	Paul McCartney & Wings	#17
1975	Rainy Day People	Gordon Lightfoot	#26
1975	Ruby, Baby	Billy "Crash" Craddock	#33
1975	Ding Dong; Ding Dong	George Harrison	#36
1975	Lizzie and the Rainman	Tanya Tucker	#37
1975	Fire on the Mountain	Marshall Tucker Band	#38
1975	Who's Sorry Now	Marie Osmond	#40
1975	Ain't That Peculiar	Diamond Reo	#44
1975	It Doesn't Matter Anymore	Linda Ronstadt	#47
1975	Skybird	Tony Orlando & Dawn	#49

GUITAR (SLIDE) (cont'd)

1975	My Elusive Dreams	Charlie Rich	#49
1975	Devil in the Bottle	T.G. Sheppard	#54
1975	What's Happened to Blue Eyes	Jessi Colter	#57
1975	If I Could Only Win Your Love	Emmylou Harris	#58
1975	Blind Man in the Bleachers	Kenny Starr	#58
1975	Linda on My Mind	Conway Twitty	#61
1975	Reconsider Me	Narvel Felts	#67
1975	The Pill	Loretta Lynn	#70
1975	Rock & Roll Runaway	Ace	#71
1975	Nothin' Heavy	David Bellamy	#77
1975	Blanket on the Ground	Billie Jo Spears	#78
1975	Live Your Life Before You Die	The Pointer Sisters	#89
1975	I'll Go to My Grave Loving You	The Statler Brothers	#93
1975	What a Man My Man Is	Lynn Anderson	#93
1975	Tryin' to Beat the Morning Home	T.G. Sheppard	#95
1975	It Do Feel Good	Donna Fargo	#98
1975	Sunday Sunrise	Anne Murray	#98
1976	The Wreck of the Edmund Fitzgerald	Gordon Lightfoot	#2
1976	Come on Over	Olivia Newton-John	#23
1976	Hello Old Friend	Eric Clapton	#24
1976	Tracks of My Tears	Linda Ronstadt	#25
1976	Banapple Gas	Cat Stevens	#41
1976	Easy as Pie	Billy "Crash" Craddock	#54
1976	If Not You	Dr. Hook	#55
1976	For a Dancer	Prelude	#63
1976	Don't Cry Joni	Conway Twitty w/Joni Lee	#63
1976	Teddy Bear's Last Ride	Diana Williams	#66
1976	Since I Fell for You	Charlie Rich	#71
1976	I'll Get Over You	Crystal Gayle	#71
1976	Amazing Grace (Used to Be Her Favorite Song)	Amazing Rhythm Aces	#72
1976	Rain, Oh Rain	Fools Gold	#76
1976	Rocky Mountain Music	Eddie Rabbitt	#76
1976	I'm So Lonesome I Could Cry	Terry Bradshaw	#91
1976	Hey Baby	J.J. Cale	#96
1976	Love Lifted Me	Kenny Rogers	#97
1976	Solitary Man	T.G. Sheppard	#100
1977	Blue Bayou	Linda Ronstadt	#3
1977	Crackerbox Palace	George Harrison	#19
1977	Luckenbach, Texas (Back to the Basics of Love)	Waylon Jennings	#25
1977	Sunflower	Glen Campbell	#39
1977	Neon Nites	Atlanta Rhythm Section	#42

GUITAR (SLIDE) (cont'd)

1977	Indian Summer	Poco	#50
1977	Race Among the Runs	Gordon Lightfoot	#65
1977	C.B. Savage	Rod Hart	#67
1977	Heaven's Just a Sin Away	The Kendalls	#69
1977	Brooklyn	Cody Jameson	#74
1977	Nothing But a Breeze	Jesse Winchester	#86
1977	Save Me	Donna McDaniel	#90
1977	Goodbye My Friend	Engelbert Humperdinck	#97
1978	Hopelessly Devoted to You	Olivia Newton-John	#3
1978	Here You Come Again	Dolly Parton	#3
1978	All I See Is Your Face	Dan Hill	#41
1978	Mammas Don't Let Your Babies Grow Up to Be Cowboys	Waylon Jennings & Willie Nelson	#42
1978	Sweet, Sweet Smile	Carpenters	#44
1979	Sail On	Commodores	#4
1979	I Just Fall in Love Again	Anne Murray	#12
1979	Heart of the Night	Poco	#20
1979	Shadows in the Moonlight	Anne Murray	#25
1979	Every Which Way but Loose	Eddie Rabbitt	#30
1979	If I Said You Have a Beautiful Body Would You Hold It Against Me	The Bellamy Brothers	#39
1979	The Football Card	Glenn Sutton	#46
1979	Four Strong Winds	Neil Young (w/Nicolette Larson)	#61
1979	Dancin' 'Round and 'Round	Olivia Newton-John	#82
1979	You and Me	Liner	#92

THE LONGEST GUITAR SOLOS OF THE 1970s

Only guitar solos that are twenty seconds or longer are included. Songs are listed in order from songs with the longest solos to the songs with the shortest solos.

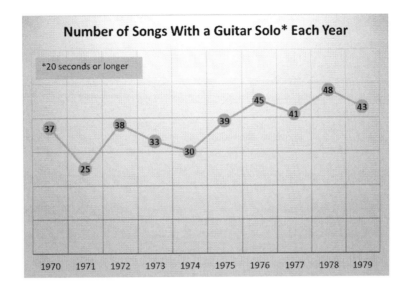

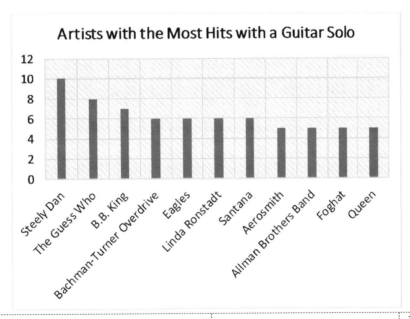

YEAR	SONG	ARTIST	HOT 100	LENGTH OF SOLO
1977	Hotel California	Eagles	#1	124, 51 sec.
1978	Yank Me, Crank Me	Ted Nugent	#58	81 sec.
1972	Black Dog	Led Zeppelin	#15	75 sec.
1970	Are You Ready?	Pacific Gas & Electric	#14	73 sec.
1975	Free Bird	Lynyrd Skynyrd	#19	69 sec.
1975	Let There Be Music	Orleans	#55	69 sec.

LONGEST GUITAR SOLOS (cont'd)

1979	Boom Boom (Out Go the Lights)	Pat Travers	#56	68, 22 sec.
1970	All Right Now	Free	#4	65 sec.
1970	Fresh Air	Quicksilver Messenger Service	#49	65 sec.
1979	One Last Kiss	The J. Geils Band	#35	65 sec.
1976	Take It Like a Man	Bachman-Turner Overdrive	#33	63 sec.
1972	That's What Love Will Make You Do	Little Milton	#59	62, 31, 28 sec.
1978	Stone Blue	Foghat	#36	62, 26 sec.
1979	Oh Well	Rockets	#30	61 sec.
1972	Goodbye to Love	Carpenters	#7	60, 25 sec.
1979	Goodbye Stranger	Supertramp	#15	60 sec.
1972	Guess Who	B.B. King	#61	58, 55 sec.
1971	Black Magic Woman	Santana	#4	58, 45 sec.
1979	Just the Same Way	Journey	#58	56 sec.
1974	Pretzel Logic	Steely Dan	#57	55 sec.
1975	Roll on Down the Highway	Bachman-Turner Overdrive	#14	54 sec.
1976	Dog Eat Dog	Ted Nugent	#91	54 sec.
1977	Watcha Gonna Do?	Pablo Cruise	#6	53 sec.
1979	Spooky	Atlanta Rhythm Section	#17	52, 36 sec.
1970	Hand Clapping Song	The Meters	#89	52 sec.
1973	Over the Hills and Far Away	Led Zeppelin	#51	52 sec.
1976	Do You Feel Like We Do	Peter Frampton	#10	51, 39 sec.
1976	Kid Charlemagne	Steely Dan	#82	51, 33 sec.
1971	Feelin' Alright	Grand Funk Railroad	#54	51, 20 sec.
1978	Like a Sunday in Salem (The Amos & Andy Song)	Gene Cotton	#40	51 sec.
1979	Roller	April Wine	#34	51 sec.
1976	Lookin' Out for #1	Bachman-Turner Overdrive	#65	50 sec.
1978	Hold Me, Touch Me	Paul Stanley	#46	50 sec.
1978	It's Late	Queen	#74	50 sec.
1979	I Want You Tonight	Pablo Cruise	#19	50 sec.
1977	Year of the Cat	Al Stewart	#8	49 sec.
1970	Only You Know and I Know	Dave Mason	#42	48 sec.
1975	Angel (What in the World's Come Over Us)	Atlanta Rhythm Section	#79	48 sec.
1974	La Grange	ZZ Top	#41	47, 45 sec.
1971	Tongue in Cheek	Sugarloaf	#55	47 sec.
1977	Barracuda	Heart	#11	47 sec.
1972	Lonesome Mary	Chilliwack	#75	46 sec.
1972	Sweet Sixteen	B.B. King	#93	45 sec.
1976	Blue Guitar	Justin Hayward & John Lodge	#94	45 sec.
1977	A Place in the Sun	Pablo Cruise	#42	45 sec.

LONGEST GUITAR SOLOS (cont'd)

1971	Tightrope Ride	The Doors	#71	44 sec.
1972	Footstompin' Music	Grand Funk Railroad	#29	44 sec.
1976	Fool for the City	Foghat	#45	44 sec.
1977	Dreamboat Annie	Heart	#42	44 sec.
1977	Tie Your Mother Down	Queen	#49	44 sec.
1977	Arrested for Driving While Blind	ZZ Top	#91	42, 38 sec.
1971	Oye Como Va	Santana	#13	42, 35 sec.
1972	Let It Rain	Eric Clapton	#48	42, 24 sec.
1975	Jackie Blue	Ozark Mountain Daredevils	#3	42 sec.
1975	I Am Love (Parts I & II)	The Jackson 5	#15	42 sec.
1977	Go Your Own Way	Fleetwood Mac	#10	42 sec.
1978	Hot Legs	Rod Stewart	#28	42 sec.
1976	Cowboy Song	Thin Lizzy	#77	41, 40 sec.
1973	Blue Collar	Bachman-Turner Overdrive	#68	41 sec.
1976	Sixteen Tons	The Don Harrison Band	#47	41 sec.
1979	Hold the Line	Toto	#5	41 sec.
1970	American Woman	The Guess Who	#1	41 sec.
1977	Fly at Night	Chilliwack	#75	40, 27 sec.
1976	Home Tonight	Aerosmith	#71	40, 22 sec.
1970	1984	Spirit	#69	40 sec.
1972	From the Beginning	Emerson, Lake & Palmer	#39	40 sec.
1976	Hot Stuff	The Rolling Stones	#49	40 sec.
1979	Renegade	Styx	#16	40 sec.
1979	I Do Believe in You	Pages	#84	40 sec.
1976	Magic Man	Heart	#9	39, 27 sec.
1975	Tush	ZZ Top	#20	39, 21 sec.
1972	Melissa	Allman Brothers Band	#86	39 sec.
1973	Blind Eye	Uriah Heep	#97	39 sec.
1974	Sweet Home Alabama	Lynyrd Skynyrd	#8	39 sec.
1975	Blue Sky	Joan Baez	#57	39 sec.
1976	Still the One	Orleans	#5	39 sec.
1978	Lay Down Sally	Eric Clapton	#3	39 sec.
1978	Wavelength	Van Morrison	#42	39 sec.
1979	Stormy	Santana	#32	39 sec.
1979	Lay It on the Line	Triumph	#86	39 sec.
1972	Alone Again (Naturally)	Gilbert O'Sullivan	#1	38 sec.
1972	Heartbroken Bopper	The Guess Who	#47	38 sec.
1976	I Heard It Through the Grapevine	Creedence Clearwater Revival	#43	38 sec.
1977	A Real Mother for Ya	Johnny Guitar Watson	#41	38 sec.
1978	So Long	Firefall	#48	38 sec.

LONGEST GUITAR SOLOS (cont'd)

1976	Gimme Your Money Please	Bachman-Turner Overdrive	#70	37, 35 sec.
1979	Sultans of Swing	Dire Straits	#4	37, 33 sec.
1970	Heartbreaker	Grand Funk Railroad	#72	37, 21 sec.
1978	Will You Still Love Me Tomorrow	Dave Mason	#39	37 sec.
1972	Play Me	Neil Diamond	#11	36 sec.
1974	Can't Get Enough	Bad Company	#5	36 sec.
1974	Goin' Down Slow	Bobby Blue Bland	#69	36 sec.
1976	Ophelia	The Band	#62	36 sec.
1979	Love Struck	Stonebolt	#70	36 sec.
1975	Black Friday	Steely Dan	#37	35, 33 sec.
1978	Champagne Jam	Atlanta Rhythm Section	#43	35, 32 sec.
1970	Time to Kill	The Band	#77	35 sec.
1973	Rocky Mountain Way	Joe Walsh	#23	35 sec.
1973	To Know You Is to Love You	B.B. King	#38	35 sec.
1974	Get Out of Denver	Bob Seger	#80	35 sec.
1975	It's All Right	Jim Capaldi	#55	35 sec.
1978	Poor Poor Pitiful Me	Linda Ronstadt	#31	35 sec.
1979	Every 1's a Winner	Hot Chocolate	#6	35 sec.
1971	Ask Me No Questions	B.B. King	#40	34, 32 sec.
1970	Spirit in the Sky	Norman Greenbaum	#3	34 sec.
1970	Darkness, Darkness	The Youngbloods	#86	34 sec.
1970	Johnny B. Goode	Johnny Winter	#92	34 sec.
1971	That Evil Child	B.B. King	#97	34 sec.
1975	One of These Nights	Eagles	#1	34 sec.
1975	Leona	Wet Willie	#69	34 sec.
1978	Baby Come Back	Player	#1	34 sec.
1978	Don't Look Back	Boston	#4	34 sec.
1978	Runaway	Jefferson Starship	#12	34 sec.
1978	FM (No Static at All)	Steely Dan	#22	34 sec.
1979	I Can't Stand It No More	Peter Frampton	#14	34 sec.
1970	House of the Rising Sun	Frijid Pink	#7	33 sec.
1971	Watching the River Flow	Bob Dylan	#41	33 sec.
1972	No One to Depend On	Santana	#36	33 sec.
1973	Let Us Love	Bill Withers	#47	33 sec.
1974	Rikki Don't Lose That Number	Steely Dan	#4	33 sec.
1974	Walk Like a Man	Grand Funk	#19	33 sec.
1975	Blue Eyes Crying in the Rain	Willie Nelson	#21	33 sec.
1975	Are You Sure Hank Done It This Way	Waylon Jennings	#60	33 sec.
1975	Midnight Sky (Part 1)	Isley Brothers	#73	33 sec.
1977	Walk This Way	Aerosmith	#10	33 sec.
1977	Slide	Slave	#32	33 sec.

LONGEST GUITAR SOLOS (cont'd)				
1977	Hurry Sundown	Outlaws	#60	33 sec.
1977	I'll Be Standing By	Foghat	#67	33 sec.
1977	Nothing But a Breeze	Jesse Winchester	#86	33 sec.
1978	Back in My Arms Again	Genya Ravan	#92	33 sec.
1979	Crank It Up (Funk Town) Pt. 1	Peter Brown	#86	33 sec.
1976	Hey Baby	Ted Nugent	#72	32, 22 sec.
1971	Caught in a Dream	Alice Cooper	#94	32, 21 sec.
1970	Ball and Chain	Tommy James	#57	32 sec.
1972	Rock and Roll	Led Zeppelin	#47	32 sec.
1973	Choo Choo Mama	Ten Years After	#89	32 sec.
1973	Stop, Wait & Listen	Circus	#91	32 sec.
1974	Jim Dandy	Black Oak Arkansas	#25	32 sec.
1974	Nobody	The Doobie Brothers	#58	32 sec.
1975	Sailing	Rod Stewart	#58	32 sec.
1976	Last Child	Aerosmith	#21	32 sec.
1976	Wheels of Fortune	The Doobie Brothers	#87	32 sec.
1977	Spend Some Time	Elvin Bishop w/Mickey Thomas	#93	32 sec.
1978	Hot Blooded	Foreigner	#3	32 sec.
1978	Blue Collar Man (Long Nights)	Styx	#21	32 sec.
1979	Silver Lining	Player	#62	32 sec.
1972	Lies	J.J. Cale	#42	31, 31, 21 sec.
1970	The Thrill Is Gone	B.B. King	#15	31, 29, 27, sec.
1970	Chains and Things	B.B. King	#45	31 sec.
1970	Get Down People	Fabulous Counts	#88	31 sec.
1971	Woodstock	Matthews' Southern Comfort	#23	31 sec.
1971	Love Me	The Rascals	#95	31 sec.
1972	Never Been to Spain	Three Dog Night	#5	31 sec.
1972	Fire and Water	Wilson Pickett	#24	31 sec.
1972	I Don't Need No Doctor	New Riders of the Purple Sage	#81	31 sec.
1973	Money	Pink Floyd	#13	31 sec.
1973	Steamroller Blues	Elvis Presley	#17	31 sec.
1973	Blue Suede Shoes	Johnny Rivers	#38	31 sec.
1975	Movin' On	Bad Company	#19	31 sec.
1975	What a Diff'rence a Day Makes	Esther Phillips	#20	31 sec.
1975	Dancin' Fool	The Guess Who	#28	31 sec.
1976	That'll Be the Day	Linda Ronstadt	#11	31 sec.
1976	Amazing Grace (Used to Be Her Favorite Song)	Amazing Rhythm Aces	#72	31 sec.
1977	Calling Dr. Love	Kiss	#16	31 sec.
1977	Back in the Saddle	Aerosmith	#38	31 sec.
1978	Life's Been Good	Joe Walsh	#12	31 sec.

LONGEST GUITAR SOLOS (cont'd)				
1978	Tried to Love	Peter Frampton	#41	31 sec.
1978	Takin' It Easy	Seals & Crofts	#79	31 sec.
1979	Hot Stuff	Donna Summer	#1	31 sec.
1979	Feelin' Satisfied	Boston	#46	31 sec.
1972	Rock & Roll Stew Part 1	Traffic	#93	30, 29 sec.
1977	She's Not There	Santana	#27	30, 27 sec.
1971	I'd Love to Change the World	Ten Years After	#40	30 sec.
1971	Dolly Dagger	Jimi Hendrix	#74	30 sec.
1975	How Long	Ace	#3	30 sec.
1975	I'll Still Love You	Jim Weatherly	#87	30 sec.
1976	Where Did Our Love Go	The J. Geils Band	#68	30 sec.
1976	You Got the Magic	John Fogerty	#87	30 sec.
1977	Drivin' Wheel	Foghat	#34	30 sec.
1978	Baker Street	Gerry Rafferty	#2	30 sec.
1978	The Power of Gold	Dan Fogelberg/Tim Weisberg	#24	30 sec.
1978	Josie	Steely Dan	#26	30 sec.
1979	Sad Eyes	Robert John	#1	30 sec.
1977	Fly By Night/In the Mood	Rush	#88	29, 27 sec.
1973	Reeling in the Years	Steely Dan	#11	29, 26, 22 sec.
1971	Feel so Bad	Ray Charles	#68	29 sec.
1973	Rockin' Pneumonia – Boogie Woogie Flu	Johnny Rivers	#6	29 sec.
1973	Twistin' the Night Away	Rod Stewart	#59	29 sec.
1973	Outlaw Man	David Blue	#94	29 sec.
1974	The Loco-Motion	Grand Funk	#1	29 sec.
1974	Kings of the Party	Brownsville Station	#31	29 sec.
1974	Get That Gasoline Blues	NRBQ	#70	29 sec.
1974	Kissin' Time	Kiss	#83	29 sec.
1975	Don't It Make You Wanna Dance?	Rusty Wier	#82	29 sec.
1976	Love Me Tonight	Head East	#54	29 sec.
1976	The Fez	Steely Dan	#59	29 sec.
1977	Lose Again	Linda Ronstadt	#76	29 sec.
1977	Caledonia	Robin Trower (James Dewar)	#82	29 sec.
1978	Love Will Find a Way	Pablo Cruise	#6	29 sec.
1978	Right Down the Line	Gerry Rafferty	#12	29 sec.
1978	Happy Anniversary	Little River Band	#16	29 sec.
1978	Make You Feel Love Again	Wet Willie	#45	29 sec.
1978	Lights	Journey	#68	29 sec.
1979	Don't Ever Wanna Lose Ya	New England	#40	29 sec.
1979	I Need You	Euclid Beach Band	#81	29 sec.
1970	Greenwood Mississippi	Little Richard	#85	28 sec.
1973	China Grove	The Doobie Brothers	#15	28 sec.

	LONGEST GUITAR SOLOS (cont'd)			
1974	Ride the Tiger	Jefferson Starship	#84	28 sec.
1975	The South's Gonna Do It	Charlie Daniels Band	#29	28 sec.
1975	You Ain't Never Been Loved (Like I'm Gonna Love You)	Jessi Colter	#64	28 sec.
1976	Sunrise	Eric Carmen	#34	28 sec.
1976	Struttin' My Stuff	Elvin Bishop	#68	28 sec.
1978	We Will Rock You/We are the Champions	Queen	#4	28 sec.
1978	Anytime	Journey	#83	28 sec.
1978	Louie, Louie	John Belushi	#89	28 sec.
1979	Damned if I Do	Alan Parsons Project	#27	28 sec.
1971	Wild Horses	The Rolling Stones	#28	27 sec.
1972	Take It Easy	Eagles	#12	27 sec.
1972	Conquistador	Procol Harum	#16	27 sec.
1972	One Way Out	Allman Brothers Band	#86	27 sec.
1973	Make Up Your Mind	The J. Geils Band	#98	27 sec.
1974	You Got the Love	Rufus feat. Chaka Khan	#11	27 sec.
1974	American Girls	Rick Springfield	#98	27 sec.
1975	Holdin' on to Yesterday	Ambrosia	#17	27 sec.
1975	Turn to Stone	Joe Walsh	#93	27 sec.
1976	Bohemium Rhapsody	Queen	#9	27 sec.
1976	Remember Me	Willie Nelson	#67	27 sec.
1976	Strong Enough to Be Gentle	Black Oak Arkansas	#89	27 sec.
1977	Lost Without Your Love	Bread	#9	27 sec.
1977	I Wouldn't Want to Be Like You	Alan Parsons	#36	27 sec.
1978	Wheel in the Sky	Journey	#57	27 sec.
1979	People of the South Wind	Kansas	#23	27 sec.
1979	Highway Song	Blackfoot	#26	27 sec.
1979	Killer Cut	Charlie	#60	27 sec.
1976	Devil with a Blue Dress	Pratt & McClain	#71	26, 25 sec.
1978	You Got That Right	Lynyrd Skynyrd	#69	26, 23 sec.
1973	Free Ride	Edgar Winter Group	#14	26 sec.
1973	Breaking Up Somebody's Home	Albert King	#91	26 sec.
1974	Sundown	Gordon Lightfoot	#1	26 sec.
1975	Part of the Plan	Dan Fogelberg	#31	26 sec.
1975	Long Haired Country Boy	Charlie Daniels Band	#56	26 sec.
1975	One More Tomorrow	Henry Gross	#93	26 sec.
1975	Two Lane Highway	Pure Prairie League	#97	26 sec.
1976	Everything That 'Cha Do (Will Come Back to You)	Wet Willie	#66	26 sec.
1977	I'll Always Call Your Name	Little River Band	#62	26 sec.
1977	Closer to the Heart	Rush	#76	26 sec.
1977	Ridin' the Storm Out	REO Speedwagon	#94	26 sec.

		LONGEST GUITAR SOLOS (cont'd)		
1978	Peg	Steely Dan	#11	26 sec.
1978	What's Your Name	Lynyrd Skynyrd	#13	26 sec.
1978	Rocket Ride	Kiss	#39	26 sec.
1978	Livingston Saturday Night	Jimmy Buffett	#52	26 sec.
1978	Take Me to the Kaptin	Prism	#59	26 sec.
1979	My Sharona	The Knack	#1	26 sec.
1979	Give Me an Inch	Ian Matthews	#67	26 sec.
1979	You're My Weakness	Faith Band	#76	26 sec.
1979	Keep on Running Away	Lazy Racer	#81	26 sec.
1979	Train, Train	Blackfoot	#38	25, 23 sec.
1972	Ain't Wastin' Time No More	Allman Brothers Band	#77	25, 22 sec.
1970	25 or 6 to 4	Chicago	#4	25 sec.
1970	Brown Paper Bag	Syndicate of Sound	#73	25 sec.
1971	Get It While You Can	Janis Joplin	#78	25 sec.
1972	Doctor My Eyes	Jackson Browne	#8	25 sec.
1972	It Doesn't Matter	Stephen Stills	#61	25 sec.
1972	The Jean Genie	David Bowie	#71	25 sec.
1973	You're So Vain	Carly Simon	#1	25 sec.
1973	Redneck Friend	Jackson Browne	#85	25 sec.
1974	Helen Wheels	Paul McCartney & Wings	#10	25 sec.
1974	Already Gone	Eagles	#32	25 sec.
1974	Doraville	Atlanta Rhythm Section	#35	25 sec.
1975	That's the Way of the World	Earth, Wind & Fire	#12	25 sec.
1976	It's Only Love	ZZ Top	#44	25 sec.
1976	Chain Gang Medley	Jim Croce	#63	25 sec.
1976	Flaming Youth	Kiss	#75	25 sec.
1976	Rose of Cimarron	Poco	#94	25 sec.
1977	I'm in You	Peter Frampton	#2	25 sec.
1977	The First Cut Is the Deepest	Rod Stewart	#21	25 sec.
1977	Cat Scratch Fever	Ted Nugent	#30	25 sec.
1977	Sailing Ships	Mesa	#55	25 sec.
1978	Well All Right	Santana	#69	25 sec.
1970	Tighter, Tighter	Alive & Kicking	#7	24 sec.
1970	Gimme Shelter	Merry Clayton	#73	24 sec.
1970	Down in the Alley	Ronnie Hawkins	#75	24 sec.
1971	When My Little Girl Is Smiling	Steve Alaimo	#72	24 sec.
1972	Baby Won't You Let Me Rock 'N Roll You	Ten Years After	#61	24 sec.
1974	Star Baby	The Guess Who	#39	24 sec.
1975	Heat Wave	Linda Ronstadt	#5	24 sec.
1975	It Doesn't Matter Anymore	Linda Ronstadt	#47	24 sec.
1976	Take Me	Grand Funk Railroad	#53	24 sec.

LONGEST GUITAR SOLOS (cont'd)

1977	Why Do Lovers (Break Each Other's Heart?)	Daryl Hall & John Oates	#73	24 sec.
1978	New York City	Zwol	#76	24 sec.
1979	Lady	Little River Band	#10	24 sec.
1979	Crazy Love	Allman Brothers Band	#29	24 sec.
1970	Mighty Joe	Shocking Blue	#43	23, 21 sec.
1970	Share the Land	The Guess Who	#10	23 sec.
1970	Canned Ham	Norman Greenbaum	#46	23 sec.
1970	Paranoid	Black Sabbath	#61	23 sec.
1970	Laughin' and Clownin'	Ray Charles	#98	23 sec.
1971	Rain Dance	The Guess Who	#19	23 sec.
1971	Bright Lights, Big City	Sonny James	#91	23 sec.
1972	Back off Boogaloo	Ringo Starr	#9	23 sec.
1972	Crazy Mama	J.J. Cale	#22	23 sec.
1972	Tupelo Honey	Van Morrison	#47	23 sec.
1972	Cheer	Potliquor	#65	23 sec.
1973	Wildflower	Skylark	#9	23 sec.
1973	I'm Just a Singer (In a Rock and Roll Band)	The Moody Blues	#12	23 sec.
1974	The Joker	Steve Miller Band	#1	23 sec.
1974	Candy's Going Bad	Golden Earring	#91	23 sec.
1975	Fire on the Mountain	Marshall Tucker Band	#38	23 sec.
1976	Texas	Charlie Daniels Band	#91	23 sec.
1976	Fire	Mother's Finest	#93	23 sec.
1977	Kick It Out	Heart	#79	23 sec.
1978	Come Together	Aerosmith	#23	23 sec.
1979	One Way or Another	Blondie	#24	23 sec.
1979	Our Love Is Insane	Desmond Child & Rouge	#51	23 sec.
1979	Lazy Eyes	T.M.G.	#91	23 sec.
1971	Mother Freedom	Bread	#37	22, 21 sec.
1970	After Midnight	Eric Clapton	#18	22 sec.
1970	Let's Work Together	Canned Heat	#26	22 sec.
1972	The Guitar Man	Bread	#11	22 sec.
1972	Jesus was a Capricorn	Kris Kristofferson	#91	22 sec.
1972	I Just Wanna Be Your Friend	Lighthouse	#93	22 sec.
1973	Stuck in the Middle with You	Stealers Wheel	#6	22 sec.
1973	Isn't It About Time	Stephen Stills & Manassas	#56	22 sec.
1973	Outlaw Man	Eagles	#59	22 sec.
1974	You Ain't Seen Nothing Yet	Bachman-Turner Overdrive	#1	22 sec.
1974	Teenage Lament '74	Alice Cooper	#48	22 sec.
1974	Country Side of Life	Wet Willie	#66	22 sec.
1975	Good Lovin' Gone Bad	Bad Company	#36	22 sec.
1976	More Than a Feeling	Boston	#5	22 sec.

	LONGEST GUITAR SOLOS (cont'd)			
1976	Union Man	Cate Bros.	#24	22 sec.
1976	Only Love Is Real	Carole King	#28	22 sec.
1976	Let's Live Together	The Road Apples	#35	22 sec.
1976	If Not You	Dr. Hook	#55	22 sec.
1977	In the Middle	Tim Moore	#75	22 sec.
1977	Part Time Love	Kerry Chater	#97	22 sec.
1978	Thunder Island	Jay Ferguson	#9	22 sec.
1978	Sweet, Sweet Smile	Carpenters	#44	22 sec.
1978	Arms of Mary	Chilliwack	#67	22 sec.
1979	Goodbye, I Love You	Firefall	#43	22 sec.
1970	Black Night	Deep Purple	#66	21, 21, 21 sec.
1970	The Seeker	The Who	#44	21 sec.
1971	Lowdown	Chicago	#35	21 sec.
1971	Jumpin' Jack Flash	Johnny Winter	#89	21 sec.
1972	Kate	Johnny Cash	#75	21 sec.
1973	Ramblin' Man	Allman Brothers Band	#2	21 sec.
1973	We May Never Pass This Way (Again)	Seals & Crofts	#21	21 sec.
1973	Billion Dollar Babies	Alice Cooper	#57	21 sec.
1973	My Old School	Steely Dan	#63	21 sec.
1974	Shinin' On	Grand Funk	#11	21 sec.
1975	Take Me in Your Arms (Rock Me)	The Doobie Brothers	#11	21 sec.
1975	Killer Queen	Queen	#12	21 sec.
1976	Hey Baby	J.J. Cale	#96	21 sec.
1977	Blue Bayou	Linda Ronstadt	#3	21 sec.
1977	Can't You See	Marshall Tucker Band	#75	21 sec.
1978	Running On Empty	Jackson Browne	#11	21 sec.
1979	Ain't That a Shame	Cheap Trick	#35	21 sec.
1979	Call Out My Name	Zwol	#75	21 sec.
1970	Reflections of My Life	The Marmalade	#10	20 sec.
1970	Woodstock	Crosby, Stills, Nash & Young	#11	20 sec.
1970	Engine Number 9	Wilson Pickett	#14	20 sec.
1970	Summertime Blues	The Who	#27	20 sec.
1970	Let's Make Each Other Happy	The Illusion	#98	20 sec.
1971	Hang on to Your Life	The Guess Who	#43	20 sec.
1971	Broken	The Guess Who	#55	20 sec.
1971	Red Eye Blues	Red Eye	#78	20 sec.
1972	Tumbling Dice	The Rolling Stones	#7	20 sec.
1972	Jambalaya (On the Bayou)	Nitty Gritty Dirt Band	#84	20 sec.
1973	Your Mama Don't Dance	Loggins & Messina	#4	20 sec.
1973	I Got a Name	Jim Croce	#10	20 sec.
1973	What a Shame	Foghat	#82	20 sec.

	LONGEST GUITAR SOLOS (cont'd)			
1974	Wang Dang Doodle	The Pointer Sisters	#61	20 sec.
1974	James Dean	The Eagles	#77	20 sec.
1975	Third Rate Romance	Amazing Rhythm Aces	#14	20 sec.
1975	I Don't Know Why	The Rolling Stones	#42	20 sec.
1977	Fair Game	Crosby, Stills & Nash	#43	20 sec.
1977	Good Morning Judge	10cc	#69	20 sec.
1978	I Ain't Gonna Eat Out My Heart Anymore	Angel	#44	20 sec.
1978	Long Hot Summer Nights	Wendy Waldman	#76	20 sec.
1979	Dirty White Boy	Foreigner	#12	20 sec.
1979	Another Night	Wilson Bros.	#94	20 sec.

HARMONICA

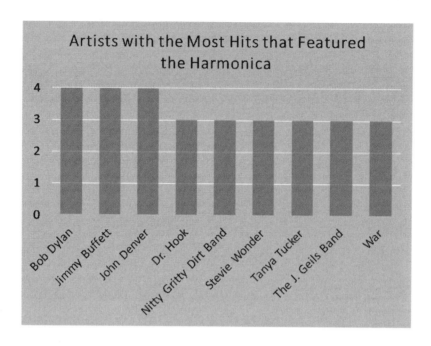

For the solo column, only harmonica solos that are ten seconds or longer are included.

YEAR	SONG	ARTIST	HOT 100	LENGTH OF SOLO
1970	Ball of Confusion (That's What the World Is Today)	The Temptations	#3	
1970	Patches	Clarence Carter	#4	
1970	Rainy Night in Georgia	Brook Benton	#4	
1970	He Ain't Heavy, He's My Brother	Hollies	#7	
1970	Hi-De-Ho	Blood, Sweat & Tears	#14	12 sec.
1970	Let's Work Together (Part 1)	Wilbert Harrison	#32	
1970	Ungena Za Ulimwengu (Unite the World)	The Temptations	#33	
1970	I Want to Take You Higher	Sly & The Family Stone	#38	18 sec.
1970	Monster	Steppenwolf	#39	
1970	Rainbow	The Marmalade	#51	16, 17, 16 sec.
1970	Screaming Night Hog	Steppenwolf	#62	
1970	Going to the Country	Steve Miller Band	#69	10 sec.
1970	Down in the Alley	Ronnie Hawkins	#75	26 sec.
1970	Beaucoups of Blues	Ringo Starr	#87	
1970	Groovin' with Mr. Bloe	Cool Heat	#89	
1970	Tobacco Road	Jamul	#93	21 sec.
1970	Rainy Days and Mondays	Carpenters	#2	
1971	Stay Awhile	The Bells	#7	20 sec.
1971	We Can Work It Out	Stevie Wonder	#13	26 sec.

HARMONICA (cont'd)

1971	All Day Music	War	#35	31 sec.
1971	Chairman of the Board	Chairman of the Board	#42	13 sec.
1971	Friends with You	John Denver	#47	19 sec.
1971	Funky Music Sho Nuff Turns Me On	Edwin Starr	#64	
1971	Some of Shelly's Blues	Nitty Gritty Dirt Band	#64	18 sec.
1971	Mixed Up Guy	Joey Scarbury	#73	
1971	I Need You	Friends of Distinction	#79	
1971	You've Got to Earn It	The Staple Singers	#97	
1972	I'll Take You There	The Staple Singers	#1	
1972	Heart of Gold	Neil Young	#1	15, 17, 17 sec.
1972	Oh Girl	Chi-Lites	#1	13 sec.
1972	Clair	Gilbert O'Sullivan	#2	15 sec.
1972	Sylvia's Mother	Dr. Hook	#5	
1972	Good Time Charlie's Got the Blues	Danny O'Keefe	#9	
1972	Join Together	The Who	#17	
1972	Long Dark Road	The Hollies	#26	11 sec.
1972	George Jackson	Bob Dylan	#33	24, 18 sec.
1972	Looking for a Love	J. Geils Band	#39	
1972	Love Me, Love Me Love	Frank Mills	#46	
1972	In the Ghetto	Candi Staton	#48	
1972	A Simple Man	Lobo	#56	
1972	Devil You	Stampeders	#61	
1972	War Song	Neil Young & Graham Nash	#61	11 sec.
1972	The Jean Genie	David Bowie	#71	
1972	Delta Dawn	Tanya Tucker	#72	
1972	Upsetter	Grand Funk Railroad	#73	
1972	Amerikan Music	Steve Alaimo	#79	
1972	Everyday	John Denver	#81	
1972	Jambalaya (On the Bayou)	Nitty Gritty Dirt Band	#84	
1972	I Received a Letter	Delbert & Glen	#90	
1972	With Pen in Hand	Bobby Goldsboro	#94	
1972	Happier Than the Morning Sun	B.J. Thomas	#100	17 sec.
1972	Don't Ever Take Away My Freedom	Peter Yarrow	#100	
1972	We're Together	The Hillside Singers	#100	
1973	Tie a Yellow Ribbon Round the Ole Oak Tree	Tony Orlando & Dawn	#1	
1973	Will It Go Round in Circles	Billy Preston	#1	
1973	The Cisco Kid	War	#2	
1973	Paper Roses	Marie Osmond	#5	
1973	Danny's Song	Anne Murray	#7	
1973	Don't Expect Me to Be Your Friend	Lobo	#8	12 sec.
1973	Long Train Runnin'	The Doobie Brothers	#8	24 sec.

HARMONICA (cont'd)

1973	Gypsy Man	War	#8	80 sec.
1973	Thinking of You	Loggins & Messina	#18	
1973	You Turn Me on, I'm a Radio	Joni Mitchell	#25	
1973	Teddy Bear Song	Barbara Fairchild	#32	
1973	Everybody's Had the Blues	Merle Haggard	#62	
1973	One Man Parade	James Taylor	#67	
1973	Please, Daddy	John Denver	#69	
1973	Boo, Boo, Don't 'Cha Be Blue	Tommy James	#70	10 sec.
1973	Send a Little Love My Way	Anne Murray	#72	12, 22 sec.
1973	Blood Red and Goin' Down	Tanya Tucker	#74	
1973	Roll in My Sweet Baby's Arms	Hank Wilson (Leon Russell)	#78	
1973	Sail on Sailor	The Beach Boys	#79	
1973	Roland the Roadie and Gertrude the Groupie	Dr. Hook	#83	
1973	California Saga (On My Way to Sunny Californ-i-a)	The Beach Boys	#84	
1973	Kid Stuff	Barbara Fairchild	#95	
1973	L.A. Freeway	Jerry Jeff Walker	#98	
1974	Smokin' in the Boy's Room	Brownsville Station	#3	14 sec.
1974	Back Home Again	John Denver	#5	
1974	Keep on Smilin'	Wet Willie	#10	19 sec.
1974	My Mistake (Was to Love You)	Diana Ross & Marvin Gaye	#19	
1974	If You Wanna Get to Heaven	Ozark Mountain Daredevils	#25	26, 14, 34 sec.
1974	Piano Man	Billy Joel	#25	15 sec.
1974	Son of Sagittarius	Eddie Kendricks	#28	
1974	Star	Stealers Wheel	#29	
1974	Doraville	Atlanta Rhythm Section	#35	25 sec.
1974	Three Ring Circus	Blue Magic	#36	
1974	On a Night Like This	Bob Dylan/The Band	#44	43 sec.
1974	Living in the U.S.A.	Steve Miller Band	#49	36 sec.
1974	I Am What I Am	Lois Fletcher	#64	
1974	Most Likely You Go Your Way (And I'll Go Mine)	Bob Dylan/The Band	#66	
1974	Do It, Fluid	The Blackbyrds	#69	
1974	Delta Dirt	Larry Gatlin	#84	
1975	My Eyes Adored You	Frankie Valli	#1	
1975	Boogie on Reggae Woman	Stevie Wonder	#3	31, 41 sec.
1975	The Rockford Files	Mike Post	#10	
1975	I'm a Woman	Maria Muldaur	#12	15 sec.
1975	Help Me Rhonda	Johnny Rivers	#22	
1975	Tangled Up in the Blue	Bob Dylan	#31	33 sec.
1975	It Doesn't Matter Anymore	Linda Ronstadt	#47	
1975	Take Me to the River	Syl Johnson	#48	
1975	Love Is a Rose	Linda Ronstadt	#63	

	HARMONICA (cont'd)			
1975	(All I Have to Do Is) Dream	Nitty Gritty Dirt Band	#66	20 sec.
1975	Sure Feels Good	Elvin Bishop	#83	
1975	Spider Jiving	Andy Fairweather Low	#87	18 sec.
1975	Let Me Start Tonite	Lamont Dozier	#87	
1975	Minnesota	Northern Light	#88	
1975	One Man Band	Leo Sayer	#96	
1976	Welcome Back	John Sebastian	#1	13 sec.
1976	Deep Purple	Donny & Marie Osmond	#14	
1976	Good Hearted Woman	Waylon Jennings & Willie Nelson	#25	
1976	Renegade	Michael Murphey	#39	
1976	It's Only Love	ZZ Top	#44	
1976	Bigfoot	Bro Smith	#57	
1976	BLT	Lee Oskar	#59	
1976	Baby Boy	Mary Kay Place	#60	
1976	Here, There and Everywhere	Emmylou Harris	#65	
1976	Remember Me	Willie Nelson	#67	
1976	Where Did Our Love Go	The J. Geils Band	#68	14 sec.
1976	Sally	Grand Funk Railroad	#69	29, 14 sec.
1976	Satin Sheets	Bellamy Brothers	#73	14 sec.
1976	Norma Jean Wants to Be a Movie Star	Sundown Company	#84	
1976	Kentucky Moonrunner	Cledus Maggard	#85	
1976	I'm So Lonesome I Could Cry	Terry Bradshaw	#91	15 sec.
1976	Sweet Summer Music	Attitudes	#94	
1977	Love's Grown Deep	Kenny Nolan	#20	13 sec.
1977	Cinderella	Firefall	#34	12 sec.
1977	Changes in Latitudes, Changes in Attitudes	Jimmy Buffett	#37	
1977	Walk Right In	Dr. Hook	#46	
1977	Runaway	Bonnie Raitt	#57	37 sec.
1977	Hound Dog Man (Play It Again)	Lenny LeBlanc	#58	
1977	You're the Only One	Geils	#83	16 sec.
1977	Rock and Roll Star	Champagne	#83	
1977	Light of a Clear Blue Morning	Dolly Parton	#87	27 sec.
1977	Romeo	Mr. Big	#87	17 sec.
1978	Miss You	The Rolling Stones	#1	
1978	My Angel Baby	Toby Beau	#13	22 sec.
1978	Cheeseburger in Paradise	Jimmy Buffett	#32	
1978	You	The McCrarys	#45	10 sec.
1978	Raining in My Heart	Leo Sayer	#47	
1978	Livingston Saturday Night	Jimmy Buffett	#52	25 sec.
1978	Georgia on My Mind	Willie Nelson	#84	29 sec.
1978	In for the Night	The Dirt Band	#86	

		HARMONICA (cont'd)			
1979	Send One Your Love	Stevie Wonder	#4	12, 52 sec.
1979	Take the Long Way Home	Supertramp	#10	26 sec.
1979	Good Girls Don't	The Knack	#11	10 sec.
1979	Weekend	Wet Willie	#29	16 sec.
1979	One Last Kiss	The J. Geils Band	#35	29 sec.
1979	Fins	Jimmy Buffett	#35	15 sec.
1979	Train, Train	Blackfoot	#38	35 sec.
1979	Watch Out for Lucy	Eric Clapton	#40	
1979	Then You Can Tell Me Goodbye	Toby Beau	#57	
1979	Take It Back	The J. Geils Band	#67	16, 16 sec.
1979	Not Fade Away	Tanya Tucker	#70	
1979	Bad Brakes	Cat Stevens	#83	

HARP

YEAR	SONG	ARTIST	HOT 100
1970	Trying to Make a Fool Out of Me	The Delfonics	#40
1970	And the Grass Won't Pay No Mind	Mark Lindsay	#44
1970	You've Been My Inspiration	The Main Ingredient	#64
1970	But for Love	Jerry Naylor	#69
1970	She Cried	The Lettermen	#73
1970	Baby, Is There Something on Your Mind	McKinley Travis	#91
1970	A Song that Never Comes	Mama Cass Elliot	#99
1971	How Can You Mend a Broken Heart	The Bee Gees	#1
1971	Just My Imagination (Running Away with Me)	The Temptations	#1
1971	Got to Be There	Michael Jackson	#4
1971	Don't Change on Me	Ray Charles	#36
1971	I'll Erase Away Your Pain	Whatnauts	#71
1972	Betcha By Golly, Wow	The Stylistics	#3
1972	Too Beautiful to Last	Engelbert Humperdinck	#86
1973	Neither One of Us (Wants to Be the First to Say Goodbye)	Gladys Knight & The Pips	#2
1973	You're a Special Part of Me	Diana Ross & Marvin Gaye	#12
1973	Don't Let It End ('Til You Let It Begin)	The Miracles	#56
1973	I Never Said Goodbye	Engelbert Humperdinck	#61
1973	As Time Goes By	Nilsson	#86
1974	Three Ring Circus	Blue Magic	#36
1974	You and I	Johnny Bristol	#48
1974	Tell Her Love Has Felt the Need	Eddie Kendricks	#50
1974	Between Her Goodbye and My Hello	Gladys Knight & The Pips	#57

		HARP (cont'd)	
1974	Give Me a Reason to Be Gone	Maureen McGovern	#71
1974	Stop to Start	Blue Magic	#74
1974	You Got to Be the One	The Chi-Lites	#83
1974	Best Thing That Ever Happened to Me	The Persuaders	#85
1975	Poetry Man	Phoebe Snow	#5
1975	Morning Side of the Mountain	Donny & Marie Osmond	#8
1975	Ain't No Way to Treat a Lady	Helen Reddy	#8
1975	Look in My Eyes Pretty Woman	Tony Orlando & Dawn	#11
1975	To the Door of the Sun (Alle Porte Del Sole)	Al Martino	#17
1975	Every Time You Touch Me (I Get High)	Charlie Rich	#19
1975	The Proud One	The Osmonds	#22
1975	You're All I Need to Get By	Tony Orlando & Dawn	#34
1975	Don't Take Your Love	Manhattans	#37
1975	Living a Little, Laughing a Little	The Spinners	#37
1975	Love Finds Its Own Way	Gladys Knight & The Pips	#47
1975	I Believe I'm Gonna Love You	Frank Sinatra	#47
1975	I Dreamed Last Night	Justin Hayward & John Lodge	#47
1975	Dance the Kung Fu	Carl Douglas	#48
1975	Mexico	James Taylor	#49
1975	My Little Lady	Bloodstone	#57
1975	Hoppy, Gene and Me	Roy Rogers	#65
1975	We May Never Love Like This Again	Maureen McGovern	#83
1975	Minnesota	Northern Light	#88
1976	I Write the Songs	Barry Manilow	#1
1976	Breaking Up Is Hard to Do	Neil Sedaka	#8
1976	There's a Kind of Hush (All Over the World)	Carpenters	#12
1976	Heaven Must Be Missing an Angel (Part 1)	Tavares	#15
1976	Love in the Shadows	Neil Sedaka	#16
1976	Love Ballad	L.T.D.	#20
1976	I Need to Be in Love	Carpenters	#25
1976	Don't Take Away the Music	Tavares	#34
1976	The Lonely One	Special Delivery	#75
1976	Forever Lovers	Mac Davis	#76
1976	Close to You	B.T. Express	#82
1977	Gonna Fly Now	Bill Conti	#1
1977	Boogie Nights	Heatwave	#2
1977	I Like Dreamin'	Kenny Nolan	#3
1977	Heaven on the 7th Floor	Paul Nicholas	#6
1977	After the Lovin'	Engelbert Humperdinck	#8
1977	Hello Stranger	Yvonne Elliman	#15
1977	Your Love	Marilyn McCoo & Billy Davis, Jr.	#15

		HARP (cont'd)		
1977	It Was Almost Like a Song	Ronnie Milsap	#16
1977	You're My World	Helen Reddy	#18
1977	Love's Grown Deep	Kenny Nolan	#20
1977	Daybreak	Barry Manilow	#23
1977	The Killing of Georgie (Part 1 and 2)	Rod Stewart	#30
1977	There Will Come a Day (I'm Gonna Happen to You)	Smokey Robinson	#42
1977	You're Throwing a Good Love Away	Spinners	#43
1977	You Take My Heart Away	James Darren	#52
1977	Going in with My Eyes Open	David Soul	#53
1977	Don't Turn the Light Out	Cliff Richard	#57
1977	"Roots" Medley	Quincy Jones	#57
1977	Sorry	Grace Jones	#71
1977	Could Heaven Ever Be Like This (Part 1)	Idris Muhammad	#76
1977	Break It to Me Gently	Aretha Franklin	#85
1977	Pirate	Cher	#93
1977	Goodbye My Friend	Engelbert Humperdinck	#97
1977	My Eyes Get Blurry	Kenny Nolan	#97
1978	MacArthur Park	Donna Summer	#1
1978	Too Much, Too Little, Too Late	Johnny Mathis & Deniece Williams	#1
1978	Our Love	Natalie Cole	#10
1978	Theme from "Close Encounters of the Third Kind"	John Williams	#13
1978	Thank God It's Friday	Love and Kisses	#22
1978	That Once in a Lifetime	Demis Roussos	#47
1978	You're All I Need to Get By	Johnny Mathis & Deniece Williams	#47
1978	I Believe You	Carpenters	#68
1978	God Knows	Debby Boone	#74
1978	Brandy	The O'Jays	#79
1979	Reunited	Peaches & Herb	#1
1979	I Will Survive	Gloria Gaynor	#1
1979	Mama Can't Buy You Love	Elton John	#9
1979	Come to Me	France Joli	#15
1979	Superman	Herbie Mann	#26
1979	I Will Be in Love with You	Livingston Taylor	#30
1979	Turn Off the Lights	Teddy Pendergrass	#48
1979	Can You Read My Mind	Maureen McGovern	#52
1979	Pops, We Love You (A Tribute to Father)	Diana Ross, Marvin Gaye, Smokey Robinson & Stevie Wonder	#59
1979	Theme from Ice Castles (Through the Eyes of Love)	Melissa Manchester	#76

HARPSICHORD

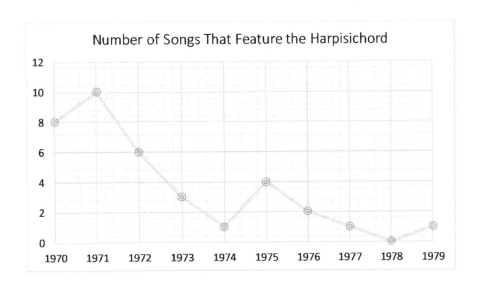

Number of Songs That Feature the Harpisichord

YEAR	SONG	ARTIST	HOT 100
1970	(They Long to Be) Close to You	Carpenters	#1
1970	I Think I Love You	The Partridge Family	#1
1970	The Tears of a Clown	Smokey Robinson & The Miracles	#1
1970	I'll Be There	The Jackson 5	#1
1970	Early in the Morning	Vanity Fare	#12
1970	Our House	Crosby, Stills, Nash & Young	#30
1970	Do You See My Love (For You Growing)	Jr. Walker/The All Stars	#32
1970	The Court of the Crimson King – Part 1	King Crimson	#80
1971	Got to Be There	Michael Jackson	#4
1971	Do You Know What I Mean	Lee Michaels	#6
1971	Desiderata	Les Crane	#8
1971	I Woke Up in Love This Morning	The Partridge Family	#13
1971	Let Your Love Go	Bread	#28
1971	Summer Sand	Dawn	#33
1971	Over and Over	The Delfonics	#58
1971	Long Ago Tomorrow	B.J. Thomas	#61
1971	Mozart Symphony No. 40 in G Minor K.550, 1st Movement	Waldo de los Rios	#67
1971	Solo	Billie Sans	#91
1972	Joy	Apollo 100	#6
1972	I Wanna Be Where You Are	Michael Jackson	#16
1972	Corner of the Sky	The Jackson 5	#18
1972	Take a Look Around	The Temptations	#30
1972	Special Someone	The Heywoods	#64
1972	Sing a Song/Make Your Own Kind of Music	Barbra Streisand	#94
1973	The Morning After	Maureen McGovern	#1

	HARPSICHORD (cont'd)		
1973	Don't Let It End ('Til You Let It Begin)	The Miracles	#56
1973	Dream On	Aerosmith	#59
1974	Never, Never Gonna Give Ya Up	Barry White	#7
1975	Lucy in the Sky with Diamonds	Elton John	#1
1975	Drive My Car	Gary Toms Empire	#69
1975	We May Never Love Like This Again	Maureen McGovern	#83
1975	Shoes	Reparata	#92
1976	My Sweet Summer Suite	The Love Unlimited Orchestra	#48
1976	Once You Hit the Road	Dionne Warwick	#79
1977	If It's the Last Thing I Do	Thelma Houston	#47
1979	Good Timin'	The Beach Boys	#40

HORNS

YEAR	SONG	ARTIST	HOT 100
1970	Raindrops Keep Fallin' on My Head	B.J. Thomas	#1
1970	(They Long to Be) Close to You	Carpenters	#1
1970	War	Edwin Starr	#1
1970	Thank You (Falettinme Be Mice Elf Again)	Sly & The Family Stone	#1
1970	We've Only Just Begun	Carpenters	#2
1970	Vehicle	The Ides of March	#2
1970	Ball of Confusion (That's What the World Is Today)	The Temptations	#3
1970	Signed, Sealed, Delivered I'm Yours	Stevie Wonder	#3
1970	25 or 6 to 4	Chicago	#4
1970	Julie, Do Ya Love Me	Bobby Sherman	#5
1970	The Letter	Joe Cocker w/Leon Russell	#7
1970	Tighter, Tighter	Alive & Kicking	#7
1970	Jam Up Jelly Tight	Tommy Roe	#8
1970	Make Me Smile	Chicago	#9
1970	Easy Come Easy Go	Bobby Sherman	#9
1970	La La La (If I Had You)	Bobby Sherman	#9
1970	Cry Me a River	Joe Cocker	#11
1970	Express Yourself	Charles Wright	#12
1970	Super Bad (Part 1 & Part 2)	James Brown	#13
1970	Hi-De-Ho	Blood, Sweat & Tears	#14
1970	It's a Shame	The Spinners	#14
1970	Look What They've Done to My Song Ma	The New Seekers	#14
1970	Celebrate	Three Dog Night	#15
1970	Rubber Duckie	Ernie (Jim Henson)	#16

HORNS (cont'd)

1970	Evil Woman Don't Play Your Games with Me	Crow	#19
1970	Walkin' in the Rain	Jay & The Americans	#19
1970	Blowing Away	The 5th Dimension	#21
1970	Solitary Man	Neil Diamond	#21
1970	You're the One – Part 2	Little Sister	#22
1970	God, Love and Rock & Roll	Teegarden & Van Winkle	#22
1970	Puppet Man	The 5th Dimension	#24
1970	Sugar Sugar	Wilson Pickett	#25
1970	You Need Love Like I Do (Don't You)	Gladys Knight & The Pips	#25
1970	Save the Country	The 5th Dimension	#27
1970	Always Something There to Remind Me	R.B. Greaves	#27
1970	Do the Funky Chicken	Rufus Thomas	#28
1970	Lucretia Mac Evil	Blood, Sweat & Tears	#29
1970	Maybe	The Three Degrees	#29
1970	It's a New Day (Part 1 & 2)	James Brown	#32
1970	Ungena Za Ulimwengu (Unite the World)	The Temptations	#33
1970	I Want to Take You Higher	Ike & Tina Turner	#34
1970	Let a Man Come in and Do the Popcorn (Part two)	James Brown	#40
1970	When Julie Comes Around	The Cuff Links	#41
1970	How Can I Forget	Marvin Gaye	#41
1970	Let's Give Adam and Eve Another Chance	Gary Puckett & The Union Gap	#41
1970	I Can't Leave Your Love Alone	Clarence Carter	#42
1970	Take a Look Around	Smith	#43
1970	Love Bones	Johnnie Taylor	#43
1970	Soul Shake	Delaney & Bonnie & Friends	#43
1970	Freedom Blues	Little Richard	#47
1970	We Can Make Music	Tommy Roe	#49
1970	Mongoose	Elephant's Memory	#50
1970	Seems Like I Gotta Do Wrong	The Whispers	#50
1970	I Just Wanna Keep It Together	Paul Davis	#51
1970	Funky Drummer (Part 1)	James Brown	#51
1970	Baby, I Need Your Loving	O.C. Smith	#52
1970	My Wife, the Dancer	Eddie & Dutch	#52
1970	You Got Me Hummin'	Cold Blood	#52
1970	Ace of Spade	O.V. Wright	#54
1970	Moon Walk Part 1	Joe Simon	#54
1970	The Cat Walk	The Village Soul Choir	#55
1970	My Honey and Me	Luther Ingram	#55
1970	Farther on Down the Road	Joe Simon	#56
1970	Rag Mama Rag	The Band	#57
1970	How Can I Tell My Mom & Dad	The Lovelites	#60

				HORNS (cont'd)	
1970	Sweet Feeling	Candi Staton	#60
1970	A Change is Gonna Come & People Gotta Be Free	The 5th Dimension	#60
1970	Big Leg Woman (With a Short Short Mini Skirt)	Israel Tolbert	#61
1970	Why Should I Cry	The Gentrys	#61
1970	Victoria	The Kinks	#62
1970	That Same Old Feeling	The Fortunes	#62
1970	Superman	The Ides of March	#64
1970	She Said Yes	Wilson Pickett	#68
1970	You, Me and Mexico	Edward Bear	#68
1970	But for Love	Jerry Naylor	#69
1970	I Need Help (I Can't Do It Alone) Pt. 1	Bobby Byrd	#69
1970	If Walls Could Talk	Little Milton	#71
1970	She's Ready	Spiral Starecase	#72
1970	I Like Your Lovin' (Do You Like Mine)	The Chi-Lites	#72
1970	Gimme Shelter	Merry Clayton	#73
1970	What Am I Gonna Do	Smith	#73
1970	Are You Getting Any Sunshine?	Lou Christie	#73
1970	Morning Much Better	Ten Wheel Drive	#74
1970	Jerusalem	Herb Alpert & The Tijuana Brass	#74
1970	Save the Country	Thelma Houston	#74
1970	Free the People	Delaney & Bonnie & Friends	#75
1970	Can You Feel It	Bobby Goldsboro	#75
1970	Keep on Doin'	Isley Brothers	#75
1970	To Be Young, Gifted and Black	Nina Simone	#76
1970	Run Sally Run	The Cuff Links	#76
1970	Yours Love	Joe Simon	#78
1970	Drop By My Place	Little Carl Carlton	#78
1970	Let the Music Take Your Mind	Kool & The Gang	#78
1970	Barbara, I Love You	New Colony Six	#78
1970	Them Changes	Buddy Miles	#81
1970	I Who Have Nothing	Liquid Smoke	#82
1970	America/Standing	The Five Stairsteps	#83
1970	Comin' Home	Delaney & Bonnie w/Eric Clapton	#84
1970	Everything Is Going to Be Alright	Teegarden & Van Winkle	#84
1970	The Gangs Back Again	Kool & The Gang	#85
1970	Compared to What	Les McCann & Eddie Harris	#85
1970	This Is My Love Song	The Intruders	#85
1970	Dreams	Buddy Miles	#86
1970	Buffalo Soldier	Flamingos	#86
1970	Funky Man	Kool & The Gang	#87
1970	Think About Your Children	Mary Hopkin	#87

	HORNS (cont'd)		
1970	Georgia Took Her Back	R.B. Greaves	#88
1970	Keep on Loving Me (You'll See the Change)	Bobby Bland	#89
1970	Get into Something	The Isley Brothers	#89
1970	I Can't Be You (You Can't Be Me)	The Glass House	#90
1970	Down By the River	The Brooklyn Bridge	#91
1970	Alright in the City	Dunn & McCashen	#91
1970	Funky Chicken (Part 1)*	Willie Henderson w/The Soul Explosions	#91
1970	Let This Be a Letter (To My Baby)	Jackie Wilson	#91
1970	I Gotta Let You Go	Martha & The Vandellas	#93
1970	That's the Way I Want Our Love	Joe Simon	#93
1970	The Lights of Tucson	Jim Campbell	#93
1970	Take It off Him and Put It on Me	Clarence Carter	#94
1970	Losers Weepers – Part 1	Etta James	#94
1970	Fire and Rain	Johnny Rivers & Friends	#94
1970	Thank You Girl	Street People	#96
1970	Bring It on Home	Lou Rawls	#96
1970	I Want To (Do Everything for You)	Raeletts	#96
1970	Day Is Done	Brooklyn Bridge	#98
1970	Message from a Black Man	The Whatnauts	#99
1971	Mr. Big Stuff	Jean Knight	#2
1971	Yo-Yo	The Osmonds	#3
1971	It Don't Come Easy	Ringo Starr	#4
1971	Draggin' the Line	Tommy James	#4
1971	Proud Mary	Ike & Tina Turner	#4
1971	Groove Me	King Floyd	#6
1971	Does Anybody Really Know What Time It Is?	Chicago	#7
1971	Beginnings	Chicago	#7
1971	If You Really Love Me	Stevie Wonder	#8
1971	Rock Steady	Aretha Franklin	#9
1971	Sooner or Later	The Grass Roots	#9
1971	Domino	Van Morrison	#9
1971	Tired of Being Alone	Al Green	#11
1971	Everybody's Everything	Santana	#12
1971	Trapped By a Thing Called Love	Denise LaSalle	#13
1971	Don't Knock My Love – Pt. 1	Wilson Pickett	#13
1971	Double Lovin'	The Osmonds	#14
1971	Funky Nassau – Part 1	Beginning of the End	#15
1971	Hot Pants (She Got to Use What She Got to Get What She Wants) (Pt. 1)	James Brown	#15
1971	Two Divided by Love	The Grass Roots	#16
1971	Cried Like a Baby	Bobby Sherman	#16

	HORNS (cont'd)		
1971	A Natural Man	Lou Rawls	#17
1971	Don't Let the Green Grass Fool You	Wilson Pickett	#17
1971	Superstar (Remember How You Got Where You Are)	The Temptations	#18
1971	Only You Know and I Know	Delaney & Bonnie	#20
1971	Free	Chicago	#20
1971	Make It Funky (Part 1)	James Brown	#22
1971	Blue Money	Van Morrison	#23
1971	Bangla-Desh	George Harrison	#23
1971	Questions 67 and 68	Chicago	#24
1971	Get It On	Chase	#24
1971	Stagger Lee	Tommy Roe	#25
1971	(Do The) Push and Pull Part 1	Rufus Thomas	#25
1971	One Tin Soldier (The Legend of Billy Jack)	Coven	#26
1971	Stop the War Now	Edwin Starr	#26
1971	Heavy Makes You Happy (Sha-Na-Boom Boom)	The Staple Singers	#27
1971	You've Got to Crawl (Before You Walk)	The 8th Day	#28
1971	Jody's Got Your Girl and Gone	Johnnie Taylor	#28
1971	Wild Night	Van Morrison	#28
1971	Soul Power (Pt. 1)	James Brown	#29
1971	Baby Let Me Kiss You	King Floyd	#29
1971	Precious, Precious	Jackie Moore	#30
1971	The Breakdown (Part 1)	Rufus Thomas	#31
1971	Go Down Gamblin'	Blood, Sweat & Tears	#32
1971	Hallelujah	Sweathog	#33
1971	1900 Yesterday	Liz Damon's Orient Express	#33
1971	Get Up, Get Into It, Get Involved (Pt. 1)	James Brown	#34
1971	Lowdown	Chicago	#35
1971	I'm a Greedy Man (Part 1)	James Brown	#35
1971	Escape-ism (Part 1)	James Brown	#35
1971	Resurrection Shuffle	Tom Jones	#38
1971	Just Seven Numbers (Can Straighten Out My Life)	Four Tops	#40
1971	Resurrection Shuffle	Ashton, Gardner & Dyke	#40
1971	The Year That Clayton Delaney Died	Tom T. Hall	#42
1971	Let It Be	Joan Baez	#49
1971	Bridget the Midget (The Queen of the Blues)	Ray Stevens	#50
1971	Rainy Jane	Davy Jones	#52
1971	Call My Name, I'll Be There	Wilson Pickett	#52
1971	He Called Me Baby	Candi Staton	#52
1971	I Hear Those Church Bells Ringing	Dusk	#53
1971	Hot Pants	Salvage	#54
1971	Waiting at the Bus Stop	Bobby Sherman	#54

		HORNS (cont'd)	
1971	Crazy About the La La La	Smokey Robinson & The Miracles	#56
1971	Roll On	The New Colony Six	#56
1971	You Think You're Hot Stuff	Jean Knight	#57
1971	Bad Water	The Raeletts	#58
1971	Whole Lotta Love	C.C.S.	#58
1971	We Were Always Sweethearts	Boz Scaggs	#61
1971	Don't Make Me Pay for Your Mistakes	Z.Z. Hill	#62
1971	Church Street Soul Revival	Tommy James	#62
1971	Funky Music Sho Nuff Turns Me On	Edwin Starr	#64
1971	Hijackin' Love	Johnnie Taylor	#64
1971	Whole Lotta Love	King Curtis	#64
1971	Feel so Bad	Ray Charles	#68
1971	Get Down	Curtis Mayfield	#69
1971	We are Neighbors	The Chi-Lites	#70
1971	What You See Is What You Get	Stoney & Meatloaf	#71
1971	Wholesale Love	Buddy Miles	#71
1971	Keep the Customer Satisfied	Gary Puckett	#71
1971	You're the One for Me	Joe Simon	#71
1971	Give It to Me	The Mob	#71
1971	Are You My Woman? (Tell Me So)	The Chi-Lites	#72
1971	Life Is a Carnival	The Band	#72
1971	Lisa, Listen to Me	Blood, Sweat & Tears	#73
1971	Your Love (Means Everything to Me)	Charles Wright	#73
1971	One Night Stand	The Magic Lanterns	#74
1971	You're the One	The Three Degrees	#77
1971	I Dig Everything About You	The Mob	#83
1971	Slipped, Tripped and Fell in Love	Clarence Carter	#84
1971	Handbags and Gladrags	Chase	#84
1971	Where are We Going	Bobby Bloom	#84
1971	Sea Cruise	Johnny Rivers	#84
1971	I Pity the Fool	Ann Peebles	#85
1971	Hot Pants – I'm Coming, Coming, I'm Coming	Bobby Byrd	#85
1971	We Got to Live Together – part 1	Buddy Miles	#86
1971	Are You Old Enough	Mark Lindsay	#87
1971	We'll Have It Made	The Spinners	#89
1971	Help the Poor	B.B. King	#90
1971	Solo	Billie Sans	#91
1971	There It Goes Again	Barbara & The Uniques	#91
1971	Chirpy Chirpy, Cheep Cheep	Lally Stott	#92
1971	Love Is Life	Earth, Wind & Fire	#93
1971	Super Highway	Ballin' Jack	#93

		HORNS (cont'd)	
1971	Adrienne	Tommy James	#93
1971	Call Me Up in Dreamland	Van Morrison	#95
1971	I Got to Tell Somebody	Betty Everett	#96
1971	Maria (You were the Only One)	Jimmy Ruffin	#97
1971	You've Got to Earn It	The Staple Singers	#97
1971	Be Good to Me Baby	Luther Ingram	#97
1971	I'm Sorry	Bobby Bland	#97
1971	I Was Wondering	The Poppy Family	#100
1972	Brandy (You're a Fine Girl)	Looking Glass	#1
1972	I Gotcha	Joe Tex	#2
1972	The Lion Sleeps Tonight	Robert John	#3
1972	(If Loving You Is Wrong) I Don't Want to Be Right	Luther Ingram	#3
1972	Saturday in the Park	Chicago	#3
1972	Down By the Lazy River	The Osmonds	#4
1972	Clean Up Woman	Betty Wright	#6
1972	Jungle Fever	The Chackachas	#8
1972	Honky Cat	Elton John	#8
1972	Power of Love	Joe Simon	#11
1972	Little Bitty Pretty One	The Jackson 5	#13
1972	Crazy Horses	The Osmonds	#14
1972	Hold Her Tight	The Osmonds	#14
1972	Slippin' into Darkness	War	#16
1972	Get on the Good Foot – Part 1	James Brown	#18
1972	Starting All Over Again	Mel and Tim	#19
1972	Suavecito	Malo	#18
1972	Happy	The Rolling Stones	#22
1972	The Day I Found Myself	Honey Cone	#23
1972	Runnin' Away	Sly & The Family Stone	#23
1972	Fire and Water	Wilson Pickett	#24
1972	Dialogue (Part 1 & 2)	Chicago	#24
1972	Elected	Alice Cooper	#26
1972	Midnight Rider	Joe Cocker w/The Chris Stainton Band	#27
1972	Do Your Thing	Isaac Hayes	#30
1972	Help Me Make It Through the Night	Gladys Knight & the Pips	#33
1972	Don't Do It	The Band	#34
1972	Glory Bound	The Grass Roots	#34
1972	Sunny Days	Lighthouse	#34
1972	This World	The Staple Singers	#38
1972	The Runway	The Grass Roots	#39
1972	King Heroin	James Brown	#40
1972	You Said a Bad Word	Joe Tex	#41

HORNS (cont'd)			
1972	Smilin'	Sly & The Family Stone	#42
1972	Handbags and Gladrags	Rod Stewart	#42
1972	Those Were the Days	Carroll O'Connor & Jean Stapleton	#43
1972	There It Is (Part 1)	James Brown	#43
1972	So Long Dixie	Blood, Sweat & Tears	#44
1972	Honky Tonk – Part 1	James Brown	#44
1972	I Got a Bag of My Own	James Brown	#44
1972	Do the Funky Penguin (Part 1)	Rufus Thomas	#44
1972	Now Run and Tell That	Denise LaSalle	#46
1972	Baby Sitter	Betty Wright	#46
1972	Ain't Nobody Home	B.B. King	#46
1972	Afro-Strut	The Nite-Liters	#49
1972	You're the Man (Part 1)	Marvin Gaye	#50
1972	Country Wine	The Raiders	#51
1972	Put It Where You Want It	The Crusaders	#52
1972	Woman Don't Go Astray	King Floyd	#53
1972	Son of Shaft	The Bar-Kays	#53
1972	A Lonely Man	The Chi-Lites	#57
1972	Funk Factory	Wilson Pickett	#58
1972	That's What Love Will Make You Do	Little Milton	#59
1972	Move 'Em Out	Delaney & Bonnie	#59
1972	Everybody Knows About My Good Thing Pt. 1	Little Johnny Taylor	#60
1972	I Love You More Than You'll Ever Know	Donny Hathaway	#60
1972	Victim of a Foolish Heart	Bettye Swann	#63
1972	Take It Slow (Out in the Country)	Lighthouse	#64
1972	Cheer	Potliquor	#65
1972	If You Can Beat Me Rockin' (You Can Have My Chair)	Laura Lee	#65
1972	Look What They've Done to My Song, Ma	Ray Charles	#65
1972	If You Let Me	Eddie Kendricks	#66
1972	Think (About It)	Lyn Collins	#66
1972	Down to the Nightclub	Tower of Power	#66
1972	Love Song	Tommy James	#67
1972	Gimme Some More	The JB's	#67
1972	Iko Iko	Dr. John	#71
1972	What It Is	The Undisputed Truth	#71
1972	Standing in for Jody	Johnnie Taylor	#74
1972	Love Potion Number Nine	Coasters	#76
1972	Butterfly	Danyel Gerard	#78
1972	What a Wonderful Thing We Have	Fabulous Rhinestones	#78
1972	Beat Me Daddy Eight to the Bar	Commander Cody	#81
1972	So Many People	Chase	#81

	HORNS (cont'd)		
1972	I Can't Turn You Loose	Edgar Winter's White Trash	#81
1972	Me and My Baby Got a Good Thing Going	Lyn Collins	#86
1972	Ain't That Loving You (For More Reasons Than One)	Isaac Hayes & David Porter	#86
1972	Country Woman	The Magic Lanterns	#88
1972	Keep on Doin' What You're Doin'	Bobby Byrd	#88
1972	Love's Street and Fool's Road	Solomon Burke	#89
1972	I Just Wanna Be Your Friend	Lighthouse	#93
1972	Whatever Turns You On	Travis Wammack	#95
1972	Turn on Your Love Light	Jerry Lee Lewis	#95
1972	Pass the Peas	The JB's	#95
1972	Willpower Weak, Temptations Strong	Bullet	#96
1972	Sittin' on a Time Bomb (Waitin' for the Hurt to Come)	Honey Cone	#96
1972	Bring It Home (And Give It to Me)	Hot Sauce	#96
1972	You Really Got a Hold on Me	Gayle McCormick	#98
1972	Where There's a Will There's a Way	Delaney & Bonnie	#99
1972	Mama Told Me Not to Come	Wilson Pickett	#99
1973	Will It Go Round in Circles	Billy Preston	#1
1973	You Are the Sunshine of My Life	Stevie Wonder	#1
1973	Superstition	Stevie Wonder	#1
1973	Just You 'N' Me	Chicago	#4
1973	Space Race	Billy Preston	#4
1973	Hello It's Me	Todd Rundgren	#5
1973	The World Is a Ghetto	War	#7
1973	Superfly	Curtis Mayfield	#8
1973	Boogie Woogie Bugle Boy	Bette Midler	#8
1973	Feelin' Stronger Every Day	Chicago	#10
1973	Here I Am (Come and Take Me)	Al Green	#10
1973	If You Want Me to Stay	Sly & The Family Stone	#12
1973	Rockin' Roll Baby	The Stylistics	#14
1973	Cheaper to Keep Her	Johnnie Taylor	#15
1973	Funky Worm	Ohio Players	#15
1973	Basketball Jones featuring Tyrone Shoelaces	Cheech & Chong	#15
1973	Steamroller Blues	Elvis Presley	#17
1973	Daddy Could Swear, I Declare	Gladys Knight & The Pips	#19
1973	Dreidel	Don McLean	#21
1973	Nutbush City Limits	Ike & Tina Turner	#22
1973	Doing It to Death	Fred Wesley/The J.B's	#22
1973	Who's in the Strawberry Patch with Sally	Tony Orlando & Dawn	#27
1973	I Got Ants in My Pants (And I Want to Dance)(Part 1)	James Brown	#27
1973	Funky Stuff	Kool & The Gang	#29
1973	Stoned Out of My Mind	The Chi-Lites	#30

		HORNS (cont'd)		
1973	Ecstasy		Ohio Players	#31
1973	The Hurt		Cat Stevens	#31
1973	There It Is		Tyrone Davis	#32
1973	Jimmy Loves Mary-Anne		Looking Glass	#33
1973	Master of Eyes (The Deepness of Your Eyes)		Aretha Franklin	#33
1973	Time to Get Down		O'Jays	#33
1973	Good Morning Heartache		Diana Ross	#34
1973	Corazon		Carole King	#37
1973	I Can't Stand the Rain		Ann Peebles	#38
1973	Future Shock		Curtis Mayfield	#39
1973	I'll Be Your Shelter (In Time of Storm)		Luther Ingram	#40
1973	Such a Night		Dr. John	#42
1973	I Can't Stand to See You Cry		Smokey Robinson & The Miracles	#45
1973	Soul Makossa		Afrique	#47
1973	I Found Sunshine		The Chi-Lites	#47
1973	Sexy, Sexy, Sexy		James Brown	#50
1973	Keep on Singing		Austin Roberts	#50
1973	Down and Out in New York City		James Brown	#50
1973	Daytime Night-Time		Keith Hampshire	#51
1973	Pardon Me Sir		Joe Cocker	#51
1973	Fencewalk		Mandrill	#52
1973	Let Me Be Your Lovemaker		Betty Wright	#55
1973	Love Is What You Make It		The Grass Roots	#55
1973	Woman to Woman		Joe Cocker w/The Chris Stainton Band	#56
1973	What My Baby Needs Now Is a Little More Lovin'		James Brown-Lyn Collins	#56
1973	Bongo Rock		The Incredible Bongo Band	#57
1973	Love and Happiness		Earnest Jackson	#58
1973	Finder's Keepers		Chairman of the Board	#59
1973	I' Been Watchin' You		The South Side Movement	#61
1973	Dancing to Your Music		Archie Bell & The Drells	#61
1973	Do It in the Name of Love		Candi Staton	#63
1973	My Old School		Steely Dan	#63
1973	Always		Luther Ingram	#64
1973	Sixty Minute Man		Clarence Carter	#65
1973	This Time It's Real		Tower of Power	#65
1973	I Don't Know What It Is, But It Sure Is Funky		Ripple	#67
1973	If I Were Only a Child Again		Curtis Mayfield	#71
1973	It's Hard to Stop (Doing Something When It's Good to You)		Betty Wright	#72
1973	Ain't Got No Home		The Band	#73
1973	Think		James Brown	#77
1973	Am I Black Enough for You		Billy Paul	#79

		HORNS (cont'd)		
1973	Frisky		Sly & The Family Stone	#79
1973	There You Go		Edwin Starr	#80
1973	Mother-In-Law		Clarence Carter	#80
1973	Big Time Operator		Keith Hampshire	#81
1973	Don't Let It Get You Down		The Crusaders	#86
1973	Girl You Need a Change of Mind (Part 1)		Eddie Kendrick	#87
1973	Bad Weather		The Supremes	#87
1973	Black Byrd		Donald Byrd	#88
1973	Take a Closer Look at the Woman You're With		Wilson Pickett	#90
1973	Breaking Up Somebody's Home		Albert King	#91
1973	Dueling Tubas		Martin Mull	#92
1973	We're Gonna Have a Good Time		Rare Earth	#93
1973	Rosanna		Dennis Yost/Classics IV	#95
1974	You Haven't Done Nothin'		Stevie Wonder	#1
1974	Nothing from Nothing		Billy Preston	#1
1974	Hooked on a Feeling		Blue Swede	#1
1974	Dancing Machine		The Jackson 5	#2
1974	Boogie Down		Eddie Kendricks	#2
1974	Don't Let the Sun Go Down on Me		Elton John	#2
1974	Jungle Boogie		Kool & The Gang	#4
1974	The Bitch Is Back		Elton John	#4
1974	Oh My My		Ringo Starr	#5
1974	Call on Me		Chicago	#6
1974	Everlasting Love		Carl Carlton	#6
1974	The Air That I Breathe		The Hollies	#6
1974	Hollywood Swinging		Kool & The Gang	#6
1974	Another Saturday Night		Cat Stevens	#6
1974	Steppin' Out (Gonna Boogie Tonight)		Tony Orlando & Dawn	#7
1974	Never My Love		Blue Swede	#7
1974	For the Love of Money		O'Jays	#9
1974	Put Your Hands Together		The O'Jays	#10
1974	Wishing You Were Here		Chicago	#11
1974	Skin Tight		Ohio Players	#13
1974	Radar Love		Golden Earring	#13
1974	Me and Baby Brother		War	#15
1974	Doo Doo Doo Doo Doo (Heartbreaker)		The Rolling Stones	#15
1974	The Payback – Part 1		James Brown	#26
1974	Don't Change Horses (In the Middle of a Stream)		Tower of Power	#26
1974	Let Your Hair Down		The Temptations	#27
1974	I Like to Live the Love		B.B. King	#28
1974	Son of Sagittarius		Eddie Kendricks	#28

	HORNS (cont'd)		
1974	My Thang	James Brown	#29
1974	Straight Shootin' Woman	Steppenwolf	#29
1974	Mighty Mighty	Earth, Wind & Fire	#29
1974	Can This Be Real	Natural Four	#31
1974	Papa Don't Take No Mess (Part 1)	James Brown	#31
1974	I'll Be the Other Woman	The Soul Children	#36
1974	Higher Plane	Kool & The Gang	#37
1974	Thanks for Saving My Life	Billy Paul	#38
1974	Whatever You Got, I Want	The Jackson 5	#38
1974	Funky President (People It's Bad)	James Brown	#44
1974	Jive Turkey (Part 1)	Ohio Players	#47
1974	Can You Handle It?	Graham Central Station	#49
1974	Eyes of Silver	The Doobie Brothers	#52
1974	Black Lassie (Featuring Johnny Stash)	Cheech & Chong	#55
1974	Virgin Man	Smokey Robinson	#56
1974	Pretzel Logic	Steely Dan	#57
1974	You're Welcome, Stop on By	Bobby Womack	#59
1974	King of Nothing	Seals & Crofts	#60
1974	Secretary	Betty Wright	#62
1974	Up for the Down Stroke	Parliament	#63
1974	That Song Is Driving Me Crazy	Tom T. Hall	#63
1974	Help Yourself	The Undisputed Truth	#63
1974	Sexy Ida (Part 1)	Ike & Tina Turner	#65
1974	Unborn Child	Seals & Crofts	#66
1974	Honey Honey	Sweet Dreams	#68
1974	The Lone Ranger	Oscar Brown Jr.	#69
1974	Goin' Down Slow	Bobby Blue Bland	#69
1974	Who Is He and What Is He to You	Creative Source	#69
1974	Do It, Fluid	The Blackbyrds	#69
1974	That's the Sound That Lonely Makes	Tavares	#70
1974	Silly Milly	Blue Swede	#71
1974	You've Got My Soul on Fire	The Temptations	#74
1974	I Feel Sanctified	Commodores	#75
1974	Power of Love	Martha Reeves	#76
1974	I've Been Born Again	Johnnie Taylor	#78
1974	Who Are You	B.B. King	#78
1974	City in the Sky	The Staple Singers	#79
1974	She	Southcote	#80
1974	Scratch	The Crusaders	#81
1974	It's Her Turn to Live	Smokey Robinson	#82
1974	Bad, Bad Leroy Brown	Frank Sinatra	#83

		HORNS (cont'd)		
1974	Fox Hunt	Herb Alpert & The TJB	#84
1974	Don't Eat the Yellow Snow	Frank Zappa	#86
1974	I Wouldn't Treat a Dog (The Way You Treated Me)	Bobby Bland	#88
1974	Can't Say Nothin'	Curtis Mayfield	#88
1974	I Wash My Hands of the Whole Damn Deal, Part 1	The New Birth	#88
1974	Ain't No Love in the Heart of the City	Bobby Bland	#91
1974	Loving You	Johnny Nash	#91
1974	What Is Hip?	Tower of Power	#91
1974	(Everybody Wanna Get Rich) Rite Away	Dr. John	#92
1974	The Real Me	The Who	#92
1974	So Good	The Eleventh Hour	#94
1974	Newsy Neighbors	First Choice	#97
1974	After Midnight	Maggie Bell	#97
1974	Funky Party	Clarence Reid	#99
1975	That's the Way (I Like It)	KC and The Sunshine Band	#1
1975	Lady Marmalade	LaBelle	#1
1975	Pick Up the Pieces	Average White Band	#1
1975	Shining Star	Earth, Wind & Fire	#1
1975	Fire	Ohio Players	#1
1975	Get Down Tonight	KC and The Sunshine Band	#1
1975	At Seventeen	Janis Ian	#3
1975	No No Song	Ringo Starr	#3
1975	Why Can't We Be Friends?	War	#6
1975	Get Down, Get Down (Get on the Floor)	Joe Simon	#8
1975	Rockin' Chair	Gwen McCrae	#9
1975	My Little Town	Simon & Garfunkel	#9
1975	Cut the Cake	Average White Band	#10
1975	Dynomite – Part 1	Bazuka	#10
1975	Get Dancin'	Disco Tex & His Sex-O-Lettes	#10
1975	Once You Get Started	Rufus feat. Chaka Khan	#10
1975	I'm a Woman	Maria Muldaur	#12
1975	Harry Truman	Chicago	#13
1975	I'll Play for You	Seals & Crofts	#18
1975	Slippery When Wet	Commodores	#19
1975	Struttin'	Billy Preston	#22
1975	I Wanna Dance Wit' Choo (Doo Dat Dance), Part 1	Disco Tex & His Sex-O-Lettes	#23
1975	Remember What I Told You to Forget	Tavares	#25
1975	Shakey Ground	The Temptations	#26
1975	Disco Queen	Hot Chocolate	#28
1975	Full of Fire	Al Green	#28
1975	Sweet Sticky Thing	Ohio Players	#33

HORNS (cont'd)

1975	Spirit of the Boogie	Kool & The Gang	#35
1975	Bluebird	Helen Reddy	#35
1975	Dream Merchant	New Birth	#36
1975	Glasshouse	The Temptations	#37
1975	Your Love	Graham Central Station	#38
1975	Letting Go	Paul McCartney & Wings	#39
1975	Happy People	The Temptations	#40
1975	Ease on Down the Road	Consumer Rapport	#42
1975	Dreaming a Dream	Crown Heights Affair	#43
1975	Give the People What They Want	The O'Jays	#45
1975	Welcome to My Nightmare	Alice Cooper	#45
1975	Keep Your Eye on the Sparrow	Merry Clayton	#45
1975	7-6-5-4-3-2-1 (Blow Your Whistle)	Gary Toms Empire	#46
1975	I Believe I'm Gonna Love You	Frank Sinatra	#47
1975	This Old Man	Purple Reign	#48
1975	Take Me to the River	Syl Johnson	#48
1975	What Can I Do for You?	LaBelle	#48
1975	Sunshine Part II	O'Jays	#48
1975	I Love Makin' Love to You	Evie Sands	#50
1975	Money	Gladys Knight & The Pips	#50
1975	As Long as He Takes Care of Home	Candi Staton	#51
1975	I Get High on You	Sly Stone	#52
1975	Growin'	Loggins & Messina	#52
1975	Mr. D.J. (5 for the D.J.)	Aretha Franklin	#53
1975	Mister Magic	Grover Washington, Jr.	#54
1975	Caribbean Festival	Kool & The Gang	#55
1975	Manhattan Spiritual	Mike Post	#56
1975	Sneakin' Up Behind You	The Brecker Brothers	#58
1975	Do It in the Name of Love	Ben E. King	#60
1975	Reach Out, I'll Be There	Gloria Gaynor	#60
1975	Hush/I'm Alive	Blue Swede	#61
1975	Got to Get You Into My Life	Blood, Sweat & Tears	#62
1975	Rhyme Tyme People	Kool & The Gang	#63
1975	Philadelphia	B.B. King	#64
1975	So in Love	Curtis Mayfield	#67
1975	Cry to Me	Loleatta Holloway	#68
1975	Drive My Car	Gary Toms Empire	#69
1975	Mamacita	The Grass Roots	#71
1975	Like They Say in L.A.	East L.A. Car Pool	#72
1975	Same Thing It Took	The Impressions	#75
1975	The Funky Gibbon	The Goodies	#79

		HORNS (cont'd)	
1975	Jam Band	Disco Tex & His Sex-O-Lettes	#80
1975	Bump Me Baby (Part 1)	Dooley Silverspoon	#80
1975	Reality	James Brown	#80
1975	Spider Jiving	Andy Fairweather Low	#87
1975	Leftovers	Millie Jackson	#87
1975	Shotgun Shuffle	The Sunshine Band	#88
1975	Baby-Get It On	Ike & Tina Turner	#88
1975	Living for the City	Ray Charles	#91
1975	Check It Out	Bobby Womack	#91
1975	Music in My Bones	Joe Simon	#92
1975	All Right Now	Lea Roberts	#92
1975	It's Alright	Graham Central Station	#92
1975	Chocolate City	Parliament	#94
1975	Believe Half of What You See (And None of What You Hear)	Leon Haywood	#94
1975	Granddaddy (Part 1)	New Birth	#95
1975	Where Is the Love	Betty Wright	#96
1975	We All Gotta Stick Together	Four Tops	#97
1976	Silly Love Songs	Paul McCartney & Wings	#1
1976	Disco Lady	Johnnie Taylor	#1
1976	Play That Funky Music	Wild Cherry	#1
1976	(Shake, Shake, Shake) Shake Your Booty	KC and The Sunshine Band	#1
1976	Love Rollercoaster	Ohio Players	#1
1976	Boogie Fever	Sylvers	#1
1976	You Should Be Dancing	Bee Gees	#1
1976	The Rubberband Man	Spinners	#2
1976	More, More, More (Pt. 1)	Andrea True Connection	#4
1976	Sing a Song	Earth, Wind & Fire	#5
1976	Got to Get You Into My Life	The Beatles	#7
1976	Summer	War	#7
1976	Getaway	Earth, Wind & Fire	#12
1976	Movin'	Brass Construction	#14
1976	Tear the Roof off the Sucker (Give Up the Funk)	Parliament	#15
1976	I Want You	Marvin Gaye	#15
1976	Who'd She Coo	Ohio Players	#18
1976	Happy Music	The Blackbyrds	#19
1976	Livin' for the Weekend	The O'Jays	#20
1976	Sophisticated Lady (She's a Different Lady)	Natalie Cole	#25
1976	A Dose of Rock 'N' Roll	Ringo Starr	#25
1976	Street Singin'	Lady Flash	#27
1976	Something He Can Feel	Aretha Franklin	#28
1976	Did You Boogie (With Your Baby)	Flash Cadillac & The Continental Kids	#29

HORNS (cont'd)

1976	I Can't Hear You More	Helen Reddy	#29
1976	Fopp	Ohio Players	#30
1976	Another Rainy Day in New York City	Chicago	#32
1976	Somebody's Gettin' It	Johnnie Taylor	#33
1976	Sunrise	Eric Carmen	#34
1976	Steppin' Out	Neil Sedaka	#36
1976	Anything You Want	John Valenti	#37
1976	Can't Hide Love	Earth, Wind & Fire	#39
1976	Framed	Cheech & Chong	#41
1976	Get Up Offa That Thing	James Brown	#45
1976	Hold On	Sons of Champlin	#47
1976	Ob-La-Di, Ob-La-Da	The Beatles	#49
1976	Foxy Lady	Crown Heights Affair	#49
1976	I Don't Wanna Lose Your Love	The Emotions	#51
1976	You Gotta Make Your Own Sunshine	Neil Sedaka	#53
1976	Keep Holding On	The Temptations	#54
1976	Dancin' Kid	Disco Tex & His Sex-O-Lettes	#60
1976	Let's Get It Together	El Coco	#61
1976	Ophelia	The Band	#62
1976	The More You Do It (The More I Like It Done to Me)	Ronnie Dyson	#62
1976	Queen of Clubs	KC and The Sunshine Band	#66
1976	You Ought to Be Havin' Fun	Tower of Power	#68
1976	Mighty High	Mighty Clouds of Joy	#69
1976	New Orleans	The Staple Singers	#70
1976	Devil with a Blue Dress	Pratt & McClain	#71
1976	Scotch on the Rocks	Band of the Black Watch	#75
1976	Soul Train "75"	Soul Train Gang	#75
1976	Wanna Make Love (Come Flick My BIC)	Sun	#76
1976	Love and Understanding (Come Together)	Kool & The Gang	#77
1976	Uptown & Country	Tom Scott	#80
1976	I'll Play the Fool	Dr. Buzzard's Original Savannah Band	#80
1976	Open	Smokey Robinson	#81
1976	Tenth Avenue Freeze-Out	Bruce Springsteen	#83
1976	Peter Gunn	Deodato	#84
1976	You're My Driving Wheel	The Supremes	#85
1976	One for the Money (Part 1)	The Whispers	#88
1976	Rattlesnake	Ohio Players	#90
1976	Laid Back Love	Major Harris	#91
1976	Let's Rock	Ellison Chase	#92
1976	Up the Creek (Without a Paddle)	The Temptations	#94
1976	I Am Somebody	Jimmy James	#94

		HORNS (cont'd)	
1976	Grasshopper	Spin	#95
1976	Hey Baby	J.J. Cale	#96
1976	Sun…Sun…Sun… Part 1	Ja-Kki	#96
1976	Valentine Love	Norman Connors	#97
1976	Touch and Go	Ecstasy, Passion & Pain	#98
1977	Sir Duke	Stevie Wonder	#1
1977	I Wish	Stevie Wonder	#1
1977	I'm Your Boogie Man	KC and The Sunshine Band	#1
1977	Keep It Comin' Love	KC and The Sunshine Band	#2
1977	(Every Time I Turn Around) Back in Love Again	L.T.D.	#4
1977	Brick House	Commodores	#5
1977	Enjoy Yourself	The Jacksons	#6
1977	You Made Me Believe in Magic	Bay City Rollers	#10
1977	Ain't Gonna Bump No More (With No Big Fat Woman)	Joe Tex	#12
1977	Isn't It Time	The Babys	#13
1977	High School Dance	The Sylvers	#17
1977	Saturday Nite	Earth, Wind & Fire	#21
1977	Save It for a Rainy Day	Stephen Bishop	#22
1977	Whodunit	Tavares	#22
1977	Shake Your Rump to the Funk	The Bar-Kays	#23
1977	Dancin' Man	Q	#23
1977	N.Y., You Got Me Dancing	Andrea True Connection	#27
1977	Gonna Fly Now (Theme from Rocky)	Maynard Ferguson	#28
1977	At Midnight (My Love Will Lift You Up)	Rufus feat. Chaka Khan	#30
1977	Hard Rock Café	Carole King	#30
1977	Another Star	Stevie Wonder	#32
1977	I Like to Do It	KC and The Sunshine Band	#37
1977	Old Fashioned Boy (You're the One)	Stallion	#37
1977	Fancy Dancer	Commodores	#39
1977	This Is the Way That I Feel	Marie Osmond	#39
1977	A Real Mother for Ya	Johnny Guitar Watson	#41
1977	Rock and Roll Never Forgets	Bob Seger	#41
1977	You're Movin' Out Today	Bette Midler	#42
1977	Dancin'	Crown Heights Affair	#42
1977	Winter Melody	Donna Summer	#43
1977	Baby Don't You Know	Wild Cherry	#43
1977	Amarillo	Neil Sedaka	#44
1977	Don't Ask My Neighbors	Emotions	#44
1977	O-H-I-O	Ohio Players	#45
1977	L.A. Sunshine	War	#45
1977	Walk Right In	Dr. Hook	#46

		HORNS (cont'd)		
1977	Little Darling (I Need You)	The Doobie Brothers	#48
1977	You are on My Mind	Chicago	#49
1977	I Wanna Do It to You	Jerry Butler	#51
1977	Open Sesame – Part 1	Kool & The Gang	#55
1977	Hold Back the Night	Graham Parker w/The Rumour	#58
1977	Feel the Beat (Everybody Disco)	Ohio Players	#61
1977	Welcome to Our World (Of Merry Music)	Mass Production	#68
1977	You're Moving Out Today	Carole Bayer Sager	#69
1977	Shakey Ground	Phoebe Snow	#70
1977	I'm Going Down	Rose Royce	#70
1977	The Doodle Song	Frankie Miller	#71
1977	Too Hot to Stop (Pt. 1)	The Bar-Kays	#74
1977	Love Is Better in the A.M. (Part 1)	Johnnie Taylor	#77
1977	Be My Lady	The Meters	#78
1977	Party Lights	Natalie Cole	#79
1977	It's Uncanny	Daryl Hall & John Oates	#80
1977	Wake Up and Be Somebody	Brainstorm	#86
1977	Disco 9000	Johnnie Taylor	#86
1977	Bodyheat (Part 1)	James Brown	#88
1977	So High (Rock Me Baby and Roll Me Away)	Dave Mason	#89
1977	Let's Clean Up the Ghetto	Philadelphia International All Stars	#91
1977	Up Your Nose	Gabriel Kaplan	#91
1977	Good Thing Man	Frank Lucas	#92
1977	Hot to Trot	Wild Cherry	#95
1977	Time Is Movin'	The Blackbyrds	#95
1977	Part Time Love	Kerry Chater	#97
1977	Ritzy Mambo	Salsoul Orchestra	#99
1978	Stayin' Alive	Bee Gees	#1
1978	If I Can't Have You	Yvonne Elliman	#1
1978	The Groove Line	Heatwave	#7
1978	Got to Get You Into My Life	Earth, Wind & Fire	#9
1978	What's Your Name	Lynyrd Skynyrd	#13
1978	You and I	Rick James	#13
1978	Serpentine Fire	Earth, Wind & Fire	#13
1978	Alive Again	Chicago	#14
1978	Oh! Darling	Robin Gibb	#15
1978	Every Kinda People	Robert Palmer	#16
1978	Deacon Blues	Steely Dan	#19
1978	Two Doors Down	Dolly Parton	#19
1978	Stuff Like That	Quincy Jones	#21
1978	Ffun	Con Funk Shun	#23

HORNS (cont'd)

1978	Lady Love	Lou Rawls	#24
1978	Too Hot Ta Trot	Commodores	#24
1978	Josie	Steely Dan	#26
1978	Chattanooga Choo Choo	Tuxedo Junction	#32
1978	Boogie Shoes	KC and The Sunshine Band	#35
1978	It's the Same Old Song	KC and The Sunshine Band	#35
1978	There'll Never Be	Switch	#36
1978	Let's All Chant	Michael Zager Band	#36
1978	Flying High	Commodores	#38
1978	On the Shelf	Donny & Marie Osmond	#38
1978	Dance Across the Floor	Jimmy "Bo" Horne	#38
1978	London Town	Paul McCartney & Wings	#39
1978	Ease on Down the Road	Diana Ross & Michael Jackson	#41
1978	Fun Time	Joe Cocker	#43
1978	Greased Lightnin'	John Travolta	#47
1978	Wrap Your Arms Around Me	KC and The Sunshine Band	#48
1978	You Can't Dance	England Dan & John Ford Coley	#49
1978	Your Love Is So Good for Me	Diana Ross	#49
1978	Livingston Saturday Night	Jimmy Buffett	#52
1978	Blame It on the Boogie	The Jacksons	#54
1978	I Want You to Be Mine	Kayak	#55
1978	What's Your Name, What's Your Number	The Andrea True Connection	#56
1978	In the Bush	Musique	#58
1978	Le Spank	Le Pamplemousse	#58
1978	Shake and Dance with Me	Con Funk Shun	#60
1978	God Only Knows	Marilyn Scott	#61
1978	Blame It on the Boogie	Mick Jackson	#61
1978	Take Me Back to Chicago	Chicago	#63
1978	Only One Love in My Life	Ronnie Milsap	#63
1978	Do You Feel All Right	KC and The Sunshine Band	#63
1978	Light the Sky on Fire	Jefferson Starship	#66
1978	Hot Shot	Karen Young	#67
1978	On the Strip	Paul Nicholas	#67
1978	Sgt. Pepper's Lonely Hearts Club Band/With a Little Help From My Friends	The Beatles	#70
1978	Dancin' Fever	Claudja Barry	#72
1978	Let's Get Crazy Tonight	Rupert Holmes	#72
1978	If It Don't Fit, Don't Force It	Kellee Patterson	#75
1978	(You Got to Walk And) Don't Look Back	Peter Tosh w/Mick Jagger	#81
1978	Africanism/Gimme Some Lovin'	Kongas	#84
1978	Georgia on My Mind	Willie Nelson	#84
1979	Bad Girls	Donna Summer	#1

			HORNS (cont'd)	
1979	Rise	Herb Alpert		#1
1979	Pop Muzik	M		#1
1979	After the Love Has Gone	Earth, Wind & Fire		#2
1979	In the Navy	Village People		#3
1979	When You're in Love with a Beautiful Woman	Dr. Hook		#6
1979	Shake Your Body (Down to the Ground)	The Jacksons		#7
1979	Tusk	Fleetwood Mac		#8
1979	September	Earth, Wind & Fire		#8
1979	What You Won't Do for Love	Bobby Caldwell		#9
1979	Heaven Must Have Sent You	Bonnie Pointer		#11
1979	Soul Man	Blues Brothers		#14
1979	No Tell Lover	Chicago		#14
1979	I Got My Mind Made Up (You Can Get It Girl)	Instant Funk		#20
1979	Don't Hold Back	Chanson		#21
1979	Hot Number	Foxy		#21
1979	I Don't Know if It's Right	Evelyn "Champagne" King		#23
1979	Baby I'm Burnin'	Dolly Parton		#25
1979	Dependin' on You	The Doobie Brothers		#25
1979	Weekend	Wet Willie		#29
1979	Arrow Through Me	Paul McCartney & Wings		#29
1979	Bustin' Loose Part 1	Chuck Brown & The Soul Searchers		#34
1979	Last of the Singing Cowboys	Marshall Tucker Band		#42
1979	Firecracker	Mass Production		#43
1979	5:15	The Who		#45
1979	Rhumba Girl	Nicolette Larson		#47
1979	I Don't Want Nobody Else (To Dance with You)	Narada Michael Walden		#47
1979	Vengeance	Carly Simon		#48
1979	Do You Wanna Go Party	KC and The Sunshine Band		#50
1979	Totally Hot	Olivia Newton-John		#52
1979	Sweets for My Sweet	Tony Orlando		#54
1979	Boogie Woogie Dancin' Shoes	Claudja Barry		#56
1979	Star Love	Cheryl Lynn		#62
1979	I Just Can't Control Myself	Nature's Divine		#65
1979	Contact	Edwin Starr		#65
1979	I'm Not Gonna Cry Anymore	Nancy Brooks		#66
1979	Motown Review	Philly Cream		#67
1979	Who Do Ya Love	KC and The Sunshine Band		#68
1979	Best Beat in Town	Switch		#69
1979	Bustin' Out	Rick James		#71
1979	I'm So Anxious	Southside Johnny & The Asbury Jukes		#71
1979	High on Your Love Suite	Rick James		#72

	HORNS (cont'd)		
1979	I've Got the Next Dance	Deniece Williams	#73
1979	Music Box	Evelyn "Champagne" King	#75
1979	H.A.P.P.Y. Radio	Edwin Starr	#79
1979	You Can't Win (Part 1)	Michael Jackson	#81
1979	Dancin'	Grey & Hanks	#83
1979	Crank It Up (Funk Town) Pt. 1	Peter Brown	#86
1979	In the Midnight Hour	Samantha Sang	#88
1979	Shoot Me (With Your Love)	Tasha Thomas	#91
1979	When You're #1	Gene Chandler	#99

JINGLE BELLS

YEAR	SONG	ARTIST	HOT 100
1970	Add Some Music to Your Day	The Beach Boys	#64
1971	The Green Grass Starts to Grow	Dionne Warwick	#43
1975	Ding Dong; Ding Dong	George Harrison	#36
1977	Do Ya Wanna Get Funky with Me	Peter Brown	#18
1977	I Like to Do It	KC and The Sunshine Band	#37

KAZOO

*There are conflicting reports on the kazoo played in "You're Sixteen", by Ringo Starr. Some say an actual kazoo was used in the song, others say the sound was made by Paul McCartney imitating a kazoo with his voice.

YEAR	SONG	ARTIST	HOT 100
1971	Uncle Albert/Admiral Halsey	Paul & Linda McCartney	#1
1974	You're Sixteen*	Ringo Starr	#1
1974	Star	Stealers Wheel	#29
1979	The Logical Song	Supertramp	#6

MANDOLIN

YEAR	SONG	ARTIST	HOT 100
1970	El Condor Pasa (If I Could)	Paul Simon	#18
1970	Rag Mama Rag	The Band	#57
1971	Maggie May	Rod Stewart	#1
1971	Mr. Bojangles	Nitty Gritty Dirt Band	#9

	MANDOLIN (cont'd)		
1971	When I'm Dead and Gone	McGuinness Flint	#47
1971	Call Me Up in Dreamland	Van Morrison	#95
1972	Mary Had a Little Lamb	Paul McCartney & Wings	#28
1972	No Sad Song	Helen Reddy	#61
1972	Speak Softly Love	Al Martino	#80
1973	Daisy a Day	Jud Strunk	#14
1974	Annie's Song	John Denver	#1
1974	Oh Very Young	Cat Stevens	#10
1974	Piano Man	Billy Joel	#25
1975	Lyin' Eyes	The Eagles	#2
1975	Dance with Me	Orleans	#6
1975	If I Could Only Win Your Love	Emmylou Harris	#58
1975	(All I Have to Do Is) Dream	Nitty Gritty Dirt Band	#66
1975	Shoes	Reparata	#92
1976	The White Knight	Cledus Maggard	#19
1976	Eh! Cumpari	Gaylord & Holiday	#72
1976	Kentucky Moonrunner	Cledus Maggard	#85
1977	Freddie	Charlene	#96
1978	Forever Autumn	Justin Hayward	#47
1979	It Hurts So Bad	Kim Carnes	#56

MELODICA

YEAR	SONG	ARTIST	HOT 100
1972	Oh Girl	Chi-Lites	#1
1973	Will It Go Round in Circles	Billy Preston	#1
1975	Dance with Me	Orleans	#6

OBOE

YEAR	SONG	ARTIST	HOT 100
1970	I've Lost You	Elvis Presley	#32
1971	Superstar	Carpenters	#2
1971	For All We Know	Carpenters	#3
1971	Stop, Look, Listen (To Your Heart)	The Stylistics	#39
1971	Friends with You	John Denver	#47
1971	I'm so Proud	The Main Ingredient	#49
1971	Beautiful People	New Seekers	#67

	OBOE (cont'd)		
1971	(She's A) Very Lovely Woman	Linda Ronstadt	#70
1971	Never Dreamed You'd Leave in Summer	Stevie Wonder	#78
1972	Betcha By Golly, Wow	The Stylistics	#3
1972	Goodbye to Love	Carpenters	#7
1972	My Boy	Richard Harris	#41
1972	Handbags and Gladrags	Rod Stewart	#42
1972	Waking Up Alone	Paul Williams	#60
1972	(Love Me) Love the Life I Lead	The Fantastics	#86
1972	I Could Never Be Happy	The Emotions	#93
1973	Yesterday Once More	Carpenters	#2
1973	Masterpiece	The Temptations	#7
1973	Peaceful	Helen Reddy	#12
1973	Don't Let It End ('Til You Let It Begin)	The Miracles	#56
1973	As Time Goes By	Nilsson	#86
1973	I Won't Last a Day Without You	Maureen McGovern	#89
1974	The Way We Were	Barbra Streisand	#1
1974	Annie's Song	John Denver	#1
1974	I Won't Last a Day Without You	Carpenters	#11
1974	Do It Baby	The Miracles	#13
1974	We're Getting Careless with Our Love	Johnnie Taylor	#34
1974	Tell Her Love Has Felt the Need	Eddie Kendricks	#50
1974	Between Her Goodbye and My Hello	Gladys Knight & The Pips	#57
1974	Door to Your Heart	The Dramatics	#62
1974	All in Love Is Fair	Barbra Streisand	#63
1974	Sleepin'	Diana Ross	#70
1974	Put a Little Love Away	The Emotions	#73
1975	Only Yesterday	Carpenters	#4
1975	I Want'a Do Something Freaky to You	Leon Haywood	#15
1975	Solitaire	Carpenters	#17
1975	Ride 'Em Cowboy	Paul Davis	#23
1975	Send in the Clowns	Judy Collins	#36
1975	Baby, Hang Up the Phone	Carl Graves	#50
1975	I Am I Am	Smokey Robinson	#56
1975	Like a Sunday Morning	Lana Cantrell	#63
1975	Somewhere in the Night	Batdorf & Rodney	#69
1975	Don't Cha Love It	The Miracles	#78
1976	Theme from Mahogany (Do You Know Where You're Going To)	Diana Ross	#1
1976	Breaking Up Is Hard to Do	Neil Sedaka	#8
1976	Tryin' to Get the Feeling Again	Barry Manilow	#10
1976	I Need to Be in Love	Carpenters	#25
1976	The Homecoming	Hagood Hardy	#41

	OBOE (cont'd)		
1976	I Thought It Took a Little Time (But Today I Fell in Love)	Diana Ross	#47
1977	I Like Dreamin'	Kenny Nolan	#3
1977	My Heart Belongs to Me	Barbra Streisand	#4
1977	Weekend in New England	Barry Manilow	#10
1977	Send in the Clowns	Judy Collins	#19
1977	Going in with My Eyes Open	David Soul	#53
1977	Fire Sign	Cory	#89
1977	Feelings	Walter Jackson	#93
1978	Last Dance	Donna Summer	#3
1978	Run for Home	Lindisfarne	#33
1978	I Believe You	Carpenters	#68
1978	I Believe You	Carpenters	#68
1979	I Never Said I Love You	Orsa Lia	#84
1979	The Man with the Child in His Eyes	Kate Bush	#85

ORCHESTRA

YEAR	SONG	ARTIST	HOT 100
1970	Bridge Over Troubled Waters	Simon & Garfunkel	#1
1970	Ain't No Mountain High Enough	Diana Ross	#1
1970	Everything Is Beautiful	Ray Stevens	#1
1970	The Long and Winding Road	The Beatles	#1
1970	Cracklin' Rosie	Neil Diamond	#1
1970	My Sweet Lord	George Harrison	#1
1970	One Less Bell to Answer	The 5th Dimension	#2
1970	Hey There Lonely Girl	Eddie Holman	#2
1970	Candida	Dawn	#3
1970	Turn Back the Hands of Time	Tyrone Davis	#3
1970	Give Me Just a Little More Time	Chairmen of the Board	#3
1970	Patches	Clarence Carter	#4
1970	Love Grows (Where My Rosemary Goes)	Edison Lighthouse	#5
1970	Without Love (There Is Nothing)	Tom Jones	#5
1970	Love or Let Me Be Lonely	The Friends of Distinction	#6
1970	I'll Never Fall in Love Again	Dionne Warwick	#6
1970	Don't Cry Daddy	Elvis Presley	#6
1970	Stoned Love	The Supremes	#7
1970	O-o-h Child	The 5 Stairsteps	#8
1970	The Wonder of You	Elvis Presley	#9
1970	Heaven Help Us All	Stevie Wonder	#9

	ORCHESTRA (cont'd)		
1970	I Just Can't Help Believing	B.J. Thomas	#9
1970	Reflections of My Life	The Marmalade	#10
1970	Arizona	Mark Lindsay	#10
1970	Midnight Cowboy	Ferrante & Teicher	#10
1970	Didn't I (Blow Your Mind This Time)	The Delfonics	#10
1970	Up the Ladder to the Roof	The Supremes	#10
1970	It's Only Make Believe	Glen Campbell	#10
1970	You Don't Have to Say You Love Me	Elvis Presley	#11
1970	Don't Play That Song	Aretha Franklin w/The Dixie Flyers	#11
1970	5-10-15-20 (25-30 Years of Love)	The Presidents	#11
1970	Groovy Situation	Gene Chandler	#12
1970	The Bells	The Originals	#12
1970	For the Love of Him	Bobby Martin	#13
1970	Daughter of Darkness	Tom Jones	#13
1970	My Baby Loves Lovin'	White Plains	#13
1970	United We Stand	Brotherhood of Man	#13
1970	A Song of Joy (Himno a la Elegria)	Miguel Ríos	#14
1970	I (Who Have Nothing)	Tom Jones	#14
1970	Kentucky Rain	Elvis Presley	#16
1970	Overture from Tommy (A Rock Opera)	Assembled Multitude	#16
1970	Love Land	Charles Wright	#16
1970	Winter World of Love	Engelbert Humperdinck	#16
1970	Come Saturday Morning	The Sandpipers	#17
1970	Honey Come Back	Glen Campbell	#19
1970	He Ain't Heavy, He's My Brother	Neil Diamond	#20
1970	Oh Me Oh My I'm a Fool for You Baby	Lulu	#22
1970	Baby Take Me in Your Arms	Jefferson	#23
1970	Hey, Mister Sun	Bobby Sherman	#24
1970	Stand By Your Man	Candi Staton	#24
1970	Can't Stop Loving You	Tom Jones	#25
1970	Silver Bird	Mark Lindsay	#25
1970	Everybody's Out of Town	B.J. Thomas	#26
1970	Never Had a Dream Come True	Stevie Wonder	#26
1970	Check Out Your Mind	The Impressions	#28
1970	That's Where I Went Wrong	The Poppy Family	#29
1970	Fancy	Bobbie Gentry	#31
1970	Airport Love Theme (Gwen and Vern)	Vincent Bell	#31
1970	I've Lost You	Elvis Presley	#32
1970	Let Me Go to Him	Dionne Warwick	#32
1970	Breaking Up Is Hard to Do	Lenny Welch	#34
1970	One Tin Soldier	The Original Caste	#34

ORCHESTRA (cont'd)

1970	Baby Hold On	The Grass Roots	#35
1970	Do What You Wanna Do	Five Flights Up	#37
1970	Make It Easy on Yourself	Dionne Warwick	#37
1970	Everything's Tuesday	Chairman of the Board	#38
1970	Temma Harbour	Mary Hopkin	#39
1970	The End of Our Road	Marvin Gaye	#40
1970	Trying to Make a Fool Out of Me	The Delfonics	#40
1970	Wigwam	Bob Dylan	#41
1970	New World Coming	Mama Cass Elliot	#42
1970	My Woman, My Woman, My Wife	Marty Robbins	#42
1970	I Stand Accused	Isaac Hayes	#42
1970	Oh What a Day	The Dells	#43
1970	The Girls' Song	The 5th Dimension	#43
1970	My Marie	Engelbert Humperdinck	#43
1970	Paper Maché	Dionne Warwick	#43
1970	And the Grass Won't Pay No Mind	Mark Lindsay	#44
1970	Walking Through the Country	The Grass Roots	#44
1970	If I Didn't Care	The Moments	#44
1970	Miss America	Mark Lindsay	#44
1970	Tonight I'll Say a Prayer	Eydie Gormé	#45
1970	Ain't That Loving You (For More Reasons Than One)	Luther Ingram	#45
1970	When We Get Married	The Intruders	#45
1970	Good Guys Only Win in the Movies	Mel and Tim	#45
1970	America, Communicate with Me	Ray Stevens	#45
1970	Sunday Morning Coming Down	Johnny Cash	#46
1970	Who's Gonna Take the Blame	Smokey Robinson & The Miracles	#46
1970	I Could Write a Book	Jerry Butler	#46
1970	If I Never Knew Your Name	Vic Dana	#47
1970	Come to Me	Tommy James & The Shondells	#47
1970	Traces/Memories Medley	The Lettermen	#47
1970	I Do Take You	The Three Degrees	#48
1970	Don't Stop Now	Eddie Holman	#48
1970	So Close	Jake Holmes	#49
1970	The Touch of You	Brenda & The Tabulations	#50
1970	It's All in Your Mind	Clarence Carter	#51
1970	Open Up My Heart	The Dells	#51
1970	Children	Joe South	#51
1970	Everything a Man Could Ever Need	Glen Campbell	#52
1970	I'll Be Right Here	Tyrone Davis	#53
1970	Whoever Finds This, I Love You	Mac Davis	#53
1970	Until it's Time for You to Go	Neil Diamond	#53

ORCHESTRA (cont'd)			
1970	When You Get Right Down to It	The Delfonics	#53
1970	Ticket to Ride	Carpenters	#54
1970	On the Beach (In the Summertime)	The 5th Dimension	#54
1970	Something	Shirley Bassey	#55
1970	(Baby) Turn on to Me	The Impressions	#56
1970	Black Fox	Freddy Robinson	#56
1970	Let Me Back In	Tyrone Davis	#58
1970	The Funniest Thing	Dennis Yost/Classics IV	#59
1970	Time Waits for No One	Friends of Distinction	#60
1970	Where are You Going to My Love	Brotherhood of Man	#61
1970	Stand By Me	David & Jimmy Ruffin	#61
1970	She Lets Her Hair Down (Early in the Morning)	The Tokens	#61
1970	I Just Don't Know What to do with Myself	Gary Puckett	#61
1970	Nothing Succeeds Like Success	Bill Deal/The Rhondels	#62
1970	Got to See if I Can't Get Mommy (To Come Back Home)	Jerry Butler	#62
1970	I Love You	Otis Leavill	#63
1970	And My Heart Sang (Tra La La)	Brenda & The Tabulations	#64
1970	Our World	Blue Mink	#64
1970	You've Been My Inspiration	The Main Ingredient	#64
1970	Deeper (In Love with You)	The O'Jays	#64
1970	The Declaration	The 5th Dimension	#64
1970	Dear Prudence	The 5 Stairsteps	#66
1970	Stay Away from Me (I Love You Too Much)	Major Lance	#67
1970	Where Did All the Good Times Go	Dennis Yost/Classics IV	#69
1970	Song from M*A*S*H	Al DeLory	#70
1970	Grover Henson Feels Forgotten	Bill Cosby	#70
1970	He Made a Woman Out of Me	Bobbie Gentry	#71
1970	When the Party Is Over	Robert John	#71
1970	Red Red Wine	Vic Dana	#72
1970	Love Uprising	Otis Leavill	#72
1970	My Way	Brook Benton	#72
1970	Long Lonely Nights	The Dells	#74
1970	Superstar	Murray Head w/The Trinidad Singers	#74
1970	Killer Joe	Quincy Jones	#74
1970	Simply Call It Love	Gene Chandler	#75
1970	Girls Will Be Girls, Boys Will Be Boys	Isley Brothers	#75
1970	Silly, Silly, Fool	Dusty Springfield	#76
1970	One Day of Your Life	Andy Williams	#77
1970	Don't Make Me Over	Brenda & The Tabulations	#77
1970	Mornin' Mornin'	Bobby Goldsboro	#78
1970	Woodstock	The Assembled Multitude	#79

ORCHESTRA (cont'd)

1970	Apartment 21	Bobbie Gentry	#81
1970	Baby I Love You	Little Milton	#82
1970	Groovin' (Out on Life)	The Newbeats	#82
1970	Brighton Hill	Jackie DeShannon	#82
1970	Fire and Rain	R.B. Greaves	#82
1970	Lovin' You Baby	White Plains	#82
1970	Destiny	José Feliciano	#83
1970	It's so Nice	Jackie DeShannon	#84
1970	Susie-Q	José Feliciano	#84
1970	Primrose Lane	O.C. Smith	#86
1970	Melanie Makes Me Smile	Tony Burrows	#87
1970	Loving You Is a Natural Thing	Ronnie Milsap	#87
1970	Shades of Green	The Flaming Ember	#88
1970	I Would Be in Love (Anyway)	Frank Sinatra	#88
1970	Can't Help Falling in Love	Andy Williams	#88
1970	She Lets Her Hair Down (Early in the Morning)	Gene Pitney	#89
1970	Come into My Life	Jimmy Cliff	#89
1970	After the Feeling Is Gone	Five Flights Up	#89
1970	More Than I Can Stand	Bobby Womack	#90
1970	Friend in the City	Andy Kim	#90
1970	A World Without Music	Archie Bell & The Drells	#90
1970	Baby, Is There Something on Your Mind	McKinley Travis	#91
1970	I'm Better off Without You	The Main Ingredient	#91
1970	Help Me Find a Way (To Say I Love You)	Little Anthony & The Imperials	#92
1970	Wrap It Up	Archie Bell & The Drells	#93
1970	Hang on Sloopy	The Lettermen	#93
1970	Heighdy-Ho Princess	Neon Philharmonic	#94
1970	One Light Two Lights	The Satisfactions	#94
1970	A Woman's Way	Rozetta Johnson	#94
1970	You've Made Me so Very Happy	Lou Rawls	#95
1970	Where are You Going	Jerry Butler	#95
1970	If You've Got a Heart	Bobby Bland	#96
1970	Baby Don't Take Your Love	Faith, Hope & Charity	#96
1970	You Keep Me Hangin' On/Hurt so Bad	Jackie DeShannon	#96
1970	Angelica	Oliver	#97
1970	I Think I Love You Again	Brenda Lee	#97
1970	Check Yourself	I.A.P. CO.	#97
1970	Give a Woman Love	Bobbi Martin	#97
1970	Looky Looky (Look at Me Girl)	The O'Jays	#98
1970	If My Heart Could Speak	The Manhattans	#98
1970	A Song that Never Comes	Mama Cass Elliot	#99

	ORCHESTRA (cont'd)		
1970	Spirit in the Sky	Dorothy Morrison	#99
1970	Alone Again Or	Love	#99
1970	Sing Out the Love (In My Heart)	Arkade	#99
1970	Lady Lay Lay	Ferrante & Teicher	#99
1970	Don't Let the Music Slip Away	Archie Bell & The Drells	#100
1970	My Soul's Got a Hole in It	Howard Tate	#100
1971	One Bad Apple	The Osmonds	#1
1971	How Can You Mend a Broken Heart	The Bee Gees	#1
1971	Knock Three Times	Dawn	#1
1971	Go Away Little Girl	Donny Osmond	#1
1971	Just My Imagination (Running Away with Me)	The Temptations	#1
1971	Theme from Shaft	Isaac Hayes	#1
1971	Indian Reservation (The Lament of the Cherokee Reservation Indian)	Raiders	#1
1971	Uncle Albert/Admiral Halsey	Paul & Linda McCartney	#1
1971	Superstar	Carpenters	#2
1971	She's a Lady	Tom Jones	#2
1971	For All We Know	Carpenters	#3
1971	Smiling Faces Sometimes	The Undisputed Truth	#3
1971	Lonely Days	Bee Gees	#3
1971	Don't Pull Your Love	Hamilton, Joe Frank & Reynolds	#4
1971	I Am… I Said	Neil Diamond	#4
1971	I've Found Someone of My Own	The Free Movement	#5
1971	Stoney End	Barbra Streisand	#6
1971	All I Ever Need Is You	Sonny & Cher	#7
1971	Your Song	Elton John	#8
1971	What the World Needs Now Is Love/Abraham, Martin and John	Tom Clay	#8
1971	Cherish	David Cassidy	#9
1971	Whatcha See Is Whatcha Get	Dramatics	#9
1971	(Where Do I Begin) Love Story	Andy Williams	#9
1971	What Is Life	George Harrison	#10
1971	Watching Scotty Grow	Bobby Goldsboro	#11
1971	Never My Love	The 5th Dimension	#12
1971	Pay to the Piper	Chairmen of the Board	#13
1971	Theme from Love Story	Henry Mancini	#13
1971	River Deep – Mountain High	Supremes & Four Tops	#14
1971	Remember Me	Diana Ross	#16
1971	Nathan Jones	The Supremes	#16
1971	No Love at All	B.J. Thomas	#16
1971	Timothy	The Buoys	#17
1971	I Don't Blame You at All	Smokey Robinson & The Miracles	#18

	ORCHESTRA (cont'd)		
1971	Love's Lines, Angles and Rhymes	The 5th Dimension	#19
1971	Maybe Tomorrow	The Jackson 5	#20
1971	Theme from "Summer of '42"	Peter Nero	#21
1971	I Really Don't Want to Know	Elvis Presley	#21
1971	Birds of a Feather	Raiders	#23
1971	One Fine Morning	Lighthouse	#24
1971	I Play and Sing	Dawn	#25
1971	Loving Her Was Easier (Than Anything I'll Ever Do Again)	Kris Kristofferson	#26
1971	I Don't Know How to Love Him	Yvonne Elliman	#28
1971	You've Got a Friend	Roberta Flack & Donny Hathaway	#29
1971	The Drum	Bobby Sherman	#29
1971	(Don't Worry) If There's a Hell Below We're All Going to Go	Curtis Mayfield	#29
1971	The Love We Had (Stays on My Mind)	The Dells	#30
1971	Theme from Love Story	Francis Lai	#31
1971	Dream Baby (How Long Must I Dream)	Glen Campbell	#31
1971	Summer Sand	Dawn	#33
1971	Burning Bridges	Mike Curb Congregation	#34
1971	Friends	Elton John	#34
1971	I Ain't Got Time Anymore	The Glass Bottle	#36
1971	MacArthur Park (Part 2)	Four Tops	#38
1971	Surrender	Diana Ross	#38
1971	Most of All	B.J. Thomas	#38
1971	Stop, Look, Listen (To Your Heart)	The Stylistics	#39
1971	She's All I Got	Freddie North	#39
1971	What are You Doing Sunday	Dawn featuring Tony Orlando	#39
1971	Till	Tom Jones	#41
1971	Do Me Right	Detroit Emeralds	#43
1971	The Green Grass Starts to Grow	Dionne Warwick	#43
1971	Another Time, Another Place	Engelbert Humperdinck	#43
1971	It's a Cryin' Shame	Gayle McCormick	#43
1971	Cherish What Is Dear to You (While It's Near to You)	Freda Payne	#44
1971	Light Sings	The 5th Dimension	#44
1971	When There's No You	Engelbert Humperdinck	#45
1971	Annabella	Hamilton, Joe Frank & Reynolds	#46
1971	I'm so Proud	The Main Ingredient	#49
1971	I Cried	James Brown	#50
1971	Take Me Girl, I'm Ready	Jr. Walker/The All Stars	#50
1971	Someone Who Cares	Kenny Rogers & The First Edition	#51
1971	Time and Love	Barbra Streisand	#51
1971	It's Summer	The Temptations	#51
1971	It's Only Love	Elvis Presley	#51

		ORCHESTRA (cont'd)		
1971	Spinning Around (I Must Be Falling in Love)	The Main Ingredient	#52
1971	Hey! Love	The Delfonics	#52
1971	I Think of You	Perry Como	#53
1971	Life	Elvis Presley	#53
1971	Ain't Got Time	Impressions	#53
1971	Do I Love You	Paul Anka	#53
1971	You Gotta Have Love in Your Heart	Supremes & Four Tops	#55
1971	(I Can Feel Those Vibrations) This Love Is Real	Jackie Wilson	#56
1971	Talk It Over in the Morning	Anne Murray	#57
1971	Who Gets the Guy	Dionne Warwick	#57
1971	Over and Over	The Delfonics	#58
1971	Is That the Way	Tin Tin	#59
1971	Could I Forget You	Tyrone Davis	#60
1971	Jennifer	Bobby Sherman	#60
1971	The Morning of Our Lives	Arkade	#60
1971	The Last Time I Saw Her	Glen Campbell	#61
1971	The Court Room	Clarence Carter	#61
1971	Long Ago Tomorrow	B.J. Thomas	#61
1971	Cheryl Moana Marie	John Rowles	#64
1971	Done Too Soon	Neil Diamond	#65
1971	Mozart Symphony No. 40 in G Minor K.550, 1st Movement	Waldo de los Rios	#67
1971	Beautiful People	New Seekers	#67
1971	Triangle of Love (Hey Diddle Diddle)	The Presidents	#68
1971	Help Me Make It Through the Night	Joe Simon	#69
1971	If It's Real What I Feel	Jerry Butler w/Brenda Lee Eager	#69
1971	All My Trials	Ray Stevens	#70
1971	(She's A) Very Lovely Woman	Linda Ronstadt	#70
1971	Touch	The Supremes	#71
1971	I'll Erase Away Your Pain	Whatnauts	#71
1971	Freedom Come, Freedom Go	The Fortunes	#72
1971	Freedom	Isley Brothers	#72
1971	Everything Is Good About You	The Lettermen	#74
1971	Pin the Tail on the Donkey	The Newcomers	#74
1971	One-Way Ticket	Tyrone Davis	#75
1971	Hill Where the Lord Hides	Chuck Mangione	#76
1971	Try Some, Buy Some	Ronnie Spector	#77
1971	Reach Out Your Hand	Brotherhood of Man	#77
1971	Never Dreamed You'd Leave in Summer	Stevie Wonder	#78
1971	Fool Me	Joe South	#78
1971	I Need You	Friends of Distinction	#79
1971	The Look of Love	Isaac Hayes	#79

		ORCHESTRA (cont'd)	
1971	Suspicious Minds	Dee Dee Warwick	#80
1971	Problem Child	Mark Lindsay	#80
1971	I Say a Little Prayer/By the Time I Get to Phoenix	Glen Campbell/Anne Murray	#81
1971	Walk Right Up to the Sun	The Delfonics	#81
1971	Didn't It Looks so Easy	The Stairsteps	#81
1971	Flim Flam Man	Barbra Streisand	#82
1971	A Song for You	Andy Williams	#82
1971	He'd Rather Have the Rain	Heaven Bound with Tony Scotti	#83
1971	Love Makes the World Go Round	Odds & Ends	#83
1971	Amanda	Dionne Warwick	#83
1971	Gonna Be Alright Now	Gayle McCormick	#84
1971	How Did We Lose It Baby	Jerry Butler	#85
1971	I Need Someone (To Love Me)	Z.Z. Hill	#86
1971	Love Makes the World Go Round	Kiki Dee	#87
1971	The Girl Who Loved Me When	Glass Bottle	#87
1971	1927 Kansas City	Mike Reilly	#88
1971	It's so Hard for Me to Say Good-Bye	Eddie Kendricks	#88
1971	Wear This Ring (With Love)	Detroit Emeralds	#91
1971	Help Me Make It Through the Night	O.C. Smith	#91
1971	Everything's Alright	Yvonne Elliman	#92
1971	The Glory of Love	The Dells	#92
1971	Be My Baby	Cissy Houston	#92
1971	I Bet He Don't Love You (Like I Love You)	The Intruders	#92
1971	We're All Goin' Home	Bobby Bloom	#93
1971	Now I'm a Woman	Nancy Wilson	#93
1971	Walk Easy My Son	Jerry Butler	#93
1971	Your Love Is so Doggone Good	The Whispers	#93
1971	All My Hard Times	Joe Simon	#93
1971	Mandrill	Mandrill	#94
1971	You Just Can't Win (By Making the Same Mistake)	Gene Chandler & Jerry Butler	#94
1971	A Part of You	Brenda & The Tabulations	#94
1971	Love Me	The Impressions	#94
1971	You Keep Me Holding On	Tyrone Davis	#94
1971	When You Get Right Down to It	Ronnie Dyson	#94
1971	I Want to Pay You Back (For Loving Me)	The Chi-Lites	#95
1971	Love Is Funny That Way	Jackie Wilson	#95
1971	Medley from "Superstar" (A Rock Opera)	The Assembled Multitude	#95
1971	If It's Alright with You	Rose Colored Glass	#95
1971	The Electronic Magnetism (That's Heavy, Baby)	Solomon Burke	#96
1971	I'll Be Home	Vikki Carr	#96
1971	Stop! In the Name of Love	Margie Joseph	#96

		ORCHESTRA (cont'd)		
1971	Solution for Pollution		Charles Wright	#96
1971	Black Seeds Keep on Growing		The Main Ingredient	#97
1971	Lucky Me		Moments	#98
1971	There's so Much Love All Around Me		The Three Degrees	#98
1971	Been Too Long on the Road		Mark Lindsay	#98
1971	The Sound of Silence		Peaches & Herb	#100
1971	The Language of Love		The Intrigues	#100
1971	We're Friends by Day (And Lovers by Night)		Whatnauts	#100
1972	Alone Again (Naturally)		Gilbert O'Sullivan	#1
1972	Without You		Nilsson	#1
1972	Me and Mrs. Jones		Billy Paul	#1
1972	The Candy Man		Sammy Davis, Jr. w/The Mike Curb Congregation	#1
1972	Let's Stay Together		Al Green	#1
1972	I Am Woman		Helen Reddy	#1
1972	Oh Girl		Chi-Lites	#1
1972	Ben		Michael Jackson	#1
1972	Papa Was a Rolling Stone		The Temptations	#1
1972	Song Sung Blue		Neil Diamond	#1
1972	Precious and Few		Climax	#3
1972	You Ought to Be with Me		Al Green	#3
1972	I'm Still in Love with You		Al Green	#3
1972	If You Don't Know Me By Now		Harold Melvin	#3
1972	I'll Be Around		The Spinners	#3
1972	Back Stabbers		O'Jays	#3
1972	Betcha By Golly, Wow		The Stylistics	#3
1972	Everybody Plays the Fool		The Main Ingredient	#3
1972	Puppy Love		Donny Osmond	#3
1972	Daddy Don't You Walk so Fast		Wayne Newton	#4
1972	Freddie's Dead (Theme from "Superfly")		Curtis Mayfield	#4
1972	Look What You Done for Me		Al Green	#4
1972	It Never Rains in Southern California		Albert Hammond	#5
1972	Where Is the Love		Roberta Flack & Donny Hathaway	#5
1972	In the Rain		Dramatics	#5
1972	Goodbye to Love		Carpenters	#7
1972	The Way of Love		Cher	#7
1972	How Do You Do?		Mouth & MacNeal	#8
1972	(Last Night) I Didn't Get to Sleep at All		The 5th Dimension	#8
1972	A Cowboy's Work Is Never Done		Sonny & Cher	#8
1972	You Are Everything		The Stylistics	#9
1972	Hey Girl		Donny Osmond	#9
1972	I'm Stone in Love with You		The Stylistics	#10

	ORCHESTRA (cont'd)		
1972	Sugar Daddy	The Jackson 5	#10
1972	If I Could Reach You	The 5th Dimension	#10
1972	Play Me	Neil Diamond	#11
1972	Drowning in the Sea of Love	Joe Simon	#11
1972	It's Going to Take Some Time	Carpenters	#12
1972	Too Young	Donny Osmond	#13
1972	Why	Donny Osmond	#13
1972	Walkin' in the Rain with the One I Love	Love Unlimited	#14
1972	Don't Say You Don't Remember	Beverly Bremers	#15
1972	One Monkey Don't Stop No Show (Part 1)	Honey Cone	#15
1972	I Wanna Be Where You Are	Michael Jackson	#16
1972	Lookin' Through the Window	The Jackson 5	#16
1972	Run to Me	Bee Gees	#16
1972	My World	Bee Gees	#16
1972	Conquistador	Procol Harum	#16
1972	Corner of the Sky	The Jackson 5	#18
1972	Sealed with a Kiss	Bobby Vinton	#19
1972	It's One of Those Nights (Yes Love)	The Partridge Family	#20
1972	Ain't Understanding Mellow	Jerry Butler & Brenda Lee Eager	#21
1972	I Can't Help Myself (Sugar Pie, Honey Bunch)	Donnie Elbert	#22
1972	Living in a House Divided	Cher	#22
1972	Gone	Joey Heatherton	#24
1972	Every Day of My Life	Bobby Vinton	#24
1972	Baby Let Me Take You (In My Arms)	Detroit Emeralds	#24
1972	People Make the World Go Round	The Stylistics	#25
1972	We've Got to Get It on Again	The Addrisi Brothers	#25
1972	How Can I Be Sure	David Cassidy	#25
1972	An American Trilogy	Mickey Newbury	#26
1972	Ask Me What You Want	Millie Jackson	#27
1972	Make Me the Woman That You Go Home To	Gladys Knight & The Pips	#27
1972	Breaking Up Is Hard to Do	The Partridge Family	#28
1972	Isn't Life Strange	The Moody Blues	#29
1972	Loving You Just Crossed My Mind	Sam Neely	#29
1972	Softly Whispering I Love You	English Congregation	#29
1972	You're Still a Young Man	Tower of Power	#29
1972	Take a Look Around	The Temptations	#30
1972	Help Me Make It Through the Night	Gladys Knight & the Pips	#33
1972	Love Theme from "The Godfather" (Speak Softly Love)	Andy Williams	#34
1972	Alive	The Bee Gees	#34
1972	You Want It, You Got It	Detroit Emeralds	#36
1972	Together Let's Find Love	The 5th Dimension	#37

		ORCHESTRA (cont'd)		
1972	Sweet Inspiration/Where You Lead	Barbra Streisand	#37
1972	Could It Be Forever	David Cassidy	#37
1972	Theme from "The Men"	Isaac Hayes	#38
1972	Mister Can't You See	Buffy Sainte-Marie	#38
1972	We're Free	Beverly Bremers	#40
1972	Me and Bobby McGee	Jerry Lee Lewis	#40
1972	My Boy	Richard Harris	#41
1972	Daisy Mae	Hamilton, Joe Frank & Reynolds	#41
1972	My Man, A Sweet Man	Millie Jackson	#42
1972	Pool of Bad Luck	Joe Simon	#42
1972	We're on Our Way	Chris Hodge	#44
1972	Everything Good Is Bad	100 Proof	#45
1972	We've Come Too Far to End It Now	Smokey Robinson & The Miracles	#46
1972	Don't Hide Your Love	Cher	#46
1972	The Coldest Days of My Life (Part 1)	The Chi-Lites	#47
1972	In the Ghetto	Candi Staton	#48
1972	Can't You Hear the Song?	Wayne Newton	#48
1972	Let's Stay Together	Isaac Hayes	#48
1972	Satisfaction	Smokey Robinson & The Miracles	#49
1972	The Harder I Try (The Bluer I Get)	Free Movement	#50
1972	Trouble in My Home	Joe Simon	#50
1972	You are the One	Sugar Bears	#51
1972	Way Back Home	Jr. Walker/The All Stars	#52
1972	Life and Breath	Climax	#52
1972	Show Me How	The Emotions	#52
1972	One Night Affair	Jerry Butler	#52
1972	(It's the Way) Nature Planned It	Four Tops	#53
1972	Brian's Song	Michel LeGrand	#56
1972	Diamonds are Forever	Shirley Bassey	#57
1972	992 Arguments	The O'Jays	#57
1972	Why Can't We Be Lovers	Holland-Dozier	#57
1972	Woman Is the Nigger of the World	John Lennon	#57
1972	I Had It All the Time	Tyrone Davis	#61
1972	I Will Never Pass This Way Again	Glen Campbell	#61
1972	Guess Who	B.B. King	#61
1972	Louisiana	Mike Kennedy	#62
1972	I'll Make You Music	Beverly Bremers	#63
1972	Papa Was a Rolling Stone	The Undisputed Truth	#63
1972	Special Someone	The Heywoods	#64
1972	(Oh Lord Won't You Buy Me A) Mercedes Benz	Goose Creek Symphony	#64
1972	Jubilation	Paul Anka	#65

	ORCHESTRA (cont'd)		
1972	Love Theme from "The Godfather"	Carlo Savina	#66
1972	Colorado	Danny Holien	#66
1972	An American Trilogy	Elvis Presley	#66
1972	Bless the Beasts and Children	Carpenters	#67
1972	Toast to the Fool	Dramatics	#67
1972	In the Quiet Morning	Joan Baez	#69
1972	In Time	Engelbert Humperdinck	#69
1972	My Guy	Petula Clark	#70
1972	Bed and Board	Barbara Mason	#70
1972	You Make Your Own Heaven and Hell Right Here on Earth	The Undisputed Truth	#72
1972	Since I Fell for You	Laura Lee	#76
1972	I've Got to Have You	Sammi Smith	#77
1972	I Wrote a Simple Song	Billy Preston	#77
1972	How Could I Let You Get Away	The Spinners	#77
1972	I Found My Dad	Joe Simon	#78
1972	Get Up and Get Down	Dramatics	#78
1972	The Young New Mexican Puppeteer	Tom Jones	#80
1972	Speak Softly Love	Al Martino	#80
1972	Giving Up	Donny Hathaway	#81
1972	Taos New Mexico	R. Dean Taylor	#83
1972	Just as Long as You Need Me, Part 1	Independents	#84
1972	Music from Across the Way	James Last	#84
1972	If We Only Have Love	Dionne Warwick	#84
1972	I Only Have Eyes for You	Jerry Butler	#85
1972	(Love Me) Love the Life I Lead	The Fantastics	#86
1972	Too Beautiful to Last	Engelbert Humperdinck	#86
1972	Tell Me This Is a Dream	Delfonics	#86
1972	A Simple Game	Four Tops	#90
1972	(They Long to Be) Close to You	Jerry Butler w/Brenda Lee Eager	#91
1972	Together Again	Bobby Sherman	#91
1972	Brandy	Scott English	#91
1972	The People Tree	Sammy Davis, Jr. w/The Mike Curb Congregation	#92
1972	Knock Knock Who's There	Mary Hopkin	#92
1972	Mother Nature	The Temptations	#92
1972	You Were Made for Me	Luther Ingram	#93
1972	I Could Never Be Happy	The Emotions	#93
1972	Long Time to Be Alone	New Colony Six	#93
1972	You Got Me Walking	Jackie Wilson	#93
1972	It's the Same Old Love	The Courtship	#93
1972	I Thank You	Donny Hathaway & June Conquest	#94
1972	It's All Up to You	The Dells	#94

	ORCHESTRA (cont'd)		
1972	Sing a Song/Make Your Own Kind of Music	Barbra Streisand	#94
1972	Mendelssohn's 4th (Second Movement)	Apollo 100	#94
1972	Number Wonderful	Rock Flowers	#95
1972	Suite: Man and Woman	Tony Cole	#97
1973	My Love	Paul McCartney & Wings	#1
1973	Keep on Truckin' (Part 1)	Eddie Kendricks	#1
1973	Midnight Train to Georgia	Gladys Knight & The Pips	#1
1973	The Night the Lights Went Out in Georgia	Vicki Lawrence	#1
1973	Touch Me in the Morning	Diana Ross	#1
1973	Delta Dawn	Helen Reddy	#1
1973	Love Train	O'Jays	#1
1973	Photograph	Ringo Starr	#1
1973	Live and Let Die	Paul McCartney & Wings	#2
1973	Neither One of Us (Wants to Be the First to Say Goodbye)	Gladys Knight & The Pips	#2
1973	Yesterday Once More	Carpenters	#2
1973	Also Sprach Zarathustra (2001)	Deodato	#2
1973	Last Song	Edward Bear	#3
1973	Sing	Carpenters	#3
1973	Leave Me Alone (Ruby Red Dress)	Helen Reddy	#3
1973	Say, Has Anybody Seen My Sweet Gypsy Rose	Dawn featuring Tony Orlando	#3
1973	Could It Be I'm Falling in Love	Spinners	#4
1973	Ain't No Woman (Like the One I've Got)	Four Tops	#4
1973	The Love I Lost (Part 1)	Harold Melvin	#7
1973	Masterpiece	The Temptations	#7
1973	Keeper of the Castle	The Four Tops	#10
1973	Call Me (Come Back Home)	Al Green	#10
1973	I Believe in You (You Believe in Me)	Johnnie Taylor	#11
1973	Peaceful	Helen Reddy	#12
1973	Stir It Up	Johnny Nash	#12
1973	You're a Special Part of Me	Diana Ross & Marvin Gaye	#12
1973	Space Oddity	David Bowie	#15
1973	Are You Man Enough	Four Tops	#15
1973	Love Jones	Brighter Side of Darkness	#16
1973	I'm Doin' Fine Now	New York City	#17
1973	So Very Hard to Go	Tower of Power	#17
1973	Do You Want to Dance?	Bette Midler	#17
1973	Out of the Question	Gilbert O'Sullivan	#17
1973	Theme from Cleopatra Jones	Joe Simon w/The Mainstreeters	#18
1973	Angel	Aretha Franklin	#20
1973	Hummingbird	Seals & Crofts	#20
1973	Leaving Me	The Independents	#21

	ORCHESTRA (cont'd)		
1973	You'll Never Get to Heaven (If You Break My Heart)	The Stylistics	#23
1973	A Million to One	Donny Osmond	#23
1973	Hurts So Good	Millie Jackson	#24
1973	Smoke Gets in Your Eyes	Blue Haze	#27
1973	Get It Together	The Jackson 5	#28
1973	Armed and Extremely Dangerous	First Choice	#28
1973	Believe in Humanity	Carole King	#28
1973	One Man Band (Plays All Alone)	Ronnie Dyson	#28
1973	And I Love You So	Perry Como	#29
1973	Ghetto Child	Spinners	#29
1973	Nobody Wants You When You're Down and Out	Bobby Womack	#29
1973	Pinball Wizard/See Me, Feel Me	The New Seekers	#29
1973	Give Me Your Love	Barbara Mason	#31
1973	Living Together, Growing Together	The 5th Dimension	#32
1973	I've Got so Much to Give	Barry White	#32
1973	Give Your Baby a Standing Ovation	The Dells	#34
1973	Be	Neil Diamond	#34
1973	Hey Girl (I Like Your Style)	The Temptations	#35
1973	Check It Out	Tavares	#35
1973	Let Me In	The Osmonds	#36
1973	I'll Always Love My Mama (Part 1)	The Intruders	#36
1973	Step By Step	Joe Simon	#37
1973	Looking Through the Eyes of Love	The Partridge Family	#39
1973	Some Guys Have All the Luck	The Persuaders	#39
1973	The Plastic Man	The Temptations	#40
1973	Friends	Bette Midler	#40
1973	Baby I've Been Missing You	The Independents	#41
1973	Rhapsody in Blue	Deodato	#41
1973	Hey You! Get off My Mountain	Dramatics	#43
1973	Love, Love, Love	Donny Hathaway	#43
1973	Fell for You	The Dramatics	#45
1973	You've Got to Take It (If You Want It)	The Main Ingredient	#46
1973	Today I Started Loving You Again	Bettye Swann	#46
1973	Sweet Harmony	Smokey Robinson	#48
1973	Never, Never, Never (Grande, Grande, Grande)	Shirley Bassey	#48
1973	A Song I'd Like to Sing	Kris Kristofferson & Rita Coolidge	#49
1973	You're a Lady	Peter Skellern	#50
1973	My Pretending Days Are Over	The Dells	#51
1973	Ashes to Ashes	The 5th Dimension	#52
1973	Don't Leave Me Starvin' for Your Love (Part 1)	Holland-Dozier	#52
1973	Pretty Lady	Lighthouse	#53

	ORCHESTRA (cont'd)		
1973	"Having a Party" Medley	The Ovations	#56
1973	Don't Let It End ('Til You Let It Begin)	The Miracles	#56
1973	Smarty Pants	First Choice	#56
1973	Tweedlee Dee	Little Jimmy Osmond	#59
1973	I Wanna Know Your Name	The Intruders	#60
1973	Letter to Lucille	Tom Jones	#60
1973	Just Don't Want to Be Lonely	Ronnie Dyson	#60
1973	All I Need Is Time	Gladys Knight & The Pips	#61
1973	I Never Said Goodbye	Engelbert Humperdinck	#61
1973	Freedom for the Stallion	The Hues Corporation	#63
1973	Lost Horizon	Shawn Phillips	#63
1973	Let Me Try Again	Frank Sinatra	#63
1973	Yesterday I Had the Blues	Harold Melvin	#63
1973	Without You in My Life	Tyrone Davis	#64
1973	Slick	Willie Hutch	#65
1973	Anthem	Wayne Newton	#65
1973	It's All Over	The Independents	#65
1973	Be What You Are	The Staple Singers	#66
1973	Brother's Gonna Work It Out	Willie Hutch	#67
1973	You Light Up My Life	Carole King	#67
1973	Happy	Bobby Darin	#67
1973	Gotta Find a Way	Moments	#68
1973	It's Forever	The Ebonys	#68
1973	First Cut Is the Deepest	Keith Hampshire	#70
1973	Send a Little Love My Way	Anne Murray	#72
1973	Back for a Taste of Your Love	Syl Johnson	#72
1973	I'm Coming Home	Johnny Mathis	#75
1973	He Did with Me	Vicki Lawrence	#75
1973	Wish That I Could Talk to You	The Sylvers	#77
1973	You'd Better Believe It	Manhattans	#77
1973	One Last Time	Glen Campbell	#78
1973	Slow Motion (Part 1)	Johnny Williams	#78
1973	Don't Burn Me	Paul Kelly	#79
1973	That's Why You Remember	Kenny Karen	#82
1973	Didn't We	Barbra Streisand	#82
1973	You're the Best Thing That Ever Happened to Me	Ray Price	#82
1973	But I Do	Bobby Vinton	#82
1973	Cosmic Sea	The Mystic Moods	#83
1973	It May Be Winter Outside, (But in My Heart It's Spring)	Love Unlimited	#83
1973	You Can Do Magic	Limmie & Family Cookin'	#84
1973	As Time Goes By	Nilsson	#86

	ORCHESTRA (cont'd)		
1973	Delta Queen	Don Fardon	#86
1973	I Won't Last a Day Without You	Maureen McGovern	#89
1973	Stay Away from Me	The Sylvers	#89
1973	On and Off (Part 1)	Anacostia	#90
1973	I Don't Want to Make You Wait	The Delfonics	#91
1973	Love Is All	Engelbert Humperdinck	#91
1973	Make Me Twice the Man	New York City	#93
1973	Fool Like You	Tim Moore	#93
1973	She's Got to Be a Saint	Ray Price	#93
1973	Somebody Loves You	The Whispers	#94
1973	We Did It	Syl Johnson	#95
1974	The Way We Were	Barbra Streisand	#1
1974	Annie's Song	John Denver	#1
1974	TSOP (The Sound of Philadelphia)	MFSB/Three Degrees	#1
1974	Then Came You	Dionne Warwicke & Spinners	#1
1974	Love's Theme	Love Unlimited Orchestra	#1
1974	Show and Tell	Al Wilson	#1
1974	Sunshine on My Shoulders	John Denver	#1
1974	Rock the Boat	The Hues Corporation	#1
1974	You Make Me Feel Brand New	The Stylistics	#2
1974	When Will I See You Again	The Three Degrees	#2
1974	The Entertainer	Marvin Hamlisch	#3
1974	Rock and Roll Heaven	The Righteous Brothers	#3
1974	Until You Come Back to Me (That's What I'm Gonna Do)	Aretha Franklin	#3
1974	I've Got to Use My Imagination	Gladys Knight & The Pips	#4
1974	Beach Baby	First Class	#4
1974	I'm Leaving It (All) Up to You	Donny & Marie Osmond	#4
1974	The Lord's Prayer	Sister Janet Mead	#4
1974	Americans	Byron MacGregor	#4
1974	Rock On	David Essex	#5
1974	Sha-La-La (Make Me Happy)	Al Green	#7
1974	You Won't See Me	Anne Murray	#8
1974	Sideshow	Blue Magic	#8
1974	Hang on in There Baby	Johnny Bristol	#8
1974	You and Me Against the World	Helen Reddy	#9
1974	Eres Tu (Touch the Wind)	Mocedades	#9
1974	Stop and Smell the Roses	Mac Davis	#9
1974	Love Me for a Reason	The Osmonds	#10
1974	I Won't Last a Day Without You	Carpenters	#11
1974	The Need to Be	Jim Weatherly	#11
1974	I've Got the Music in Me	The Kiki Dee Band	#12

		ORCHESTRA (cont'd)	
1974	You Little Trustmaker	The Tymes	#12
1974	Do It Baby	The Miracles	#13
1974	Last Time I Saw Him	Diana Ross	#14
1974	Haven't Got Time for the Pain	Carly Simon	#14
1974	Who Do You Think You Are	Bo Donaldson & The Heywoods	#15
1974	Keep on Singing	Helen Reddy	#15
1974	Finally Got Myself Together (I'm a Changed Man)	The Impressions	#17
1974	If You Talk in Your Sleep	Elvis Presley	#17
1974	Rockin' Soul	The Hues Corporation	#18
1974	Let's Put It All Together	The Stylistics	#18
1974	I'm Coming Home	Spinners	#18
1974	I'm in Love	Aretha Franklin	#19
1974	Midnight Rider	Gregg Allman	#19
1974	Livin' for You	Al Green	#19
1974	Give It to the People	The Righteous Brothers	#20
1974	Mighty Love – Pt. 1	Spinners	#20
1974	I Feel a Song (In My Heart)	Gladys Knight & The Pips	#21
1974	Woman to Woman	Shirley Brown	#22
1974	Touch a Hand, Make a Friend	The Staple Singers	#23
1974	This Heart	Gene Redding	#24
1974	The Americans (A Canadian's Opinion)	Gordon Sinclair	#24
1974	Fish Ain't Bitin'	Lamont Dozier	#26
1974	Baby Come Close	Smokey Robinson	#27
1974	Train of Thought	Cher	#27
1974	Distant Lover	Marvin Gaye	#28
1974	"Joy" Pt. 1	Isaac Hayes	#30
1974	La La Peace Song	Al Wilson	#30
1974	Let's Get Married	Al Green	#32
1974	Dream On	The Righteous Brothers	#32
1974	Outside Woman	Bloodstone	#34
1974	We're Getting Careless with Our Love	Johnnie Taylor	#34
1974	Three Ring Circus	Blue Magic	#36
1974	Kung Fu	Curtis Mayfield	#40
1974	Heavy Fallin' Out	The Stylistics	#41
1974	One Chain Don't Make No Prison	Four Tops	#41
1974	I Saw a Man and He Danced with His Wife	Cher	#42
1974	Heavenly	The Temptations	#43
1974	Wildflower	The New Birth	#45
1974	Don't Knock My Love	Diana Ross & Marvin Gaye	#46
1974	Ain't Nothing Like the Real Thing	Aretha Franklin	#47
1974	You and I	Johnny Bristol	#48

	ORCHESTRA (cont'd)		
1974	Tell Her Love Has Felt the Need	Eddie Kendricks	#50
1974	In the Mood	Bette Midler	#51
1974	Ask Me	Ecstasy, Passion & Pain	#52
1974	Homely Girl	The Chi-Lites	#54
1974	Midnight Flower	Four Tops	#55
1974	Touch and Go	Al Wilson	#57
1974	I Wish It Was Me	Tyrone Davis	#57
1974	Between Her Goodbye and My Hello	Gladys Knight & The Pips	#57
1974	Satisfaction Guaranteed (Or Take Your Love Back)	Harold Melvin	#58
1974	Too Late	Tavares	#59
1974	My Country	Jud Strunk	#59
1974	She's Gone	Daryl Hall & John Oates	#60
1974	Happiness Is Me and You	Gilbert O'Sullivan	#62
1974	I Just Can't Get You Out of My Mind	Four Tops	#62
1974	La La Peace Song	O.C. Smith	#62
1974	Door to Your Heart	The Dramatics	#62
1974	I'll Be Your Everything	Percy Sledge	#62
1974	Rhapsody in White	Barry White	#63
1974	All in Love Is Fair	Barbra Streisand	#63
1974	It's Been a Long Time	The New Birth	#66
1974	Shoe Shoe Shine	Dynamic Superiors	#68
1974	Time Will Tell	Tower of Power	#69
1974	The Player – Part 1	First Choice	#70
1974	Sleepin'	Diana Ross	#70
1974	Wonderful	Isaac Hayes	#71
1974	Give Me a Reason to Be Gone	Maureen McGovern	#71
1974	Put a Little Love Away	The Emotions	#73
1974	Stop to Start	Blue Magic	#74
1974	Skybird	Neil Diamond	#75
1974	California My Way	The Main Ingredient	#75
1974	Under the Influence of Love	Love Unlimited	#76
1974	My Main Man	The Staple Singers	#76
1974	How Do You Feel the Morning After	Millie Jackson	#77
1974	Where are All My Friends	Harold Melvin	#80
1974	You Turned My World Around	Frank Sinatra	#83
1974	Dreams are Ten a Penny	The First Class	#83
1974	Tell Me That I'm Wrong	Blood, Sweat & Tears	#83
1974	You Got to Be the One	The Chi-Lites	#83
1974	Loose Booty	Sly & The Family Stone	#84
1974	Best Thing That Ever Happened to Me	The Persuaders	#85
1974	Love Is the Message	MFSB/Three Degrees	#85

ORCHESTRA (cont'd)			
1974	I'm Falling in Love with You	Little Anthony & The Imperials	#86
1974	Let This Be a Lesson to You	The Independents	#88
1974	What Goes Up (Must Come Down)	Tyrone Davis	#89
1974	Ma! (He's Making Eyes at Me)	Lena Zavaroni	#91
1974	Ms. Grace	The Tymes	#91
1974	What's Your Name	Andy & David Williams	#92
1974	A Mother for My Children	The Whispers	#92
1974	Good Things Don't Last Forever	Ecstasy, Passion & Pain	#93
1974	I Wish It Was Me You Loved	The Dells	#94
1974	Love That Really Counts	Natural Four	#98
1975	He Don't Love You (Like I Love You)	Tony Orlando & Dawn	#1
1975	Philadelphia Freedom	Elton John	#1
1975	My Eyes Adored You	Frankie Valli	#1
1975	The Hustle	Van McCoy & The Soul City Symphony	#1
1975	I'm Sorry	John Denver	#1
1975	Sky High	Jigsaw	#3
1975	Express	B.T. Express	#4
1975	Only Yesterday	Carpenters	#4
1975	Run Joey Run	David Geddes	#4
1975	Love Won't Let Me Wait	Major Harris	#5
1975	They Just Can't Stop The (Games People Play)	Spinners	#5
1975	Old Days	Chicago	#5
1975	Could It Be Magic	Barry Manilow	#6
1975	Feelings	Morris Albert	#6
1975	This Will Be	Natalie Cole	#6
1975	Swearin' to God	Frankie Valli	#6
1975	Morning Side of the Mountain	Donny & Marie Osmond	#8
1975	What Am I Gonna Do with You	Barry White	#8
1975	Never Can Say Goodbye	Gloria Gaynor	#9
1975	It Only Takes a Minute	Tavares	#10
1975	Brazil	The Ritchie Family	#11
1975	Take Me in Your Arms (Rock Me)	The Doobie Brothers	#11
1975	Our Day Will Come	Frankie Valli	#11
1975	Look in My Eyes Pretty Woman	Tony Orlando & Dawn	#11
1975	The Way We Were/Try to Remember	Gladys Knight & The Pips	#11
1975	Doctor's Orders	Carol Douglas	#11
1975	Only Women	Alice Cooper	#12
1975	That's the Way of the World	Earth, Wind & Fire	#12
1975	Bungle in the Jungle	Jethro Tull	#12
1975	L-O-V-E (Love)	Al Green	#13
1975	Sweet Surrender	John Denver	#13

	ORCHESTRA (cont'd)		
1975	Something Better to Do	Olivia Newton-John	#13
1975	Mornin' Beautiful	Tony Orlando & Dawn	#14
1975	Bad Luck (Part 1)	Harold Melvin	#15
1975	I Want'a Do Something Freaky to You	Leon Haywood	#15
1975	(I Believe) There's Nothing Stronger Than Our Love	Paul Anka with Odia Coates	#15
1975	Up in a Puff of Smoke	Polly Brown	#16
1975	Solitaire	Carpenters	#17
1975	The Last Game of the Season (A Blind Man in the Bleachers)	David Geddes	#18
1975	Shoeshine Boy	Eddie Kendricks	#18
1975	The Last Farewell	Roger Whittaker	#19
1975	My Boy	Elvis Presley	#20
1975	Attitude Dancing	Carly Simon	#21
1975	Satin Soul	The Love Unlimited Orchestra	#22
1975	Just a Little Bit of You	Michael Jackson	#23
1975	Ride 'Em Cowboy	Paul Davis	#23
1975	Peace Pipe	B.T. Express	#31
1975	Main Title (Theme from "Jaws")	John Williams	#32
1975	'Til the World Ends	Three Dog Night	#32
1975	Send in the Clowns	Judy Collins	#36
1975	Look at Me (I'm in Love)	Moments	#39
1975	Give It What You Got	B.T. Express	#40
1975	Love Power	Willie Hutch	#41
1975	Hope That We Can Be Together Soon	Sharon Paige/Harold Melvin	#42
1975	Sexy	MFSB	#42
1975	If Loving You Is Wrong I Don't Want to Be Right	Millie Jackson	#42
1975	Make the World Go Away	Donny & Marie Osmond	#44
1975	Every Day I Have to Cry Some	Arthur Alexander	#45
1975	Change with the Times	Van McCoy	#46
1975	Star on a TV Show	The Stylistics	#47
1975	Sugar Pie Guy (Pt. 1)	The Joneses	#47
1975	Me and Mrs. Jones	Ron Banks/Dramatics	#47
1975	Love Finds Its Own Way	Gladys Knight & The Pips	#47
1975	I Dreamed Last Night	Justin Hayward & John Lodge	#47
1975	Please Pardon Me (You Remind Me of a Friend)	Rufus feat. Chaka Khan	#48
1975	Oh Me, Oh My (Dreams in My Arms)	Al Green	#48
1975	One Beautiful Day	Ecstasy, Passion & Pain	#48
1975	Skybird	Tony Orlando & Dawn	#49
1975	Baby, Hang Up the Phone	Carl Graves	#50
1975	To Each His Own	Faith, Hope & Charity	#50
1975	Get the Cream off the Top	Eddie Kendricks	#50
1975	Can't Give You Anything (But My Love)	The Stylistics	#51

	ORCHESTRA (cont'd)		
1975	Burnin' Thing	Mac Davis	#53
1975	We're Almost There	Michael Jackson	#54
1975	I Am I Am	Smokey Robinson	#56
1975	My Little Lady	Bloodstone	#57
1975	Summer of '42	Biddu Orchestra	#57
1975	Forever Came Today	The Jackson 5	#60
1975	Free Man	South Shore Commission	#61
1975	Brand New Love Affair (Part I & II)	Chicago	#61
1975	Like a Sunday Morning	Lana Cantrell	#63
1975	Happy	Eddie Kendricks	#66
1975	I Got to Pieces	Cotton, Lloyd & Christian	#66
1975	Sooner or Later	The Impressions	#68
1975	I Won't Last a Day Without You/Let Me Be the One	Al Wilson	#70
1975	Thank You Baby	The Stylistics	#70
1975	Flyin' High	The Blackbyrds	#70
1975	Seven Lonely Nights	Four Tops	#71
1975	Showdown	Odia Coates	#71
1975	Alvin Stone (The Birth & Death of a Gangster)	Fantastic Four	#74
1975	Funny How Love Can Be	First Class	#74
1975	Let Me Make Love to You	The O'Jays	#75
1975	Salsoul Hustle	Salsoul Orchestra	#76
1975	Party Music	Pat Lundi	#78
1975	Toby	The Chi-Lites	#78
1975	Don't Cha Love It	The Miracles	#78
1975	The Other Woman	Vicki Lawrence	#81
1975	(I'm Going By) The Stars in Your Eyes	The Dramatics	#81
1975	A Hurricane Is Coming Tonite	Carol Douglas	#81
1975	We May Never Love Like This Again	Maureen McGovern	#83
1975	I Want to Dance with You (Dance with Me)	The Ritchie Family	#84
1975	Isn't It Lonely Together	Stark & McBrien	#85
1975	I'll Be Holding On	Al Downing	#85
1975	Life and Death in G & A	Love Childs Afro Cuban Blues Band	#90
1975	The Zip	MFSB	#91
1975	99 Miles from L.A.	Albert Hammond	#91
1975	When You're Young and in Love	The Choice Four	#91
1975	Don't Leave Me in the Morning	Odia Coates	#91
1975	For Your Love	Christopher Paul & Shawn	#91
1975	Shackin' Up	Barbara Mason	#91
1975	Rolling Down a Mountainside	The Main Ingredient	#92
1975	Chocolate Chip	Isaac Hayes	#92
1975	House of Strangers	Jim Gilstrap	#93

	ORCHESTRA (cont'd)		
1975	Three Steps from True Love	The Reflections	#94
1975	When You're Young and in Love	Ralph Carter	#95
1975	I Believe in Father Christmas	Greg Lake	#95
1975	I Just Can't Say Goodbye	Philly Devotions	#95
1975	The Little Drummer Boy	Moonlion	#95
1975	Chase the Clouds Away	Chuck Mangione	#96
1975	One Man Band	Leo Sayer	#96
1975	Hurt	The Manhattans	#97
1975	Honey Trippin'	The Mystic Moods	#98
1975	Sunday Sunrise	Anne Murray	#98
1975	(If You Want It) Do It Yourself	Gloria Gaynor	#98
1975	Walk on By	Gloria Gaynor	#98
1975	I Don't Want to Be a Lone Ranger	Johnny "Guitar" Watson	#99
1975	(Call Me Your) Anything Man	Bobby Moore	#99
1975	Where Have They Gone	Jimmy Beaumont & The Skyliners	#100
1975	Remember the Rain?	The 21st Century	#100
1976	Kiss and Say Goodbye	Manhattans	#1
1976	If You Leave Me Now	Chicago	#1
1976	A Fifth of Beethoven	Walter Murphy	#1
1976	Disco Duck (Part 1)	Rick Dees	#1
1976	I Write the Songs	Barry Manilow	#1
1976	Theme from Mahogany (Do You Know Where You're Going To)	Diana Ross	#1
1976	Theme from S.W.A.T.	Rhythm Heritage	#1
1976	You'll Never Find Another Love Like Mine	Lou Rawls	#2
1976	I Love Music (Part 1)	O'Jays	#5
1976	Sweet Love	Commodores	#5
1976	Times of Your Life	Paul Anka	#7
1976	Just to Be Close to You	Commodores	#7
1976	Beth	Kiss	#7
1976	Breaking Up Is Hard to Do	Neil Sedaka	#8
1976	Walk Away From Love	David Ruffin	#9
1976	Turn the Beat Around	Vickie Sue Robinson	#10
1976	Tryin' to Get the Feeling Again	Barry Manilow	#10
1976	Let Her In	John Travolta	#10
1976	Never Gonna Fall in Love Again	Eric Carmen	#11
1976	A Little Bit More	Dr. Hook	#11
1976	If You Know What I Mean	Neil Diamond	#11
1976	Wake Up Everybody (Part 1)	Harold Melvin	#12
1976	Fanny (Be Tender with My Love)	Bee Gees	#12
1976	I Only Want to Be with You	Bay City Rollers	#12

		ORCHESTRA (cont'd)	
1976	Baby Face	The Wing and a Prayer Fife and Drum Corps.	#14
1976	Heaven Must Be Missing an Angel (Part 1)	Tavares	#15
1976	Love in the Shadows	Neil Sedaka	#16
1976	The Best Disco in Town	The Ritchie Family	#17
1976	Tangerine	The Salsoul Orchestra	#18
1976	Love Ballad	L.T.D.	#20
1976	Baretta's Theme ("Keep Your Eye on the Sparrow")	Rhythm Heritage	#20
1976	Young Hearts Run Free	Candi Staton	#20
1976	I Need to Be in Love	Carpenters	#25
1976	One Love in My Lifetime	Diana Ross	#25
1976	Just You and I	Melissa Manchester	#27
1976	Save Your Kisses for Me	Brotherhood of Man	#27
1976	I've Got a Feeling (We'll Be Seeing Each Other Again)	Al Wilson	#29
1976	Looking for Space	John Denver	#29
1976	I Can't Hear You More	Helen Reddy	#29
1976	Nice 'N' Naasty	The Salsoul Orchestra	#30
1976	Love Fire	Jigsaw	#30
1976	Inseparable	Natalie Cole	#32
1976	Anytime (I'll Be There)	Paul Anka	#33
1976	Don't Take Away the Music	Tavares	#34
1976	I.O.U.	Jimmy Dean	#35
1976	He's a Friend	Eddie Kendricks	#36
1976	Love or Leave	Spinners	#36
1976	C'mon Marianne	Donny Osmond	#38
1976	It's Over	Boz Scaggs	#38
1976	Give It Up (Turn It Loose)	Tyrone Davis	#38
1976	Silver Star	The Four Seasons	#38
1976	Whenever I'm Away from You	John Travolta	#38
1976	Still Crazy After All These Years	Paul Simon	#40
1976	I'm Gonna Let My Heart Do the Walking	The Supremes	#40
1976	The Homecoming	Hagood Hardy	#41
1976	Flight '76	Walter Murphy	#44
1976	Venus	Frankie Avalon	#46
1976	I Can't Live a Dream	The Osmonds	#46
1976	Down to Love Town	The Originals	#47
1976	Heavy Love	David Ruffin	#47
1976	I Thought It Took a Little Time (But Today I Fell in Love)	Diana Ross	#47
1976	My Sweet Summer Suite	The Love Unlimited Orchestra	#48
1976	Mr. Melody	Natalie Cole	#49
1976	Everything's Coming Up Love	David Ruffin	#49
1976	Message in Our Music	The O'Jays	#49

	ORCHESTRA (cont'd)		
1976	Can't Stop Groovin' Now, Wanna Do It Some More	B.T. Express	#52
1976	Ten Percent	Double Exposure	#54
1976	Let's Be Young Tonight	Jermaine Jackson	#55
1976	Street Talk	B.C.G. (B.C. Generation)	#56
1976	Wake Up Susan	Spinners	#56
1976	Baby, I'll Give It to You	Seals & Crofts	#58
1976	Vaya Con Dios	Freddy Fender	#59
1976	I Cheat the Hangman	The Doobie Brothers	#60
1976	Lipstick	Michel Polnareff	#61
1976	Everyday Without You	Hamilton, Joe Frank & Reynolds	#62
1976	Breezin'	George Benson	#63
1976	Daylight	Vickie Sue Robinson	#63
1976	Groovy People	Lou Rawls	#64
1976	Sixteen Reasons	LaVerne & Shirley	#65
1976	Growin' Up	Dan Hill	#67
1976	It's Cool	The Tymes	#68
1976	Party	Van McCoy	#69
1976	Catfish	Four Tops	#71
1976	I Could Have Danced All Night	Biddu Orchestra	#72
1976	There Won't Be No Country Music (There Won't Be No Rock 'N' Roll)	C.W. McCall	#73
1976	The Lonely One	Special Delivery	#75
1976	Save Your Kisses for Me	Bobby Vinton	#75
1976	Funky Weekend	The Stylistics	#76
1976	Make Love to Your Mind	Bill Withers	#76
1976	We're All Alone	Frankie Valli	#78
1976	You Are Beautiful	The Stylistics	#78
1976	The Game Is Over (What's the Matter with You)	Brown Sugar	#79
1976	Party Line	The Andrea True Connection	#80
1976	Once a Fool	Kiki Dee	#82
1976	Close to You	B.T. Express	#82
1976	Every Beat of My Heart	Crown Heights Affair	#83
1976	Train Called Freedom	South Shore Commission	#86
1976	Words (Are Impossible)	Donny Gerrard	#87
1976	You're Fooling You	The Dramatics	#87
1976	You're Just the Right Size	Salsoul Orchestra	#88
1976	Music	John Miles	#88
1976	Daydreamer	C.C. & Company	#91
1976	This Is It	Melba Moore	#91
1976	Disco Sax	Houston Person	#91
1976	Full Time Thing (Between Dusk and Dawn)	Whirlwind	#91
1976	Happy Man (Pt. 1)	Impact	#94

	ORCHESTRA (cont'd)		
1976	Wow	Andre Gagnon	#95
1976	Night Walk	Van McCoy	#96
1976	All Roads (Lead Back to You)	Donny Most	#97
1976	Moonlight Serenade	Bobby Vinton	#97
1976	Tubular Bells	Champs' Boys Orchestra	#98
1976	Tonight's the Night	S.S.O.	#99
1976	I Don't Wanna Leave You	Debbie Taylor	#100
1977	Best of My Love	Emotions	#1
1977	Star Wars Theme/Cantina Band	Meco	#1
1977	Car Wash	Rose Royce	#1
1977	You Don't Have to Be a Star (To Be in My Show)	Marilyn McCoo & Billy Davis, Jr.	#1
1977	Gonna Fly Now	Bill Conti	#1
1977	Don't Give Up on Us	David Soul	#1
1977	Looks Like We Made It	Barry Manilow	#1
1977	Nobody Does It Better	Carly Simon	#2
1977	My Heart Belongs to Me	Barbra Streisand	#4
1977	Easy	Commodores	#4
1977	It's Ecstasy When You Lady Down Next to Me	Barry White	#4
1977	Baby, What a Big Surprise	Chicago	#4
1977	I've Got Love on My Mind	Natalie Cole	#5
1977	After the Lovin'	Engelbert Humperdinck	#8
1977	You and Me	Alice Cooper	#9
1977	Weekend in New England	Barry Manilow	#10
1977	Boogie Child	Bee Gees	#12
1977	Your Love	Marilyn McCoo & Billy Davis, Jr.	#15
1977	You're My World	Helen Reddy	#18
1977	Slow Dancin' Don't Turn Me On	Addrisi Bros.	#20
1977	Love's Grown Deep	Kenny Nolan	#20
1977	Disco Lucy (I Love Lucy Theme)	Wilton Place Street Band	#24
1977	Uptown Festival (Part 1)	Shalamar	#25
1977	Gloria	Enchantment	#25
1977	I Believe You	Dorothy Moore	#27
1977	Whispering/Cherchez La Femme/Se Si Bon	Dr. Buzzard's Original Savannah Band	#27
1977	Slide	Slave	#32
1977	Calling Occupants of Interplanetary Craft	Carpenters	#32
1977	Slowdown	John Miles	#34
1977	All You Get from Love Is a Love Song	Carpenters	#35
1977	Love in 'C' Minor – Pt. 1	Cerrone	#36
1977	Devil's Gun	C.J. & Co.	#36
1977	Keep Me Cryin'	Al Green	#37
1977	Somethin' 'Bout 'Cha	Latimore	#37

		ORCHESTRA (cont'd)	
1977	Magical Mystery Tour	Ambrosia	#39
1977	Do Your Dance – Part 1	Rose Royce	#39
1977	Doctor Love	First Choice	#41
1977	I Don't Love You Anymore	Teddy Pendergrass	#41
1977	You're Throwing a Good Love Away	Spinners	#43
1977	Do It to My Mind	Johnny Bristol	#43
1977	Sunshine	Enchantment	#45
1977	Theme from Charlie's Angels	Henry Mancini	#45
1977	Love in 'C' Minor	Heart & Soul Orchestra	#46
1977	If It's the Last Thing I Do	Thelma Houston	#47
1977	You + Me = Love	Undisputed Truth	#48
1977	Ha Cha Cha (Funktion)	Brass Construction	#51
1977	Silver Lady	David Soul	#52
1977	Baby Don't Change Your Mind	Gladys Knight & The Pips	#52
1977	You Take My Heart Away	James Darren	#52
1977	Be My Girl	The Dramatics	#53
1977	Disco Inferno	The Trammps	#53
1977	Going in with My Eyes Open	David Soul	#53
1977	Dis-Gorilla (Part 1)	Rick Dees	#56
1977	Don't Turn the Light Out	Cliff Richard	#57
1977	"Roots" Medley	Quincy Jones	#57
1977	Sing	Tony Orlando & Dawn	#58
1977	When Love Is New	Arthur Prysock	#64
1977	I Gotta Keep Dancin'	Carrie Lucas	#64
1977	It Feels So Good to Be Loved So Bad	The Manhattans	#66
1977	See You When I Git There	Lou Rawls	#66
1977	Theme from King Kong (Pt. 1)	Love Unlimited Orchestra	#68
1977	Gonna Love You More	George Benson	#71
1977	Sorry	Grace Jones	#71
1977	Any Way You Want Me	The Sylvers	#72
1977	Dreamin'	Loleatta Holloway	#72
1977	Darlin' Darlin' Baby (Sweet, Tender, Love)	O'Jays	#72
1977	Reaching for the World	Harold Melvin	#74
1977	Does She Do It Like She Dances	Addrisi Brothers	#74
1977	Everybody Ought to Be in Love	Paul Anka	#75
1977	Still the Lovin' Is Fun	B.J. Thomas	#77
1977	Never My Love	Addrisi Brothers	#80
1977	Here Is Where Your Love Belongs	The Sons of Champlin	#80
1977	Bless the Beasts and Children	Barry DeVorzon & Perry Botkin, Jr.	#82
1977	Look Into Your Heart	Aretha Franklin	#82
1977	Land of Make Believe	Chuck Mangione w/Esther Saterfield	#86

	ORCHESTRA (cont'd)		
1977	Heaven on Earth (So Fine)	Spinners	#89
1977	Fire Sign	Cory	#89
1977	This Will Be a Night to Remember	Eddie Holman	#90
1977	Feel the Need	Detroit Emeralds	#90
1977	Save Me	Donna McDaniel	#90
1977	Some Enchanted Evening	Jane Olivor	#91
1977	C'est La Vie	Greg Lake	#91
1977	My Cherie Amour	Soul Train Gang	#92
1977	I Caught Your Act	The Hues Corporation	#92
1977	Feelings	Walter Jackson	#93
1977	If I Have to Go Away	Jigsaw	#93
1977	Make It with You	The Whispers	#94
1977	Theme from "Rocky" (Gonna Fly Now)	Rhythm Heritage	#94
1977	Since I Fell for You/I'm Falling in Love	Hodges, James and Smith	#96
1977	Ma Baker	Boney M	#96
1977	My Eyes Get Blurry	Kenny Nolan	#97
1977	Discomania	The Lovers	#100
1977	For Elise	The Philharmonics	#100
1977	Dance Little Lady Dance	Danny White	#100
1978	Shadow Dancing	Andy Gibb	#1
1978	MacArthur Park	Donna Summer	#1
1978	Grease	Frankie Valli	#1
1978	Last Dance	Donna Summer	#3
1978	Reminiscing	Little River Band	#3
1978	Use Ta Be My Girl	The O'Jays	#4
1978	Dance, Dance, Dance (Yowsah, Yowsah, Yowsah)	Chic	#6
1978	Dance with Me	Peter Brown w/Betty Wright	#8
1978	Copacabana (At the Copa)	Barry Manilow	#8
1978	Ready to Take a Chance Again	Barry Manilow	#11
1978	Theme from "Close Encounters of the Third Kind"	John Williams	#13
1978	Falling	LeBlanc & Carr	#13
1978	Don't Let Me Be Misunderstood	Santa Esmeralda w/ Leroy Gomez	#15
1978	Desiree	Neil Diamond	#16
1978	Sweet Life	Paul Davis	#17
1978	I Can't Stand the Rain	Eruption	#17
1978	Native New Yorker	Odyssey	#21
1978	Thank God It's Friday	Love and Kisses	#22
1978	If Ever I See You Again	Robert Flack	#24
1978	Theme from "Close Encounters of the Third Kind"	Meco	#25
1978	Macho Man	Village People	#25

	ORCHESTRA (cont'd)		
1978	Close the Door	Teddy Pendergrass	#25
1978	Lovely Day	Bill Withers	#30
1978	Fantasy	Earth, Wind & Fire	#32
1978	More Than a Woman	Tavares	#32
1978	Run for Home	Lindisfarne	#33
1978	It's You That I Need	Enchantment	#33
1978	Themes from "The Wizard of Oz"	Meco	#35
1978	Will You Still Love Me Tomorrow	Dave Mason	#39
1978	I Don't Wanna Go	Joey Travolta	#43
1978	Got to Have Loving	Don Ray	#44
1978	Cocomotion	El Coco	#44
1978	Little One	Chicago	#44
1978	Holding On (When Love Is Gone)	L.T.D.	#49
1978	The Next Hundred Years	Al Martino	#49
1978	If My Friends Could See Me Now	Linda Clifford	#54
1978	Never Get Enough of Your Love	L.T.D.	#56
1978	Put Your Head on My Shoulder	Leif Garrett	#58
1978	Your Sweetness Is My Weakness	Barry White	#60
1978	I Believe You	Carpenters	#68
1978	Let's Live Together	Cazz	#70
1978	Cuz It's You, Girl	James Walsh Gypsy Band	#71
1978	Ooh Boy	Rose Royce	#72
1978	Runaway Love	Linda Clifford	#76
1978	The House of the Rising Sun	Santa Esmeralda	#78
1978	Love Me Right	Denise LaSalle	#80
1978	We Fell in Love While Dancing	Bill Brandon	#80
1978	I Can't Wait Any Longer	Bill Anderson	#80
1978	I Love You, I Love You, I Love You	Ronnie McDowell	#81
1978	Come Go with Me	Pockets	#84
1978	Take Me I'm Yours	Michael Henderson	#88
1978	Dancing in Paradise	El Coco	#91
1978	Don't Let It Show	Alan Parsons Project	#92
1978	Ain't Gonna Hurt Nobody	Brick	#92
1978	Miss Broadway	Belle Epoque	#92
1978	Number One	Eloise Laws	#97
1979	Reunited	Peaches & Herb	#1
1979	I Will Survive	Gloria Gaynor	#1
1979	Too Much Heaven	Bee Gees	#1
1979	Tragedy	Bee Gees	#1
1979	No More Tears (Enough Is Enough)	Barbra Streisand/Donna Summer	#1
1979	Still	Commodores	#1

	ORCHESTRA (cont'd)		
1979	Don't Stop 'til You Get Enough	Michael Jackson	#1
1979	Y.M.C.A.	Village People	#2
1979	The Main Event/Fight	Barbara Streisand	#3
1979	Heaven Knows	Donna Summer w/Brooklyn Dreams	#4
1979	Sail On	Commodores	#4
1979	Shake Your Groove Thing	Peaches & Herb	#5
1979	I'll Never Love This Way Again	Dionne Warwick	#5
1979	Makin' It	David Naughton	#5
1979	Boogie Wonderland	Earth, Wind & Fire/The Emotions	#6
1979	I Want Your Love	Chic	#7
1979	Mama Can't Buy You Love	Elton John	#9
1979	Ships	Barry Manilow	#9
1979	Somewhere in the Night	Barry Manilow	#9
1979	I Was Made for Dancin'	Leif Garrett	#10
1979	Got to Be Real	Cheryl Lynn	#12
1979	Every Time I Think of You	The Babys	#13
1979	Come to Me	France Joli	#15
1979	Born to Be Alive	Patrick Hernandez	#16
1979	Different Worlds	Maureen McGovern	#18
1979	The Boss	Diana Ross	#19
1979	What Cha Gonna Do with My Lovin'	Stephanie Mills	#22
1979	Damned if I Do	Alan Parsons Project	#27
1979	Up on the Roof	James Taylor	#28
1979	Every Which Way but Loose	Eddie Rabbitt	#30
1979	Don't You Write Her Off	McGuinn, Clark & Hillman	#33
1979	Saturday Night, Sunday Morning	Thelma Houston	#34
1979	Found a Cure	Ashford & Simpson	#36
1979	Street Life	Crusaders	#36
1979	You Can Do It	Niteflyte	#37
1979	Good Friend	Mary MacGregor	#39
1979	Bridge Over Troubled Waters	Linda Clifford	#41
1979	Let Me Know (I Have a Right)	Gloria Gaynor	#42
1979	Got to Give in to Love	Bonnie Boyer	#43
1979	Get It Up	Ronnie Milsap	#43
1979	Diamonds	Chris Rea	#44
1979	We've Got Love	Peaches & Herb	#44
1979	Go West	Village People	#45
1979	Ghost Dancer	Addrisi Brothers	#45
1979	You Stepped Into My Life	Melba Moore	#47
1979	Turn Off the Lights	Teddy Pendergrass	#48
1979	I Need Your Help Barry Manilow	Ray Stevens	#49

	ORCHESTRA (cont'd)		
1979	One More Minute	Saint Tropez	#49
1979	Ready for the 80's	Village People	#52
1979	Can You Read My Mind	Maureen McGovern	#52
1979	At Midnight	T-Connection	#56
1979	In the Stone	Earth, Wind & Fire	#58
1979	This Moment in Time	Engelbert Humperdinck	#58
1979	Pops, We Love You (A Tribute to Father)	Diana Ross, Marvin Gaye, Smokey Robinson & Stevie Wonder	#59
1979	Make Love to Me	Helen Reddy	#60
1979	A Little Lovin' (Keeps the Doctor Away)	The Raes	#61
1979	Roller-Skatin' Mate (Part 1)	Peaches & Herb	#66
1979	Light My Fire/137 Disco Heaven	Amii Stewart	#69
1979	Dance with You	Carrie Lucas	#70
1979	Sinner Man	Sarah Dash	#71
1979	Night Dancin'	Taka Boom	#74
1979	Theme from Ice Castles (Through the Eyes of Love)	Melissa Manchester	#76
1979	Pow Wow	Cory Daye	#76
1979	Take That to the Bank	Shalamar	#79
1979	Cuba	Gibson Brothers	#81
1979	Theme from Superman (Main Title)	John Williams	#81
1979	Rocky II Disco	Maynard Ferguson	#82
1979	Touch Me Baby	Ultimate	#82
1979	I Never Said I Love You	Orsa Lia	#84
1979	The Man with the Child in His Eyes	Kate Bush	#85
1979	Whole Lotta Love	The Wonder Band	#87
1979	Ain't That Enough for You	John Davis	#89
1979	This Is It	Dan Hartman	#91

ORGAN

For the "length of solo" column, only organ solos that are ten seconds or longer are included.

YEAR	SONG	ARTIST	HOT 100	LENGTH OF SOLO
1970	Venus	The Shocking Blue	#1	
1970	The Rapper	The Jaggerz	#2	
1970	Ball of Confusion (That's What the World Is Today)	The Temptations	#3	
1970	Gypsy Woman	Brian Hyland	#3	
1970	Green-Eyed Lady	Sugarloaf	#3	32 sec.
1970	Rainy Night in Georgia	Brook Benton	#4	
1970	Ma Belle Amie	The Tee Set	#5	

ORGAN (cont'd)				
1970	Tighter, Tighter	Alive & Kicking	#7	
1970	Evil Ways	Santana	#9	35 sec.
1970	Cry Me a River	Joe Cocker	#11	28 sec.
1970	Lay a Little Lovin' on Me	Robin McNamara	#11	
1970	Hi-De-Ho	Blood, Sweat & Tears	#14	
1970	Out in the Country	Three Dog Night	#15	23 sec.
1970	Celebrate	Three Dog Night	#15	
1970	Be My Baby	Andy Kim	#17	16 sec.
1970	After Midnight	Eric Clapton	#18	
1970	God, Love and Rock & Roll	Teegarden & Van Winkle	#22	10 sec.
1970	Spirit in the Dark	Aretha Franklin w/The Dixie Flyers	#23	
1970	Ain't It Funky Now (Part 1)	James Brown	#24	
1970	Sugar Sugar	Wilson Pickett	#25	
1970	Up on Cripple Creek	The Band	#25	
1970	Save the Country	The 5th Dimension	#27	
1970	Viva Tirado – Part 1	El Chicano	#28	
1970	She Came in Through the Bathroom Window	Joe Cocker	#30	22 sec.
1970	As the Years Go By	Mashmakhan	#31	
1970	Ungena Za Ulimwengu (Unite the World)	The Temptations	#33	
1970	Jennifer Tomkins	Street People	#36	
1970	Point It Out	Smokey Robinson & The Miracles	#37	
1970	Border Song (Holy Moses)	Aretha Franklin	#37	
1970	Monster	Steppenwolf	#39	
1970	When Julie Comes Around	The Cuff Links	#41	
1970	How Can I Forget	Marvin Gaye	#41	
1970	Take a Look Around	Smith	#43	
1970	Soul Shake	Delaney & Bonnie & Friends	#43	
1970	Gotta Get Back to You	Tommy James & The Shondells	#45	
1970	We Can Make Music	Tommy Roe	#49	
1970	Pearl	Tommy Roe	#50	11 sec.
1970	To the Other Woman (I'm the Other Woman)	Doris Duke	#50	
1970	Chicken Strut	The Meters	#50	
1970	(Don't Try to Lay No Boogie Woogie on the) "King of Rock & Roll"	Crow	#52	25 sec.
1970	Who Needs Ya	Steppenwolf	#54	
1970	Something	Shirley Bassey	#55	
1970	Cottage Cheese	Crow	#56	12 sec.
1970	Look-Ka Py Py	The Meters	#56	
1970	Je T'Aime…Moi Non Plus	Jane Birkin & Serge Gainsbourg	#58	
1970	Glory Glory	The Rascals	#58	
1970	Big Leg Woman (With a Short Short Mini Skirt)	Israel Tolbert	#61	

	ORGAN (cont'd)			
1970	Why Should I Cry	The Gentrys	#61	
1970	Screaming Night Hog	Steppenwolf	#62	
1970	Superman	The Ides of March	#64	
1970	Easy Rider (Let the Wind Pay the Way)	Iron Butterfly	#66	
1970	You, Me and Mexico	Edward Bear	#68	
1970	1984	Spirit	#69	
1970	Just Let It Come	Alive 'N Kickin'	#69	
1970	If Walls Could Talk	Little Milton	#71	
1970	My Way	Brook Benton	#72	
1970	What Am I Gonna Do	Smith	#73	
1970	Empty Pages	Traffic	#74	
1970	Long and Lonesome Road	The Shocking Blue	#75	
1970	Something	Booker T. & The M.G.'s	#76	
1970	Stoned Cowboy	Fantasy	#77	
1970	Black Hands White Cotton	The Caboose	#79	
1970	I Got a Thing, You Got a Thing, Everybody's Got a Thing	Funkadelic	#80	
1970	Got to Believe in Love	Robin McNamara	#80	
1970	I Who Have Nothing	Liquid Smoke	#82	
1970	Whiter Shade of Pale	R.B. Greaves	#82	22, 18 sec.
1970	This Is My Love Song	The Intruders	#85	
1970	Dreams	Buddy Miles	#86	
1970	Country Preacher	Cannonball Adderley	#86	
1970	Think About Your Children	Mary Hopkin	#87	
1970	Get Down People	Fabulous Counts	#88	46 sec.
1970	Take It off Him and Put It on Me	Clarence Carter	#94	
1970	Don't Worry Baby	The Tokens	#95	11 sec.
1970	Time to Get It Together	Country Coalition	#96	
1970	Want You to Know	Rotary Connection	#96	
1970	Oh My My	The Monkees	#98	
1970	Laughin' and Clownin'	Ray Charles	#98	
1970	I Heard the Voice of Jesus	Turley Richards	#99	
1970	Sing Out the Love (In My Heart)	Arkade	#99	
1970	Move Me, O Wondrous Music	Ray Charles Singers	#99	
1970	Listen Here	Brian Auger/The Trinity	#100	
1970	Don't Let the Music Slip Away	Archie Bell & The Drells	#100	
1970	Sparkle and Shine	The Clique	#100	
1971	Maggie May	Rod Stewart	#1	
1971	Me and Bobby McGee	Janis Joplin	#1	11 sec.
1971	Mr. Big Stuff	Jean Knight	#2	
1971	Spanish Harlem	Aretha Franklin	#2	
1971	Signs	Five Man Electrical Band	#3	

		ORGAN (cont'd)			
1971	Black Magic Woman	Santana	#4	
1971	Draggin' the Line	Tommy James	#4	
1971	Do You Know What I Mean	Lee Michaels	#6	
1971	Liar	Three Dog Night	#7	
1971	Sweet Mary	Wadsworth Mansion	#7	
1971	Chick-A-Boom (Don't Ya Jes' Love It)	Daddy Dewdrop	#9	
1971	Sooner or Later	The Grass Roots	#9	
1971	Lover Her Madly	The Doors	#11	
1971	Everybody's Everything	Santana	#12	27 sec.
1971	I Don't Know How to Love Him	Helen Reddy	#13	
1971	Oye Como Va	Santana	#13	
1971	Love the One You're With	Stephen Stills	#14	
1971	Won't Get Fooled Again	The Who	#15	
1971	Easy Loving	Freddie Hart	#17	
1971	Born to Wander	Rare Earth	#17	
1971	Don't Let the Green Grass Fool You	Wilson Pickett	#17	
1971	One Man Band	Three Dog Night	#19	
1971	Only You Know and I Know	Delaney & Bonnie	#20	15 sec.
1971	Get It On	Chase	#24	13 sec.
1971	I Don't Know How to Love Him	Yvonne Elliman	#28	
1971	Cool Aid	Paul Humphrey	#29	
1971	Baby Let Me Kiss You	King Floyd	#29	
1971	Hallelujah	Sweathog	#33	
1971	Where Did They Go, Lord	Elvis Presley	#33	
1971	Chicago	Graham Nash	#34	
1971	Lowdown	Chicago	#35	
1971	All Day Music	War	#35	13 sec.
1971	D.O.A.	Bloodrick	#36	
1971	Resurrection Shuffle	Tom Jones	#38	
1971	I Likes to Do It	The People's Choice	#38	
1971	Can I Get a Witness	Lee Michaels	#39	
1971	Where You Lead	Barbra Streisand	#40	
1971	I'm Comin' Home	Tommy James	#40	
1971	Marianne	Stephen Stills	#42	
1971	Cry Baby	Janis Joplin	#42	
1971	Melting Pot	Booker T. & The M.G.'s	#45	
1971	She Didn't Do Magic	Lobo	#46	
1971	13 Questions	Seatrain	#49	
1971	Bridget the Midget (The Queen of the Blues)	Ray Stevens	#50	
1971	They Can't Take Away Our Music	Eric Burdon & War	#50	
1971	I'm a Believer	Neil Diamond	#51	

		ORGAN (cont'd)			
1971	Ride with Me	Steppenwolf	#52	
1971	God Bless Whoever Sent You	The Originals	#53	
1971	Lonely Teardrops	Brian Hyland	#54	
1971	Tongue in Cheek	Sugarloaf	#55	35 sec.
1971	Follow Me	Mary Travers	#56	
1971	It's for You	Springwell	#60	
1971	We Were Always Sweethearts	Boz Scaggs	#61	
1971	Reason to Believe	Rod Stewart	#62	
1971	Gypsy Queen – Part 1	Gypsy	#62	45 sec.
1971	For Ladies Only	Steppenwolf	#64	
1971	Gimme Some Lovin'-Pt. 1	Traffic	#68	
1971	Nevada Fighter	Michael Nesmith	#70	35 sec.
1971	Tightrope Ride	The Doors	#71	
1971	What You See Is What You Get	Stoney & Meatloaf	#71	
1971	You're a Big Girl Now	The Stylistics	#73	
1971	Holly Holy	Jr. Walker/The All Stars	#75	
1971	You Send Me	Ponderosa Twins + One	#78	
1971	Get It While You Can	Janis Joplin	#78	
1971	Mother	Barbra Streisand	#79	
1971	It's the Real Thing – Pt. 1	The Electric Express	#81	
1971	Amanda	Dionne Warwick	#83	
1971	Handbags and Gladrags	Chase	#84	
1971	We Got to Live Together – part 1	Buddy Miles	#86	
1971	Mother Nature's Wine	Sugarloaf	#88	
1971	Spinning Wheel (Pt. 1)	James Brown	#90	
1971	My Sweet Lord	Billy Preston	#90	
1971	Take My Hand	Kenny Rogers & The First Edition	#91	30 sec.
1971	A Long Time, A Long Way to Go	Todd Rundgren	#92	
1971	Mandrill	Mandrill	#94	
1971	Love Me	The Rascals	#95	
1971	Stop! In the Name of Love	Margie Joseph	#96	
1971	Near You	Boz Scaggs	#96	
1971	I Been Moved	Andy Kim	#97	
1972	Outa-Space	Billy Preston	#2	
1972	Mother and Child Reunion	Paul Simon	#4	
1972	Never Been to Spain	Three Dog Night	#5	
1972	Hold Your Head Up	Argent	#5	
1972	Joy	Apollo 100	#6	
1972	Good Time Charlie's Got the Blues	Danny O'Keefe	#9	
1972	Sweet Seasons	Carole King	#9	
1972	The Family of Man	Three Dog Night	#12	

		ORGAN (cont'd)		
1972	Roundabout	Yes	#13	12 sec.
1972	You Wear It Well	Rod Stewart	#13	
1972	Slippin' into Darkness	War	#16	
1972	Conquistador	Procol Harum	#16	
1972	Hey Big Brother	Rare Earth	#19	
1972	Long Dark Road	The Hollies	#26	
1972	Ask Me What You Want	Millie Jackson	#27	
1972	Rock 'N Roll Soul	Grand Funk Railroad	#29	
1972	Small Beginnings	Flash	#29	
1972	Footstompin' Music	Grand Funk Railroad	#29	33, 14 sec.
1972	Don't Do It	The Band	#34	
1972	All the Young Dudes	Mott the Hoople	#37	
1972	Easy Livin	Uriah Heep	#39	
1972	Looking for a Love	J. Geils Band	#39	
1972	Ain't Nobody Home	B.B. King	#46	
1972	Slaughter	Billy Preston	#50	16, 26 sec.
1972	Trouble in My Home	Joe Simon	#50	
1972	Hot 'N' Tasty	Humble Pie	#52	
1972	I'm Movin' On	John Kay	#52	
1972	Woman Don't Go Astray	King Floyd	#53	
1972	Son of Shaft	The Bar-Kays	#53	
1972	In a Broken Dream	Python Lee Jackson (Rod Stewart)	#56	
1972	It Doesn't Matter	Stephen Stills	#61	
1972	What'd I Say	Rare Earth	#61	
1972	That's the Way God Planned It	Billy Preston	#65	
1972	If You Let Me	Eddie Kendricks	#66	
1972	What Would the Children Think	Rick Springfield	#70	
1972	After All This Time	Merry Clayton	#71	
1972	If I Were a Carpenter	Bob Seger	#76	44 sec.
1972	I Wrote a Simple Song	Billy Preston	#77	
1972	Get Up and Get Down	Dramatics	#78	
1972	What a Wonderful Thing We Have	Fabulous Rhinestones	#78	
1972	Amerikan Music	Steve Alaimo	#79	
1972	The Young New Mexican Puppeteer	Tom Jones	#80	
1972	Best Thing	Styx	#82	
1972	Simple Song of Freedom	Buckwheat	#84	
1972	The Mosquito	The Doors	#85	26 sec.
1972	Summer Sun	Jamestown Massacre	#90	
1972	Eve	Jim Capaldi	#91	
1972	I Got a Thing About You Baby	Billy Lee Riley	#93	
1972	Mendelssohn's 4th (Second Movement)	Apollo 100	#94	

ORGAN (cont'd)

1972	Celebration	Tommy James	#95	
1972	Hushabye	Robert John	#99	
1972	The Road We Didn't Take	Freda Payne	#100	
1973	Will It Go Round in Circles	Billy Preston	#1	
1973	Playground in My Mind	Clint Holmes	#2	15 sec.
1973	Why Can't We Live Together	Timmy Thomas	#3	
1973	Space Race	Billy Preston	#4	
1973	Smoke on the Water	Deep Purple	#4	
1973	Hello It's Me	Todd Rundgren	#5	
1973	Hocus Pocus	Focus	#9	
1973	Rockin' Roll Baby	The Stylistics	#14	
1973	Let Me Serenade You	Three Dog Night	#17	
1973	Give It to Me	The J. Geils Band	#30	34 sec.
1973	Ecstasy	Ohio Players	#31	
1973	Jimmy Loves Mary-Anne	Looking Glass	#33	13 sec.
1973	A Letter to Myself	The Chi-Lites	#33	
1973	Sweet Understanding Love	Four Tops	#33	
1973	Oh La De Da	The Staple Singers	#33	
1973	Jesus Is Just Alright	The Doobie Brothers	#35	
1973	Goin' Home	The Osmonds	#36	
1973	Close Your Eyes	Edward Bear	#37	
1973	I Can't Stand the Rain	Ann Peebles	#38	
1973	I'll Be Your Shelter (In Time of Storm)	Luther Ingram	#40	
1973	Tell Her She's Lovely	El Chicano	#40	
1973	Drinking Wine Spo-Dee O'Dee	Jerry Lee Lewis	#41	
1973	You Can't Always Get What You Want	The Rolling Stones	#42	
1973	Sexy, Sexy, Sexy	James Brown	#50	
1973	Fencewalk	Mandrill	#52	
1973	Don't Leave Me Starvin' for Your Love (Part 1)	Holland-Dozier	#52	
1973	Isn't It About Time	Stephen Stills & Manassas	#56	
1973	What My Baby Needs Now Is a Little More Lovin'	James Brown-Lyn Collins	#56	
1973	Love and Happiness	Earnest Jackson	#58	
1973	Yesterday I Had the Blues	Harold Melvin	#63	
1973	Always	Luther Ingram	#64	
1973	It's All Over	The Independents	#65	
1973	First Cut Is the Deepest	Keith Hampshire	#70	
1973	If I Were Only a Child Again	Curtis Mayfield	#71	
1973	Back for a Taste of Your Love	Syl Johnson	#72	
1973	People are Changin'	Timmy Thomas	#75	29 sec.
1973	Fever	Rita Coolidge	#76	18 sec.
1973	Am I Black Enough for You	Billy Paul	#79	

		ORGAN (cont'd)			
1973	I Can Make It Thru the Days (But Oh Those Lonely Nights)	Ray Charles	#81	
1973	Hang Loose	Mandrill	#83	
1973	Love Me for What I Am	Lobo	#86	
1973	Sunshine	Mickey Newbury	#87	
1973	Girl You Need a Change of Mind (Part 1)	Eddie Kendrick	#87	
1973	Sylvia	Focus	#89	
1973	If I Could Only Be Sure	Nolan Porter	#89	
1973	We	Shawn Phillips	#89	
1973	Breaking Up Somebody's Home	Albert King	#91	
1973	Stop, Wait & Listen	Circus	#91	
1973	Mr. Skin	Spirit	#92	
1973	L.A. Freeway	Jerry Jeff Walker	#98	
1973	Soul Je T'Aime	Sylvia & Ralfi Pagan	#99	
1974	TSOP (The Sound of Philadelphia)	MFSB/Three Degrees	#1	
1974	I Can Help	Billy Swan	#1	
1974	I Shot the Sheriff	Eric Clapton	#1	
1974	On and On	Gladys Knight & The Pips	#5	
1974	Another Saturday Night	Cat Stevens	#6	
1974	Me and Baby Brother	War	#15	
1974	Save the Last Dance for Me	DeFranco Family	#18	13 sec.
1974	Willie and the Hand Jive	Eric Clapton	#26	
1974	Fallin' in Love	The Souther, Hillman, Furay Band	#27	
1974	Baby Come Close	Smokey Robinson	#27	
1974	Surfin' U.S.A.	The Beach Boys	#36	12 sec.
1974	Blood Is Thicker Than Water	William DeVaughn	#42	
1974	Living in the U.S.A.	Steve Miller Band	#49	
1974	Dance with the Devil	Cozy Powell	#49	
1974	When a Child Is Born	Michael Holm	#53	
1974	What It Comes Down To	Isley Brothers	#55	
1974	You Can't Be a Beacon (If Your Light Don't Shine)	Donna Fargo	#57	
1974	I'll Be Your Everything	Percy Sledge	#62	
1974	Help Yourself	The Undisputed Truth	#63	
1974	I Hate Hate	Razzy Bailey	#67	
1974	Goin' Down Slow	Bobby Blue Bland	#69	
1974	Silly Milly	Blue Swede	#71	
1974	Dance Master (Pt. 1)	Willie Henderson	#73	
1974	It Only Hurts When I Try to Smile	Dawn featuring Tony Orlando	#81	
1974	Love Is the Message	MFSB/Three Degrees	#85	
1974	Loving Arms	Kris Kristofferson & Rita Coolidge	#86	
1974	Just One Look	Anne Murray	#86	

ORGAN (cont'd)

Year	Title	Artist	Peak	Time
1974	I Wouldn't Treat a Dog (The Way You Treated Me)	Bobby Bland	#88	
1974	Might Just Take Your Life	Deep Purple	#91	55 sec.
1974	Mine for Me	Rod Stewart	#91	
1974	Dancin' (On a Saturday Night)	Flash Cadillac & The Continental Kids	#93	
1975	Miracles	Jefferson Starship	#3	
1975	Some Kind of Wonderful	Grand Funk	#3	
1975	Get Dancin'	Disco Tex & His Sex-O-Lettes	#10	
1975	Do It Any Way You Wanna	People's Choice	#11	
1975	L-O-V-E (Love)	Al Green	#13	
1975	Holdin' on to Yesterday	Ambrosia	#17	
1975	Operator	The Manhattan Transfer	#22	
1975	Rendezvous	Hudson Brothers	#26	
1975	Two Fine People	Cat Stevens	#33	
1975	Your Love	Graham Central Station	#38	
1975	If Loving You Is Wrong I Don't Want to Be Right	Millie Jackson	#42	
1975	Take Me to the River	Syl Johnson	#48	
1975	Oh Me, Oh My (Dreams in My Arms)	Al Green	#48	
1975	Skybird	Tony Orlando & Dawn	#49	13 sec.
1975	I Get High on You	Sly Stone	#52	
1975	Mr. D.J. (5 for the D.J.)	Aretha Franklin	#53	
1975	Nice, Nice, Very Nice	Ambrosia	#63	
1975	Department of Youth	Alice Cooper	#67	
1975	So in Love	Curtis Mayfield	#67	
1975	Never Been Any Reason	Head East	#68	
1975	Same Thing It Took	The Impressions	#75	
1975	Stars in My Eyes	Sugarloaf	#87	
1975	It's Alright	Graham Central Station	#92	
1975	Hang on Sloopy	Rick Derringer	#94	
1975	Look at You	George McCrae	#95	
1975	We All Gotta Stick Together	Four Tops	#97	17 sec.
1975	Foot Stompin' Music	Hamilton Bohannon	#98	
1976	A Fifth of Beethoven	Walter Murphy	#1	
1976	Saturday Night	Bay City Rollers	#1	
1976	Fooled Around and Fell in Love	Elvin Bishop (Mickey Thomas)	#3	
1976	Do You Feel Like We Do	Peter Frampton	#10	47 sec.
1976	Takin' It to the Streets	The Doobie Brothers	#13	
1976	Hello Old Friend	Eric Clapton	#24	
1976	Good Vibrations	Todd Rundgren	#34	
1976	Give It Up (Turn It Loose)	Tyrone Davis	#38	
1976	Banapple Gas	Cat Stevens	#41	
1976	'Til It's Time to Say Goodbye	Jonathan Cain	#44	

ORGAN (cont'd)

1976	Yes, Yes, Yes	Bill Cosby	#46	
1976	Play on Love	Jefferson Starship	#49	
1976	Roots, Rock, Reggae	Bob Marley	#51	
1976	Free Ride	Tavares	#52	
1976	You Gotta Make Your Own Sunshine	Neil Sedaka	#53	
1976	Take Me	Grand Funk Railroad	#53	
1976	Love Me Tonight	Head East	#54	
1976	Bigfoot	Bro Smith	#57	
1976	Dancin' Kid	Disco Tex & His Sex-O-Lettes	#60	
1976	The Jam	Graham Central Station	#63	
1976	Honey I	George McCrae	#65	
1976	Brand New Love Affair	Jigsaw	#66	
1976	It's Cool	The Tymes	#68	
1976	Devil with a Blue Dress	Pratt & McClain	#71	
1976	Hey Baby	Ted Nugent	#72	
1976	Uptown & Country	Tom Scott	#80	
1976	Can't Change My Heart	Cate Bros.	#91	
1976	Nursery Rhymes (Part 1)	People's Choice	#93	
1976	Sweet Summer Music	Attitudes	#94	
1976	Hideaway	John Sebastian	#95	
1976	Spirit in the Night	Manfred Mann	#97	
1977	Blinded By the Night	Manfred Mann	#1	
1977	Fly Like an Eagle	Steve Miller	#2	
1977	(Your Love Has Lifted Me) Higher and Higher	Rita Coolidge	#2	
1977	The Things We Do for Love	10 CC	#5	
1977	Right Time of the Night	Jennifer Warnes	#6	
1977	Lonely Boy	Andrew Gold	#7	
1977	Ain't Gonna Bump No More (With No Big Fat Woman)	Joe Tex	#12	
1977	Telephone Man	Meri Wilson	#18	
1977	Dusic	Brick	#18	
1977	Slow Dancin' Don't Turn Me On	Addrisi Bros.	#20	
1977	Long Time	Boston	#22	
1977	Here Come Those Tears Again	Jackson Browne	#23	
1977	Mainstreet	Bob Seger	#24	
1977	This Song	George Harrison	#25	
1977	She's Not There	Santana	#27	
1977	Thunder in My Heart	Leo Sayer	#38	
1977	A Place in the Sun	Pablo Cruise	#42	
1977	Baby Don't You Know	Wild Cherry	#43	
1977	I Think We're Alone Now	The Rubinoos	#45	
1977	Theme from Charlie's Angels	Henry Mancini	#45	

ORGAN (cont'd)

1977	Reach	Orleans	#51	17 sec.
1977	Hold Back the Night	Graham Parker w/The Rumour	#58	
1977	Hard Times	Boz Scaggs	#58	
1977	Stone Cold Sober	Crawler	#65	
1977	My Own Way to Rock	Burton Cummings	#74	16 sec.
1977	Only the Lucky	Walter Egan	#82	
1977	You're the Only One	Geils	#83	
1977	Light of a Clear Blue Morning	Dolly Parton	#87	
1977	While I'm Alone	Maze feat. Frankie Beverly	#89	
1977	Time Is Movin'	The Blackbyrds	#95	
1978	Hollywood Nights	Bob Seger	#12	
1978	Runaway	Jefferson Starship	#12	
1978	Wonderful Tonight	Eric Clapton	#16	
1978	Blue Collar Man (Long Nights)	Styx	#21	
1978	Prove It All Night	Bruce Springsteen	#33	
1978	Dance Across the Floor	Jimmy "Bo" Horne	#38	
1978	Will You Still Love Me Tomorrow	Dave Mason	#39	
1978	Curious Mind (Um, Um, Um, Um, Um, Um)	Johnny Rivers	#41	
1978	Let It Go, Let It Flow	Dave Mason	#45	
1978	Make You Feel Love Again	Wet Willie	#45	
1978	So Long	Firefall	#48	
1978	That's Your Secret	Sea Level	#50	14 sec.
1978	Flyin'	Prism	#53	
1978	I Want You to Be Mine	Kayak	#55	
1978	Roll with the Changes	REO Speedwagon	#58	18 sec.
1978	Shake and Dance with Me	Con Funk Shun	#60	
1978	Portrait (He Knew)	Kansas	#64	
1978	Lights	Journey	#68	
1978	Was Dog a Doughnut	Cat Stevens	#70	
1978	Belle	Al Green	#83	
1978	Africanism/Gimme Some Lovin'	Kongas	#84	
1978	Manana	Jimmy Buffett	#84	17 sec.
1978	Wild in the Streets	British Lions	#87	
1978	Don't Let It Show	Alan Parsons Project	#92	
1979	Heart of Glass	Blondie	#1	
1979	Fire	Pointer Sisters	#2	27 sec.
1979	The Logical Song	Supertramp	#6	
1979	Promises	Eric Clapton	#9	
1979	Take the Long Way Home	Supertramp	#10	
1979	Goodbye Stranger	Supertramp	#15	
1979	Renegade	Styx	#16	

		ORGAN (cont'd)			
1979	Spooky	Atlanta Rhythm Section	#17	32 sec.
1979	Don't You Write Her Off	McGuinn, Clark & Hillman	#33	
1979	Bustin' Loose Part 1	Chuck Brown & The Soul Searchers	#34	
1979	You Thrill Me	Exile	#40	
1979	Goodbye, I Love You	Firefall	#43	
1979	Diamonds	Chris Rea	#44	
1979	Peter Piper	Frank Mills	#48	
1979	Turn Off the Lights	Teddy Pendergrass	#48	
1979	Get Down	Gene Chandler	#53	
1979	Silver Lining	Player	#62	
1979	One Fine Day	Rita Coolidge	#66	
1979	Take It Back	The J. Geils Band	#67	
1979	Feel That You're Feelin'	Maze Featuring Frankie Beverly	#67	
1979	She's Got a Whole Number	Keith Herman	#87	

PIANO

For the "length of solo" column, only piano solos that are ten seconds or longer are included.

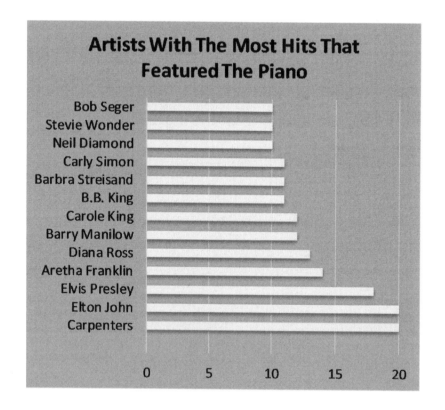

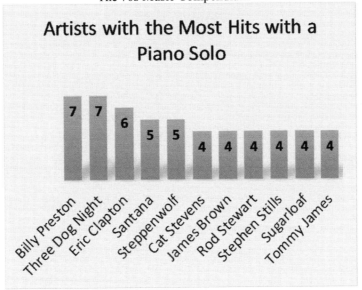

Artists with the Most Hits with a Piano Solo

YEAR	SONG	ARTIST	HOT 100	LENGTH OF SOLO
1970	Bridge Over Troubled Waters	Simon & Garfunkel	#1	22, 23 sec.
1970	(They Long to Be) Close to You	Carpenters	#1	
1970	Let It Be	The Beatles	#1	13 sec.
1970	Mama Told Me (Not to Come)	Three Dog Night	#1	
1970	ABC	The Jackson 5	#1	
1970	Everything Is Beautiful	Ray Stevens	#1	
1970	The Long and Winding Road	The Beatles	#1	
1970	I Want You Back	The Jackson 5	#1	
1970	We've Only Just Begun	Carpenters	#2	
1970	Instant Karma (We All Shine On)	John Lennon	#3	
1970	Love on a Two-Way Street	The Moments	#3	
1970	In the Summertime	Mungo Jerry	#3	16 sec.
1970	Ride Captain Ride	Blues Image	#4	
1970	Julie, Do Ya Love Me	Bobby Sherman	#5	
1970	Lay Down (Candles in the Rain)	Melanie w/Edwin Hawkins Singers	#6	
1970	I'll Never Fall in Love Again	Dionne Warwick	#6	
1970	The Letter	Joe Cocker w/Leon Russell	#7	
1970	Come and Get It	Badfinger	#7	
1970	O-o-h Child	The 5 Stairsteps	#8	
1970	The Wonder of You	Elvis Presley	#9	
1970	Heaven Help Us All	Stevie Wonder	#9	
1970	Gimme Dat Ding	The Pipkins	#9	18 sec.
1970	Share the Land	The Guess Who	#10	
1970	Midnight Cowboy	Ferrante & Teicher	#10	
1970	Don't Play That Song	Aretha Franklin w/The Dixie Flyers	#11	15, 11 sec.
1970	Cry Me a River	Joe Cocker	#11	
1970	Call Me	Aretha Franklin	#13	

	PIANO (cont'd)			
1970	Look What They've Done to My Song Ma	The New Seekers	#14	
1970	Get Up I Feel Like Being Like a Sex Machine (Part 1)	James Brown	#15	
1970	Be My Baby	Andy Kim	#17	
1970	After Midnight	Eric Clapton	#18	
1970	Walkin' in the Rain	Jay & The Americans	#19	
1970	Reach Out and Touch (Somebody's Hand)	Diana Ross	#20	
1970	Yellow River	Christie	#23	
1970	Spirit in the Dark	Aretha Franklin w/The Dixie Flyers	#23	
1970	Hey, Mister Sun	Bobby Sherman	#24	
1970	Shilo	Neil Diamond	#24	
1970	Up on Cripple Creek	The Band	#25	
1970	Never Had a Dream Come True	Stevie Wonder	#26	
1970	Save the Country	The 5th Dimension	#27	
1970	Lucretia Mac Evil	Blood, Sweat & Tears	#29	
1970	She Came in Through the Bathroom Window	Joe Cocker	#30	
1970	Our House	Crosby, Stills, Nash & Young	#30	
1970	Airport Love Theme (Gwen and Vern)	Vincent Bell	#31	
1970	I've Lost You	Elvis Presley	#32	
1970	Mississippi	John Phillips	#32	
1970	Let Me Go to Him	Dionne Warwick	#32	
1970	Breaking Up Is Hard to Do	Lenny Welch	#34	
1970	Do It	Neil Diamond	#36	
1970	Border Song (Holy Moses)	Aretha Franklin	#37	
1970	Make It Easy on Yourself	Dionne Warwick	#37	
1970	Come Running	Van Morrison	#39	
1970	Oh Happy Day	Glen Campbell	#40	
1970	Let's Give Adam and Eve Another Chance	Gary Puckett & The Union Gap	#41	
1970	New World Coming	Mama Cass Elliot	#42	
1970	My Woman, My Woman, My Wife	Marty Robbins	#42	
1970	I Stand Accused	Isaac Hayes	#42	
1970	Oh What a Day	The Dells	#43	
1970	Soul Shake	Delaney & Bonnie & Friends	#43	
1970	My Marie	Engelbert Humperdinck	#43	12 sec.
1970	Walking Through the Country	The Grass Roots	#44	
1970	If I Didn't Care	The Moments	#44	
1970	Miss America	Mark Lindsay	#44	
1970	California Girl	Eddie Floyd	#45	
1970	Tonight I'll Say a Prayer	Eydie Gormé	#45	
1970	Part Time Love	Ann Peebles	#45	
1970	Chains and Things	B.B. King	#45	
1970	When We Get Married	The Intruders	#45	

PIANO (cont'd)

1970	I've Gotta Make You Love Me	Steam	#46	
1970	(How 'Bout a Little Hand For) The Boys in the Band	The Boys in the Band	#48	
1970	Don't Stop Now	Eddie Holman	#48	
1970	Hummingbird	B.B. King	#48	
1970	Stealing in the Name of the Lord	Paul Kelly	#49	
1970	Mongoose	Elephant's Memory	#50	
1970	I Don't Wanna Cry	Ronnie Dyson	#50	
1970	You Make Me Real	The Doors	#50	
1970	I Just Wanna Keep It Together	Paul Davis	#51	
1970	Into the Mystic	Johnny Rivers	#51	
1970	A Little Bit of Soap	Paul Davis	#52	
1970	I'll Be Right Here	Tyrone Davis	#53	
1970	I'm So Glad I Fell for You	David Ruffin	#53	
1970	Ticket to Ride	Carpenters	#54	35 sec.
1970	I'm So Excited	B.B. King	#54	
1970	My Honey and Me	Luther Ingram	#55	
1970	I'm Just a Prisoner (Of Your Good Lovin')	Candi Staton	#56	
1970	Black Fox	Freddy Robinson	#56	
1970	Rag Mama Rag	The Band	#57	25, 16 sec.
1970	Won't Find Better (Than Me)	The New Hope	#57	
1970	Come Together	Ike & Tina Turner	#57	
1970	Glory Glory	The Rascals	#58	
1970	Sweet Feeling	Candi Staton	#60	
1970	Welfare Cadilac	Guy Drake	#63	
1970	Deeper (In Love with You)	The O'Jays	#64	
1970	The Declaration	The 5th Dimension	#64	
1970	Dear Prudence	The 5 Stairsteps	#66	
1970	Hello It's Me	Nazz	#66	
1970	Diane Kolby	Holy Man	#67	
1970	Song from M*A*S*H	Al DeLory	#70	
1970	He Made a Woman Out of Me	Bobbie Gentry	#71	
1970	Empty Pages	Traffic	#74	80 sec.
1970	Morning Much Better	Ten Wheel Drive	#74	16 sec.
1970	Save the Country	Thelma Houston	#74	
1970	Your Own Back Yard	Dion	#75	
1970	Can You Feel It	Bobby Goldsboro	#75	
1970	Down in the Alley	Ronnie Hawkins	#75	24 sec.
1970	I Call My Baby Candy	The Jaggerz	#75	15 sec.
1970	Girls Will Be Girls, Boys Will Be Boys	Isley Brothers	#75	
1970	Something	Booker T. & The M.G.'s	#76	
1970	Time to Kill	The Band	#77	

		PIANO (cont'd)		
1970	Barbara, I Love You	New Colony Six	#78	
1970	Got to Believe in Love	Robin McNamara	#80	
1970	Together	The Illusion	#80	
1970	Sunset Strip	Ray Stevens	#81	
1970	Gas Lamps and Clay	Blues Image	#81	
1970	Brighton Hill	Jackie DeShannon	#82	
1970	Lucifer	Bob Seger System	#84	
1970	Love Minus Zero-No Limit	Turley Richards	#84	
1970	Everything Is Going to Be Alright	Teegarden & Van Winkle	#84	19 sec.
1970	It's Your Life	Andy Kim	#85	
1970	Compared to What	Les McCann & Eddie Harris	#85	
1970	I Started Loving You Again	Al Martino	#86	
1970	The Ghetto – Part 1	Donny Hathaway	#87	
1970	Wonder Could I Live There Anymore	Charley Pride	#87	
1970	Loving You Is a Natural Thing	Ronnie Milsap	#87	
1970	Shades of Green	The Flaming Ember	#88	
1970	I Would Be in Love (Anyway)	Frank Sinatra	#88	
1970	Groovin' with Mr. Bloe	Cool Heat	#89	
1970	Keep on Loving Me (You'll See the Change)	Bobby Bland	#89	
1970	Get into Something	The Isley Brothers	#89	
1970	Mill Valley	Miss Abrams	#90	
1970	Thank God and Greyhound	Roy Clark	#90	
1970	Down By the River	The Brooklyn Bridge	#91	
1970	Let This Be a Letter (To My Baby)	Jackie Wilson	#91	
1970	Cole, Cooke & Redding	Wilson Pickett	#91	
1970	Monster Mash	Bobby (Boris) Pickett	#91	
1970	Help Me Find a Way (To Say I Love You)	Little Anthony & The Imperials	#92	
1970	Up on the Roof	Laura Nyro	#92	
1970	Run, Woman, Run	Tammy Wynette	#92	
1970	Border Song	Elton John	#92	
1970	Johnny B. Goode	Johnny Winter	#92	10 sec.
1970	Hang on Sloopy	The Lettermen	#93	
1970	Father Come on Home	Pacific Gas & Electric	#93	
1970	The Lights of Tucson	Jim Campbell	#93	
1970	Free to Carry On	The Sandpipers	#94	11 sec.
1970	Good Morning Freedom	Daybreak	#94	
1970	I Got a Problem	Jesse Anderson	#95	
1970	Lady Love	The Klowns	#95	
1970	You've Made Me so Very Happy	Lou Rawls	#95	21 sec.
1970	Where are You Going	Jerry Butler	#95	
1970	If You've Got a Heart	Bobby Bland	#96	

PIANO (cont'd)

1970	I Want To (Do Everything for You)	Raeletts	#96	
1970	I Think I Love You Again	Brenda Lee	#97	
1970	Can't Get Over Losing You	Donnie Elbert	#98	
1970	Let's Make Each Other Happy	The Illusion	#98	
1970	Looky Looky (Look at Me Girl)	The O'Jays	#98	
1970	Laughin' and Clownin'	Ray Charles	#98	15 sec.
1970	Day Is Done	Brooklyn Bridge	#98	
1970	Spirit in the Sky	Dorothy Morrison	#99	
1970	Lady Lay Lay	Ferrante & Teicher	#99	
1970	Listen Here	Brian Auger/The Trinity	#100	
1970	Darling Dear	Smokey Robinson & The Miracles	#100	
1971	Joy to the World	Three Dog Night	#1	
1971	It's Too Late	Carole King	#1	
1971	How Can You Mend a Broken Heart	The Bee Gees	#1	
1971	Brand New Key	Melanie	#1	
1971	Family Affair	Sly & The Family Stone	#1	
1971	Me and Bobby McGee	Janis Joplin	#1	23 sec.
1971	Superstar	Carpenters	#2	
1971	Rainy Days and Mondays	Carpenters	#2	
1971	Put Your Hand in the Hand	Ocean	#2	
1971	For All We Know	Carpenters	#3	
1971	Imagine	John Lennon	#3	14 sec.
1971	The Night They Drove Old Dixie Down	Joan Baez	#3	
1971	Lonely Days	Bee Gees	#3	
1971	Signs	Five Man Electrical Band	#3	
1971	Don't Pull Your Love	Hamilton, Joe Frank & Reynolds	#4	
1971	Mercy Mercy Me (The Ecology)	Marvin Gaye	#4	
1971	Doesn't Somebody Want to Be Wanted	The Partridge Family	#6	
1971	Stoney End	Barbra Streisand	#6	
1971	Bridge Over Troubled Water	Aretha Franklin	#6	
1971	Does Anybody Really Know What Time It Is?	Chicago	#7	
1971	Stay Awhile	The Bells	#7	
1971	If You Really Love Me	Stevie Wonder	#8	
1971	What the World Needs Now Is Love/Abraham, Martin and John	Tom Clay	#8	
1971	I'll Meet You Halfway	The Partridge Family	#9	
1971	If I Were Your Woman	Gladys Knight & The Pips	#9	
1971	Sooner or Later	The Grass Roots	#9	
1971	That's the Way I've Always Heard It Should Be	Carly Simon	#10	
1971	One Toke Over the Line	Brewer & Shipley	#10	
1971	It's Impossible	Perry Como	#10	
1971	Lover Her Madly	The Doors	#11	

		PIANO (cont'd)		
1971	Wild World	Cat Stevens	#11	
1971	I Don't Know How to Love Him	Helen Reddy	#13	
1971	Theme from Love Story	Henry Mancini	#13	
1971	So Far Away	Carole King	#14	
1971	Riders on the Storm	The Doors	#14	44 sec.
1971	Thin Line Between Love & Hate	The Persuaders	#15	
1971	Where Did Our Love Go	Donnie Elbert	#15	
1971	Remember Me	Diana Ross	#16	
1971	Cried Like a Baby	Bobby Sherman	#16	
1971	A Natural Man	Lou Rawls	#17	
1971	Rain Dance	The Guess Who	#19	
1971	We Gotta Get You a Woman	Runt (Todd Rundgren)	#20	
1971	Maybe Tomorrow	The Jackson 5	#20	
1971	Theme from "Summer of '42"	Peter Nero	#21	
1971	I Really Don't Want to Know	Elvis Presley	#21	
1971	Double Barrel	Dave & Ansil Collins	#22	
1971	The Story in Your Eyes	The Moody Blues	#23	
1971	Bangla-Desh	George Harrison	#23	
1971	(I Know) I'm Losing You	Rod Stewart w/Faces	#24	
1971	Stagger Lee	Tommy Roe	#25	15 sec.
1971	Absolutely Right	Five Man Electrical Band	#26	
1971	One Tin Soldier (The Legend of Billy Jack)	Coven	#26	
1971	You've Got a Friend	Roberta Flack & Donny Hathaway	#29	
1971	Albert Flasher	The Guess Who	#29	
1971	Reach Out I'll Be There	Diana Ross	#29	
1971	Theme from Love Story	Francis Lai	#31	
1971	Long Ago and Far Away	James Taylor	#31	
1971	Where Did They Go, Lord	Elvis Presley	#33	
1971	Friends	Elton John	#34	
1971	Me and My Arrow	Nilsson	#34	
1971	Booty Butt	Ray Charles Orchestra	#36	
1971	I'm Leavin'	Elvis Presley	#36	
1971	Sit Yourself Down	Stephen Stills	#37	
1971	MacArthur Park (Part 2)	Four Tops	#38	
1971	Surrender	Diana Ross	#38	
1971	Love Means (You Never Have to Say You're Sorry)	Sounds of Sunshine	#39	13 sec.
1971	She's All I Got	Freddie North	#39	
1971	Can I Get a Witness	Lee Michaels	#39	
1971	Your Time to Cry	Joe Simon	#40	
1971	Charity Ball	Fanny	#40	
1971	Ask Me No Questions	B.B. King	#40	

		PIANO (cont'd)		
1971	If You Were Mine	Ray Charles	#41	
1971	Watching the River Flow	Bob Dylan	#41	
1971	Love	The Lettermen	#42	24 sec.
1971	Silver Moon	Michael Nesmith	#42	
1971	Cry Baby	Janis Joplin	#42	
1971	Mother	John Lennon	#43	
1971	Change Partners	Stephen Stills	#43	
1971	Apeman	The Kinks	#45	
1971	When There's No You	Engelbert Humperdinck	#45	
1971	I'm so Proud	The Main Ingredient	#49	
1971	Spill the Wine	The Isley Brothers	#49	
1971	Bridget the Midget (The Queen of the Blues)	Ray Stevens	#50	
1971	I Cried	James Brown	#50	
1971	Time and Love	Barbra Streisand	#51	
1971	House at Pooh Corner	Nitty Gritty Dirt Band	#53	
1971	Bless You	Martha & The Vandellas	#53	
1971	Don't Wanna Live Inside Myself	Bee Gees	#53	
1971	Lonely Teardrops	Brian Hyland	#54	
1971	After the Fire Is Gone	Conway Twitty & Loretta Lynn	#56	
1971	Mammy Blue	Pop-Tops	#57	
1971	You Think You're Hot Stuff	Jean Knight	#57	
1971	Who Gets the Guy	Dionne Warwick	#57	
1971	Bed of Rose's	The Statler Brothers	#58	
1971	The Morning of Our Lives	Arkade	#60	
1971	Ooh Poo Pah Doo	Ike & Tina Turner	#60	62 sec.
1971	Long Ago Tomorrow	B.J. Thomas	#61	
1971	Do You Know What Time It Is?	P-Nut Gallery	#62	
1971	Don't Make Me Pay for Your Mistakes	Z.Z. Hill	#62	
1971	Reason to Believe	Rod Stewart	#62	
1971	Church Street Soul Revival	Tommy James	#62	
1971	Turn Your Radio On	Ray Stevens	#63	
1971	I Love You Lady Dawn	The Bells	#64	
1971	Rub It In	Layng Martine	#65	
1971	Done Too Soon	Neil Diamond	#65	
1971	Brownsville	Joy of Cooking	#66	26 sec.
1971	Ain't It a Sad Thing	R. Dean Taylor	#66	
1971	Ghetto Woman	B.B. King	#68	
1971	Come Back Home	Bobby Goldsboro	#69	
1971	Help Me Make It Through the Night	Joe Simon	#69	
1971	I'll Erase Away Your Pain	Whatnauts	#71	
1971	Be Nice to Me	Todd Rundgren	#71	

			PIANO (cont'd)	
1971	When My Little Girl Is Smiling	Steve Alaimo	#72	
1971	Heartbreak Hotel	Frijid Pink	#72	
1971	Freedom	Isley Brothers	#72	
1971	Deep Enough for Me	Ocean	#73	
1971	Don't Try to Lay No Boogie-Woogie on the King of Rock and Roll	John Baldry	#73	
1971	Military Madness	Graham Nash	#73	
1971	Mixed Up Guy	Joey Scarbury	#73	
1971	Holly Holy	Jr. Walker/The All Stars	#75	
1971	The Animal Trainer and the Toad	Mountain	#76	
1971	Never Dreamed You'd Leave in Summer	Stevie Wonder	#78	
1971	Get It While You Can	Janis Joplin	#78	
1971	I Need You	Friends of Distinction	#79	
1971	Didn't It Looks so Easy	The Stairsteps	#81	
1971	Flim Flam Man	Barbra Streisand	#82	
1971	We Got a Dream	Ocean	#82	
1971	A Song for You	Andy Williams	#82	
1971	A Mama and a Papa	Ray Stevens	#82	
1971	Love Makes the World Go Round	Odds & Ends	#83	
1971	And I Love You So	Bobby Goldsboro	#83	
1971	Sea Cruise	Johnny Rivers	#84	
1971	I Need Someone (To Love Me)	Z.Z. Hill	#86	
1971	Are You Old Enough	Mark Lindsay	#87	
1971	The Girl Who Loved Me When	Glass Bottle	#87	
1971	It's so Hard for Me to Say Good-Bye	Eddie Kendricks	#88	
1971	We'll Have It Made	The Spinners	#89	
1971	My Sweet Lord	Billy Preston	#90	
1971	Help the Poor	B.B. King	#90	
1971	You and Your Folks, Me and My Folks	Funkadelic	#91	
1971	Hymn 43	Jethro Tull	#91	
1971	Take My Hand	Kenny Rogers & The First Edition	#91	
1971	Be My Baby	Cissy Houston	#92	
1971	A Long Time, A Long Way to Go	Todd Rundgren	#92	
1971	Your Love Is so Doggone Good	The Whispers	#93	
1971	I Wanna Be Free	Loretta Lynn	#94	
1971	You Keep Me Holding On	Tyrone Davis	#94	19 sec.
1971	Olena	Don Nix	#94	
1971	When You Get Right Down to It	Ronnie Dyson	#94	
1971	Fly Little White Dove Fly	The Bells	#95	
1971	Call Me Up in Dreamland	Van Morrison	#95	
1971	If It's Alright with You	Rose Colored Glass	#95	
1971	I'll Be Home	Vikki Carr	#96	

		PIANO (cont'd)		
1971	I Got to Tell Somebody	Betty Everett	#96	
1971	Near You	Boz Scaggs	#96	
1971	Puff of Smoke	Roy Head	#96	
1971	Good Enough to Be Your Wife	Jeannie C. Riley	#97	
1971	Maria (You were the Only One)	Jimmy Ruffin	#97	
1971	I'm Sorry	Bobby Bland	#97	
1971	San Bernadina	Christie	#100	
1971	The Language of Love	The Intrigues	#100	
1972	Alone Again (Naturally)	Gilbert O'Sullivan	#1	
1972	American Pie (Parts 1 & 2)	Don McLean	#1	
1972	Without You	Nilsson	#1	
1972	Lean on Me	Bill Withers	#1	
1972	Black & White	Three Dog Night	#1	
1972	Too Late to Turn Back Now	Cornelius Brothers & Sister Rose	#2	
1972	Clair	Gilbert O'Sullivan	#2	
1972	Hurting Each Other	Carpenters	#2	
1972	I'd Love You to Want Me	Lobo	#2	
1972	Burning Love	Elvis Presley	#2	
1972	Saturday in the Park	Chicago	#3	
1972	Everybody Plays the Fool	The Main Ingredient	#3	
1972	Puppy Love	Donny Osmond	#3	
1972	Daddy Don't You Walk so Fast	Wayne Newton	#4	
1972	Day After Day	Badfinger	#4	
1972	It Never Rains in Southern California	Albert Hammond	#5	
1972	In the Rain	Dramatics	#5	
1972	Morning Has Broken	Cat Stevens	#6	12, 12, 14, 12, 14 sec.
1972	Rocket Man	Elton John	#6	
1972	Goodbye to Love	Carpenters	#7	
1972	Doctor My Eyes	Jackson Browne	#8	
1972	Honky Cat	Elton John	#8	
1972	Sweet Seasons	Carole King	#9	
1972	Sugar Daddy	The Jackson 5	#10	
1972	If I Could Reach You	The 5th Dimension	#10	13 sec.
1972	Layla	Derek & The Dominos	#10	24 sec.
1972	Power of Love	Joe Simon	#11	
1972	Tight Rope	Leon Russell	#11	
1972	It's Going to Take Some Time	Carpenters	#12	
1972	Anticipation	Carly Simon	#13	
1972	Day by Day	Godspell	#13	
1972	Speak to the Sky	Rick Springfield	#14	15 sec.
1972	Rock and Roll Lullaby	B.J. Thomas	#15	

	PIANO (cont'd)			
1972	I Saw the Light	Todd Rundgren	#16	
1972	My World	Bee Gees	#16	
1972	Walk on Water	Neil Diamond	#17	
1972	Thunder and Lightning	Chi Coltrane	#17	
1972	The City of New Orleans	Arlo Guthrie	#18	
1972	It's One of Those Nights (Yes Love)	The Partridge Family	#20	
1972	Ain't Understanding Mellow	Jerry Butler & Brenda Lee Eager	#21	
1972	I Can't Help Myself (Sugar Pie, Honey Bunch)	Donnie Elbert	#22	12 sec.
1972	The Day I Found Myself	Honey Cone	#23	
1972	Once You Understand	Think	#23	
1972	Don't Ever Be Lonely (A Poor Little Fool Like Me)	Cornelius Brothers & Sister Rose	#23	
1972	Taxi	Harry Chapin	#24	
1972	Pop That Thang	The Isley Brothers	#24	
1972	Levon	Elton John	#24	13 sec.
1972	Run Run Run	Jo Jo Gunne	#27	
1972	American City Suite	Cashman & West	#27	
1972	Jump Into the Fire	Nilsson	#27	
1972	Midnight Rider	Joe Cocker w/The Chris Stainton Band	#27	30 sec.
1972	Mary Had a Little Lamb	Paul McCartney & Wings	#28	
1972	Feeling Alright	Joe Cocker	#33	32 sec.
1972	Superwoman (Where Were You When I Needed You)	Stevie Wonder	#33	
1972	Love Theme from "The Godfather" (Speak Softly Love)	Andy Williams	#34	
1972	Glory Bound	The Grass Roots	#34	
1972	Sunny Days	Lighthouse	#34	
1972	Alive	The Bee Gees	#34	
1972	The Nickel Song	Melanie	#35	
1972	Together Let's Find Love	The 5th Dimension	#37	
1972	Could It Be Forever	David Cassidy	#37	
1972	Rock Me Baby	David Cassidy	#38	
1972	Looking for a Love	J. Geils Band	#39	
1972	We're Free	Beverly Bremers	#40	
1972	Me and Bobby McGee	Jerry Lee Lewis	#40	
1972	Until It's Time for You to Go	Elvis Presley	#40	
1972	My Boy	Richard Harris	#41	
1972	Daisy Mae	Hamilton, Joe Frank & Reynolds	#41	
1972	Tiny Dancer	Elton John	#41	13 sec.
1972	After Midnight	J.J. Cale	#42	
1972	Lies	J.J. Cale	#42	

	PIANO (cont'd)			
1972	I'm Coming Home	Stories	#42	20 sec.
1972	Handbags and Gladrags	Rod Stewart	#42	15 sec.
1972	Chantilly Lace	Jerry Lee Lewis	#43	
1972	Those Were the Days	Carroll O'Connor & Jean Stapleton	#43	
1972	There It Is (Part 1)	James Brown	#43	30 sec.
1972	No	Bulldog	#44	
1972	Do the Funky Penguin (Part 1)	Rufus Thomas	#44	
1972	Everything Good Is Bad	100 Proof	#45	
1972	Brown Eyed Girl	El Chicano	#45	
1972	Walk in the Night	Jr. Walker/The All Stars	#46	
1972	Ain't Nobody Home	B.B. King	#46	
1972	Love Me, Love Me Love	Frank Mills	#46	
1972	Rock and Roll	Led Zeppelin	#47	
1972	Let It Rain	Eric Clapton	#48	
1972	To Get to You	Jerry Wallace	#48	
1972	Can't You Hear the Song?	Wayne Newton	#48	
1972	Rock Me on the Water	Jackson Browne	#48	19 sec.
1972	In Heaven There Is No Beer	Clean Living	#49	14 sec.
1972	The Harder I Try (The Bluer I Get)	Free Movement	#50	
1972	Sour Suite	The Guess Who	#50	25 sec.
1972	Trouble in My Home	Joe Simon	#50	
1972	Sweet Caroline (Good Times Never Seemed So Good)	Bobby Womack	#51	
1972	Country Wine	The Raiders	#51	
1972	Life and Breath	Climax	#52	
1972	Put It Where You Want It	The Crusaders	#52	
1972	Lay-Away	The Isley Brothers	#54	
1972	What am I Living For	Ray Charles	#54	
1972	Brian's Song	Michel LeGrand	#56	
1972	992 Arguments	The O'Jays	#57	25 sec.
1972	A Lonely Man	The Chi-Lites	#57	
1972	Am I Losing You	The Partridge Family	#59	
1972	Everybody Knows About My Good Thing Pt. 1	Little Johnny Taylor	#60	
1972	Waking Up Alone	Paul Williams	#60	13 sec.
1972	I Will Never Pass This Way Again	Glen Campbell	#61	
1972	Baby Won't You Let Me Rock 'N Roll You	Ten Years After	#61	
1972	Guess Who	B.B. King	#61	
1972	Pain (Part 1)	Ohio Players	#64	
1972	Do What You Set Out to Do	Bobby Bland	#64	
1972	Cheer	Potliquor	#65	
1972	That's the Way God Planned It	Billy Preston	#65	
1972	Jubilation	Paul Anka	#65	

	PIANO (cont'd)			
1972	Look What They've Done to My Song, Ma	Ray Charles	#65	
1972	Changes	David Bowie	#66	
1972	Bless the Beasts and Children	Carpenters	#67	
1972	Rip Off	Laura Lee	#68	
1972	In Time	Engelbert Humperdinck	#69	
1972	Guns, Guns, Guns	The Guess Who	#70	
1972	Keep Playin' That Rock 'N' Roll	Edgar Winter's White Trash	#70	
1972	What Would the Children Think	Rick Springfield	#70	
1972	Carry Me, Carrie	Dr. Hook	#71	
1972	After All This Time	Merry Clayton	#71	
1972	Lay Lady Lay	The Isley Brothers	#71	
1972	Cotton Jenny	Anne Murray	#71	
1972	Cry	Lynn Anderson	#71	
1972	Iko Iko	Dr. John	#71	
1972	Money Back Guarantee	Five Man Electrical Band	#72	
1972	Oh Me Oh My (I'm a Fool for You Baby)	Aretha Franklin	#73	
1972	That's What Friends Are For	B.J. Thomas	#74	
1972	Sunday Morning Sunshine	Harry Chapin	#75	
1972	Will You Still Love Me Tomorrow	Roberta Flack	#76	
1972	Since I Fell for You	Laura Lee	#76	
1972	I Wrote a Simple Song	Billy Preston	#77	
1972	Ain't Wastin' Time No More	Allman Brothers Band	#77	
1972	Speak Softly Love	Al Martino	#80	
1972	Beat Me Daddy Eight to the Bar	Commander Cody	#81	
1972	Giving Up	Donny Hathaway	#81	
1972	I Don't Need No Doctor	New Riders of the Purple Sage	#81	
1972	Step Out	Mamas & Papas	#81	
1972	Wholy Holy	Aretha Franklin	#81	
1972	Up in Heah	Ike & Tina Turner	#83	
1972	Just as Long as You Need Me, Part 1	Independents	#84	
1972	Simple Song of Freedom	Buckwheat	#84	
1972	If We Only Have Love	Dionne Warwick	#84	
1972	Ain't That Peculiar	Fanny	#85	
1972	I Only Have Eyes for You	Jerry Butler	#85	
1972	Together Alone	Melanie	#86	
1972	Ain't That Loving You (For More Reasons Than One)	Isaac Hayes & David Porter	#86	
1972	(Love Me) Love the Life I Lead	The Fantastics	#86	
1972	Dinah Flo	Boz Scaggs	#86	
1972	Too Beautiful to Last	Engelbert Humperdinck	#86	
1972	Nobody But You	Loggins & Messina	#86	
1972	Don't Want to Say Goodbye	Raspberries	#86	

PIANO (cont'd)

1972	Hey, You Love	Mouth & MacNeal	#87	
1972	Goodbye Again	John Denver	#88	
1972	Rockin' with the King	Canned Heat w/Little Richard	#88	
1972	Country Woman	The Magic Lanterns	#88	
1972	I Received a Letter	Delbert & Glen	#90	
1972	Open the Door (Song for Judith)	Judy Collins	#90	
1972	Keep on Running	Stevie Wonder	#90	
1972	Jesus was a Capricorn	Kris Kristofferson	#91	
1972	Misty Blue	Joe Simon	#91	
1972	Eve	Jim Capaldi	#91	
1972	Deteriorata	National Lampoon	#91	
1972	It's Four in the Morning	Faron Young	#92	
1972	Rock and Roll Crazies	Stephen Stills & Manassas	#92	
1972	Sweet Baby	Donnie Elbert	#92	
1972	Mother Nature	The Temptations	#92	
1972	All His Children	Charley Pride w/Henry Mancini	#92	
1972	Long Time to Be Alone	New Colony Six	#93	
1972	Sweet Sixteen	B.B. King	#93	
1972	Roberta	Bones	#94	18 sec.
1972	With Pen in Hand	Bobby Goldsboro	#94	
1972	Celebration	Tommy James	#95	
1972	Whatever Turns You On	Travis Wammack	#95	
1972	Willpower Weak, Temptations Strong	Bullet	#96	
1972	Sittin' on a Time Bomb (Waitin' for the Hurt to Come)	Honey Cone	#96	
1972	Runnin' Back to Saskatoon	The Guess Who	#96	
1972	Song Seller	Raiders	#96	60 sec.
1972	Get Out of Bed	Livingston Taylor	#97	
1972	Thank God for You Baby	PG&E	#97	
1972	He's an Indian Cowboy in the Rodeo	Buffy Sainte-Marie	#98	
1972	Me and Jesus	Tom T. Hall	#98	
1972	Redwood Tree	Van Morrison	#98	
1973	Killing Me Softly with His Song	Roberta Flack	#1	
1973	You're So Vain	Carly Simon	#1	
1973	Crocodile Rock	Elton John	#1	
1973	Bad, Bad Leroy Brown	Jim Croce	#1	
1973	Top of the World	Carpenters	#1	
1973	Midnight Train to Georgia	Gladys Knight & The Pips	#1	
1973	Brother Louie	Stories	#1	
1973	Will It Go Round in Circles	Billy Preston	#1	
1973	The Most Beautiful Girl	Charlie Rich	#1	
1973	Touch Me in the Morning	Diana Ross	#1	

PIANO (cont'd)

1973	Delta Dawn	Helen Reddy	#1	
1973	You Are the Sunshine of My Life	Stevie Wonder	#1	
1973	Angie	The Rolling Stones	#1	25 sec.
1973	Give Me Love – (Give Me Peace on Earth)	George Harrison	#1	
1973	Goodbye Yellow Brick Road	Elton John	#2	
1973	Live and Let Die	Paul McCartney & Wings	#2	
1973	Kodachrome	Paul Simon	#2	
1973	Daniel	Elton John	#2	
1973	Ramblin' Man	Allman Brothers Band	#2	
1973	Yesterday Once More	Carpenters	#2	
1973	Also Sprach Zarathustra (2001)	Deodato	#2	
1973	Sing	Carpenters	#3	
1973	Leave Me Alone (Ruby Red Dress)	Helen Reddy	#3	
1973	Say, Has Anybody Seen My Sweet Gypsy Rose	Dawn featuring Tony Orlando	#3	
1973	I'm Gonna Love You Just a Little More Baby	Barry White	#3	
1973	Ain't No Woman (Like the One I've Got)	Four Tops	#4	
1973	Your Mama Don't Dance	Loggins & Messina	#4	
1973	Hello It's Me	Todd Rundgren	#5	
1973	That Lady (Part 1)	Isley Brothers	#6	
1973	The Cover of "Rolling Stone"	Dr. Hook	#6	
1973	Diamond Girl	Seals & Crofts	#6	
1973	Rockin' Pneumonia – Boogie Woogie Flu	Johnny Rivers	#6	32 sec.
1973	The Love I Lost (Part 1)	Harold Melvin	#7	
1973	Boogie Woogie Bugle Boy	Bette Midler	#8	
1973	All I Know	Garfunkel	#9	25, 19 sec.
1973	Reeling in the Years	Steely Dan	#11	
1973	Saturday Night's Alright for Fighting	Elton John	#12	
1973	I'm Just a Singer (In a Rock and Roll Band)	The Moody Blues	#12	
1973	You're a Special Part of Me	Diana Ross & Marvin Gaye	#12	
1973	Dancing in the Moonlight	King Harvest	#13	14 sec.
1973	Don't Let Me Be Lonely Tonight	James Taylor	#14	
1973	Rockin' Roll Baby	The Stylistics	#14	
1973	China Grove	The Doobie Brothers	#15	
1973	Cheaper to Keep Her	Johnnie Taylor	#15	
1973	Behind Closed Doors	Charlie Rich	#15	
1973	Basketball Jones featuring Tyrone Shoelaces	Cheech & Chong	#15	
1973	Sitting	Cat Stevens	#16	18, 16 sec.
1973	My Music	Loggins & Messina	#16	
1973	Let Me Serenade You	Three Dog Night	#17	
1973	Do You Want to Dance?	Bette Midler	#17	
1973	The Right Thing to Do	Carly Simon	#17	

		PIANO (cont'd)			
1973	Out of the Question	Gilbert O'Sullivan	#17	
1973	Steamroller Blues	Elvis Presley	#17	
1973	Theme from Cleopatra Jones	Joe Simon w/The Mainstreeters	#18	
1973	Angel	Aretha Franklin	#20	
1973	Separate Ways	Elvis Presley	#20	17 sec.
1973	Summer (The First Time)	Bobby Goldsboro	#21	
1973	We May Never Pass This Way (Again)	Seals & Crofts	#21	
1973	How Can I Tell Her	Lobo	#22	
1973	Been to Canaan	Carole King	#24	
1973	Who's in the Strawberry Patch with Sally	Tony Orlando & Dawn	#27	
1973	Believe in Humanity	Carole King	#28	
1973	Hallelujah Day	The Jackson 5	#28	
1973	If We Make It Through December	Merle Haggard	#28	
1973	Ghetto Child	Spinners	#29	
1973	Give It to Me	The J. Geils Band	#30	
1973	Jesse	Roberta Flack	#30	
1973	"Cherry Cherry" from Hot August Night	Neil Diamond	#31	22 sec.
1973	Ecstasy	Ohio Players	#31	
1973	Kissing My Love	Bill Withers	#31	
1973	Master of Eyes (The Deepness of Your Eyes)	Aretha Franklin	#33	
1973	Oh La De Da	The Staple Singers	#33	
1973	Good Morning Heartache	Diana Ross	#34	
1973	Let's Pretend	Raspberries	#35	
1973	Hello Hurray	Alice Cooper	#35	
1973	Check It Out	Tavares	#35	
1973	Goin' Home	The Osmonds	#36	
1973	Soul Song	Joe Stampley	#37	
1973	Step By Step	Joe Simon	#37	
1973	Corazon	Carole King	#37	
1973	To Know You Is to Love You	B.B. King	#38	
1973	Blue Suede Shoes	Johnny Rivers	#38	
1973	The Plastic Man	The Temptations	#40	17 sec.
1973	Back When My Hair Was Short	Gunhill Road	#40	
1973	Friends	Bette Midler	#40	
1973	Drinking Wine Spo-Dee O'Dee	Jerry Lee Lewis	#41	18 sec.
1973	Baby I've Been Missing You	The Independents	#41	
1973	Rhapsody in Blue	Deodato	#41	
1973	Roll Over Beethoven	Electric Light Orchestra	#42	
1973	Such a Night	Dr. John	#42	
1973	You Can't Always Get What You Want	The Rolling Stones	#42	
1973	Rosalie	Sam Neely	#43	

	PIANO (cont'd)			
1973	Hey You! Get off My Mountain	Dramatics	#43	
1973	I Knew Jesus (Before He was a Star)	Glen Campbell	#45	
1973	I Can't Stand to See You Cry	Smokey Robinson & The Miracles	#45	
1973	Fell for You	The Dramatics	#45	
1973	Clouds	David Gates	#47	
1973	I Found Sunshine	The Chi-Lites	#47	
1973	Let Us Love	Bill Withers	#47	
1973	Cindy Incidentally	Faces	#48	10 sec.
1973	The Free Electric Band	Albert Hammond	#48	
1973	Country Sunshine	Dottie West	#49	
1973	You're a Lady	Peter Skellern	#50	
1973	Mammy Blue	Stories	#50	
1973	With a Child's Heart	Michael Jackson	#50	
1973	Pardon Me Sir	Joe Cocker	#51	
1973	Remember (Christmas)	Nilsson	#53	36 sec.
1973	Pretty Lady	Lighthouse	#53	
1973	Let Me Be Your Lovemaker	Betty Wright	#55	
1973	Woman from Tokyo	Deep Purple	#60	
1973	Only in Your Heart	America	#62	
1973	My Old School	Steely Dan	#63	
1973	What About Me	Anne Murray	#64	
1973	The Lord Knows I'm Drinking	Cal Smith	#64	
1973	It's All Over	The Independents	#65	
1973	You Light Up My Life	Carole King	#67	
1973	Boogie Woogie Man	Paul Davis	#68	
1973	Music Everywhere	Tufano & Giammarese	#68	
1973	How Can I Tell You	Travis Wammack	#68	
1973	Tonight	Raspberries	#69	
1973	You're a Lady	Dawn featuring Tony Orlando	#70	
1973	Nobody Wins	Brenda Lee	#70	
1973	Everything's Been Changed	The 5th Dimension	#70	
1973	Ain't Got No Home	The Band	#73	
1973	Blood Red and Goin' Down	Tanya Tucker	#74	
1973	I'm a Stranger Here	Five Man Electrical Band	#76	
1973	Avenging Annie	Andy Pratt	#78	
1973	Sail on Sailor	The Beach Boys	#79	
1973	You're in Good Hands	Jermaine Jackson	#79	
1973	I Can Make It Thru the Days (But Oh Those Lonely Nights)	Ray Charles	#81	
1973	That's Why You Remember	Kenny Karen	#82	
1973	Didn't We	Barbra Streisand	#82	
1973	Will You Love Me Tomorrow?	Melanie	#82	

		PIANO (cont'd)			
1973	Giving It All Away	Roger Daltrey	#83	
1973	It May Be Winter Outside, (But in My Heart It's Spring)	Love Unlimited	#83	
1973	Redneck Friend	Jackson Browne	#85	
1973	Good Morning	Michael Redway	#85	
1973	This Is Your Song	Don Goodwin	#86	
1973	River Road	Uncle Dog	#86	
1973	Don't Let It Get You Down	The Crusaders	#86	
1973	I'm Sorry	Joey Heatherton	#87	
1973	Girl You Need a Change of Mind (Part 1)	Eddie Kendrick	#87	
1973	Queen of the Roller Derby	Leon Russell	#89	
1973	Stay Away from Me	The Sylvers	#89	
1973	We	Shawn Phillips	#89	
1973	Names, Tags, Numbers & Labels	The Association	#91	10 sec.
1973	The Long Way Home	Neil Diamond	#91	
1973	Love Is All	Engelbert Humperdinck	#91	
1973	Sugar Magnolia	Grateful Dead	#91	
1973	You Were Always There	Donna Fargo	#93	
1973	Fool Like You	Tim Moore	#93	
1973	She's Got to Be a Saint	Ray Price	#93	
1973	Somebody Loves You	The Whispers	#94	
1973	I Miss You Baby	Millie Jackson	#95	
1973	L.A. Freeway	Jerry Jeff Walker	#98	
1973	Make Up Your Mind	The J. Geils Band	#98	
1973	Friend and a Lover	The Partridge Family	#99	
1974	The Way We Were	Barbra Streisand	#1	
1974	Kung Fu Fighting	Carl Douglas	#1	
1974	I Honestly Love You	Olivia Newton-John	#1	
1974	Bennie and the Jets	Elton John	#1	21 sec.
1974	Nothing from Nothing	Billy Preston	#1	16 sec.
1974	You're Sixteen	Ringo Starr	#1	
1974	I Shot the Sheriff	Eric Clapton	#1	
1974	Whatever Gets You Thru the Night	John Lennon	#1	
1974	Boogie Down	Eddie Kendricks	#2	
1974	Don't Let the Sun Go Down on Me	Elton John	#2	14 sec.
1974	Jazzman	Carole King	#2	
1974	My Melody of Love	Bobby Vinton	#3	
1974	Rock and Roll Heaven	The Righteous Brothers	#3	
1974	Until You Come Back to Me (That's What I'm Gonna Do)	Aretha Franklin	#3	
1974	Tin Man	America	#4	
1974	I've Got to Use My Imagination	Gladys Knight & The Pips	#4	

		PIANO (cont'd)			
1974	I'm Leaving It (All) Up to You	Donny & Marie Osmond	#4	
1974	Rikki Don't Lose That Number	Steely Dan	#4	
1974	Longfellow Serenade	Neil Diamond	#5	
1974	Mockingbird	Carly Simon & James Taylor	#5	
1974	Oh My My	Ringo Starr	#5	
1974	Midnight at the Oasis	Maria Muldaur	#6	
1974	Clap for the Wolfman	The Guess Who	#6	
1974	Waterloo	ABBA	#6	
1974	Wildwood Weed	Jim Stafford	#7	
1974	Tubular Bells	Mike Oldfield	#7	
1974	Sweet Home Alabama	Lynyrd Skynyrd	#8	28 sec.
1974	Stop and Smell the Roses	Mac Davis	#9	
1974	Oh Very Young	Cat Stevens	#10	
1974	Wishing You Were Here	Chicago	#11	
1974	A Very Special Love Song	Charlie Rich	#11	
1974	I Won't Last a Day Without You	Carpenters	#11	
1974	The Need to Be	Jim Weatherly	#11	
1974	Takin' Care of Business	Bachman-Turner Overdrive	#12	
1974	My Girl Bill	Jim Stafford	#12	
1974	I've Got the Music in Me	The Kiki Dee Band	#12	
1974	Promised Land	Elvis Presley	#14	
1974	Are You Lonesome Tonight	Donny Osmond	#14	
1974	Haven't Got Time for the Pain	Carly Simon	#14	
1974	Trying to Hold on to My Woman	Lamont Dozier	#15	
1974	Keep on Singing	Helen Reddy	#15	
1974	Love Don't Love Nobody – Pt. 1	Spinners	#15	44 sec.
1974	Rub It In	Billy "Crash" Craddock	#16	
1974	Sure as I'm Sittin' Here	Three Dog Night	#16	
1974	Don't You Worry 'Bout a Thing	Stevie Wonder	#16	
1974	There Won't Be Anymore	Charlie Rich	#18	
1974	I'm Coming Home	Spinners	#18	
1974	Overnight Sensation (Hit Record)	Raspberries	#18	28 sec.
1974	This Heart	Gene Redding	#24	
1974	I Love My Friend	Charlie Rich	#24	
1974	Piano Man	Billy Joel	#25	13 sec.
1974	Fire, Baby I'm on Fire	Andy Kim	#28	
1974	Star	Stealers Wheel	#29	20 sec.
1974	"Joy" Pt. 1	Isaac Hayes	#30	
1974	Dream On	The Righteous Brothers	#32	
1974	Play Something Sweet (Brickyard Blues)	Three Dog Night	#33	
1974	Second Avenue	Garfunkel	#34	

		PIANO (cont'd)		
1974	Outside Woman	Bloodstone	#34	
1974	You Can Have Her	Sam Neely	#34	
1974	W*O*L*D*	Harry Chapin	#36	
1974	I'll Be the Other Woman	The Soul Children	#36	
1974	Sugar Baby Love	The Rubettes	#37	
1974	One Day at a Time	Marilyn Sellars	#37	
1974	Thanks for Saving My Life	Billy Paul	#38	
1974	I've Got a Thing About You Baby	Elvis Presley	#39	
1974	Daybreak	Nilsson	#39	
1974	Star Baby	The Guess Who	#39	
1974	Heartbreak Kid	Bo Donaldson & The Heywoods	#39	
1974	Without Love	Aretha Franklin	#45	
1974	Put Out the Light	Joe Cocker	#46	
1974	It Could Have Been Me	Sami Jo	#46	
1974	She Called Me Baby	Charlie Rich	#47	
1974	Ain't Nothing Like the Real Thing	Aretha Franklin	#47	
1974	You're So Unique	Billy Preston	#48	
1974	Room Full of Roses	Mickey Gilley	#50	33 sec.
1974	Tell Her Love Has Felt the Need	Eddie Kendricks	#50	
1974	River of Love	B.W. Stevenson	#53	
1974	When the Morning Comes	Hoyt Axton	#54	15 sec.
1974	Don't Send Nobody Else	Ace Spectrum	#57	
1974	Someday	Dave Loggins	#57	
1974	Satisfaction Guaranteed (Or Take Your Love Back)	Harold Melvin	#58	
1974	Second Avenue	Tim Moore	#58	24 sec.
1974	My Country	Jud Strunk	#59	
1974	Summer Breeze (Part 1)	Isley Brothers	#60	
1974	King of Nothing	Seals & Crofts	#60	
1974	Wang Dang Doodle	The Pointer Sisters	#61	
1974	Travelin' Shoes	Elvin Bishop	#61	
1974	Happiness Is Me and You	Gilbert O'Sullivan	#62	
1974	All in Love Is Fair	Barbra Streisand	#63	
1974	I Am What I Am	Lois Fletcher	#64	
1974	Hangin' Around	Edgar Winter Group	#65	
1974	Jessica	Allman Brothers Band	#65	
1974	Country Side of Life	Wet Willie	#66	
1974	I Hate Hate	Razzy Bailey	#67	
1974	Houston (I'm Comin' to See You)	Glen Campbell	#68	
1974	Early Morning Love	Sammy Johns	#68	
1974	Shoe Shoe Shine	Dynamic Superiors	#68	
1974	Goin' Down Slow	Bobby Blue Bland	#69	

	PIANO (cont'd)			
1974	Time Will Tell	Tower of Power	#69	
1974	Get That Gasoline Blues	NRBQ	#70	
1974	Mississippi Cotton Picking Delta Town	Charley Pride	#70	
1974	Lamplight	David Essex	#71	
1974	Boogie Bands and One Night Stands	Kathy Dalton	#72	
1974	Moonlight Special	Ray Stevens	#73	
1974	Power of Love	Martha Reeves	#76	
1974	How Do You Feel the Morning After	Millie Jackson	#77	
1974	Travelin' Prayer	Billy Joel	#77	18 sec.
1974	Who Are You	B.B. King	#78	
1974	Beyond the Blue Horizon	Lou Christie	#80	
1974	Let Me Get to Know You	Paul Anka	#80	
1974	Get Out of Denver	Bob Seger	#80	
1974	Worse Comes to Worst	Billy Joel	#80	
1974	You Turned My World Around	Frank Sinatra	#83	
1974	Easy Street	Edgar Winter Group	#83	
1974	All Shook Up	Suzi Quatro	#85	
1974	I'm Falling in Love with You	Little Anthony & The Imperials	#86	
1974	The Man That Turned My Mama On	Tanya Tucker	#86	
1974	Just One Look	Anne Murray	#86	
1974	Bring Back the Love of Yesterday	The Dells	#87	
1974	If It Feels Good, Do It	Ian Lloyd & Stories	#88	
1974	Let This Be a Lesson to You	The Independents	#88	
1974	What's Your Name	Andy & David Williams	#92	
1974	Georgia Porcupine	George Fischoff	#93	
1974	Wake Up and Love Me	April Stevens	#93	
1974	Tell Laura I Love Her	Johnny T. Angel	#94	
1974	The Golden Age of Rock 'N' Roll	Mott The Hoople	#96	
1974	After Midnight	Maggie Bell	#97	
1974	Funky Party	Clarence Reid	#99	
1975	One of These Nights	Eagles	#1	
1975	Love Will Keep Us Together	The Captain & Tennille	#1	
1975	Fly, Robin, Fly	Silver Convention	#1	
1975	Island Girl	Elton John	#1	
1975	Lucy in the Sky with Diamonds	Elton John	#1	
1975	Before the Next Teardrop Falls	Freddy Fender	#1	
1975	Laughter in the Rain	Neil Sedaka	#1	
1975	(Hey Won't You Play) Another Somebody Done Somebody Wrong Song	B.J. Thomas	#1	
1975	Fallin' in Love	Hamilton, Joe Frank & Reynolds	#1	
1975	Mandy	Barry Manilow	#1	
1975	Boogie on Reggae Woman	Stevie Wonder	#3	

	PIANO (cont'd)			
1975	Who Loves You	Four Seasons	#3	
1975	I'm Not Lisa	Jessi Colter	#4	
1975	Someone Saved My Life Tonight	Elton John	#4	14 sec.
1975	The Way I Want to Touch You	Captain & Tennille	#4	
1975	How Sweet It Is (To Be Loved By You)	James Taylor	#5	
1975	They Just Can't Stop The (Games People Play)	Spinners	#5	
1975	Old Days	Chicago	#5	
1975	You are So Beautiful to Me	Joe Cocker	#5	
1975	Lonely People	America	#5	12 sec.
1975	Could It Be Magic	Barry Manilow	#6	22, 27 sec.
1975	Lady	Styx	#6	14 sec.
1975	Feelings	Morris Albert	#6	
1975	This Will Be	Natalie Cole	#6	15 sec.
1975	Why Can't We Be Friends?	War	#6	
1975	Midnight Blue	Melissa Manchester	#6	
1975	Nights on Broadway	Bee Gees	#7	
1975	Get Down, Get Down (Get on the Floor)	Joe Simon	#8	
1975	Ain't No Way to Treat a Lady	Helen Reddy	#8	
1975	I Don't Like to Sleep Alone	Paul Anka with Odia Coates	#8	16 sec.
1975	Long Tall Glasses (I Can Dance)	Leo Sayer	#9	12 sec.
1975	Rocky	Austin Roberts	#9	
1975	My Little Town	Simon & Garfunkel	#9	
1975	Nightingale	Carole King	#9	
1975	Dynomite – Part 1	Bazuka	#10	
1975	Get Dancin'	Disco Tex & His Sex-O-Lettes	#10	
1975	Take Me in Your Arms (Rock Me)	The Doobie Brothers	#11	
1975	Killer Queen	Queen	#12	
1975	I'm a Woman	Maria Muldaur	#12	
1975	Bungle in the Jungle	Jethro Tull	#12	
1975	I Must of Got Lost	J. Geils Band	#12	
1975	Venus and Mars Rock Show	Paul McCartney & Wings	#12	
1975	Something Better to Do	Olivia Newton-John	#13	
1975	Harry Truman	Chicago	#13	
1975	Misty	Ray Stevens	#14	
1975	Mornin' Beautiful	Tony Orlando & Dawn	#14	
1975	Eighteen with a Bullet	Pete Wingfield	#15	
1975	SOS	ABBA	#15	
1975	(I Believe) There's Nothing Stronger Than Our Love	Paul Anka with Odia Coates	#15	
1975	I Am Love (Parts I & II)	The Jackson 5	#15	
1975	Rock N' Roll (I Gave You the Best Years of My Life)	Mac Davis	#15	
1975	Solitaire	Carpenters	#17	

PIANO (cont'd)

1975	The Last Game of the Season (A Blind Man in the Bleachers)	David Geddes	#18	
1975	Every Time You Touch Me (I Get High)	Charlie Rich	#19	
1975	Secret Love	Freddy Fender	#20	
1975	My Boy	Elvis Presley	#20	
1975	Daisy Jane	America	#20	
1975	Carolina in the Pines	Michael Murphey	#21	
1975	Attitude Dancing	Carly Simon	#21	
1975	Struttin'	Billy Preston	#22	
1975	Operator	The Manhattan Transfer	#22	
1975	Gone at Last	Paul Simon/Phoebe Snow	#23	20 sec.
1975	Your Bulldog Drinks Champagne	Jim Stafford	#24	
1975	Ready	Cat Stevens	#26	
1975	I Belong to You	Love Unlimited	#27	
1975	That's When the Music Takes Me	Neil Sedaka	#27	
1975	Don't Tell Me Goodnight	Lobo	#27	
1975	Rockin' All Over the World	John Fogerty	#27	14 sec.
1975	Dancin' Fool	The Guess Who	#28	
1975	Young Americans	David Bowie	#28	
1975	The South's Gonna Do It	Charlie Daniels Band	#29	29 sec.
1975	Shaving Cream	Benny Bell	#30	
1975	It's All Down to Goodnight Vienna	Ringo Starr	#31	
1975	Two Fine People	Cat Stevens	#33	
1975	Ruby, Baby	Billy "Crash" Craddock	#33	
1975	The Entertainer	Billy Joel	#34	
1975	I've Been This Way Before	Neil Diamond	#34	
1975	T-R-O-U-B-L-E	Elvis Presley	#35	
1975	Bluebird	Helen Reddy	#35	
1975	Send in the Clowns	Judy Collins	#36	
1975	I Get Lifted	George McCrae	#37	
1975	I Got Stoned and I Missed It	Jim Stafford	#37	
1975	Living a Little, Laughing a Little	The Spinners	#37	
1975	Glasshouse	The Temptations	#37	
1975	Your Love	Graham Central Station	#38	
1975	Sweet Maxine	The Doobie Brothers	#40	
1975	Good Times, Rock & Roll	Flash Cadillac & The Continental Kids	#41	
1975	Love Power	Willie Hutch	#41	
1975	Hope That We Can Be Together Soon	Sharon Paige/Harold Melvin	#42	
1975	I Don't Know Why	The Rolling Stones	#42	
1975	El Bimbo	Bimbo Jet	#43	
1975	Katmandu	Bob Seger	#43	

PIANO (cont'd)

1975	I Wanna Learn a Love Song	Harry Chapin	#44	
1975	Runaway	Charlie Kulis	#46	
1975	Please Pardon Me (You Remind Me of a Friend)	Rufus feat. Chaka Khan	#48	
1975	What Can I Do for You?	LaBelle	#48	
1975	My Elusive Dreams	Charlie Rich	#49	
1975	Carry Me	David Crosby/Graham Nash	#52	
1975	I'm Her Fool	Billy Swan	#53	
1975	Mr. D.J. (5 for the D.J.)	Aretha Franklin	#53	
1975	Burnin' Thing	Mac Davis	#53	
1975	Sadie	Spinners	#54	
1975	Long Haired Country Boy	Charlie Daniels Band	#56	
1975	Don't Let Go	Commander Cody	#56	
1975	Blue Sky	Joan Baez	#57	
1975	Summer of '42	Biddu Orchestra	#57	
1975	What's Happened to Blue Eyes	Jessi Colter	#57	13 sec.
1975	If I Could Only Win Your Love	Emmylou Harris	#58	
1975	Blind Man in the Bleachers	Kenny Starr	#58	
1975	Day Tripper	Anne Murray	#59	
1975	Pinball	Brian Protheroe	#60	
1975	Please, Mr. President	Paula Webb	#60	
1975	Thanks for the Smiles	Charlie Ross	#61	
1975	Going Down Slowly	The Pointer Sisters	#61	
1975	Love Corporation	Hues Corporation	#62	
1975	Help Me Make It (To My Rockin' Chair)	B.J. Thomas	#64	
1975	Bringing It Back	Elvis Presley	#65	16 sec.
1975	Hoppy, Gene and Me	Roy Rogers	#65	
1975	Happy	Eddie Kendricks	#66	
1975	I Got to Pieces	Cotton, Lloyd & Christian	#66	
1975	Hey There Little Firefly (Part 1)	Firefly	#67	
1975	Nevertheless	Allman Brothers Band	#67	10 sec.
1975	Reconsider Me	Narvel Felts	#67	
1975	Come and Get Your Love	Roger Daltrey	#68	
1975	Cry to Me	Loleatta Holloway	#68	
1975	Leona	Wet Willie	#69	
1975	Somewhere in the Night	Batdorf & Rodney	#69	
1975	The Pill	Loretta Lynn	#70	
1975	Fancy Lady	Billy Preston	#71	
1975	Rock & Roll Runaway	Ace	#71	
1975	Mamacita	The Grass Roots	#71	
1975	Like They Say in L.A.	East L.A. Car Pool	#72	
1975	How Glad I Am	Kiki Dee	#74	

	PIANO (cont'd)			
1975	Same Thing It Took	The Impressions	#75	
1975	Costafine Town	Splinter	#77	
1975	Nothin' Heavy	David Bellamy	#77	17 sec.
1975	Louisiana Lou and Three Card Monty John	Allman Brothers Band	#78	19 sec.
1975	Waterfall	Carly Simon w/James Taylor	#78	
1975	The Other Woman	Vicki Lawrence	#81	
1975	(I'm Going By) The Stars in Your Eyes	The Dramatics	#81	
1975	Don't It Make You Wanna Dance?	Rusty Wier	#82	
1975	Art for Art's Sake	10cc	#83	
1975	Sure Feels Good	Elvin Bishop	#83	
1975	Please Tell Him That I Said Hello	Debbie Campbell	#84	
1975	Isn't It Lonely Together	Stark & McBrien	#85	
1975	I'll Still Love You	Jim Weatherly	#87	
1975	Live Your Life Before You Die	The Pointer Sisters	#89	
1975	A Lover's Question	Loggins & Messina	#89	
1975	Keep Our Love Alive	Paul Davis	#90	
1975	You're a Part of Me	Susan Jacks	#90	
1975	We Been Singin' Songs	Baron Stewart	#91	
1975	Everything's the Same (Ain't Nothing Changed)	Billy Swan	#91	
1975	For Your Love	Christopher Paul & Shawn	#91	
1975	No Charge	Shirley Caesar	#91	
1975	Charmer	Tim Moore	#91	
1975	Cry Cry Cry	Shirley & Company	#91	
1975	Love Don't You Go Through No Changes on Me	Sister Sledge	#92	
1975	Everybody Wants to Find a Bluebird	Randy Edelman	#92	
1975	I'll Go to My Grave Loving You	The Statler Brothers	#93	
1975	Run Tell the People	Daniel Boone	#93	
1975	Chocolate City	Parliament	#94	
1975	It Ain't No Fun	Shirley Brown	#94	
1975	More and More	Carly Simon	#94	23 sec.
1975	Our Last Song Together	Bo Donaldson & The Heywoods	#95	
1975	Tryin' to Beat the Morning Home	T.G. Sheppard	#95	
1975	Chico and the Man	José Feliciano	#96	
1975	Walk on By	Gloria Gaynor	#98	
1975	Where Have They Gone	Jimmy Beaumont & The Skyliners	#100	
1976	Silly Love Songs	Paul McCartney & Wings	#1	
1976	December, 1963 (Oh, What a Night)	The Four Seasons	#1	
1976	Love Hangover	Diana Ross	#1	
1976	I Write the Songs	Barry Manilow	#1	
1976	Theme from Mahogany (Do You Know Where You're Going To)	Diana Ross	#1	
1976	Convoy	C.W. McCall	#1	

PIANO (cont'd)

1976	Welcome Back	John Sebastian	#1	
1976	The Rubberband Man	Spinners	#2	
1976	Get Up and Boogie (That's Right)	Silver Convention	#2	
1976	All By Myself	Eric Carmen	#2	20 sec.
1976	I'd Really Love to See You Tonight	England Dan & John Ford Coley	#2	
1976	Love So Right	Bee Gees	#3	
1976	Misty Blue	Dorothy Moore	#3	
1976	Let 'Em In	Paul McCartney & Wings	#3	
1976	Fooled Around and Fell in Love	Elvin Bishop (Mickey Thomas)	#3	
1976	Shop Around	Captain & Tennille	#4	
1976	More, More, More (Pt. 1)	Andrea True Connection	#4	
1976	Sorry Seems to Be the Hardest Word	Elton John	#6	
1976	Get Closer	Seals & Crofts w/Carolyn Willis	#6	
1976	Summer	War	#7	
1976	Beth	Kiss	#7	16 sec.
1976	Nadia's Theme (The Young and The Restless)	Barry DeVorzon & Perry Botkin, Jr.	#8	
1976	Breaking Up Is Hard to Do	Neil Sedaka	#8	
1976	Bohemium Rhapsody	Queen	#9	
1976	Money Honey	Bay City Rollers	#9	
1976	Evil Woman	Electric Light Orchestra	#10	14 sec.
1976	This Masquerade	George Benson	#10	
1976	Tryin' to Get the Feeling Again	Barry Manilow	#10	
1976	Say You Love Me	Fleetwood Mac	#11	
1976	Never Gonna Fall in Love Again	Eric Carmen	#11	
1976	If You Know What I Mean	Neil Diamond	#11	
1976	Wake Up Everybody (Part 1)	Harold Melvin	#12	
1976	Takin' It to the Streets	The Doobie Brothers	#13	
1976	I Do, I Do, I Do, I Do, I Do	ABBA	#15	
1976	Somewhere in the Night	Helen Reddy	#19	
1976	The White Knight	Cledus Maggard	#19	
1976	Young Blood	Bad Company	#20	
1976	Livin' for the Weekend	The O'Jays	#20	
1976	Winners and Losers	Hamilton, Joe Frank & Reynolds	#21	
1976	Come on Over	Olivia Newton-John	#23	
1976	Today's the Day	America	#23	
1976	I Need to Be in Love	Carpenters	#25	
1976	Don't Pull Your Love/Then You Can Tell Me Goodbye	Glen Campbell	#27	
1976	Just You and I	Melissa Manchester	#27	
1976	Save Your Kisses for Me	Brotherhood of Man	#27	
1976	Only Love Is Real	Carole King	#28	
1976	Hurt	Elvis Presley	#28	

		PIANO (cont'd)		
1976	This One's for You	Barry Manilow	#29	
1976	Did You Boogie (With Your Baby)	Flash Cadillac & The Continental Kids	#29	
1976	I Can't Hear You More	Helen Reddy	#29	
1976	One Piece at a Time	Johnny Cash	#29	
1976	Mamma Mia	ABBA	#32	
1976	Inseparable	Natalie Cole	#32	
1976	You'll Lose a Good Thing	Freddy Fender	#32	
1976	Let the Music Play	Barry White	#32	
1976	Another Rainy Day in New York City	Chicago	#32	
1976	Take It Like a Man	Bachman-Turner Overdrive	#33	
1976	Sunrise	Eric Carmen	#34	
1976	Fallen Angel	Frankie Valli	#36	
1976	Steppin' Out	Neil Sedaka	#36	
1976	Give It Up (Turn It Loose)	Tyrone Davis	#38	
1976	Silver Star	The Four Seasons	#38	
1976	Teddy Bear	Red Sovine	#40	
1976	The Homecoming	Hagood Hardy	#41	
1976	Take a Hand	Rick Springfield	#41	
1976	Yesterday's Hero	John Paul Young	#42	
1976	'Til It's Time to Say Goodbye	Jonathan Cain	#44	
1976	Can You Do It	Grand Funk Railroad	#45	
1976	So Sad the Song	Gladys Knight & The Pips	#47	
1976	Hold On	Sons of Champlin	#47	
1976	I Thought It Took a Little Time (But Today I Fell in Love)	Diana Ross	#47	
1976	Falling Apart at the Seams	Marmalade	#49	
1976	Mr. Melody	Natalie Cole	#49	
1976	Foxy Lady	Crown Heights Affair	#49	
1976	Play on Love	Jefferson Starship	#49	
1976	I Don't Wanna Lose Your Love	The Emotions	#51	
1976	You Gotta Make Your Own Sunshine	Neil Sedaka	#53	
1976	Easy as Pie	Billy "Crash" Craddock	#54	
1976	Goofus	Carpenters	#56	
1976	Funny How Time Slips Away	Dorothy Moore	#58	
1976	You're My Everything	Lee Garrett	#58	
1976	The Fez	Steely Dan	#59	
1976	No, No, Joe	Silver Convention	#60	
1976	It Makes Me Giggle	John Denver	#60	
1976	Locomotive Breath	Jethro Tull	#62	
1976	The More You Do It (The More I Like It Done to Me)	Ronnie Dyson	#62	
1976	Chain Gang Medley	Jim Croce	#63	

	PIANO (cont'd)			
1976	Don't Cry Joni	Conway Twitty w/Joni Lee	#63	
1976	TVC 15	David Bowie	#64	
1976	Groovy People	Lou Rawls	#64	
1976	Sixteen Reasons	LaVerne & Shirley	#65	
1976	Brand New Love Affair	Jigsaw	#66	
1976	Teddy Bear's Last Ride	Diana Williams	#66	
1976	California Day	Starland Vocal Band	#66	
1976	Remember Me	Willie Nelson	#67	25 sec.
1976	Light up the World with Sunshine	Hamilton, Joe Frank & Reynolds	#67	
1976	Where Did Our Love Go	The J. Geils Band	#68	
1976	Highfly	John Miles	#68	
1976	Since I Fell for You	Charlie Rich	#71	
1976	Home Tonight	Aerosmith	#71	
1976	Don't Fight the Hands (That Need You)	Hamilton, Joe Frank & Reynolds	#72	
1976	Eh! Cumpari	Gaylord & Holiday	#72	
1976	Living It Down	Freddy Fender	#72	
1976	Rain, Oh Rain	Fools Gold	#76	
1976	High Out of Time	Carole King	#76	19 sec.
1976	The Princess and the Punk	Barry Mann	#78	
1976	Rescue Me	Melissa Manchester	#78	
1976	We're All Alone	Frankie Valli	#78	
1976	I Can't Ask for Anymore Than You	Cliff Richard	#80	
1976	Party Line	The Andrea True Connection	#80	
1976	The Hungry Years	Wayne Newton	#82	
1976	Jukin'	Atlanta Rhythm Section	#82	
1976	Tenth Avenue Freeze-Out	Bruce Springsteen	#83	
1976	'Til I Can Make It on My Own	Tammy Wynette	#84	
1976	Someday (I Didn't Want to Have to Be the One)	Henry Gross	#85	
1976	Train Called Freedom	South Shore Commission	#86	
1976	Better Place to Be (Parts 1 & 2)	Harry Chapin	#86	
1976	Words (Are Impossible)	Donny Gerrard	#87	
1976	Music	John Miles	#88	
1976	Things	Anne Murray	#89	
1976	Out of the Darkness	David Crosby/Graham Nash	#89	15 sec.
1976	Rattlesnake	Ohio Players	#90	
1976	The Fonz Song	The Heyettes	#91	
1976	Texas	Charlie Daniels Band	#91	20 sec.
1976	Laid Back Love	Major Harris	#91	
1976	Let's Rock	Ellison Chase	#92	
1976	Sweet Loving Man	Morris Albert	#93	
1976	Find 'Em, Fool 'Em & Forget 'Em	Dobie Gray	#94	

PIANO (cont'd)				
1976	Wow	Andre Gagnon	#95	
1976	Hideaway	John Sebastian	#95	
1976	Sun…Sun…Sun… Part 1	Ja-Kki	#96	
1976	Love Lifted Me	Kenny Rogers	#97	
1976	Can't You See	Waylon Jennings	#97	
1976	You to Me Are Everything, Part 1	Revelation	#98	
1976	Touch and Go	Ecstasy, Passion & Pain	#98	
1976	Say You Love Me	D.J. Rogers	#98	
1976	Abyssinia Jones	Edwin Starr	#98	
1976	Solitary Man	T.G. Sheppard	#100	
1976	I Don't Wanna Leave You	Debbie Taylor	#100	
1977	You Light Up My Life	Debby Boone	#1	
1977	Evergreen (Love Theme from "A Star Is Born")	Barbra Streisand	#1	
1977	You Don't Have to Be a Star (To Be in My Show)	Marilyn McCoo & Billy Davis, Jr.	#1	
1977	Dancing Queen	ABBA	#1	
1977	Southern Nights	Glen Campbell	#1	
1977	Gonna Fly Now	Bill Conti	#1	
1977	Don't Give Up on Us	David Soul	#1	
1977	I'm Your Boogie Man	KC and The Sunshine Band	#1	
1977	Looks Like We Made It	Barry Manilow	#1	
1977	Don't It Make My Brown Eyes Blue	Crystal Gayle	#2	
1977	Nobody Does It Better	Carly Simon	#2	
1977	Keep It Comin' Love	KC and The Sunshine Band	#2	
1977	I'm in You	Peter Frampton	#2	
1977	That's Rock 'N' Roll	Shaun Cassidy	#3	
1977	Don't Stop	Fleetwood Mac	#3	
1977	My Heart Belongs to Me	Barbra Streisand	#4	
1977	Easy	Commodores	#4	10 sec.
1977	Night Moves	Bob Seger	#4	
1977	Do You Wanna Make Love	Peter McCann	#5	16 sec.
1977	Strawberry Letter 23	The Brothers Johnson	#5	
1977	The Things We Do for Love	10 CC	#5	
1977	I've Got Love on My Mind	Natalie Cole	#5	
1977	Angel in Your Arms	Hot	#6	
1977	Right Time of the Night	Jennifer Warnes	#6	
1977	Cold as Ice	Foreigner	#6	
1977	Lonely Boy	Andrew Gold	#7	
1977	Year of the Cat	Al Stewart	#8	16 sec.
1977	After the Lovin'	Engelbert Humperdinck	#8	
1977	You and Me	Alice Cooper	#9	
1977	Lost Without Your Love	Bread	#9	

PIANO (cont'd)

1977	Weekend in New England	Barry Manilow	#10	
1977	I Wanna Get Next to You	Rose Royce	#10	
1977	Maybe I'm Amazed	Paul McCartney & Wings	#10	
1977	Carry on Wayward Son	Kansas	#11	
1977	We Just Disagree	Dave Mason	#12	
1977	Somebody to Love	Queen	#13	
1977	Isn't It Time	The Babys	#13	
1977	The King Is Gone	Ronnie McDowell	#13	
1977	Can't Stop Dancin'	Captain & Tennille	#13	
1977	Heard It in a Love Song	Marshall Tucker Band	#14	
1977	Help Is on Its Way	Little River Band	#14	
1977	Say You'll Stay Until Tomorrow	Tom Jones	#15	
1977	Your Love	Marilyn McCoo & Billy Davis, Jr.	#15	
1977	It Was Almost Like a Song	Ronnie Milsap	#16	26, 13 sec.
1977	How Much Love	Leo Sayer	#17	
1977	Way Down	Elvis Presley	#18	
1977	Sam	Olivia Newton-John	#20	
1977	My Way	Elvis Presley	#22	
1977	Whodunit	Tavares	#22	
1977	Here Come Those Tears Again	Jackson Browne	#23	
1977	Gone Too Far	England Dan & John Ford Coley	#23	
1977	Daybreak	Barry Manilow	#23	
1977	The Greatest Love of All	George Benson	#24	25 sec.
1977	Mainstreet	Bob Seger	#24	
1977	Christine Sixteen	Kiss	#25	
1977	This Song	George Harrison	#25	
1977	Ariel	Dean Friedman	#26	
1977	I Believe You	Dorothy Moore	#27	
1977	N.Y., You Got Me Dancing	Andrea True Connection	#27	
1977	Bite Your Lip (Get Up and Dance!)	Elton John	#28	
1977	Hard Rock Café	Carole King	#30	
1977	Moody Blue	Elvis Presley	#31	
1977	Sometimes	Facts of Life	#31	
1977	Calling Occupants of Interplanetary Craft	Carpenters	#32	
1977	Another Star	Stevie Wonder	#32	
1977	(Remember the Days of The) Old Schoolyard	Cat Stevens	#33	
1977	Spring Rain	Silvetti	#39	
1977	In the Mood	Henhouse Five Plus Too (Ray Stevens)	#40	
1977	People in Love	10cc	#40	
1977	Rock and Roll Never Forgets	Bob Seger	#41	
1977	On the Border	Al Stewart	#42	

PIANO (cont'd)

1977	I Just Can't Say No to You	Parker McGee	#42	
1977	Someone to Lay Down Beside Me	Linda Ronstadt	#42	12 sec.
1977	A Place in the Sun	Pablo Cruise	#42	
1977	You're Throwing a Good Love Away	Spinners	#43	
1977	Phantom Writer	Gary Wright	#43	
1977	Something About You	LeBlanc & Carr	#48	
1977	Sleepwalker	The Kinks	#48	
1977	You are on My Mind	Chicago	#49	
1977	I'm Dreaming	Jennifer Warnes	#50	
1977	Silver Lady	David Soul	#52	
1977	Going in with My Eyes Open	David Soul	#53	
1977	Sailing Ships	Mesa	#55	
1977	Money, Money, Money	ABBA	#56	
1977	From Graceland to the Promised Land	Merle Haggard	#58	
1977	Hound Dog Man (Play It Again)	Lenny LeBlanc	#58	
1977	The Pretender	Jackson Browne	#58	
1977	Come in from the Rain	Captain & Tennille	#61	
1977	I'm Scared	Burton Cummings	#61	
1977	Feel the Beat (Everybody Disco)	Ohio Players	#61	
1977	Sub-Rosa Subway	Klaatu	#62	
1977	Platinum Heroes	Bruce Foster	#63	
1977	Man Smart, Woman Smarter	Robert Palmer	#63	
1977	Dog Days	Atlanta Rhythm Section	#64	
1977	Down the Hall	The Four Seasons	#65	
1977	Ten to Eight	David Castle	#68	
1977	Georgia Rhythm	Atlanta Rhythm Section	#68	
1977	Welcome to Our World (Of Merry Music)	Mass Production	#68	
1977	You're Moving Out Today	Carole Bayer Sager	#69	
1977	I'm Going Down	Rose Royce	#70	
1977	Gonna Love You More	George Benson	#71	
1977	Hail! Hail! Rock and Roll!	Starland Vocal Band	#71	
1977	The Doodle Song	Frankie Miller	#71	
1977	Why Do Lovers (Break Each Other's Heart?)	Daryl Hall & John Oates	#73	
1977	My Own Way to Rock	Burton Cummings	#74	
1977	Brooklyn	Cody Jameson	#74	
1977	Hey Baby	Ringo Starr	#74	
1977	Everybody Ought to Be in Love	Paul Anka	#75	
1977	Lose Again	Linda Ronstadt	#76	
1977	I Can't Help Myself	Eddie Rabbitt	#77	
1977	Still the Lovin' Is Fun	B.J. Thomas	#77	
1977	Kick It Out	Heart	#79	

PIANO (cont'd)

1977	Never My Love	Addrisi Brothers	#80	
1977	You Light Up My Life	Kacey Cisyk	#80	
1977	It's Uncanny	Daryl Hall & John Oates	#80	
1977	My Best Friend's Wife	Paul Anka	#80	
1977	I Need a Man	Grace Jones	#83	
1977	Rock and Roll Star	Champagne	#83	
1977	Time Bomb	Lake	#83	
1977	Red Hot	Robert Gordon w/Link Wray	#83	16 sec.
1977	Break It to Me Gently	Aretha Franklin	#85	
1977	Prisoner (Captured by Your Eyes)	L.A. Jets	#86	
1977	Making a Good Thing Better	Olivia Newton-John	#87	
1977	Avenging Annie	Roger Daltrey	#88	
1977	So High (Rock Me Baby and Roll Me Away)	Dave Mason	#89	
1977	This Will Be a Night to Remember	Eddie Holman	#90	
1977	Flame	Steve Sperry	#91	
1977	Some Enchanted Evening	Jane Olivor	#91	
1977	Up Your Nose	Gabriel Kaplan	#91	
1977	Love to the World	L.T.D.	#91	
1977	It Ain't Love	Tom Powers	#92	16 sec.
1977	Love Bug	Bumble Bee Unlimited	#92	
1977	Moondance	Van Morrison	#92	28 sec.
1977	Good Thing Man	Frank Lucas	#92	
1977	Spend Some Time	Elvin Bishop w/Mickey Thomas	#93	
1977	Dance and Shake Your Tambourine	Universal Robot Band	#93	
1977	Deeply	Anson Williams	#93	
1977	Make It with You	The Whispers	#94	
1977	Theme from "Rocky" (Gonna Fly Now)	Current	#94	
1977	Freddie	Charlene	#96	
1977	It Ain't Easy Coming Down	Charlene	#97	
1977	Goodbye My Friend	Engelbert Humperdinck	#97	
1977	I've Never Been to Me	Charlene	#97	
1977	Part Time Love	Kerry Chater	#97	
1977	My Pearl	Automatic Man	#97	
1977	For Elise	The Philharmonics	#100	
1978	Kiss You All Over	Exile	#1	
1978	Three Times a Lady	Commodores	#1	
1978	You Don't Bring Me Flowers	Barbra Streisand & Neil Diamond	#1	
1978	You're the One That I Want	John Travolta & Olivia Newton-John	#1	
1978	Short People	Randy Newman	#2	
1978	The Closer I Get to You	Roberta Flack & Donny Hathaway	#2	
1978	Can't Smile Without You	Barry Manilow	#3	

PIANO (cont'd)

1978	How Much I Feel	Ambrosia	#3	
1978	Sometimes When We Touch	Dan Hill	#3	
1978	Here You Come Again	Dolly Parton	#3	
1978	We Will Rock You/We are the Champions	Queen	#4	
1978	Still the Same	Bob Seger	#4	11 sec.
1978	I Go Crazy	Paul Davis	#7	
1978	Hey Deanie	Shaun Cassidy	#7	
1978	Imaginary Lover	Atlanta Rhythm Section	#7	
1978	Dance with Me	Peter Brown w/Betty Wright	#8	
1978	Count on Me	Jefferson Starship	#8	14 sec.
1978	Come Sail Away	Styx	#8	12 sec.
1978	Thunder Island	Jay Ferguson	#9	
1978	We'll Never Have to Say Goodbye Again	England Dan & John Ford Coley	#9	
1978	Our Love	Natalie Cole	#10	
1978	Ready to Take a Chance Again	Barry Manilow	#11	
1978	Two Out of Three Ain't Bad	Meat Loaf	#11	11 sec.
1978	Running on Empty	Jackson Browne	#11	
1978	Peg	Steely Dan	#11	
1978	How You Gonna See Me Now	Alice Cooper	#12	
1978	Bluer Than Blue	Michael Johnson	#12	
1978	Fool (If You Think It's Over)	Chris Rea	#12	
1978	Hollywood Nights	Bob Seger	#12	
1978	What's Your Name	Lynyrd Skynyrd	#13	
1978	Because the Night	Patti Smith Group	#13	
1978	I'm Not Gonna Let It Bother Me Tonight	Atlanta Rhythm Section	#14	
1978	Goodbye Girl	David Gates	#15	
1978	Back in the U.S.A.	Linda Ronstadt	#16	11, 17 sec.
1978	Desiree	Neil Diamond	#16	
1978	She's Always a Woman	Billy Joel	#17	
1978	Sweet Life	Paul Davis	#17	
1978	Please Come Home for Christmas	Eagles	#18	
1978	Talking in Your Sleep	Crystal Gayle	#18	
1978	Even Now	Barry Manilow	#19	
1978	The Way You Do the Things You Do	Rita Coolidge	#20	
1978	I'm Every Woman	Chaka Khan	#21	
1978	Native New Yorker	Odyssey	#21	
1978	Werewolves of London	Warren Zevon	#21	
1978	Love Theme from "Eyes of Laura Mars" (Prisoner)	Barbra Streisand	#21	13 sec.
1978	I Was Only Joking	Rod Stewart	#22	
1978	Part-Time Love	Elton John	#22	
1978	FM (No Static at All)	Steely Dan	#22	

PIANO (cont'd)				
1978	Before My Heart Finds Out	Gene Cotton	#23	
1978	The Way I Feel Tonight	Bay City Rollers	#24	
1978	The Power of Gold	Dan Fogelberg/Tim Weisberg	#24	
1978	Heartless	Heart	#24	
1978	Only the Good Die Young	Billy Joel	#24	11 sec.
1978	If Ever I See You Again	Robert Flack	#24	
1978	Thank You for Being a Friend	Andrew Gold	#25	
1978	Getting' Ready for Love	Diana Ross	#27	
1978	Hot Legs	Rod Stewart	#28	
1978	Can We Still Be Friends	Todd Rundgren	#29	
1978	Took the Last Train	David Gates	#30	
1978	Street Corner Serenade	Wet Willie	#30	
1978	Tumbling Dice	Linda Ronstadt	#32	
1978	Chattanooga Choo Choo	Tuxedo Junction	#32	
1978	Love or Something Like It	Kenny Rogers	#32	
1978	The Circle Is Small (I Can See It in Your Eyes)	Gordon Lightfoot	#33	
1978	Prove It All Night	Bruce Springsteen	#33	
1978	Ego	Elton John	#34	
1978	Think It Over	Cheryl Ladd	#34	13 sec.
1978	You're a Part of Me	Gene Cotton w/Kim Carnes	#36	
1978	Easy to Love	Leo Sayer	#36	
1978	Let's All Chant	Michael Zager Band	#36	
1978	Heartbreaker	Dolly Parton	#37	17 sec.
1978	Everybody Dance	Chic	#38	
1978	Paradise by the Dashboard Light	Meat Loaf	#39	
1978	Galaxy	War	#39	
1978	Ease on Down the Road	Diana Ross & Michael Jackson	#41	
1978	All I See Is Your Face	Dan Hill	#41	
1978	(I Will Be Your) Shadow in the Street	Allan Clarke	#41	
1978	Badlands	Bruce Springsteen	#42	
1978	Mammas Don't Let Your Babies Grow Up to Be Cowboys	Waylon Jennings & Willie Nelson	#42	
1978	I Don't Wanna Go	Joey Travolta	#43	
1978	Sweet, Sweet Smile	Carpenters	#44	
1978	How Can I Leave You Again	John Denver	#44	
1978	Little One	Chicago	#44	
1978	Make You Feel Love Again	Wet Willie	#45	
1978	Hold Me, Touch Me	Paul Stanley	#46	
1978	Since You Been Gone	Head East	#46	
1978	Greased Lightnin'	John Travolta	#47	
1978	The Dream Never Dies	Cooper Brothers	#48	
1978	The Next Hundred Years	Al Martino	#49	

		PIANO (cont'd)			
1978	If You Wanna Do a Dance	Spinners	#49	
1978	That's Your Secret	Sea Level	#50	
1978	Darlin'	Paul Davis w/Susan Collins	#51	
1978	Livingston Saturday Night	Jimmy Buffett	#52	
1978	You Don't Love Me Anymore	Eddie Rabbitt	#53	
1978	I Want to Live	John Denver	#55	12 sec.
1978	I Want You to Be Mine	Kayak	#55	
1978	Music, Harmony and Rhythm	Brooklyn Dreams	#57	
1978	Storybook Children (Daybreak)	Bette Midler	#57	
1978	Roll with the Changes	REO Speedwagon	#58	
1978	New Orleans Ladies	Louisiana's Le Roux	#59	
1978	Miles Away	Fotomaker	#63	14 sec.
1978	Only One Love in My Life	Ronnie Milsap	#63	11 sec.
1978	This Night Won't Last Forever	Bill LaBounty	#65	
1978	Hot Shot	Karen Young	#67	
1978	I Believe You	Carpenters	#68	
1978	Lights	Journey	#68	
1978	You Got That Right	Lynyrd Skynyrd	#69	
1978	Let's Live Together	Cazz	#70	15 sec.
1978	You'll Love Again	Hotel	#71	
1978	Cuz It's You, Girl	James Walsh Gypsy Band	#71	
1978	Until Now	Bobby Arvon	#72	
1978	Martha (Your Lovers Come and Go)	Gabriel	#73	15 sec.
1978	God Knows	Debby Boone	#74	
1978	I'm on My Way	Captain & Tennille	#74	
1978	It's Over	Electric Light Orchestra	#75	
1978	Don't Cost You Nothing	Ashford & Simpson	#79	
1978	What a Difference You've Made in My Life	Ronnie Milsap	#80	
1978	Georgia on My Mind	Willie Nelson	#84	
1978	Manana	Jimmy Buffett	#84	
1978	It's Really You	Tarney/Spencer Band	#86	
1978	Get Back	Billy Preston	#86	
1978	Never Had a Love	Pablo Cruise	#87	
1978	Disco Rufus	Stargard	#88	
1978	Boats Against the Current	Eric Carmen	#88	20 sec.
1978	The Loneliest Man on the Moon	David Castle	#89	
1978	Louie, Louie	John Belushi	#89	
1978	Let the Song Last Forever	Dan Hill	#91	
1978	Don't Let It Show	Alan Parsons Project	#92	
1978	Back in My Arms Again	Genya Ravan	#92	
1979	Bad Girls	Donna Summer	#1	

PIANO (cont'd)

1979	Rise	Herb Alpert	#1	
1979	No More Tears (Enough Is Enough)	Barbra Streisand/Donna Summer	#1	
1979	Still	Commodores	#1	
1979	What a Fool Believes	The Doobie Brothers	#1	
1979	Good Times	Chic	#1	
1979	After the Love Has Gone	Earth, Wind & Fire	#2	
1979	Fire	Pointer Sisters	#2	
1979	We Are Family	Sister Sledge	#2	
1979	The Devil Went Down to Georgia	Charlie Daniels Band	#3	
1979	Music Box Dancer	Frank Mills	#3	
1979	Sail On	Commodores	#4	
1979	She Believes in Me	Kenny Rogers	#5	
1979	Hold the Line	Toto	#5	19 sec.
1979	You're Only Lonely	J.D. Souther	#7	
1979	You Decorated My Life	Kenny Rogers	#7	10 sec.
1979	Ooh Baby Baby	Linda Ronstadt	#7	
1979	I Want Your Love	Chic	#7	
1979	Mama Can't Buy You Love	Elton John	#9	
1979	Somewhere in the Night	Barry Manilow	#9	
1979	Lady	Little River Band	#10	
1979	You Take My Breath Away	Rex Smith	#10	
1979	Take the Long Way Home	Supertramp	#10	
1979	Love Takes Time	Orleans	#11	
1979	Deeper Than the Night	Olivia Newton-John	#11	
1979	I Just Fall in Love Again	Anne Murray	#12	
1979	Broken Hearted Me	Anne Murray	#12	13, 13, 20 sec.
1979	Disco Nights (Rock-Freak)	G.Q.	#12	
1979	We've Got Tonite	Bob Seger	#13	14 sec.
1979	Every Time I Think of You	The Babys	#13	
1979	Soul Man	Blues Brothers	#14	
1979	I Can't Stand It No More	Peter Frampton	#14	
1979	Big Shot	Billy Joel	#14	
1979	Goodbye Stranger	Supertramp	#15	
1979	Blue Morning, Blue Day	Foreigner	#15	
1979	Lovin', Touchin', Squeezin'	Journey	#16	
1979	The Gambler	Kenny Rogers	#16	
1979	If You Remember Me	Chris Thompson & Night	#17	
1979	Dancin' Shoes	Nigel Olsson	#18	
1979	I Want You Tonight	Pablo Cruise	#19	
1979	This Night Won't Last Forever	Michael Johnson	#19	
1979	Get Used to It	Roger Voudouris	#21	

		PIANO (cont'd)			
1979	People of the South Wind	Kansas	#23	
1979	Honesty	Billy Joel	#24	
1979	Bicycle Race	Queen	#24	
1979	Baby I'm Burnin'	Dolly Parton	#25	
1979	Dependin' on You	The Doobie Brothers	#25	
1979	Old Time Rock & Roll	Bob Seger	#28	
1979	Up on the Roof	James Taylor	#28	
1979	Weekend	Wet Willie	#29	
1979	So Good, So Right	Brenda Russell	#30	
1979	Oh Well	Rockets	#30	
1979	Happiness	Pointer Sisters	#30	
1979	(If Loving You Is Wrong) I Don't Want to Be Right	Barbara Mandrell	#31	
1979	A Man I'll Never Be	Boston	#31	
1979	Shakedown Cruise	Jay Ferguson	#31	
1979	One Last Kiss	The J. Geils Band	#35	
1979	Fins	Jimmy Buffett	#35	
1979	Found a Cure	Ashford & Simpson	#36	
1979	Rubber Biscuit	Blues Brothers	#37	
1979	You Took the Words Right Out of My Mouth	Meat Loaf	#39	
1979	Video Killed the Radio Star	The Buggles	#40	
1979	Get It Up	Ronnie Milsap	#43	
1979	Dance Away	Roxy Music	#44	
1979	I've Never Been in Love	Suzi Quatro	#44	
1979	Diamonds	Chris Rea	#44	
1979	Just One Look	Linda Ronstadt	#44	
1979	Dancin' Fool	Frank Zappa	#45	
1979	Who Listens to the Radio	The Sports	#45	
1979	5:15	The Who	#45	
1979	I Go to Rio	Pablo Cruise	#46	
1979	Get a Move On	Eddie Money	#46	
1979	Dancer	Gino Soccio	#48	
1979	Georgy Porgy	Toto w/Cheryl Lynn	#48	
1979	Peter Piper	Frank Mills	#48	
1979	Vengeance	Carly Simon	#48	
1979	I Need Your Help Barry Manilow	Ray Stevens	#49	
1979	Do You Wanna Go Party	KC and The Sunshine Band	#50	
1979	Can You Read My Mind	Maureen McGovern	#52	
1979	Sweets for My Sweet	Tony Orlando	#54	
1979	Dancin' Shoes	Faith Band	#54	
1979	At Midnight	T-Connection	#56	
1979	Since You Been Gone	Rainbow	#57	

		PIANO (cont'd)		
1979	Then You Can Tell Me Goodbye	Toby Beau	#57	
1979	This Is Love	Oak	#58	
1979	Pops, We Love You (A Tribute to Father)	Diana Ross, Marvin Gaye, Smokey Robinson & Stevie Wonder	#59	
1979	You're the Only One	Dolly Parton	#59	
1979	Moment by Moment	Yvonne Elliman	#59	
1979	My Love Is Music	Space	#60	
1979	Heartaches	BTO	#60	
1979	Killer Cut	Charlie	#60	
1979	Easy to Be Hard	Cheryl Barnes	#64	
1979	Heart to Heart	Errol Sober	#65	28 sec.
1979	One Fine Day	Rita Coolidge	#66	
1979	Take It Back	The J. Geils Band	#67	
1979	Just Another Night	Ian Hunter	#68	
1979	You've Really Got a Hold on Me	Eddie Money	#72	
1979	Animal House	Stephen Bishop	#73	
1979	In Thee	Blue Öyster Cult	#74	
1979	Theme from Ice Castles (Through the Eyes of Love)	Melissa Manchester	#76	13 sec.
1979	Hey, St. Peter	Flash and The Pan	#76	
1979	Plain Jane	Sammy Hagar	#77	
1979	Hold on to the Night	Hotel	#80	
1979	I Need You	Euclid Beach Band	#81	
1979	Cuba	Gibson Brothers	#81	15, 23 sec.
1979	I'll Come Running	Livingston Taylor	#82	
1979	Dancin'	Grey & Hanks	#83	
1979	I Never Said I Love You	Orsa Lia	#84	
1979	I Do Believe in You	Pages	#84	
1979	The Man with the Child in His Eyes	Kate Bush	#85	
1979	Don't Stop Me Now	Queen	#86	
1979	Aqua Boogie (A Psychoalphadiscobetabioaquadoloop)	Parliament	#89	
1979	Ain't That Enough for You	John Davis	#89	
1979	You've Lost That Lovin' Feelin'	Long John Baldry & Kathi MacDonald	#89	
1979	Frederick	Patti Smith Group	#90	
1979	I Do the Rock	Tim Curry	#91	
1979	This Is It	Dan Hartman	#91	
1979	What's A Matter Baby	Ellen Foley	#92	
1979	Pinball, That's All	Bill Wray	#96	
1979	When You're #1	Gene Chandler	#99	

SAXOPHONE

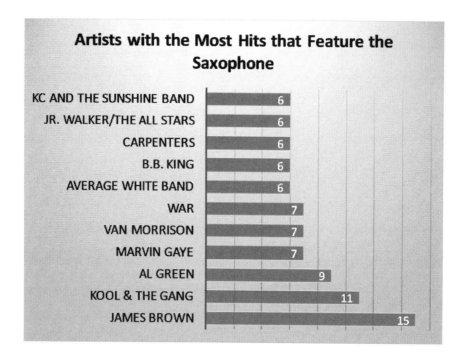

YEAR	SONG	ARTIST	HOT 100	Length of Solo
1970	Thank You (Falettinme Be Mice Elf Again)	Sly & The Family Stone	#1	
1970	Travelin' Band	Creedence Clearwater Revival	#2	
1970	Get Ready	Rare Earth	#4	
1970	The Letter	Joe Cocker w/Leon Russell	#7	18 sec.
1970	Easy Come Easy Go	Bobby Sherman	#9	
1970	Super Bad (Part 1 & Part 2)	James Brown	#13	
1970	Celebrate	Three Dog Night	#15	
1970	Gotta Hold on to this Feeling	Jr. Walker/The All Stars	#21	55, 17, 22, 16 sec.
1970	Blowing Away	The 5th Dimension	#21	
1970	You're the One – Part 2	Little Sister	#22	
1970	Fancy	Bobbie Gentry	#31	
1970	Do You See My Love (For You Growing)	Jr. Walker/The All Stars	#32	
1970	Steal Away	Johnnie Taylor	#37	
1970	Come Running	Van Morrison	#39	
1970	I Can't Leave Your Love Alone	Clarence Carter	#42	
1970	Oh What a Day	The Dells	#43	
1970	Soul Shake	Delaney & Bonnie & Friends	#43	25 sec.
1970	Part Time Love	Ann Peebles	#45	

SAXOPHONE (cont'd)					
1970	Freedom Blues	Little Richard	#47	29 sec.
1970	So Much Love	Faith, Hope & Charity	#51	13 sec.
1970	Into the Mystic	Johnny Rivers	#51	23 sec.
1970	Open Up My Heart	The Dells	#51	
1970	Funky Drummer (Part 1)	James Brown	#51	44 sec.
1970	I'll Be Right Here	Tyrone Davis	#53	
1970	Moon Walk Part 1	Joe Simon	#54	
1970	I'm So Excited	B.B. King	#54	
1970	I'm Just a Prisoner (Of Your Good Lovin')	Candi Staton	#56	
1970	Where Did All the Good Times Go	Dennis Yost/Classics IV	#69	11 sec.
1970	I Need Help (I Can't Do It Alone) Pt. 1	Bobby Byrd	#69	
1970	When the Party Is Over	Robert John	#71	
1970	If Walls Could Talk	Little Milton	#71	
1970	We Can Make It Baby	The Originals	#74	
1970	Superstar	Murray Head w/The Trinidad Singers	#74	
1970	Let the Music Take Your Mind	Kool & The Gang	#78	
1970	Them Changes	Buddy Miles	#81	
1970	The Gangs Back Again	Kool & The Gang	#85	
1970	Compared to What	Les McCann & Eddie Harris	#85	
1970	This Is My Love Song	The Intruders	#85	
1970	Man of Constant Sorrow	Ginger Baker's Air Force (Denny Laine)	#85	
1970	Country Preacher	Cannonball Adderley	#86	
1970	Funky Man	Kool & The Gang	#87	
1970	Get Down People	Fabulous Counts	#88	
1970	Keep on Loving Me (You'll See the Change)	Bobby Bland	#89	
1970	Get into Something	The Isley Brothers	#89	
1970	Funky Chicken (Part 1)	Willie Henderson w/The Soul Explosions	#91	
1970	Wrap It Up	Archie Bell & The Drells	#93	
1970	I Gotta Let You Go	Martha & The Vandellas	#93	
1970	That's the Way I Want Our Love	Joe Simon	#93	
1970	The Lights of Tucson	Jim Campbell	#93	
1970	Bring It on Home	Lou Rawls	#96	
1970	Baby Don't Take Your Love	Faith, Hope & Charity	#96	14 sec.
1970	Darling Dear	Smokey Robinson & The Miracles	#100	
1971	It's Too Late	Carole King	#1	
1971	Brown Sugar	The Rolling Stones	#1	28 sec.
1971	What's Going On	Marvin Gaye	#2	
1971	Mr. Big Stuff	Jean Knight	#2	
1971	Rainy Days and Mondays	Carpenters	#2	13 sec.
1971	It Don't Come Easy	Ringo Starr	#4	
1971	Mercy Mercy Me (The Ecology)	Marvin Gaye	#4	18 sec.

				SAXOPHONE (cont'd)	
1971	Proud Mary	Ike & Tina Turner	#4	
1971	Bridge Over Troubled Water	Aretha Franklin	#6	
1971	Domino	Van Morrison	#9	
1971	Power to the People	John Lennon	#11	17 sec.
1971	Tired of Being Alone	Al Green	#11	
1971	Trapped By a Thing Called Love	Denise LaSalle	#13	
1971	Hot Pants (She Got to Use What She Got to Get What She Wants) (Pt. 1)	James Brown	#15	
1971	A Natural Man	Lou Rawls	#17	
1971	Bangla-Desh	George Harrison	#23	
1971	Stagger Lee	Tommy Roe	#25	
1971	Stop the War Now	Edwin Starr	#26	
1971	Wild Night	Van Morrison	#28	12 sec.
1971	Precious, Precious	Jackie Moore	#30	
1971	Get Up, Get Into It, Get Involved (Pt. 1)	James Brown	#34	
1971	All Day Music	War	#35	
1971	Booty Butt	Ray Charles Orchestra	#36	
1971	Resurrection Shuffle	Tom Jones	#38	
1971	K-Jee	The Nite-Liters	#39	
1971	Resurrection Shuffle	Ashton, Gardner & Dyke	#40	
1971	Do Me Right	Detroit Emeralds	#43	
1971	Bridget the Midget (The Queen of the Blues)	Ray Stevens	#50	
1971	They Can't Take Away Our Music	Eric Burdon & War	#50	
1971	Take Me Girl, I'm Ready	Jr. Walker/The All Stars	#50	20 sec.
1971	Call My Name, I'll Be There	Wilson Pickett	#52	
1971	I Hear Those Church Bells Ringing	Dusk	#53	
1971	Angel Baby	Dusk	#57	
1971	Bad Water	The Raeletts	#58	
1971	Whole Lotta Love	C.C.S.	#58	
1971	I Can't Get Next to You	Al Green	#60	
1971	Ooh Poo Pah Doo	Ike & Tina Turner	#60	25 sec.
1971	The Court Room	Clarence Carter	#61	
1971	Whole Lotta Love	King Curtis	#64	
1971	Gimme Some Lovin'-Pt. 1	Traffic	#68	
1971	Life Is a Carnival	The Band	#72	
1971	Freedom	Isley Brothers	#72	
1971	Don't Try to Lay No Boogie-Woogie on the King of Rock and Roll	John Baldry	#73	
1971	Lisa, Listen to Me	Blood, Sweat & Tears	#73	25 sec.
1971	Your Love (Means Everything to Me)	Charles Wright	#73	
1971	Indian Summer	Audience	#74	
1971	Holly Holy	Jr. Walker/The All Stars	#75	45 sec.

		SAXOPHONE (cont'd)		
1971	Hill Where the Lord Hides	Chuck Mangione	#76	
1971	You're the One	The Three Degrees	#77	35 sec.
1971	Suspicious Minds	Dee Dee Warwick	#80	
1971	It's the Real Thing – Pt. 1	The Electric Express	#81	
1971	Sea Cruise	Johnny Rivers	#84	
1971	We Got to Live Together – part 1	Buddy Miles	#86	
1971	We'll Have It Made	The Spinners	#89	
1971	Spinning Wheel (Pt. 1)	James Brown	#90	
1971	The Glory of Love	The Dells	#92	
1971	Love Is Life	Earth, Wind & Fire	#93	23 sec.
1971	Super Highway	Ballin' Jack	#93	
1971	Call Me Up in Dreamland	Van Morrison	#95	27 sec.
1971	Near You	Boz Scaggs	#96	
1971	Puff of Smoke	Roy Head	#96	
1971	Be Good to Me Baby	Luther Ingram	#97	
1971	I'm Sorry	Bobby Bland	#97	
1971	My Heart Is Yours	Wilbert Harrison	#98	
1972	Me and Mrs. Jones	Billy Paul	#1	
1972	I'll Take You There	The Staple Singers	#1	
1972	I Gotcha	Joe Tex	#2	
1972	You Ought to Be with Me	Al Green	#3	
1972	Jungle Fever	The Chackachas	#8	
1972	Honky Cat	Elton John	#8	
1972	Bang a Gong (Get It On)	T. Rex	#10	
1972	Power of Love	Joe Simon	#11	
1972	One Monkey Don't Stop No Show (Part 1)	Honey Cone	#15	
1972	Thunder and Lightning	Chi Coltrane	#17	
1972	Get on the Good Foot – Part 1	James Brown	#18	
1972	Starting All Over Again	Mel and Tim	#19	
1972	Baby Let Me Take You (In My Arms)	Detroit Emeralds	#24	
1972	Talking Loud and Saying Nothing – Part 1	James Brown	#27	
1972	White Lies, Blue Eyes	Bullet	#28	
1972	You're Still a Young Man	Tower of Power	#29	
1972	Mister Can't You See	Buffy Sainte-Marie	#38	
1972	You Said a Bad Word	Joe Tex	#41	
1972	Lies	J.J. Cale	#42	
1972	Those Were the Days	Carroll O'Connor & Jean Stapleton	#43	
1972	There It Is (Part 1)	James Brown	#43	
1972	Hearsay	The Soul Children	#44	
1972	Honky Tonk – Part 1	James Brown	#44	
1972	Walk in the Night	Jr. Walker/The All Stars	#46	

	SAXOPHONE (cont'd)			
1972	Now Run and Tell That	Denise LaSalle	#46	
1972	Tupelo Honey	Van Morrison	#47	24 sec.
1972	Let's Stay Together	Isaac Hayes	#48	
1972	Way Back Home	Jr. Walker/The All Stars	#52	
1972	Put It Where You Want It	The Crusaders	#52	
1972	Man Sized Job	Denise LaSalle	#55	
1972	Why Can't We Be Lovers	Holland-Dozier	#57	22 sec.
1972	Woman Is the Nigger of the World	John Lennon	#57	
1972	Under My Wheels	Alice Cooper	#59	
1972	That's What Love Will Make You Do	Little Milton	#59	
1972	Move 'Em Out	Delaney & Bonnie	#59	19 sec.
1972	Everybody Knows About My Good Thing Pt. 1	Little Johnny Taylor	#60	
1972	Waking Up Alone	Paul Williams	#60	15 sec.
1972	I Love You More Than You'll Ever Know	Donny Hathaway	#60	
1972	Jackie Wilson Said (I'm in Heaven When You Smile)	Van Morrison	#61	
1972	I Had It All the Time	Tyrone Davis	#61	
1972	What'd I Say	Rare Earth	#61	32 sec.
1972	Guess Who	B.B. King	#61	
1972	Victim of a Foolish Heart	Bettye Swann	#63	
1972	Take It Slow (Out in the Country)	Lighthouse	#64	
1972	Cheer	Potliquor	#65	
1972	Day and Night	The Wackers	#65	
1972	Think (About It)	Lyn Collins	#66	
1972	Down to the Nightclub	Tower of Power	#66	
1972	Changes	David Bowie	#66	
1972	Gimme Some More	The JB's	#67	
1972	Keep Playin' That Rock 'N' Roll	Edgar Winter's White Trash	#70	
1972	After All This Time	Merry Clayton	#71	
1972	Iko Iko	Dr. John	#71	
1972	What It Is	The Undisputed Truth	#71	
1972	What a Wonderful Thing We Have	Fabulous Rhinestones	#78	38 sec.
1972	Beat Me Daddy Eight to the Bar	Commander Cody	#81	14 sec.
1972	Giving Up	Donny Hathaway	#81	
1972	Me and My Baby Got a Good Thing Going	Lyn Collins	#86	
1972	Rockin' with the King	Canned Heat w/Little Richard	#88	38 sec.
1972	Eve	Jim Capaldi	#91	
1972	Sweet Sixteen	B.B. King	#93	
1972	It's the Same Old Love	The Courtship	#93	
1972	Celebration	Tommy James	#95	18 sec.
1972	Number Wonderful	Rock Flowers	#95	16 sec.
1972	Turn on Your Love Light	Jerry Lee Lewis	#95	14 sec.

	SAXOPHONE (cont'd)			
1972	Pass the Peas	The JB's	#95	
1972	America	Simon & Garfunkel	#97	
1972	Redwood Tree	Van Morrison	#98	
1972	You Really Got a Hold on Me	Gayle McCormick	#98	
1972	Southbound Train	Graham Nash & David Crosby	#99	13, 34, 34 sec.
1973	Let's Get It On	Marvin Gaye	#1	
1973	Will It Go Round in Circles	Billy Preston	#1	
1973	Frankenstein	Edgar Winter Group	#1	
1973	Superstition	Stevie Wonder	#1	
1973	Photograph	Ringo Starr	#1	13 sec.
1973	The Cisco Kid	War	#2	
1973	Oh, Babe, What Would You Say?	Hurricane Smith	#3	32, 30 sec.
1973	Why Can't We Live Together	Timmy Thomas	#3	
1973	Just You 'N' Me	Chicago	#4	30 sec.
1973	Space Race	Billy Preston	#4	
1973	Your Mama Don't Dance	Loggins & Messina	#4	
1973	Hello It's Me	Todd Rundgren	#5	
1973	Diamond Girl	Seals & Crofts	#6	23 sec.
1973	The World Is a Ghetto	War	#7	
1973	Trouble Man	Marvin Gaye	#7	
1973	Money	Pink Floyd	#13	32 sec.
1973	Don't Let Me Be Lonely Tonight	James Taylor	#14	34 sec.
1973	Cheaper to Keep Her	Johnnie Taylor	#15	
1973	Walk on the Wild Side	Lou Reed	#16	23 sec.
1973	My Music	Loggins & Messina	#16	11 sec.
1973	So Very Hard to Go	Tower of Power	#17	15 sec.
1973	Angel	Aretha Franklin	#20	10 sec.
1973	Come Get to This	Marvin Gaye	#21	
1973	I Was Checkin' out She Was Checkin' In	Don Covay	#29	13 sec.
1973	Give Me Your Love	Barbara Mason	#31	
1973	I've Got so Much to Give	Barry White	#32	
1973	There It Is	Tyrone Davis	#32	
1973	Good Morning Heartache	Diana Ross	#34	
1973	Hey Girl (I Like Your Style)	The Temptations	#35	
1973	Soul Makossa	Manu Dibango	#35	
1973	Bitter Bad	Melanie	#36	
1973	To Know You Is to Love You	B.B. King	#38	
1973	I Can't Stand the Rain	Ann Peebles	#38	
1973	Soul Makossa	Afrique	#47	16 sec.
1973	The Message	Cymande	#48	10 sec.

	SAXOPHONE (cont'd)			
1973	Who Was It?	Hurricane Smith	#49	16, 16 sec.
1973	Sexy, Sexy, Sexy	James Brown	#50	
1973	Daytime Night-Time	Keith Hampshire	#51	
1973	Pardon Me Sir	Joe Cocker	#51	16 sec.
1973	Let Me Be Your Lovemaker	Betty Wright	#55	
1973	River	Joe Simon	#62	
1973	Yesterday I Had the Blues	Harold Melvin	#63	
1973	Slick	Willie Hutch	#65	
1973	Sixty Minute Man	Clarence Carter	#65	
1973	Brother's Gonna Work It Out	Willie Hutch	#67	
1973	Didn't I	Sylvia	#70	10 sec.
1973	Parrty – Part 1	Maceo and The Macks	#71	22, 42, 25 sec.
1973	Hot Wire	Al Green	#71	
1973	Ain't Got No Home	The Band	#73	16 sec.
1973	Am I Black Enough for You	Billy Paul	#79	
1973	What a Shame	Foghat	#82	
1973	But I Do	Bobby Vinton	#82	
1973	You Can Do Magic	Limmie & Family Cookin'	#84	14 sec.
1973	River Road	Uncle Dog	#86	38 sec.
1973	Don't Let It Get You Down	The Crusaders	#86	
1973	Breaking Up Somebody's Home	Albert King	#91	
1973	A Little Bit Like Magic	King Harvest	#91	15 sec.
1973	Mr. Skin	Spirit	#92	19 sec.
1973	Until It's Time for You to Go	The New Birth	#97	
1974	The Night Chicago Died	Paper Lace	#1	
1974	Whatever Gets You Thru the Night	John Lennon	#1	13, 16, 14, 16 sec.
1974	Do It ('Til You're Satisfied)	B.T. Express	#2	
1974	Jazzman	Carole King	#2	12, 16, 31 sec.
1974	Jungle Boogie	Kool & The Gang	#4	
1974	The Bitch Is Back	Elton John	#4	18 sec.
1974	Mockingbird	Carly Simon & James Taylor	#5	15, 40 sec.
1974	Oh My My	Ringo Starr	#5	26 sec.
1974	Waterloo	ABBA	#6	
1974	Hollywood Swinging	Kool & The Gang	#6	
1974	Help Me	Joni Mitchell	#7	
1974	Me and Baby Brother	War	#15	
1974	Trying to Hold on to My Woman	Lamont Dozier	#15	
1974	Doo Doo Doo Doo Doo (Heartbreaker)	The Rolling Stones	#15	

SAXOPHONE (cont'd)

Year	Title	Artist	Peak	Time
1974	There Won't Be Anymore	Charlie Rich	#18	
1974	Overnight Sensation (Hit Record)	Raspberries	#18	13 sec.
1974	Livin' for You	Al Green	#19	
1974	Don't Change Horses (In the Middle of a Stream)	Tower of Power	#26	
1974	Let Your Hair Down	The Temptations	#27	
1974	Distant Lover	Marvin Gaye	#28	
1974	I Like to Live the Love	B.B. King	#28	
1974	Son of Sagittarius	Eddie Kendricks	#28	
1974	Straight Shootin' Woman	Steppenwolf	#29	
1974	My Thang	James Brown	#29	
1974	Can This Be Real	Natural Four	#31	19, 19 sec.
1974	I'm a Train	Albert Hammond	#31	
1974	Papa Don't Take No Mess (Part 1)	James Brown	#31	
1974	Let's Get Married	Al Green	#32	
1974	Happiness Is Just Around the Bend	The Main Ingredient	#35	
1974	I'll Be the Other Woman	The Soul Children	#36	
1974	Higher Plane	Kool & The Gang	#37	17 sec.
1974	Thanks for Saving My Life	Billy Paul	#38	
1974	Whatever You Got, I Want	The Jackson 5	#38	
1974	I Shall Sing	Garfunkel	#38	13 sec.
1974	Rock Around the Clock	Bill Haley & His Comets	#39	14 sec.
1974	Heartbreak Kid	Bo Donaldson & The Heywoods	#39	
1974	Kung Fu	Curtis Mayfield	#40	
1974	The Black-Eyed Boys	Paper Lace	#41	13 sec.
1974	Chameleon	Herbie Hancock	#42	
1974	Put Out the Light	Joe Cocker	#46	17, 24 sec.
1974	Can You Handle It?	Graham Central Station	#49	
1974	You Sure Love to Ball	Marvin Gaye	#50	
1974	Keep It in the Family	Leon Haywood	#50	
1974	In the Mood	Bette Midler	#51	
1974	Virgin Man	Smokey Robinson	#56	
1974	Stoned to the Bone – Part 1	James Brown	#58	
1974	You're Welcome, Stop on By	Bobby Womack	#59	
1974	Wang Dang Doodle	The Pointer Sisters	#61	
1974	Travelin' Shoes	Elvin Bishop	#61	
1974	There Will Never Be Any Peace (Until God Is Seated at the Conference Table)	The Chi-Lites	#63	
1974	Raised on Robbery	Joni Mitchell	#65	
1974	Unborn Child	Seals & Crofts	#66	
1974	The Lone Ranger	Oscar Brown Jr.	#69	
1974	Do It, Fluid	The Blackbyrds	#69	22 sec.

	SAXOPHONE (cont'd)			
1974	Boogie Bands and One Night Stands	Kathy Dalton	#72	
1974	I Feel Sanctified	Commodores	#75	
1974	Who Are You	B.B. King	#78	
1974	Scratch	The Crusaders	#81	
1974	It's Her Turn to Live	Smokey Robinson	#82	
1974	Bad, Bad Leroy Brown	Frank Sinatra	#83	
1974	Easy Street	Edgar Winter Group	#83	48 sec.
1974	Love Is the Message	MFSB/Three Degrees	#85	
1974	I Wouldn't Treat a Dog (The Way You Treated Me)	Bobby Bland	#88	
1974	Let This Be a Lesson to You	The Independents	#88	
1974	(Everybody Wanna Get Rich) Rite Away	Dr. John	#92	
1975	Laughter in the Rain	Neil Sedaka	#1	19 sec.
1975	Lady Marmalade	LaBelle	#1	
1975	Pick Up the Pieces	Average White Band	#1	
1975	Listen to What the Man Said	Paul McCartney & Wings	#1	15 sec.
1975	Please Mr. Postman	Carpenters	#1	15 sec.
1975	Miracles	Jefferson Starship	#3	
1975	No No Song	Ringo Starr	#3	
1975	Express	B.T. Express	#4	
1975	Only Yesterday	Carpenters	#4	13 sec.
1975	Love Won't Let Me Wait	Major Harris	#5	
1975	How Sweet It Is (To Be Loved By You)	James Taylor	#5	17 sec.
1975	Poetry Man	Phoebe Snow	#5	29 sec.
1975	Low Rider	War	#7	
1975	Cut the Cake	Average White Band	#10	
1975	Brazil	The Ritchie Family	#11	
1975	Our Day Will Come	Frankie Valli	#11	15 sec.
1975	Shame, Shame, Shame	Shirley (And Company)	#12	17 sec.
1975	It's a Miracle	Barry Manilow	#12	
1975	Harry Truman	Chicago	#13	
1975	Sad Sweet Dreamer	Sweet Sensation	#14	
1975	Lady Blue	Leon Russell	#14	11 sec.
1975	Eighteen with a Bullet	Pete Wingfield	#15	12 sec.
1975	Up in a Puff of Smoke	Polly Brown	#16	
1975	You	George Harrison	#20	10, 14 sec.
1975	Stand By Me	John Lennon	#20	
1975	Black Superman – "Muhammad Ali"	Johnny Wakelin	#21	22 sec.
1975	Operator	The Manhattan Transfer	#22	30 sec.
1975	Help Me Rhonda	Johnny Rivers	#22	13 sec.
1975	Born to Run	Bruce Springsteen	#23	15 sec.
1975	Shakey Ground	The Temptations	#26	18 sec.

		SAXOPHONE (cont'd)		
1975	Full of Fire	Al Green	#28	
1975	Young Americans	David Bowie	#28	21, 11 sec.
1975	Butter Boy	Fanny	#29	18 sec.
1975	Shaving Cream	Benny Bell	#30	
1975	Just Too Many People	Melissa Manchester	#30	
1975	Peace Pipe	B.T. Express	#31	
1975	It's All Down to Goodnight Vienna	Ringo Starr	#31	
1975	School Boy Crush	Average White Band	#33	
1975	Sweet Sticky Thing	Ohio Players	#33	30, 29 sec.
1975	You're All I Need to Get By	Tony Orlando & Dawn	#34	20 sec.
1975	Spirit of the Boogie	Kool & The Gang	#35	
1975	Bloody Well Right	Supertramp	#35	25 sec.
1975	Bluebird	Helen Reddy	#35	18 sec.
1975	Ding Dong; Ding Dong	George Harrison	#36	
1975	Glasshouse	The Temptations	#37	
1975	Your Love	Graham Central Station	#38	
1975	If I Ever Lose This Heaven	Average White Band	#39	22 sec.
1975	Letting Go	Paul McCartney & Wings	#39	
1975	Give It What You Got	B.T. Express	#40	
1975	Good Times, Rock & Roll	Flash Cadillac & The Continental Kids	#41	
1975	Sexy	MFSB	#42	
1975	If Loving You Is Wrong I Don't Want to Be Right	Millie Jackson	#42	
1975	Sun Goddess	Ramsey Lewis & Earth, Wind & Fire	#44	
1975	Give the People What They Want	The O'Jays	#45	
1975	Welcome to My Nightmare	Alice Cooper	#45	
1975	Keep Your Eye on the Sparrow	Merry Clayton	#45	16 sec.
1975	This Old Man	Purple Reign	#48	
1975	Take Me to the River	Syl Johnson	#48	
1975	Oh Me, Oh My (Dreams in My Arms)	Al Green	#48	
1975	You Brought the Woman Out of Me	Evie Sands	#50	
1975	Money	Gladys Knight & The Pips	#50	
1975	Growin'	Loggins & Messina	#52	
1975	I'm Her Fool	Billy Swan	#53	
1975	Mister Magic	Grover Washington, Jr.	#54	
1975	Caribbean Festival	Kool & The Gang	#55	
1975	(Just Like) Romeo and Juliet	Sha Na Na	#55	
1975	Don't Let Go	Commander Cody	#56	
1975	Sneakin' Up Behind You	The Brecker Brothers	#58	
1975	Day Tripper	Anne Murray	#59	
1975	Pinball	Brian Protheroe	#60	19 sec.

	SAXOPHONE (cont'd)			
1975	Got to Get You Into My Life	Blood, Sweat & Tears	#62	
1975	Rhyme Tyme People	Kool & The Gang	#63	
1975	So in Love	Curtis Mayfield	#67	
1975	Come and Get Your Love	Roger Daltrey	#68	
1975	Drive My Car	Gary Toms Empire	#69	
1975	Alvin Stone (The Birth & Death of a Gangster)	Fantastic Four	#74	
1975	Same Thing It Took	The Impressions	#75	
1975	The Funky Gibbon	The Goodies	#79	
1975	Jam Band	Disco Tex & His Sex-O-Lettes	#80	
1975	Reality	James Brown	#80	
1975	Gee Baby	Peter Shelley	#81	17 sec.
1975	The Music Never Stopped	The Grateful Dead	#81	
1975	I Like It Like That	Loggins & Messina	#84	15 sec.
1975	I Want to Dance with You (Dance with Me)	The Ritchie Family	#84	
1975	Shotgun Shuffle	The Sunshine Band	#88	
1975	Baby-Get It On	Ike & Tina Turner	#88	13 sec.
1975	A Lover's Question	Loggins & Messina	#89	
1975	The Zip	MFSB	#91	
1975	Smokin' Room	Carl Carlton	#91	
1975	All Right Now	Lea Roberts	#92	
1975	Chocolate Chip	Isaac Hayes	#92	
1975	It's Alright	Graham Central Station	#92	
1975	Chocolate City	Parliament	#94	
1975	My First Day Without Her	Dennis Yost/Classics IV	#94	
1975	Granddaddy (Part 1)	New Birth	#95	
1975	You and Your Baby Blues	Solomon Burke	#96	
1975	We All Gotta Stick Together	Four Tops	#97	
1976	Tonight's the Night (Gonna Be Alright)	Rod Stewart	#1	21 sec.
1976	Silly Love Songs	Paul McCartney & Wings	#1	
1976	Play That Funky Music	Wild Cherry	#1	
1976	December, 1963 (Oh, What a Night)	The Four Seasons	#1	
1976	Kiss and Say Goodbye	Manhattans	#1	
1976	Let 'Em In	Paul McCartney & Wings	#3	
1976	More Than a Feeling	Boston	#5	
1976	Get Closer	Seals & Crofts w/Carolyn Willis	#6	
1976	There's a Kind of Hush (All Over the World)	Carpenters	#12	
1976	Takin' It to the Streets	The Doobie Brothers	#13	24 sec.
1976	I Do, I Do, I Do, I Do, I Do	ABBA	#15	15 sec.
1976	Tangerine	The Salsoul Orchestra	#18	
1976	Young Hearts Run Free	Candi Staton	#20	
1976	Making Our Dreams Come True	Cyndi Grecco	#25	

		SAXOPHONE (cont'd)		
1976	You Are My Starship	Norman Connors	#27	23 sec.
1976	Only Love Is Real	Carole King	#28	
1976	Did You Boogie (With Your Baby)	Flash Cadillac & The Continental Kids	#29	
1976	Nice 'N' Naasty	The Salsoul Orchestra	#30	
1976	Love Is the Drug	Roxy Music	#30	
1976	Anytime (I'll Be There)	Paul Anka	#33	
1976	Anything You Want	John Valenti	#37	
1976	Give It Up (Turn It Loose)	Tyrone Davis	#38	
1976	Still Crazy After All These Years	Paul Simon	#40	19 sec.
1976	Queen of My Soul	Average White Band	#40	37 sec.
1976	What Can I Say	Boz Scaggs	#42	14 sec.
1976	Livin' Ain't Livin'	Firefall	#42	
1976	Hard Work	John Handy	#46	
1976	Ob-La-Di, Ob-La-Da	The Beatles	#49	
1976	I Wanna Stay with You	Gallagher and Lyle	#49	16 sec.
1976	Roots, Rock, Reggae	Bob Marley	#51	
1976	Can't Stop Groovin' Now, Wanna Do It Some More	B.T. Express	#52	
1976	Gotta Be the One	Maxine Nightingale	#53	
1976	You Gotta Make Your Own Sunshine	Neil Sedaka	#53	13 sec.
1976	Ten Percent	Double Exposure	#54	
1976	Goofus	Carpenters	#56	23 sec.
1976	Dancin' Kid	Disco Tex & His Sex-O-Lettes	#60	
1976	Lipstick	Michel Polnareff	#61	
1976	If I Only Knew	The Ozark Mountain Daredevils	#65	
1976	Queen of Clubs	KC and The Sunshine Band	#66	
1976	California Day	Starland Vocal Band	#66	
1976	Tell It Like It Is	Andy Williams	#72	
1976	Love and Understanding (Come Together)	Kool & The Gang	#77	
1976	Rescue Me	Melissa Manchester	#78	
1976	Party Line	The Andrea True Connection	#80	
1976	Uptown & Country	Tom Scott	#80	
1976	Open	Smokey Robinson	#81	
1976	Once a Fool	Kiki Dee	#82	17 sec.
1976	This Old Heart of Mine	Rod Stewart	#83	
1976	Tenth Avenue Freeze-Out	Bruce Springsteen	#83	
1976	Peter Gunn	Deodato	#84	
1976	Wheels of Fortune	The Doobie Brothers	#87	
1976	Makes You Blind	The Glitter Band	#91	
1976	Laid Back Love	Major Harris	#91	
1976	Hey Baby	J.J. Cale	#96	
1976	Listen to the Buddha	Ozo	#96	12 sec.

		SAXOPHONE (cont'd)		
1976	Valentine Love	Norman Connors	#97	
1976	Touch and Go	Ecstasy, Passion & Pain	#98	
1976	Tonight's the Night	S.S.O.	#99	
1976	I Don't Wanna Leave You	Debbie Taylor	#100	
1977	Sir Duke	Stevie Wonder	#1	
1977	I Wish	Stevie Wonder	#1	
1977	Da Doo Ron Ron	Shaun Cassidy	#1	11 sec.
1977	I'm Your Boogie Man	KC and The Sunshine Band	#1	
1977	Dazz	Brick	#3	15, 15 sec.
1977	That's Rock 'N' Roll	Shaun Cassidy	#3	15 sec.
1977	(Every Time I Turn Around) Back in Love Again	L.T.D.	#4	
1977	Year of the Cat	Al Stewart	#8	18, 19 sec.
1977	Smoke from a Distant Fire	Sanford/Townsend Band	#9	13 sec.
1977	Just Remember I Love You	Firefall	#11	
1977	Ain't Gonna Bump No More (With No Big Fat Woman)	Joe Tex	#12	
1977	Boogie Child	Bee Gees	#12	
1977	Give a Little Bit	Supertramp	#15	
1977	Do Ya Wanna Get Funky with Me	Peter Brown	#18	18 sec.
1977	Surfin' USA	Leif Garrett	#20	
1977	Saturday Nite	Earth, Wind & Fire	#21	
1977	Save It for a Rainy Day	Stephen Bishop	#22	
1977	Dancin' Man	Q	#23	
1977	This Song	George Harrison	#25	36 sec.
1977	Ariel	Dean Friedman	#26	32 sec.
1977	I Believe You	Dorothy Moore	#27	
1977	Back Together Again	Daryl Hall & John Oates	#28	
1977	Gonna Fly Now (Theme from Rocky)	Maynard Ferguson	#28	
1977	All You Get from Love Is a Love Song	Carpenters	#35	28 sec.
1977	Keep Me Cryin'	Al Green	#37	
1977	Somethin' 'Bout 'Cha	Latimore	#37	
1977	Old Fashioned Boy (You're the One)	Stallion	#37	
1977	In the Mood	Henhouse Five Plus Too (Ray Stevens)	#40	
1977	A Real Mother for Ya	Johnny Guitar Watson	#41	
1977	Rock and Roll Never Forgets	Bob Seger	#41	
1977	Winter Melody	Donna Summer	#43	16 sec.
1977	L.A. Sunshine	War	#45	
1977	Walk Right In	Dr. Hook	#46	
1977	I Wanna Do It to You	Jerry Butler	#51	
1977	You Take My Heart Away	James Darren	#52	19 sec.
1977	Goin' Places	The Jacksons	#52	

SAXOPHONE (cont'd)

1977	Open Sesame – Part 1	Kool & The Gang	#55	
1977	Spring Affair	Donna Summer	#58	
1977	Hold Back the Night	Graham Parker w/The Rumour	#58	
1977	Feel the Beat (Everybody Disco)	Ohio Players	#61	
1977	When Love Is New	Arthur Prysock	#64	17 sec.
1977	Welcome to Our World (Of Merry Music)	Mass Production	#68	
1977	Any Way You Want Me	The Sylvers	#72	
1977	My Own Way to Rock	Burton Cummings	#74	
1977	Too Hot to Stop (Pt. 1)	The Bar-Kays	#74	
1977	Could Heaven Ever Be Like This (Part 1)	Idris Muhammad	#76	
1977	Be My Lady	The Meters	#78	
1977	Disco 9000	Johnnie Taylor	#86	
1977	Bodyheat (Part 1)	James Brown	#88	
1977	Moondance	Van Morrison	#92	28 sec.
1977	If I Have to Go Away	Jigsaw	#93	22 sec.
1977	Six Packs a Day	Billy Lemmons	#93	
1977	Ashes and Sand	Johnny Rivers	#96	
1977	Ritzy Mambo	Salsoul Orchestra	#99	
1977	For Elise	The Philharmonics	#100	
1978	Baker Street	Gerry Rafferty	#2	17, 24 sec.
1978	Just the Way You Are	Billy Joel	#3	34, 15 sec.
1978	I Just Wanna Stop	Gino Vannelli	#4	20 sec.
1978	Feels So Good	Chuck Mangione	#4	
1978	I Love the Nightlife (Disco 'Round)	Alicia Bridges	#5	18 sec.
1978	Whenever I Call You "Friend"	Kenny Loggins & Stevie Nicks	#5	
1978	Dance, Dance, Dance (Yowsah, Yowsah, Yowsah)	Chic	#6	
1978	You Belong to Me	Carly Simon	#6	17 sec.
1978	Time Passages	Al Stewart	#7	55 sec.
1978	Shame	Evelyn "Champagne" King	#9	
1978	Fool (If You Think It's Over)	Chris Rea	#12	18 sec.
1978	You and I	Rick James	#13	
1978	Serpentine Fire	Earth, Wind & Fire	#13	
1978	Runaround Sue	Leif Garrett	#13	13 sec.
1978	Alive Again	Chicago	#14	
1978	Flash Light	Parliament	#16	
1978	Movin' Out (Anthony's Song)	Billy Joel	#17	13 sec.
1978	King Tut	Steve Martin and The Toot Uncommons	#17	
1978	Deacon Blues	Steely Dan	#19	28 sec.
1978	Long, Long Way from Home	Foreigner	#20	15 sec.
1978	It's a Laugh	Daryl Hall & John Oates	#20	17 sec.

	SAXOPHONE (cont'd)			
1978	Native New Yorker	Odyssey	#21	18 sec.
1978	Stuff Like That	Quincy Jones	#21	
1978	Too Hot Ta Trot	Commodores	#24	
1978	Only the Good Die Young	Billy Joel	#24	12 sec.
1978	Close the Door	Teddy Pendergrass	#25	
1978	Josie	Steely Dan	#26	
1978	Getting' Ready for Love	Diana Ross	#27	29 sec.
1978	Almost Summer	Celebration featuring Mike Love	#28	16 sec.
1978	Took the Last Train	David Gates	#30	39, 18 sec.
1978	Street Corner Serenade	Wet Willie	#30	14, 16 sec.
1978	Chattanooga Choo Choo	Tuxedo Junction	#32	
1978	Almost Like Being in Love	Michael Johnson	#32	28 sec.
1978	Prove It All Night	Bruce Springsteen	#33	19 sec.
1978	It's the Same Old Song	KC and The Sunshine Band	#35	
1978	There'll Never Be	Switch	#36	
1978	On the Shelf	Donny & Marie Osmond	#38	
1978	Dance Across the Floor	Jimmy "Bo" Horne	#38	
1978	Galaxy	War	#39	
1978	Curious Mind (Um, Um, Um, Um, Um, Um)	Johnny Rivers	#41	
1978	Badlands	Bruce Springsteen	#42	15 sec.
1978	Fun Time	Joe Cocker	#43	19 sec.
1978	Let Me Party with You (Party, Party, Party)(Part 1)	Bunny Sigler	#43	
1978	Little One	Chicago	#44	
1978	Make You Feel Love Again	Wet Willie	#45	
1978	Ca Plane Pour Moi	Plastic Bertrand	#47	
1978	Greased Lightnin'	John Travolta	#47	
1978	Wrap Your Arms Around Me	KC and The Sunshine Band	#48	
1978	You Can't Dance	England Dan & John Ford Coley	#49	
1978	The Wanderer	Leif Garrett	#49	
1978	Darlin'	Paul Davis w/Susan Collins	#51	
1978	Ready for the Times to Get Better	Crystal Gayle	#52	
1978	Livingston Saturday Night	Jimmy Buffett	#52	
1978	What's Your Name, What's Your Number	The Andrea True Connection	#56	
1978	Weekend Lover	Odyssey	#57	15 sec.
1978	Le Spank	Le Pamplemousse	#58	
1978	Driftwood	The Moody Blues	#59	
1978	Peggy Sue	The Beach Boys	#59	
1978	Your Sweetness Is My Weakness	Barry White	#60	
1978	Honey Don't Leave L.A.	James Taylor	#61	13 sec.
1978	Do You Feel All Right	KC and The Sunshine Band	#63	

		SAXOPHONE (cont'd)			
1978	Never Let Her Slip Away	Andrew Gold	#67	16 sec.
1978	Hot Shot	Karen Young	#67	
1978	On the Strip	Paul Nicholas	#67	
1978	Let's Live Together	Cazz	#70	
1978	Bombs Away	Bob Weir	#70	
1978	Whatever Happened to Benny Santini?	Chris Rea	#71	17 sec.
1978	He's So Fine	Jane Olivor	#77	
1978	We Fell in Love While Dancing	Bill Brandon	#80	
1978	(You Got to Walk And) Don't Look Back	Peter Tosh w/Mick Jagger	#81	21 sec.
1978	#1 Dee Jay	Goody Goody	#82	16 sec.
1978	Come Go with Me	Pockets	#84	
1978	In for the Night	The Dirt Band	#86	21 sec.
1978	Take Me I'm Yours	Michael Henderson	#88	
1978	Shaker Song	Spyro Gyra	#90	
1979	Da Ya Think I'm Sexy?	Rod Stewart	#1	35 sec.
1979	Pop Muzik	M	#1	
1979	Don't Stop 'til You Get Enough	Michael Jackson	#1	
1979	After the Love Has Gone	Earth, Wind & Fire	#2	10 sec.
1979	The Logical Song	Supertramp	#6	20 sec.
1979	Boogie Wonderland	Earth, Wind & Fire/The Emotions	#6	
1979	Ooh Baby Baby	Linda Ronstadt	#7	30 sec.
1979	Lotta Love	Nicolette Larson	#8	15 sec.
1979	Love Is the Answer	England Dan & John Ford Coley	#10	
1979	Shake It	Ian Matthews	#13	15 sec.
1979	Soul Man	Blues Brothers	#14	
1979	Big Shot	Billy Joel	#14	
1979	Come to Me	France Joli	#15	
1979	Hold On	Ian Gomm	#18	
1979	Does Your Mother Know	ABBA	#19	
1979	I Got My Mind Made Up (You Can Get It Girl)	Instant Funk	#20	
1979	Heart of the Night	Poco	#20	20 sec.
1979	Don't Hold Back	Chanson	#21	
1979	Get It Right Next Time	Gerry Rafferty	#21	16 sec.
1979	Maybe I'm a Fool	Eddie Money	#22	19 sec.
1979	I Don't Know if It's Right	Evelyn "Champagne" King	#23	
1979	Morning Dance	Spyro Gyra	#24	
1979	Please Don't Leave	Lauren Wood	#24	14 sec.
1979	Shadows in the Moonlight	Anne Murray	#25	26 sec.
1979	Old Time Rock & Roll	Bob Seger	#28	14 sec.
1979	Instant Replay	Dan Hartman	#29	
1979	Weekend	Wet Willie	#29	

	SAXOPHONE (cont'd)			
1979	Song on the Radio	Al Stewart	#29	15, 17, 71, 34 sec.
1979	Arrow Through Me	Paul McCartney & Wings	#29	
1979	Street Life	Crusaders	#36	34 sec.
1979	Married Men	Bette Midler	#40	
1979	Young Blood	Rickie Lee Jones	#40	
1979	I Don't Wanna Lose You	Daryl Hall & John Oates	#42	
1979	Firecracker	Mass Production	#43	
1979	Dancing in the City	Marshall Hain	#43	
1979	Goodbye, I Love You	Firefall	#43	
1979	Here Comes the Night	The Beach Boys	#44	20 sec.
1979	Elena	The Marc Tanner Band	#45	
1979	Dancer	Gino Soccio	#48	
1979	Vengeance	Carly Simon	#48	
1979	Wasn't It Good	Cher	#49	13, 14 sec.
1979	Totally Hot	Olivia Newton-John	#52	
1979	Since I Don't Have You	Art Garfunkel	#53	31 sec.
1979	Sweets for My Sweet	Tony Orlando	#54	
1979	Groove Me	Fern Kinney	#54	
1979	California Dreamin'	America	#56	32 sec.
1979	Easy Driver	Kenny Loggins	#60	
1979	My Love Is Music	Space	#60	
1979	Easy to Be Hard	Cheryl Barnes	#64	
1979	One Fine Day	Rita Coolidge	#66	27 sec.
1979	Who Do Ya Love	KC and The Sunshine Band	#68	
1979	The Topical Song	The Barron Knights	#70	11 sec.
1979	Sinner Man	Sarah Dash	#71	14 sec.
1979	Run Home Girl	Sad Café	#71	13 sec.
1979	Bustin' Out	Rick James	#71	
1979	Stillsane	Carolyne Mas	#71	13, 13 sec.
1979	You've Really Got a Hold on Me	Eddie Money	#72	17 sec.
1979	I've Got the Next Dance	Deniece Williams	#73	
1979	Animal House	Stephen Bishop	#73	
1979	Night Dancin'	Taka Boom	#74	
1979	Music Box	Evelyn "Champagne" King	#75	
1979	Here I Go (Fallin' in Love Again)	Frannie Golde	#76	15 sec.
1979	You're My Weakness	Faith Band	#76	22 sec.
1979	Pow Wow	Cory Daye	#76	
1979	When I Think of You	Leif Garrett	#78	
1979	I'll Know Her When I See Her	Cooper Brothers Band	#79	12 sec.

SAXOPHONE (cont'd)			
1979	Voulez-Vous	ABBA	#80	
1979	I'll Come Running	Livingston Taylor	#82	17 sec.
1979	Rocky II Disco	Maynard Ferguson	#82	
1979	Crank It Up (Funk Town) Pt. 1	Peter Brown	#86	
1979	In the Midnight Hour	Samantha Sang	#88	
1979	You Stepped Into My Life	Wayne Newton	#90	10 sec.
1979	Shoot Me (With Your Love)	Tasha Thomas	#91	
1979	I Do the Rock	Tim Curry	#91	
1979	This Is It	Dan Hartman	#91	32 sec.
1979	Walk on By	Average White Band	#92	
1979	You and Me	Liner	#92	10 sec.
1979	Pinball, That's All	Bill Wray	#96	

SITAR

The Sitar became popular in American pop music in the mid-sixties after George Harrison played it on the Beatles' "Norwegian Wood (This Bird Has Flown)". The sitar craze lasted mostly from 1966-1973. Then its use in pop songs faded dramatically. It was still used, just rarely. Some of the sitars used in the songs below are electric.

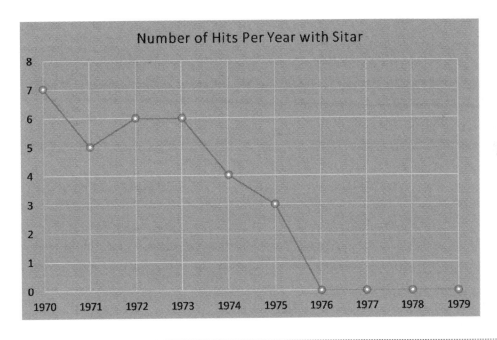

YEAR	SONG	ARTIST	HOT 100
1970	Signed, Sealed, Delivered I'm Yours	Stevie Wonder	#3
1970	Band of Gold	Freda Payne	#3
1970	Snowbird	Anne Murray	#8
1970	Didn't I (Blow Your Mind This Time)	The Delfonics	#10
1970	Everybody's Got the Right to Love	The Supremes	#21
1970	Trying to Make a Fool Out of Me	The Delfonics	#40

		SITAR (cont'd)		
1971	Maybe Tomorrow	The Jackson 5	#20
1971	Where Evil Grows	The Poppy Family	#45
1971	Over and Over	The Delfonics	#58
1971	You've Lost That Lovin' Feelin'	Roberta Flack & Donny Hathaway	#71
1971	Sing High – Sing Low	Anne Murray	#83
1972	You Are Everything	The Stylistics	#9
1972	Corner of the Sky	The Jackson 5	#18
1972	Glory Bound	The Grass Roots	#34
1972	We're on Our Way	Chris Hodge	#44
1972	How Could I Let You Get Away	The Spinners	#77
1972	Tell Me This Is a Dream	Delfonics	#86
1973	Do It Again	Steely Dan	#6
1973	You're a Special Part of Me	Diana Ross & Marvin Gaye	#12
1973	Magic Woman Touch	The Hollies	#60
1973	Wish That I Could Talk to You	The Sylvers	#77
1973	I Don't Want to Make You Wait	The Delfonics	#91
1973	Make Me Twice the Man	New York City	#93
1974	You Make Me Feel Brand New	The Stylistics	#2
1974	Who Do You Think You Are	Bo Donaldson & The Heywoods	#15
1974	Outside Woman	Bloodstone	#34
1974	Keep Your Head to the Sky	Earth, Wind & Fire	#52
1975	Lucy in the Sky with Diamonds	Elton John	#1
1975	Thank You Baby	The Stylistics	#70
1975	You're a Part of Me	Susan Jacks	#90

STEEL DRUMS

YEAR	SONG	ARTIST	HOT 100
1971	Co-Co	The Sweet	#99
1972	Vanilla Olay	Jackie DeShannon	#76
1972	Vahevala	Loggins & Messina	#84
1973	Darling Come Back Home	Eddie Kendricks	#67
1973	Hey, Little Girl	Foster Sylvers	#92
1974	Worse Comes to Worst	Billy Joel	#80
1974	Mine for Me	Rod Stewart	#91
1975	It's All Right	Jim Capaldi	#55
1975	Hang on Sloopy	Rick Derringer	#94
1976	Another Rainy Day in New York City	Chicago	#32
1977	Man Smart, Woman Smarter	Robert Palmer	#63

STEEL DRUMS (cont'd)			
1978	Every Kinda People	Robert Palmer	#16
1978	Street Corner Serenade	Wet Willie	#30
1978	Mary's Boy Child/Oh My Lord	Boney M	#85
1979	Morning Dance	Spyro Gyra	#24
1979	Fins	Jimmy Buffett	#35

STRINGS

These songs have strings without horns. If you're looking for songs with strings *and* horns, check the "orchestra" section.

YEAR	SONG	ARTIST	HOT 100
1970	Make It with You	Bread	#1
1970	Love on a Two-Way Street	The Moments	#3
1970	Band of Gold	Freda Payne	#3
1970	Rainy Night in Georgia	Brook Benton	#4
1970	He Ain't Heavy, He's My Brother	Hollies	#7
1970	Snowbird	Anne Murray	#8
1970	(If You Let Me Make Love to You Then) Why Can't I Touch You?	Ronnie Dyson	#8
1970	Call Me	Aretha Franklin	#13
1970	The Thrill Is Gone	B.B. King	#15
1970	What Is Truth	Johnny Cash	#19
1970	Reach Out and Touch (Somebody's Hand)	Diana Ross	#20
1970	Everybody's Got the Right to Love	The Supremes	#21
1970	Closer to Home (I'm Your Captain)	Grand Funk Railroad	#22
1970	She	Tommy James & The Shondells	#23
1970	Deeper & Deeper	Freda Payne	#24
1970	Shilo	Neil Diamond	#24
1970	It's All in the Game	Four Tops	#24
1970	Long Long Time	Linda Ronstadt	#25
1970	Wonderful World, Beautiful People	Jimmy Cliff	#25
1970	All I Have to do Is Dream	Bobbie Gentry & Glen Campbell	#27
1970	The Sly, Slick and the Wicked	The Lost Generation	#30
1970	I'm Not My Brothers Keeper	The Flaming Ember	#34
1970	(You've Got Me) Dangling on a String	Chairmen of the Board	#38
1970	I Am Somebody (Part 2)	Johnnie Taylor	#39
1970	Cupid	Johnny Nash	#39
1970	Oh Happy Day	Glen Campbell	#40

	STRINGS (cont'd)		
1970	California Girl	Eddie Floyd	#45
1970	Chains and Things	B.B. King	#45
1970	Don't It Make You Want to Go Home	Brook Benton	#45
1970	My Elusive Dreams	Bobby Vinton	#46
1970	Sweetheart	Engelbert Humperdinck	#47
1970	Morning	Jim Ed Brown	#47
1970	Hummingbird	B.B. King	#48
1970	Pearl	Tommy Roe	#50
1970	To the Other Woman (I'm the Other Woman)	Doris Duke	#50
1970	I Don't Wanna Cry	Ronnie Dyson	#50
1970	The Onion Song	Marvin Gaye & Tammi Terrell	#50
1970	Into the Mystic	Johnny Rivers	#51
1970	Can't Help Falling in Love with You	Al Martino	#51
1970	I'm So Glad I Fell for You	David Ruffin	#53
1970	California Soul	Marvin Gaye & Tammi Terrell	#56
1970	Capture the Moment	Jay & The Americans	#57
1970	Je T'Aime…Moi Non Plus	Jane Birkin & Serge Gainsbourg	#58
1970	Add Some Music to Your Day	The Beach Boys	#64
1970	Gonna Give Her All the Love I've Got	Marvin Gaye	#67
1970	That Same Old Feeling	Pickettywitch	#67
1970	She Didn't Know (She Kept on Talking)	Dee Dee Warwick	#70
1970	She Cried	The Lettermen	#73
1970	Carolina in My Mind	Crystal Mansion	#73
1970	We Can Make It Baby	The Originals	#74
1970	The Witch	The Rattles	#79
1970	If You Do Believe in Love	The Tee Set	#81
1970	I Can't Tell the Bottom from the Top	Hollies	#82
1970	Love Minus Zero-No Limit	Turley Richards	#84
1970	Man of Constant Sorrow	Ginger Baker's Air Force (Denny Laine)	#85
1970	I Started Loving You Again	Al Martino	#86
1970	I'm Gonna Love You	The Intrigues	#86
1970	I Have Learned to Do Without You	Mavis Staples	#87
1970	Cole, Cooke & Redding	Wilson Pickett	#91
1970	If Only I Had My Mind on Something Else	Bee Gees	#91
1970	No Arms Can Ever Hold You	Bobby Vinton	#93
1970	Where Have All Our Heroes Gone	Bill Anderson	#93
1970	Patch of Blue	Frankie Valli/4 Seasons	#94
1970	Free to Carry On	The Sandpipers	#94
1970	Then She's a Lover	Roy Clark	#94
1970	This Bitter Earth	The Satisfactions	#96
1970	Can't Get Over Losing You	Donnie Elbert	#98

	STRINGS (cont'd)		
1970	I Heard the Voice of Jesus	Turley Richards	#99
1970	Darling Dear	Smokey Robinson & The Miracles	#100
1971	Want Ads	The Honey Cone	#1
1971	What's Going On	Marvin Gaye	#2
1971	Rainy Days and Mondays	Carpenters	#2
1971	Spanish Harlem	Aretha Franklin	#2
1971	Mama's Pearl	The Jackson 5	#2
1971	Rose Garden	Lynn Anderson	#3
1971	Ain't No Sunshine	Bill Withers	#3
1971	Imagine	John Lennon	#3
1971	Baby I'm – A Want You	Bread	#3
1971	Mercy Mercy Me (The Ecology)	Marvin Gaye	#4
1971	Got to Be There	Michael Jackson	#4
1971	If	Bread	#4
1971	If You Could Read My Mind	Gordon Lightfoot	#5
1971	Sweet and Innocent	Donny Osmond	#7
1971	Help Me Make It Through the Night	Sammi Smith	#8
1971	I'll Meet You Halfway	The Partridge Family	#9
1971	If I Were Your Woman	Gladys Knight & The Pips	#9
1971	That's the Way I've Always Heard It Should Be	Carly Simon	#10
1971	It's Impossible	Perry Como	#10
1971	Stick-Up	Honey Cone	#11
1971	For the Good Times	Ray Price	#11
1971	Bring the Boys Home	Freda Payne	#12
1971	I Don't Know How to Love Him	Helen Reddy	#13
1971	Stones	Neil Diamond	#14
1971	Here Comes That Rainy Day Feeling Again	The Fortunes	#15
1971	Thin Line Between Love & Hate	The Persuaders	#15
1971	I Don't Want to Do Wrong	Gladys Knight & The Pips	#17
1971	You're All I Need to Get By	Aretha Franklin	#19
1971	Chirpy Chirpy Cheep Cheep	Mac and Katie Kissoon	#20
1971	I Love You for All Seasons	The Fuzz	#21
1971	Right on the Tip of My Tongue	Brenda & The Tabulations	#23
1971	Saturday Morning Confusion	Bobby Russell	#28
1971	Reach Out I'll Be There	Diana Ross	#29
1971	Don't Change on Me	Ray Charles	#36
1971	Love Means (You Never Have to Say You're Sorry)	Sounds of Sunshine	#39
1971	Your Time to Cry	Joe Simon	#40
1971	I Won't Mention It Again	Ray Price	#42
1971	You're the Reasons Why	The Ebonys	#51
1971	Ruby Tuesday	Melanie	#52

	STRINGS (cont'd)		
1971	Bless You	Martha & The Vandellas	#53
1971	God Bless Whoever Sent You	The Originals	#53
1971	Don't Wanna Live Inside Myself	Bee Gees	#53
1971	Can't Find the Time	Rose Colored Glasses	#54
1971	Flesh and Blood	Johnny Cash	#54
1971	All I Have	The Moments	#56
1971	Angel Baby	Dusk	#57
1971	I Wish I Were	Andy Kim	#62
1971	How Can I Unlove You	Lynn Anderson	#63
1971	I'm Still Waiting	Diana Ross	#63
1971	You're My Man	Lynn Anderson	#63
1971	Ain't It a Sad Thing	R. Dean Taylor	#66
1971	Shoes	Brook Benton	#67
1971	Gotta See Jane	R. Dean Taylor	#67
1971	Ghetto Woman	B.B. King	#68
1971	Come Back Home	Bobby Goldsboro	#69
1971	I'd Rather Be Sorry	Ray Price	#70
1971	In These Changing Times	Four Tops	#70
1971	You've Lost That Lovin' Feelin'	Roberta Flack & Donny Hathaway	#71
1971	Hot Love	T. Rex	#72
1971	It's Up to You Petula	Edison Lighthouse	#72
1971	Mixed Up Guy	Joey Scarbury	#73
1971	Like an Open Door	The Fuzz	#77
1971	Nickel Song	The New Seekers	#81
1971	A Mama and a Papa	Ray Stevens	#82
1971	And I Love You So	Bobby Goldsboro	#83
1971	Sing High – Sing Low	Anne Murray	#83
1971	Day by Day (Every Minute of the Hour)	The Continental 4	#84
1971	Give Up Your Guns	The Buoys	#84
1971	I Don't Wanna Lose You	Johnnie Taylor	#86
1971	I'm Girl Scoutin'	The Intruders	#88
1971	Baby, I'm Yours	Jody Miller	#91
1971	Beginning to Feel the Pain	Mac Davis	#92
1971	Valerie	Cymarron	#96
1971	California on My Mind	Morning Mist	#96
1971	I Been Moved	Andy Kim	#97
1971	Wild World	The Gentrys	#97
1972	The First Time Ever I Saw Your Face	Roberta Flack	#1
1972	Baby Don't Get Hooked on Me	Mac Davis	#1
1972	Lean on Me	Bill Withers	#1
1972	Too Late to Turn Back Now	Cornelius Brothers & Sister Rose	#2

		STRINGS (cont'd)		
1972	Nights in White Satin		The Moody Blues	#2
1972	Clair		Gilbert O'Sullivan	#2
1972	Hurting Each Other		Carpenters	#2
1972	I'd Like to Teach the World to Sing (In Perfect Harmony)		The New Seekers	#7
1972	The Happiest Girl in the Whole U.S.A.		Donna Fargo	#11
1972	Something's Wrong with Me		Austin Roberts	#12
1972	Vincent (Starry, Starry Night)		Don McLean	#12
1972	Sweet Surrender		Bread	#15
1972	The Witch Queen of New Orleans		Redbone	#21
1972	I Believe in Music		Gallery	#22
1972	Spaceman		Nilsson	#23
1972	Taxi		Harry Chapin	#24
1972	All the King's Horses		Aretha Franklin	#26
1972	American City Suite		Cashman & West	#27
1972	Ring the Living Bell		Melanie	#31
1972	When You Say Love		Sonny & Cher	#32
1972	If You Leave Me Tonight I'll Cry		Jerry Wallace	#28
1972	What Am I Crying For?		Dennis Yost/Classics IV	#39
1972	Until It's Time for You to Go		Elvis Presley	#40
1972	Tiny Dancer		Elton John	#41
1972	Walk in the Night		Jr. Walker/The All Stars	#46
1972	To Get to You		Jerry Wallace	#48
1972	Sour Suite		The Guess Who	#50
1972	Sweet Caroline (Good Times Never Seemed So Good)		Bobby Womack	#51
1972	What am I Living For		Ray Charles	#54
1972	A Simple Man		Lobo	#56
1972	I Miss You (Part 1)		Harold Melvin	#58
1972	Carolyn		Merle Haggard	#58
1972	Am I Losing You		The Partridge Family	#59
1972	Everybody Loves a Love Song		Mac Davis	#63
1972	Zing Went the Strings of My Heart		The Trammps	#64
1972	Love Gonna Pack Up (And Walk Out)		The Persuaders	#64
1972	Do What You Set Out to Do		Bobby Bland	#64
1972	Starman		David Bowie	#65
1972	What Would the Children Think		Rick Springfield	#70
1972	Cotton Jenny		Anne Murray	#71
1972	Cry		Lynn Anderson	#71
1972	That's What Friends are For		B.J. Thomas	#74
1972	Will You Still Love Me Tomorrow		Roberta Flack	#76
1972	Keep on Keeping On		N.F. Porter	#77
1972	Amerikan Music		Steve Alaimo	#79

		STRINGS (cont'd)	
1972	Runaway/Happy Together	Dawn featuring Tony Orlando	#79
1972	Lovin' You, Lovin' Me	Candi Staton	#83
1972	I Guess I'll Miss the Man	The Supremes	#85
1972	Together Alone	Melanie	#86
1972	Don't Want to Say Goodbye	Raspberries	#86
1972	Circles	The New Seekers	#87
1972	Goodbye Again	John Denver	#88
1972	Tell 'em Willie Boy's A'Comin'	Tommy James	#89
1972	Misty Blue	Joe Simon	#91
1972	Dedicated to the One I Love	The Temprees	#93
1972	With Pen in Hand	Bobby Goldsboro	#94
1972	Vaya con Dios	Dawn featuring Tony Orlando	#95
1972	A Sunday Kind of Love	Lenny Welch	#96
1972	Hushabye	Robert John	#99
1972	The Road We Didn't Take	Freda Payne	#100
1972	Don't Ever Take Away My Freedom	Peter Yarrow	#100
1973	Tie a Yellow Ribbon Round the Ole Oak Tree	Tony Orlando & Dawn	#1
1973	You're So Vain	Carly Simon	#1
1973	Let's Get It On	Marvin Gaye	#1
1973	Top of the World	Carpenters	#1
1973	Brother Louie	Stories	#1
1973	Half-Breed	Cher	#1
1973	The Most Beautiful Girl	Charlie Rich	#1
1973	The Morning After	Maureen McGovern	#1
1973	Angie	The Rolling Stones	#1
1973	I'm Gonna Love You Just a Little More Baby	Barry White	#3
1973	Oh, Babe, What Would You Say?	Hurricane Smith	#3
1973	Paper Roses	Marie Osmond	#5
1973	Funny Face	Donna Fargo	#5
1973	Break Up to Make Up	The Stylistics	#5
1973	Danny's Song	Anne Murray	#7
1973	Don't Expect Me to Be Your Friend	Lobo	#8
1973	The Twelth of Never	Donny Osmond	#8
1973	Wildflower	Skylark	#9
1973	Daddy's Home	Jermaine Jackson	#9
1973	All I Know	Garfunkel	#9
1973	I Got a Name	Jim Croce	#10
1973	Natural High	Bloodstone	#10
1973	I Believe in You (You Believe in Me)	Johnnie Taylor	#11
1973	Daisy a Day	Jud Strunk	#14
1973	Aubrey	Bread	#15

		STRINGS (cont'd)		
1973	Behind Closed Doors		Charlie Rich	#15
1973	Walk on the Wild Side		Lou Reed	#16
1973	Love Jones		Brighter Side of Darkness	#16
1973	The Right Thing to Do		Carly Simon	#17
1973	Summer (The First Time)		Bobby Goldsboro	#21
1973	We May Never Pass This Way (Again)		Seals & Crofts	#21
1973	Young Love		Donny Osmond	#25
1973	Jesse		Roberta Flack	#30
1973	Harry Hippie		Bobby Womack	#31
1973	Sweet Understanding Love		Four Tops	#33
1973	Soul Song		Joe Stampley	#37
1973	Close Your Eyes		Edward Bear	#37
1973	I'm Never Gonna Be Alone Anymore		Cornelius Brothers & Sister Rose	#37
1973	Back When My Hair Was Short		Gunhill Road	#40
1973	Roll Over Beethoven		Electric Light Orchestra	#42
1973	Rosalie		Sam Neely	#43
1973	Never Let You Go		Bloodstone	#43
1973	There's No Me Without You		Manhattans	#43
1973	Country Sunshine		Dottie West	#49
1973	Who Was It?		Hurricane Smith	#49
1973	Sail Around the World		David Gates	#50
1973	Mammy Blue		Stories	#50
1973	Remember (Christmas)		Nilsson	#53
1973	The Last Thing on My Mind		Neil Diamond	#56
1973	Across 110th Street		Bobby Womack	#56
1973	Little Girl Gone		Donna Fargo	#57
1973	Oh! No Not My Baby		Rod Stewart	#59
1973	Songman		Cashman & West	#59
1973	I'd Rather Be a Cowboy		John Denver	#62
1973	Silly Wasn't I		Valerie Simpson	#63
1973	I Like You		Donovan	#66
1973	Darling Come Back Home		Eddie Kendricks	#67
1973	Nobody Wins		Brenda Lee	#70
1973	Everything's Been Changed		The 5th Dimension	#70
1973	Oh No, Not My Baby		Merry Clayton	#72
1973	Dream Me Home		Mac Davis	#73
1973	Rock 'N Roll (I Gave You the Best Years of My Life)		Kevin Johnson	#73
1973	Top of the World		Lynn Anderson	#74
1973	Blood Red and Goin' Down		Tanya Tucker	#74
1973	My Merry-Go-Round		Johnny Nash	#77
1973	You're in Good Hands		Jermaine Jackson	#79

STRINGS (cont'd)

1973	Will You Love Me Tomorrow?	Melanie	#82
1973	Come Live with Me	Ray Charles	#82
1973	Good Morning	Michael Redway	#85
1973	This Is Your Song	Don Goodwin	#86
1973	Only Love	Bill Quateman	#86
1973	What's Your Mama's Name	Tanya Tucker	#86
1973	I'm Sorry	Joey Heatherton	#87
1973	Sunshine	Mickey Newbury	#87
1973	Half a Million Miles from Home	Albert Hammond	#87
1973	Your Side of the Bed	Mac Davis	#88
1973	Vado Via	Drupi	#88
1973	Farewell Andromeda (Welcome to My Morning)	John Denver	#89
1973	Come Live with Me	Roy Clark	#89
1973	Names, Tags, Numbers & Labels	The Association	#91
1973	Together We Can Make Such Sweet Music	The Spinners	#91
1973	You Were Always There	Donna Fargo	#93
1973	Kid Stuff	Barbara Fairchild	#95
1973	I Miss You Baby	Millie Jackson	#95
1973	Working Class Hero	Tommy Roe	#97
1973	Mr. Magic Man	Wilson Pickett	#98
1973	I'm Leavin' You	Engelbert Humperdinck	#99
1974	Angie Baby	Helen Reddy	#1
1974	Cat's in the Cradle	Harry Chapin	#1
1974	Dark Lady	Cher	#1
1974	The Night Chicago Died	Paper Lace	#1
1974	Can't Get Enough of Your Love, Babe	Barry White	#1
1974	Best Thing That Ever Happened to Me	Gladys Knight & The Pips	#3
1974	Come and Get Your Love	Redbone	#5
1974	Back Home Again	John Denver	#5
1974	I'll Have to Say I Love You in a Song	Jim Croce	#9
1974	Carefree Highway	Gordon Lightfoot	#10
1974	A Very Special Love Song	Charlie Rich	#11
1974	I Love	Tom T. Hall	#12
1974	Trying to Hold on to My Woman	Lamont Dozier	#15
1974	Love Don't Love Nobody – Pt. 1	Spinners	#15
1974	Sexy Mama	Moments	#17
1974	I Love My Friend	Charlie Rich	#24
1974	Come Monday	Jimmy Buffett	#30
1974	American Tune	Paul Simon	#35
1974	Happiness Is Just Around the Bend	The Main Ingredient	#35
1974	Sugar Baby Love	The Rubettes	#37

STRINGS (cont'd)

1974	One Day at a Time	Marilyn Sellars	#37
1974	Without Love	Aretha Franklin	#45
1974	She Called Me Baby	Charlie Rich	#47
1974	I Don't See Me in Your Eyes Anymore	Charlie Rich	#47
1974	Love Has No Pride	Linda Ronstadt	#51
1974	Don't Send Nobody Else	Ace Spectrum	#57
1974	There Will Never Be Any Peace (Until God Is Seated at the Conference Table)	The Chi-Lites	#63
1974	Houston (I'm Comin' to See You)	Glen Campbell	#68
1974	My Love	Margie Joseph	#69
1974	Let Me Get to Know You	Paul Anka	#80
1974	It Only Hurts When I Try to Smile	Dawn featuring Tony Orlando	#81
1974	Something	Johnny Rodriguez	#85
1974	U.S. of A	Donna Fargo	#86
1974	Daybreaker	Electric Light Orchestra	#87
1974	Bring Back the Love of Yesterday	The Dells	#87
1974	Feel Like Making Love	Bob James	#88
1974	Try (Try to Fall in Love)	Cooker	#88
1974	Christmas Dream	Perry Como	#92
1975	Fly, Robin, Fly	Silver Convention	#1
1975	Rhinestone Cowboy	Glen Campbell	#1
1975	Laughter in the Rain	Neil Sedaka	#1
1975	(Hey Won't You Play) Another Somebody Done Somebody Wrong Song	B.J. Thomas	#1
1975	You're the First, the Last, My Everything	Barry White	#2
1975	Miracles	Jefferson Starship	#3
1975	Who Loves You	Four Seasons	#3
1975	I'm Not Lisa	Jessi Colter	#4
1975	Ain't No Way to Treat a Lady	Helen Reddy	#8
1975	Can't Get It Out of My Head	Electric Light Orchestra	#9
1975	#9 Dream	John Lennon	#9
1975	Rock N' Roll (I Gave You the Best Years of My Life)	Mac Davis	#15
1975	To the Door of the Sun (Alle Porte Del Sole)	Al Martino	#17
1975	Every Time You Touch Me (I Get High)	Charlie Rich	#19
1975	Daisy Jane	America	#20
1975	Emotion	Helen Reddy	#22
1975	I Belong to You	Love Unlimited	#27
1975	Never Let Her Go	David Gates	#29
1975	Beer Barrel Polka	Bobby Vinton	#33
1975	Volare	Al Martino	#33
1975	Judy Mae	Boomer Castleman	#33
1975	You're All I Need to Get By	Tony Orlando & Dawn	#34

	STRINGS (cont'd)		
1975	Diamonds and Rust	Joan Baez	#35
1975	Living a Little, Laughing a Little	The Spinners	#37
1975	Lizzie and the Rainman	Tanya Tucker	#37
1975	I'll Do for You Anything You Want Me To	Barry White	#40
1975	I Wanna Learn a Love Song	Harry Chapin	#44
1975	Since I Met You Baby	Freddy Fender	#45
1975	It Doesn't Matter Anymore	Linda Ronstadt	#47
1975	Dance the Kung Fu	Carl Douglas	#48
1975	Rag Doll	Sammy Johns	#52
1975	(If You Add) All the Love in the World	Mac Davis	#54
1975	Lonely School Year	The Hudson Brothers	#57
1975	Love Corporation	Hues Corporation	#62
1975	Hoppy, Gene and Me	Roy Rogers	#65
1975	Hey There Little Firefly (Part 1)	Firefly	#67
1975	A Friend of Mine Is Going Blind	John Dawson Read	#72
1975	Anytime (I'll Be There)	Frank Sinatra	#75
1975	How High the Moon	Gloria Gaynor	#75
1975	Inside My Love	Minnie Riperton	#76
1975	Gee Baby	Peter Shelley	#81
1975	Out of Time	The Rolling Stones	#81
1975	Please Tell Him That I Said Hello	Debbie Campbell	#84
1975	You Are a Song	Batdorf & Rodney	#87
1975	Let Me Start Tonite	Lamont Dozier	#87
1975	Heartbreak Road	Bill Withers	#89
1975	Smokin' Room	Carl Carlton	#91
1975	No Charge	Shirley Caesar	#91
1975	Words (Are Impossible)	Margie Joseph	#91
1975	Charmer	Tim Moore	#91
1975	Cry Cry Cry	Shirley & Company	#91
1975	Love Don't You Go Through No Changes on Me	Sister Sledge	#92
1975	What Time of Day	Billy Thunderkloud	#92
1975	My First Day Without Her	Dennis Yost/Classics IV	#94
1975	Love Hurts	Jim Capaldi	#97
1976	Tonight's the Night (Gonna Be Alright)	Rod Stewart	#1
1976	Don't Go Breaking My Heart	Elton John & Kiki Dee	#1
1976	Love Hangover	Diana Ross	#1
1976	Afternoon Delight	Starland Vocal Band	#1
1976	Convoy	C.W. McCall	#1
1976	Get Up and Boogie (That's Right)	Silver Convention	#2
1976	Right Back Where We Started From	Maxine Nightingale	#2
1976	Misty Blue	Dorothy Moore	#3

		STRINGS (cont'd)		
1976	You Sexy Thing	Hot Chocolate	#3
1976	Sara Smile	Daryl Hall & John Oates	#4
1976	Take It to the Limit	Eagles	#4
1976	Evil Woman	Electric Light Orchestra	#10
1976	This Masquerade	George Benson	#10
1976	Love Me	Yvonne Elliman	#14
1976	This One's for You	Barry Manilow	#29
1976	Fallen Angel	Frankie Valli	#36
1976	We Can't Hide It Anymore	Larry Santos	#36
1976	I Kinda Miss You	The Manhattans	#46
1976	So Sad the Song	Gladys Knight & The Pips	#47
1976	Could It Be Magic	Donna Summer	#52
1976	Easy as Pie	Billy "Crash" Craddock	#54
1976	Ode to Billie Joe	Bobbie Gentry	#54
1976	Funny How Time Slips Away	Dorothy Moore	#58
1976	No, No, Joe	Silver Convention	#60
1976	Jealousy	Major Harris	#73
1976	Amber Cascades	America	#75
1976	Try Me, I Know We Can Make It	Donna Summer	#80
1976	Norma Jean Wants to Be a Movie Star	Sundown Company	#84
1976	'Til I Can Make It on My Own	Tammy Wynette	#84
1976	Better Place to Be (Parts 1 & 2)	Harry Chapin	#86
1976	Find 'Em, Fool 'Em & Forget 'Em	Dobie Gray	#94
1976	We're on the Right Track	South Shore Commission	#94
1976	Bad Luck	The Atlanta Disco Band	#94
1976	Will You Love Me Tomorrow	Dana Valery	#95
1976	Love Lifted Me	Kenny Rogers	#97
1976	You to Me Are Everything, Part 1	Revelation	#98
1976	Abyssinia Jones	Edwin Starr	#98
1977	You Light Up My Life	Debby Boone	#1
1977	Rich Girl	Daryl Hall & John Oates	#1
1977	Dancing Queen	ABBA	#1
1977	(Your Love Has Lifted Me) Higher and Higher	Rita Coolidge	#2
1977	Angel in Your Arms	Hot	#6
1977	Livin' Thing	Electric Light Orchestra	#13
1977	It Was Almost Like a Song	Ronnie Milsap	#16
1977	Don't Worry Baby	B.J. Thomas	#17
1977	How Much Love	Leo Sayer	#17
1977	Sam	Olivia Newton-John	#20
1977	Ain't Nothing Like the Real Thing	Donny & Marie Osmond	#21
1977	Back Together Again	Daryl Hall & John Oates	#28

		STRINGS (cont'd)	
1977	Moody Blue	Elvis Presley	#31
1977	So You Win Again	Hot Chocolate	#31
1977	Sometimes	Facts of Life	#31
1977	Changes in Latitudes, Changes in Attitudes	Jimmy Buffett	#37
1977	Thunder in My Heart	Leo Sayer	#38
1977	Spring Rain	Silvetti	#39
1977	People in Love	10cc	#40
1977	Superman	Celi Bee & The Buzzy Bunch	#41
1977	Someone to Lay Down Beside Me	Linda Ronstadt	#42
1977	There Will Come a Day (I'm Gonna Happen to You)	Smokey Robinson	#42
1977	Look What You've Done to My Heart	Marilyn McCoo & Billy Davis, Jr.	#51
1977	Save Me	Merrilee Rush	#54
1977	From Graceland to the Promised Land	Merle Haggard	#58
1977	Spring Affair	Donna Summer	#58
1977	Hooked on You	Bread	#60
1977	Come in from the Rain	Captain & Tennille	#61
1977	Platinum Heroes	Bruce Foster	#63
1977	Daddy Cool	Boney M	#65
1977	Ten to Eight	David Castle	#68
1977	I Need a Man	Grace Jones	#83
1977	Break It to Me Gently	Aretha Franklin	#85
1977	Making a Good Thing Better	Olivia Newton-John	#87
1977	Flame	Steve Sperry	#91
1977	Deeply	Anson Williams	#93
1977	Pirate	Cher	#93
1977	We Never Danced to a Love Song	The Manhattans	#93
1977	It Ain't Easy Coming Down	Charlene	#97
1977	Only Love Can Break a Heart	Bobby Vinton	#99
1978	Le Freak	Chic	#1
1978	You Don't Bring Me Flowers	Barbra Streisand & Neil Diamond	#1
1978	Our Love	Natalie Cole	#10
1978	Turn to Stone	Electric Light Orchestra	#13
1978	Sweet Talkin' Woman	Electric Light Orchestra	#17
1978	Talking in Your Sleep	Crystal Gayle	#18
1978	Getting' Ready for Love	Diana Ross	#27
1978	Mr. Blue Sky	Electric Light Orchestra	#35
1978	This Is Love	Paul Anka	#35
1978	How Can I Leave You Again	John Denver	#44
1978	That Once in a Lifetime	Demis Roussos	#47
1978	You're All I Need to Get By	Johnny Mathis & Deniece Williams	#47
1978	Silver Dreams	The Babys	#53

	STRINGS (cont'd)		
1978	I Want to Live	John Denver	#55
1978	You Keep Me Dancing	Samantha Sang	#56
1978	Storybook Children (Daybreak)	Bette Midler	#57
1978	This Night Won't Last Forever	Bill LaBounty	#65
1978	You'll Love Again	Hotel	#71
1978	Ready or Not	Helen Reddy	#73
1978	It's Over	Electric Light Orchestra	#75
1978	He's So Fine	Jane Olivor	#77
1978	Brandy	The O'Jays	#79
1978	What a Difference You've Made in My Life	Ronnie Milsap	#80
1978	On the Wrong Track	Kevin Lamb	#82
1978	The Loneliest Man on the Moon	David Castle	#89
1978	Let the Song Last Forever	Dan Hill	#91
1979	Good Times	Chic	#1
1979	Music Box Dancer	Frank Mills	#3
1979	Take Me Home	Cher	#8
1979	Shine a Little Love	Electric Light Orchestra	#8
1979	He's the Greatest Dancer	Sister Sledge	#9
1979	Don't Cry Out Loud	Melissa Manchester	#10
1979	Half the Way	Crystal Gayle	#15
1979	Maybe I'm a Fool	Eddie Money	#22
1979	Where Were You When I Was Falling in Love	Lobo	#23
1979	Rainbow Connection	Kermit (Jim Henson)	#25
1979	(If Loving You Is Wrong) I Don't Want to Be Right	Barbara Mandrell	#31
1979	It Must Be Love	Alton McClain & Destiny	#32
1979	Love Pains	Yvonne Elliman	#34
1979	Kiss in the Dark	Pink Lady	#37
1979	Married Men	Bette Midler	#40
1979	My Baby's Baby	Liquid Gold	#45
1979	Why Leave Us Alone	Five Special	#55
1979	Baby, I Need Your Lovin'	Eric Carmen	#62
1979	Fancy Dancer	Frankie Valli	#77
1979	When I Dream	Crystal Gayle	#84

TUBULAR/CHURCH BELLS

YEAR	SONG	ARTIST	HOT 100
1970	Share the Land	The Guess Who	#10
1970	The Bells	The Originals	#12

	TUBULAR/CHURCH BELLS (cont'd)		
1970	Overture from Tommy (A Rock Opera)	Assembled Multitude	#16
1971	I Hear Those Church Bells Ringing	Dusk	#53
1971	Hot Pants	Salvage	#54
1971	1927 Kansas City	Mike Reilly	#88
1971	Adrienne	Tommy James	#93
1971	Your Love Is so Doggone Good	The Whispers	#93
1973	Close Your Eyes	Edward Bear	#37
1973	Somebody Loves You	The Whispers	#94
1974	Sugar Baby Love	The Rubettes	#37
1974	It Could Have Been Me	Sami Jo	#46
1974	Shoe Shoe Shine	Dynamic Superiors	#68
1974	Flashback	The 5th Dimension	#82
1975	Lucy in the Sky with Diamonds	Elton John	#1
1975	Please Mr. Postman	Carpenters	#1
1975	Ding Dong; Ding Dong	George Harrison	#36
1975	Reality	James Brown	#80
1976	I Do, I Do, I Do, I Do, I Do	ABBA	#15
1976	There Won't Be No Country Music (There Won't Be No Rock 'N' Roll)	C.W. McCall	#73
1976	Scotch on the Rocks	Band of the Black Watch	#75
1976	It Should Have Been Me	Yvonne Fair	#85
1977	Amarillo	Neil Sedaka	#44
1977	Closer to the Heart	Rush	#76
1978	Theme from "Close Encounters of the Third Kind"	Meco	#25
1979	I Want Your Love	Chic	#7
1979	Heaven Must Have Sent You	Bonnie Pointer	#11

VIBRASLAP

YEAR	SONG	ARTIST	HOT 100
1970	Engine Number 9	Wilson Pickett	#14
1971	Feelin' Alright	Grand Funk Railroad	#54
1971	It's so Hard for Me to Say Good-Bye	Eddie Kendricks	#88
1972	Corner of the Sky	The Jackson 5	#18
1972	Fire and Water	Wilson Pickett	#24
1972	Feeling Alright	Joe Cocker	#33
1972	Louisiana	Mike Kennedy	#62
1972	Iko Iko	Dr. John	#71
1972	What a Wonderful Thing We Have	Fabulous Rhinestones	#78
1972	Tell 'em Willie Boy's A'Comin'	Tommy James	#89

VIBRASLAP (cont'd)

1973	Master of Eyes (The Deepness of Your Eyes)	Aretha Franklin	#33
1973	A Song I'd Like to Sing	Kris Kristofferson & Rita Coolidge	#49
1973	Black Byrd	Donald Byrd	#88
1974	Do It Baby	The Miracles	#13
1974	My Thang	James Brown	#29
1974	Tell Her Love Has Felt the Need	Eddie Kendricks	#50
1974	Captain Howdy	Simon Stokes	#90
1975	Fame	David Bowie	#1
1975	I Dreamed Last Night	Justin Hayward & John Lodge	#47
1975	Sneakin' Up Behind You	The Brecker Brothers	#58
1975	Hush/I'm Alive	Blue Swede	#61
1975	Alvin Stone (The Birth & Death of a Gangster)	Fantastic Four	#74
1975	Don't Cha Love It	The Miracles	#78
1975	Smokin' Room	Carl Carlton	#91
1975	Love Don't You Go Through No Changes on Me	Sister Sledge	#92
1976	A Fifth of Beethoven	Walter Murphy	#1
1976	(Don't Fear) The Reaper	Blue Öyster Cult	#12
1976	Somebody's Gettin' It	Johnnie Taylor	#33
1976	Banapple Gas	Cat Stevens	#41
1976	Roots, Rock, Reggae	Bob Marley	#51
1976	You Got the Magic	John Fogerty	#87
1976	Night Walk	Van McCoy	#96
1977	Uptown Festival (Part 1)	Shalamar	#25
1977	Slide	Slave	#32
1977	On the Border	Al Stewart	#42
1977	Man Smart, Woman Smarter	Robert Palmer	#63
1977	Dance Little Lady Dance	Danny White	#100
1978	You and I	Rick James	#13
1978	Street Corner Serenade	Wet Willie	#30
1978	Never Had a Love	Pablo Cruise	#87
1979	What Cha Gonna Do with My Lovin'	Stephanie Mills	#22
1979	Ghost Dancer	Addrisi Brothers	#45
1979	You Stepped Into My Life	Melba Moore	#47
1979	Reason to Be	Kansas	#52
1979	Groove Me	Fern Kinney	#54
1979	Why Leave Us Alone	Five Special	#55
1979	I Just Can't Control Myself	Nature's Divine	#65
1979	High on Your Love Suite	Rick James	#72
1979	Pow Wow	Cory Daye	#76
1979	Mirror Star	Fabulous Poodles	#81
1979	Shoot Me (With Your Love)	Tasha Thomas	#91

VIOLIN

Songs in this list use only *one* violin. If you're looking for songs with a whole section of violins, check the "strings" or "orchestra" lists.

YEAR	SONG	ARTIST	HOT 100
1970	Mississippi	John Phillips	#32
1970	Rag Mama Rag	The Band	#56
1970	Carolina in My Mind	James Taylor	#67
1970	Going to the Country	Steve Miller Band	#69
1970	Is Anybody Goin' to San Antone	Charley Pride	#70
1970	Darkness, Darkness	The Youngbloods	#86
1970	Beaucoups of Blues	Ringo Starr	#87
1970	Wonder Could I Live There Anymore	Charley Pride	#87
1970	Dear Ann	George Baker Selection	#93
1971	13 Questions	Seatrain	#49
1971	Reason to Believe	Rod Stewart	#62
1971	Ride a White Swan	Tyrannosaurus Rex	#76
1971	Soldier's Last Letter	Merle Haggard	#90
1971	I'm Just Me	Charley Pride	#94
1972	You Wear It Well	Rod Stewart	#13
1972	Kiss an Angel Good Mornin'	Charley Pride	#21
1972	Pretty as You Feel	Jefferson Airplane	#60
1972	Changes	David Bowie	#66
1972	Guilty	Al Green	#69
1972	Jambalaya (On the Bayou)	Nitty Gritty Dirt Band	#84
1972	It's Four in the Morning	Faron Young	#92
1973	Dead Skunk	Loudon Wainwright III	#16
1973	Thinking of You	Loggins & Messina	#18
1973	If We Make It Through December	Merle Haggard	#28
1973	Superman	Donna Fargo	#41
1973	Everybody's Had the Blues	Merle Haggard	#62
1973	Roll in My Sweet Baby's Arms	Hank Wilson (Leon Russell)	#78
1973	You Always Come Back (To Hurting Me)	Johnny Rodriguez	#86
1973	My Heart Just Keeps on Breakin'	The Chi-Lites	#92
1973	Smoke! Smoke! Smoke! (That Cigarette)	Commander Cody	#94
1974	Rub It In	Billy "Crash" Craddock	#16
1974	Workin' at the Car Wash Blues	Jim Croce	#32
1974	Time for Livin'	Sly & The Family Stone	#32
1974	W*O*L*D*	Harry Chapin	#36

VIOLIN (cont'd)

1974	(I'm A) YoYo Man	Rick Cunha	#61
1974	Silver Threads and Golden Needles	Linda Ronstadt	#67
1974	I Hate Hate	Razzy Bailey	#67
1974	Mississippi Cotton Picking Delta Town	Charley Pride	#70
1974	Battle of New Orleans	Nitty Gritty Dirt Band	#72
1974	Travelin' Prayer	Billy Joel	#77
1975	Black Water	The Doobie Brothers	#1
1975	Thank God I'm a Country Boy	John Denver	#1
1975	Holdin' on to Yesterday	Ambrosia	#17
1975	Sally G	Paul McCartney & Wings	#17
1975	The South's Gonna Do It	Charlie Daniels Band	#29
1975	Ruby, Baby	Billy "Crash" Craddock	#33
1975	Fire on the Mountain	Marshall Tucker Band	#38
1975	Blind Man in the Bleachers	Kenny Starr	#58
1975	Linda on My Mind	Conway Twitty	#61
1975	Love Is a Rose	Linda Ronstadt	#63
1975	This Ol' Cowboy	Marshall Tucker Band	#78
1975	Changes	Loggins & Messina	#84
1975	Live Your Life Before You Die	The Pointer Sisters	#89
1975	A Lover's Question	Loggins & Messina	#89
1976	Fly Away	John Denver	#13
1976	Play on Love	Jefferson Starship	#49
1976	Mozambique	Bob Dylan	#54
1976	I'll Get Over You	Crystal Gayle	#71
1976	Rocky Mountain Music	Eddie Rabbitt	#76
1976	Texas	Charlie Daniels Band	#91
1976	Rose of Cimarron	Poco	#94
1976	Solitary Man	T.G. Sheppard	#100
1977	Sunflower	Glen Campbell	#39
1977	White Bird	David LaFlamme	#89
1977	For a While	Mary MacGregor	#90
1978	You're In My Heart	Rod Stewart	#4
1978	Dust in the Wind	Kansas	#6
1978	Point of Know Return	Kansas	#28
1978	Sweet, Sweet Smile	Carpenters	#44
1978	Ready for the Times to Get Better	Crystal Gayle	#52
1979	The Devil Went Down to Georgia	Charlie Daniels Band	#3
1979	Sweets for My Sweet	Tony Orlando	#54
1979	Lonely Wind	Kansas	#60
1979	Four Strong Winds	Neil Young (w/Nicolette Larson)	#61

WHISTLE

YEAR	SONG	ARTIST	HOT 100
1972	Taurus	Dennis Coffey	#18
1973	Funky Stuff	Kool & The Gang	#29
1973	Bad Weather	The Supremes	#87
1974	Up for the Down Stroke	Parliament	#63
1975	7-6-5-4-3-2-1 (Blow Your Whistle)	Gary Toms Empire	#46
1975	Hollywood Hot	The Eleventh Hour	#55
1976	Hold On	Sons of Champlin	#47
1977	O-H-I-O	Ohio Players	#45
1977	Up Your Nose	Gabriel Kaplan	#91
1977	Dance and Shake Your Tambourine	Universal Robot Band	#93
1978	Let Me Party with You (Party, Party, Party)(Part 1)	Bunny Sigler	#43
1979	Bad Girls	Donna Summer	#1
1979	Keep on Dancin'	Gary's Gang	#41

MISCELLANEOUS INSTRUMENTS

Instruments that were featured in fewer than three songs are listed here. Songs are listed alphabetically by instrument.

YEAR	SONG	ARTIST	HOT 100	INSTRUMENT
1972	Amazing Grace	Royal Scots Dragoon Guards	#11	Bagpipes
1976	Scotch on the Rocks	Band of the Black Watch	#75	Bagpipes
1970	The Tears of a Clown	Smokey Robinson & The Miracles	#1	Bassoon
1970	The Tears of a Clown	Smokey Robinson & The Miracles	#1	Calliope
1973	I'm Just a Singer (In a Rock and Roll Band)	The Moody Blues	#12	Chamberlin
1979	Ring My Bell	Anita Ward	#1	Chimes
1970	The Rapper	The Jaggerz	#2	Cowbell
1972	Me and Julio Down by the Schoolyard	Paul Simon	#22	Cuica
1970	I Do Take You	The Three Degrees	#48	English Horn
1975	Have You Never Been Mellow	Olivia Newton-John	#1	English Horn
1976	Bohemium Rhapsody	Queen	#9	Gong
1972	Isn't Life Strange	The Moody Blues	#29	Harmonium
1970	In the Summertime	Mungo Jerry	#3	Jug
1979	Tusk	Fleetwood Mac	#8	Kleenex box
1979	Tusk	Fleetwood Mac	#8	Lamb chops w/spatula
1973	Space Oddity	David Bowie	#15	Mellotron

MICELLANEOUS INSTRUMENTS (cont'd)

1973	Dream On	Aerosmith	#59	Mellotron
1972	Join Together	The Who	#17	Mouth Harp
1974	Travelin' Prayer	Billy Joel	#77	Mouth Harp
1970	The Tears of a Clown	Smokey Robinson & The Miracles	#1	Piccolo
1970	Hitchin' A Ride	Vanity Fare	#5	Recorder
1979	The Logical Song	Supertramp	#6	Siren whistle
1970	Fire and Rain	James Taylor	#3	String Bass
1973	Space Oddity	David Bowie	#15	Stylophone
1976	Good Vibrations	Todd Rundgren	#34	Theremin
1978	The Next Hundred Years	Al Martino	#49	Ukulele
1970	My Sweet Lord	George Harrison	#1	Zither

TOP ARTISTS

To appear on the "Top Solo Artists" chart, an artist had to have at least 15 Hot 100 hits. Elvis Presley and James Brown both had the most Hot 100 hits with 36. What's amazing about Presley is he also had the most hits in the sixties. While Brown had a lot of Hot 100 hits in the 70s, he never had a song crack the top ten. His highest charting hit was "Super Bad (Part 1 & Part 2)" from 1970. It peaked at #13.

So, who <u>was</u> the top solo artist of the 70s? Though Presley and Brown had the most hits, I think they both get disqualified since neither one of them had a #1 hit. Based on the data, I'd rank the top solo artists like this: #1- Elton John, #2- Paul McCartney, #3- Stevie Wonder.

You could make an argument for moving Wonder up to #2 or even #1 based not only on his steady hit production, but also on the fact that he won 12 Grammy awards during the decade, including Album of the Year in 1973, 1974, and 1976. He was so dominant, that when Paul Simon won the Grammy for Album of the Year in 1975, he thanked Stevie Wonder for not putting out an album that year.

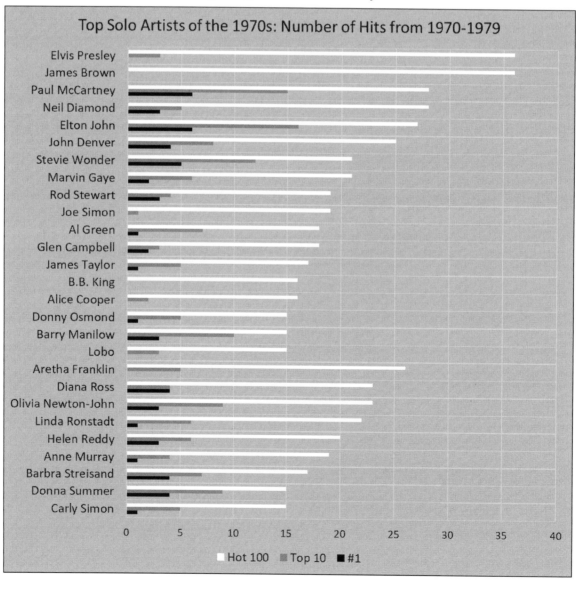

Who was the top group of the 1970s? Chicago easily had the most Hot 100 hits of the decade, but they only had one #1 hit. The Jackson 5, Carpenters, and Bee Gees all tied for the 2nd most hits of the decade. The Bee Gees had the most #1 hits, with the Eagles in 2nd place, and The Jackson 5 having the third most #1 hits.

If we base it on the chart data alone, I'd rank the top groups of the 1970s like this: #1- Bee Gees, #2- The Eagles, #3- The Jackson 5, #4- The Carpenters, #5- Chicago.

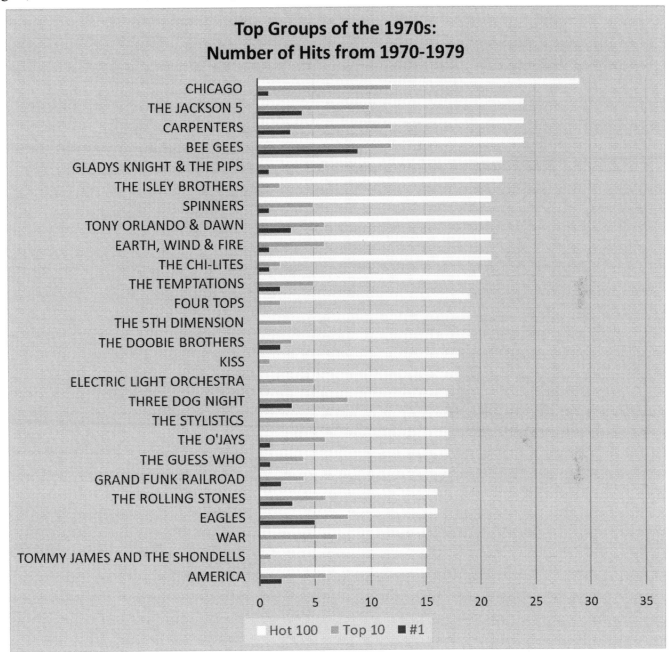

The charts that follow for each artist help show how successful each was over a period of time. Many of them had a couple of years where they were white-hot. For example, look at Donna Summer from 1978-1980. Nine top five hits, including four #1 hits. Impressive! Also take a look at Elton John from 1973-1975, The Jackson 5's first six hits, and The Bee Gees from 1977-1979. Other artists, such as Paul McCartney and The Commodores just had a long period of sustained success.

The bold horizontal gridline near the middle of each chart represents the top 40 line. Hits above the line made the top 40, while hits below the line peaked outside the top 40.

The Bee Gees

Illustration by Nigel Vu

"When we get together and write it's not like three individuals, it's like one person in the room."
~Maurice Gibb[1]

"You can't put us in a category. We're part folk, pop, rock, R&B, everything. The tags rarely fit. What is disco? What is rock? It's all pretty vague and ambiguous.''
~Barry Gibb[2]

"The Bee Gees were an early inspiration for me, Kelly Rowland and Michelle. We loved their songwriting and beautiful harmonies."
~Beyoncé[3]

"I cried listening to their music. I knew every note, every instrument."
~Michael Jackson[4]

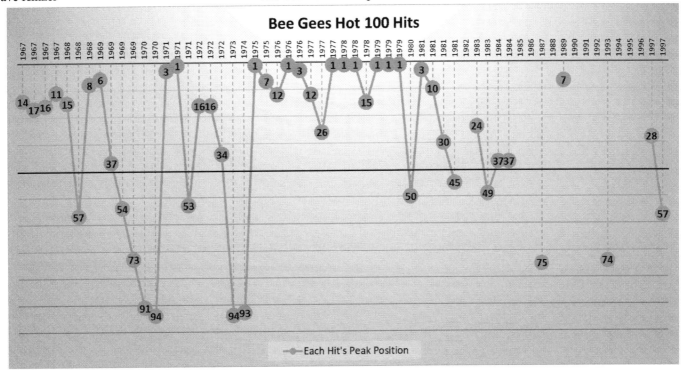

Bee Gees Hot 100 Hits

The Carpenters

Illustration by Dankugaru

"She has the best female voice in the world: melodic, tuneful and distinctive."
~Paul McCartney, on Karen Carpenter[5]

"One of the greatest voices of our lifetime..."
~Elton John, on Karen Carpenter[6]

"Karen Carpenter had a great sound, but if you've got three guys out on the ballfield and one of them started humming [a Carpenters song], the other two guys would pants him."
~John Fogerty[7]

"Let's hope we can have some hits!"
~A&M owner Herb Alpert, on meeting Richard and Karen Carpenter[8]

Carpenters Hot 100 Hits

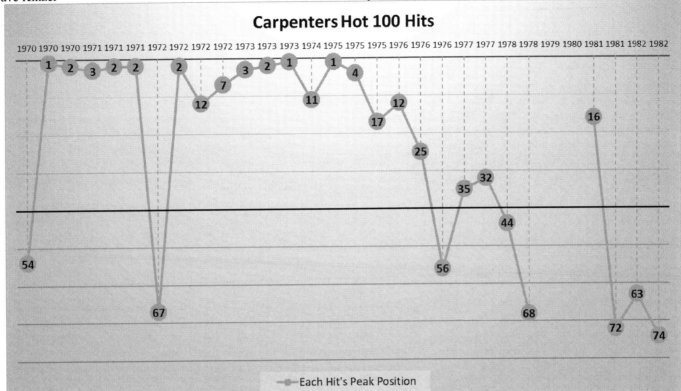

1970 1970 1970 1971 1971 1971 1972 1972 1972 1972 1973 1973 1973 1974 1975 1975 1975 1976 1976 1976 1977 1977 1978 1978 1979 1980 1981 1981 1982 1982

Each Hit's Peak Position

The Commodores

Illustration by Claire Starling

"I think the whole world is dying to hear someone say, "I love you". I think that if I can leave the legacy of love and passion in the world, then I think I've done my job in a world that's getting colder and colder by the day."
~Lionel Richie[9]

"I think the hidden gem is the subtleties of a lot of the nuances that are in our music, that penetrates through the hearts and the souls of people. You can't listen to a song by the Commodores and not be touched in some way."
~Thomas McClary, founder of The Commodores[10]

"I miss the fun we had. The memories of the fun stand out over everything. I'm disappointed that we couldn't work things out and stay together."
~William King, on Lionel Richie leaving the group[11]

"We were terrible. We played two songs by James Brown… We did not do a good job."
~William King, on the Commodores first ever performance at a talent show at Tuskegee University[12]

Commodores Hot 100 Hits

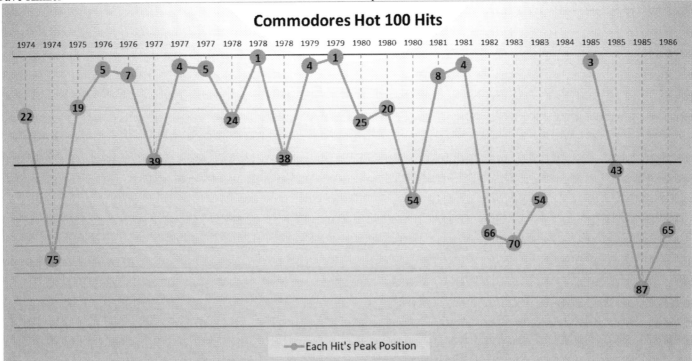

1974 1974 1975 1976 1976 1977 1977 1977 1978 1978 1978 1979 1979 1980 1980 1980 1981 1981 1982 1983 1983 1984 1985 1985 1985 1986

Each Hit's Peak Position

John Denver

Illustration by Matt Cleveland

"John Denver was someone I truly respected as a singer and a songwriter. He wrote songs that truly touched my heart."
~Olivia Newton-John[13]

"He was certainly one of the best, if not the best entertainer and vocalist I've ever worked with."
~Chris Nole, Denver's last pianist[14]

"I was never trying to write a hit. I was just trying to write good songs and get a message out, and it was my great good fortune to be popular."
~Denver[15]

"I write songs about real things, from the perspective that all people are the same and that these songs will touch them all in the same place."
~Denver[16]

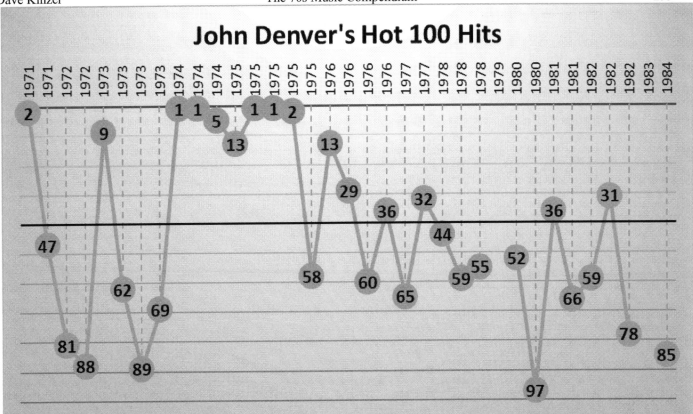

John Denver's Hot 100 Hits

Each Hit's Peak Position

Neil Diamond

Illustration by Eric Eckert

"Performing is the easiest part of what I do, and songwriting is the hardest."
~Diamond[17]

"Before he became the Jewish Elvis, I would say that he was really the prophet for the upcoming singer/songwriter revolution. He was a first."
~Paul Shaffer, David Letterman's musical director[18]

"I can't tell you how many people have been brought kicking and screaming to a Neil show, who after two and a half hours are genuflecting at the altar of Diamond."
~Richard Bennett, Diamond's guitarist[19]

"Is there any more wonderful, infectious, irresistible hook to a pop song? I don't think so."
~John Lithgow, actor, on "Sweet Caroline"[20]

Neil Diamond Hot 100 Hits

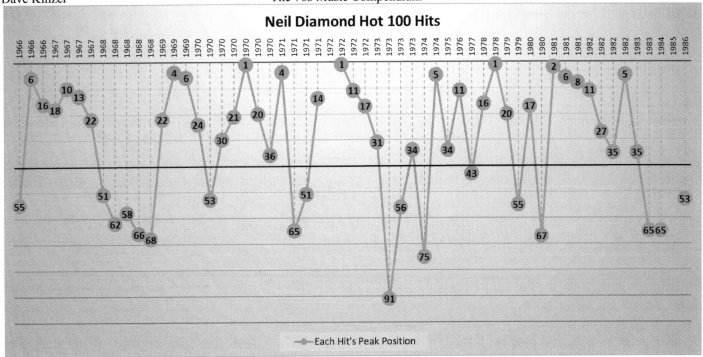

Each Hit's Peak Position

Jackson 5

Illustration by Matt Cleveland

"One day our television broke down. We took it to the shop and the guy was late fixin' it. So we started singin' country western around the house with our mom."
~Marlon Jackson, on the beginning of the Jackson 5[21]

"We're brothers first, and entertainers second."
~Tito Jackson[22]

"I was sitting in my dressing room on the second floor when I heard these little voices… As young as I was, I knew talent when I saw it. Even with their little children voices I heard their potential and knew what these guys could achieve."
~Gladys Knight[23]

"They played to sold-out arenas around the world. We had to have such heavy security on the Jackson 5. Not to keep the fans from hurting them, but to keep them from loving them to death."
~Barry Gordy, founder of Motown[24]

The Jackson 5 Hot 100 Hits

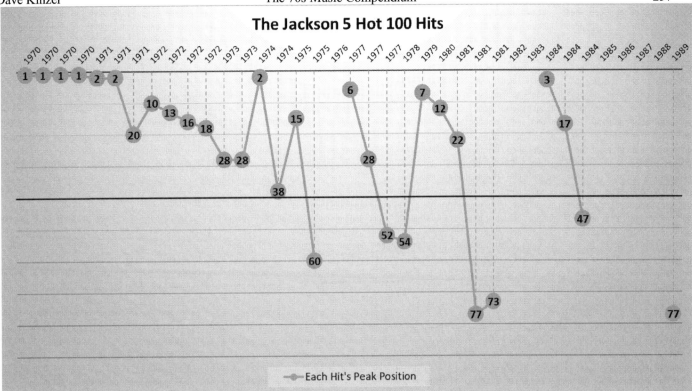

Each Hit's Peak Position

Elton John

Illustration by Justin Witt

"The great thing about rock and roll is that someone like me can be a star."
~John[25]

"I wrote some sort of nonsensical psychedelic lyrics that were plagiarized from a conglomerate of things in vogue, and actually got a reply. So I went to London and this guy said, 'I've got this kid. He wants to write songs, but he doesn't write lyrics. He's auditioned for us, and everyone said no. Maybe you two guys should hook up.' It's kismet. Elton had answered the same ad."
~Bernie Taupin, John's longtime lyricist, on how he met Elton John[26]

"Elton John has never gone out of style because his music isn't seasonal, it's perennial. It comes down to these timeless melodies and the ever-resonant words of your collaborator, Bernie Taupin."
~Robert Downey Jr., at the 2004 Kennedy Center Honors[27]

"I'm not everybody's cup of tea. But sometimes criticism can be hurtful. Be respectful. I'm a good piano player, I can sing well, I write good songs. If you don't like it, fair enough. But give me a break."
~John[28]

Elton John Hot 100 Hits

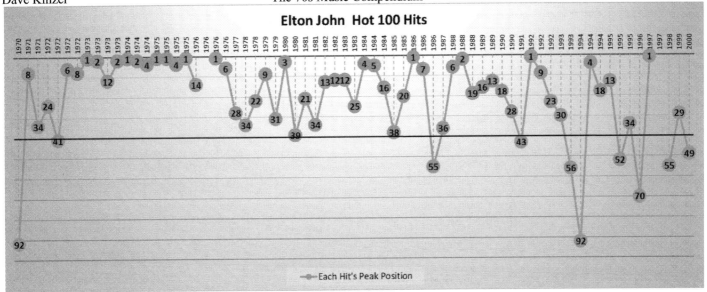

Each Hit's Peak Position

Paul McCartney

Illustration by Jace King

"In the '60s, [my ambition] was to get a car ... And I got one. We used to always say it when we were kids: Get a guitar, a car, and a house. That was the height of our ambition ... It wasn't to rule the world."
~McCartney[29]

"I'm in awe of McCartney. He can do it all. And he's never let up. He's got the gift for melody, he's got the rhythm, he can play any instrument... And his melodies are effortless, that's what you have to be in awe of."
~Bob Dylan[30]

"Paul McCartney is a genius. Paul married rock and roll to beauty and forever raised the bar for composers, musicians, and fans."
~Alec Baldwin, at the 2010 Kennedy Center Honors[31]

"I should be able to look at my accolades and go, 'Come on, Paul. That's enough.' But there's still this little voice ... that goes, 'No, no, no. You could do better. This person over here is excelling. Try harder!'"
~McCartney[32]

Paul McCartney Hot 100 Hits

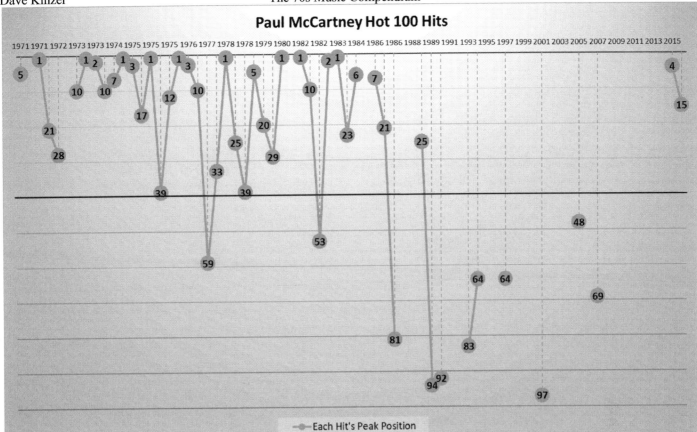

Each Hit's Peak Position

Linda Ronstadt

Illustration by Margee Bright-Ragland

"I had a terrible crush on Smokey Robinson, like every other female on the planet."
~Ronstadt[33]

"Linda lives in a place where art trumps commerce, where self-exploration trumps self-exploitation, where hard work and integrity trump fame and failure. She never wanted to be a star, she just wanted to make good music."
~Glen Frey, inducting Ronstadt into the Rock and Roll hall of fame in 2014[34]

"Her lower register was her glory, and she was the full master of it. She could bend it to her will, shade pitches, float ballads, belt imperiously and blend with most anyone in harmony singing."
~www.rockhall.com[35]

"Singing with Aaron Neville, he pulled stuff out of my voice I never could have gotten, because if he's providing XYZ, I have to put in ABC, and usually I don't have to put in ABC."
~Ronstadt[36]

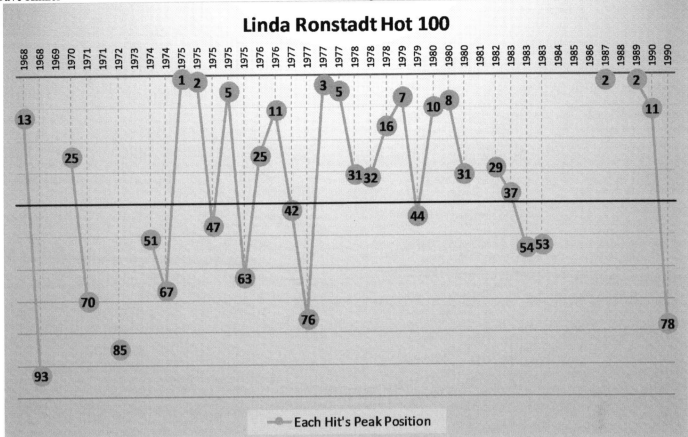

Linda Ronstadt Hot 100

Diana Ross

Illustration by Izabel Piña

"Diana Ross is more than just an ageless beauty. She is a force that has helped to shape our culture."
~Oprah Winfrey[37]

"I like songs that are positive and say something inspirational and makes a difference in people's lives."
~Ross, on what makes the perfect pop song[38]

"Ain't No Mountain High Enough."
~Ross, on her favorite song to perform[39]

"Although never a commanding instrument, Ross's small, syrupy voice with its dash of vinegar can convey a certain calculated poignancy."
~Stephen Holden[40]

Diana Ross Hot 100 Hits

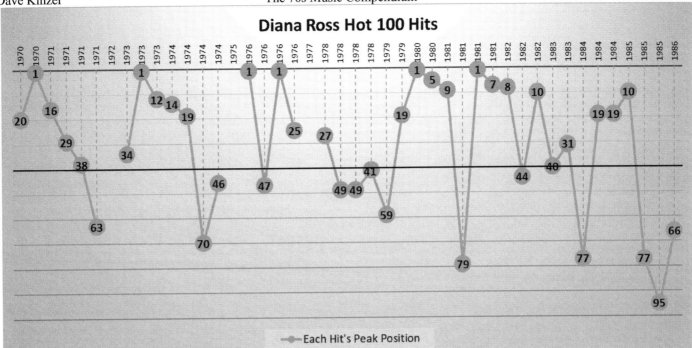

Each Hit's Peak Position

Donna Summer

Illustration by Justin Witt

"Donna Summer made music that moved me both emotionally and physically to get up and dance. You could always hear the deep passion in her voice. She was so much more than the queen of disco she became known for, she was an honest and gifted singer with flawless vocal talent."
~Beyoncé[41]

"Donna changed the face of pop culture forever. There is no doubt that music would sound different today if she had never graced us with her talent. She was a super-diva and a true superstar who never compromised when it came to her career or her family. She always did it with class, dignity, grace and zero attitude."
~David Foster, 16-time Grammy Award winner[42]

"People didn't know what to do with me when I first came out. There was no category for dance."
~Summer[43]

"Rest in Peace, dear Donna Summer. Your voice was the heartbeat and soundtrack of a decade."
~Quincy Jones, on hearing of Summer's death[44]

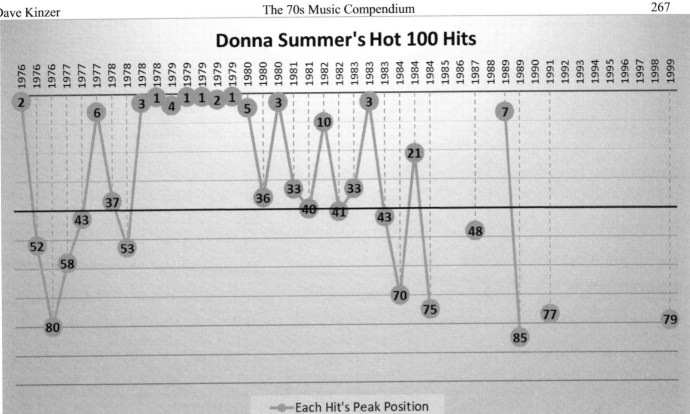

Stevie Wonder

Illustration by Leon

"He was blind and shy and only 11 years old, but he played the piano like nothing I had ever heard."
~Berry Gordy, founder of Motown, on meeting Stevie Wonder for the first time[45]

"Everyone that was over eleven years old was my parent... All of the Marvelettes saw themselves as being my parents. All of the Supremes, even though they were just a little older than me..."
~Wonder, on how the other Motown musicians treated him, at age eleven[46]

"I used Stevie Wonder as an inspiration, whom I look up to a great deal... For the way that he crafted music... I used him as a role model in trying to play all the instruments."
~Prince[47]

"He is the universal poet, who celebrates our humanity and challenges us to do more and to be better, and to do it all with a smile on our face, and laughter in our hearts."
~Halle Berry, actress, at the 1999 Kennedy Center Honors[48]

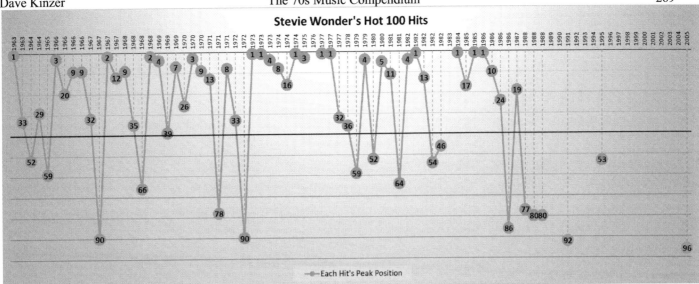

Stevie Wonder's Hot 100 Hits

Each Hit's Peak Position

MUSIC THEORY

SONGS THAT MODULATE

Modulation is when a song modulates, or changes keys. Usually, this will happen towards the end of a song when the artist wants the song's intensity or level of excitement to increase. Almost all songs that modulate do it only once, but a few songs will modulate two or three times.

The ten highest charting songs from each year that modulated are listed below.

YEAR	SONG	ARTIST	HOT 100
1970	My Sweet Lord	George Harrison	#1
1970	Ain't No Mountain High Enough	Diana Ross	#1
1970	Everything Is Beautiful	Ray Stevens	#1
1970	Cracklin' Rosie	Neil Diamond	#1
1970	Love Grows (Where My Rosemary Goes)	Edison Lighthouse	#5
1970	It's Only Make Believe	Glen Campbell	#10
1970	Look What They've Done to My Song Ma	The New Seekers	#14
1970	Little Green Bag	George Baker Selection	#21
1970	God, Love and Rock & Roll	Teegarden & Van Winkle	#22
1970	Summertime Blues	The Who	#27
1971	Me and Bobby McGee	Janis Joplin	#1
1971	Sooner or Later	The Grass Roots	#9
1971	Theme from Love Story	Henry Mancini	#13
1971	Friends with You	John Denver	#47
1971	Rainy Jane	Davy Jones	#52
1971	He's So Fine	Jody Miller	#53
1971	Life	Elvis Presley	#53
1971	Roll On	The New Colony Six	#56
1971	Whole Lotta Love	C.C.S.	#58
1971	Cheryl Moana Marie	John Rowles	#64
1972	The Candy Man	Sammy Davis, Jr. w/The Mike Curb Congregation	#1
1972	Clair	Gilbert O'Sullivan	#2
1972	Precious and Few	Climax	#3
1972	Freddie's Dead (Theme from "Superfly")	Curtis Mayfield	#4
1972	I'd Like to Teach the World to Sing (In Perfect Harmony)	The Hillside Singers	#13
1972	Beautiful Sunday	Daniel Boone	#15
1972	Don't Say You Don't Remember	Beverly Bremers	#15

SONGS THAT MODULATE (cont'd)

1972	My World	Bee Gees	#16
1972	Sealed with a Kiss	Bobby Vinton	#19
1972	Once You Understand	Think	#23
1973	Leave Me Alone (Ruby Red Dress)	Helen Reddy	#3
1973	Funny Face	Donna Fargo	#5
1973	You're a Special Part of Me	Diana Ross & Marvin Gaye	#12
1973	Behind Closed Doors	Charlie Rich	#15
1973	Teddy Bear Song	Barbara Fairchild	#32
1973	Soul Song	Joe Stampley	#37
1973	Sixty Minute Man	Clarence Carter	#65
1973	Shambala	B.W. Stevenson	#66
1973	Boo, Boo, Don't 'Cha Be Blue	Tommy James	#70
1973	Hot Wire	Al Green	#71
1974	Seasons in the Sun	Terry Jacks	#1
1974	Dark Lady	Cher	#1
1974	I'm Leaving It (All) Up to You	Donny & Marie Osmond	#4
1974	Mockingbird	Carly Simon & James Taylor	#5
1974	Let Me Be There	Olivia Newton-John	#6
1974	Another Saturday Night	Cat Stevens	#6
1974	Life Is a Rock (But the Radio Rolled Me)	Reunion	#8
1974	Eres Tu (Touch the Wind)	Mocedades	#9
1974	Stop and Smell the Roses	Mac Davis	#9
1974	Last Time I Saw Him	Diana Ross	#14
1975	Love Will Keep Us Together	The Captain & Tennille	#1
1975	Fire	Ohio Players	#1
1975	Rocky	Austin Roberts	#9
1975	Rock N' Roll (I Gave You the Best Years of My Life)	Mac Davis	#15
1975	The Proud One	The Osmonds	#22
1975	Beer Barrel Polka	Bobby Vinton	#33
1975	Don't Take Your Love	Manhattans	#37
1975	Make the World Go Away	Donny & Marie Osmond	#44
1975	Every Day I Have to Cry Some	Arthur Alexander	#45
1975	My Elusive Dreams	Charlie Rich	#49
1976	I Write the Songs	Barry Manilow	#1
1976	Bohemium Rhapsody	Queen	#9
1976	Fanny (Be Tender with My Love)	Bee Gees	#12
1976	Cupid	Tony Orlando & Dawn	#22
1976	Good Hearted Woman	Waylon Jennings & Willie Nelson	#25
1976	Don't Take Away the Music	Tavares	#34
1976	Whenever I'm Away from You	John Travolta	#38
1976	Take a Hand	Rick Springfield	#41

	SONGS THAT MODULATE (cont'd)		
1976	Down to the Line	Bachman-Turner Overdrive	#43
1976	I Can't Live a Dream	The Osmonds	#46
1977	Don't Give Up on Us	David Soul	#1
1977	Looks Like We Made It	Barry Manilow	#1
1977	(Your Love Has Lifted Me) Higher and Higher	Rita Coolidge	#2
1977	Angel in Your Arms	Hot	#6
1977	Right Time of the Night	Jennifer Warnes	#6
1977	Weekend in New England	Barry Manilow	#10
1977	Whodunit	Tavares	#22
1977	Ariel	Dean Friedman	#26
1977	Old Fashioned Boy (You're the One)	Stallion	#37
1977	Amarillo	Neil Sedaka	#44
1978	Can't Smile Without You	Barry Manilow	#3
1978	Last Dance	Donna Summer	#3
1978	Ready to Take a Chance Again	Barry Manilow	#11
1978	Runaround Sue	Leif Garrett	#13
1978	The Way I Feel Tonight	Bay City Rollers	#24
1978	Street Corner Serenade	Wet Willie	#30
1978	Devoted to You	Carly Simon & James Taylor	#36
1978	Mammas Don't Let Your Babies Grow Up to Be Cowboys	Waylon Jennings & Willie Nelson	#42
1978	I Don't Wanna Go	Joey Travolta	#43
1978	Dreadlock Holiday	10 CC	#44
1979	Sad Eyes	Robert John	#1
1979	Got to Be Real	Cheryl Lynn	#12
1979	New York Groove	Ace Frehley	#13
1979	Half the Way	Crystal Gayle	#15
1979	Morning Dance	Spyro Gyra	#24
1979	Rainbow Connection	Kermit (Jim Henson)	#25
1979	Love Pains	Yvonne Elliman	#34
1979	I Need Your Help Barry Manilow	Ray Stevens	#49
1979	Can You Read My Mind	Maureen McGovern	#52
1979	Sweets for My Sweet	Tony Orlando	#54

SONGS WITH OSTINATOS

An ostinato is a short, repetitive rhythmic or melodic phrase. An ostinato can be an instrumental or a vocal part. The key, though, is that it is a short phrase that repeats. I only included songs that had distinctive or especially important ostinatos, or ostinatos that dominated the music. James Brown's songs are usually filled with ostinatos of all kinds.

YEAR	SONG	ARTIST	HOT 100
1970	American Woman	The Guess Who	#1
1970	War	Edwin Starr	#1
1970	Green-Eyed Lady	Sugarloaf	#3
1970	Spill the Wine	Eric Burdon & War	#3
1970	Whole Lotta Love	Led Zeppelin	#4
1970	25 or 6 to 4	Chicago	#4
1970	Evil Ways	Santana	#9
1970	Still Water (Love)	Four Tops	#11
1970	Express Yourself	Charles Wright	#12
1970	Celebrate	Three Dog Night	#15
1970	Get Up I Feel Like Being Like a Sex Machine (Part 1)	James Brown	#15
1970	You're the One – Part 2	Little Sister	#22
1970	Ain't It Funky Now (Part 1)	James Brown	#24
1970	Do the Funky Chicken	Rufus Thomas	#28
1970	Viva Tirado – Part 1	El Chicano	#28
1970	It's a New Day (Part 1 & 2)	James Brown	#32
1970	Brother Rapp (Part 1)	James Brown	#32
1970	Let a Man Come in and Do the Popcorn (Part two)	James Brown	#40
1970	Mighty Joe	Shocking Blue	#43
1970	Chains and Things	B.B. King	#45
1970	Mongoose	Elephant's Memory	#50
1970	Funky Drummer (Part 1)	James Brown	#51
1970	On the Beach (In the Summertime)	The 5th Dimension	#54
1970	Sing a Song for Freedom	Frijid Pink	#55
1970	Cryin' in the Streets (Part 1)	George Perkins	#61
1970	Gonna Give Her All the Love I've Got	Marvin Gaye	#67
1970	I Need Help (I Can't Do It Alone) Pt. 1	Bobby Byrd	#69
1970	Stoned Cowboy	Fantasy	#77
1970	Let the Music Take Your Mind	Kool & The Gang	#78
1970	Country Preacher	Cannonball Adderley	#86
1970	Funky Man	Kool & The Gang	#87
1970	Lady Love	The Klowns	#95
1970	Love Like a Man	Ten Years After	#98
1971	Hot Pants (She Got to Use What She Got to Get What She Wants) (Pt. 1)	James Brown	#15
1971	Immigrant Song	Led Zeppelin	#16
1971	Make It Funky (Part 1)	James Brown	#22
1971	Soul Power (Pt. 1)	James Brown	#29
1971	(Don't Worry) If There's a Hell Below We're All Going to Go	Curtis Mayfield	#29
1971	Get Up, Get Into It, Get Involved (Pt. 1)	James Brown	#34
1971	I'm a Greedy Man (Part 1)	James Brown	#35

SONGS WITH OSTINATOS (cont'd)

1971	Escape-ism (Part 1)	James Brown	#35
1971	Do Me Right	Detroit Emeralds	#43
1971	Whole Lotta Love	C.C.S.	#58
1971	Whole Lotta Love	King Curtis	#64
1971	Gimme Some Lovin'-Pt. 1	Traffic	#68
1971	Give It to Me	The Mob	#71
1971	You've Lost That Lovin' Feelin'	Roberta Flack & Donny Hathaway	#71
1971	Don't Try to Lay No Boogie-Woogie on the King of Rock and Roll	John Baldry	#73
1971	Your Love (Means Everything to Me)	Charles Wright	#73
1971	Where are We Going	Bobby Bloom	#84
1971	Adrienne	Tommy James	#93
1971	Be Good to Me Baby	Luther Ingram	#97
1972	I'll Be Around	The Spinners	#3
1972	Freddie's Dead (Theme from "Superfly")	Curtis Mayfield	#4
1972	Troglodyte (Cave Man)	Jimmy Castor Bunch	#6
1972	Clean Up Woman	Betty Wright	#6
1972	Rock and Roll Part 2	Gary Glitter	#7
1972	Jungle Fever	The Chackachas	#8
1972	Sweet Seasons	Carole King	#9
1972	Join Together	The Who	#17
1972	Get on the Good Foot – Part 1	James Brown	#18
1972	Once You Understand	Think	#23
1972	Feeling Alright	Joe Cocker	#33
1972	Do the Funky Penguin (Part 1)	Rufus Thomas	#44
1972	Son of My Father	Giorgio	#46
1972	Afro-Strut	The Nite-Liters	#49
1972	Jubilation	Paul Anka	#65
1972	Gimme Some More	The JB's	#67
1972	The Jean Genie	David Bowie	#71
1972	You Were Made for Me	Luther Ingram	#93
1972	Pass the Peas	The JB's	#95
1973	Superstition	Stevie Wonder	#1
1973	I'm Gonna Love You Just a Little More Baby	Barry White	#3
1973	Why Can't We Live Together	Timmy Thomas	#3
1973	Walk on the Wild Side	Lou Reed	#16
1973	Theme from Cleopatra Jones	Joe Simon w/The Mainstreeters	#18
1973	Summer (The First Time)	Bobby Goldsboro	#21
1973	Doing It to Death	Fred Wesley/The J.B's	#22
1973	I Got Ants in My Pants (And I Want to Dance)(Part 1)	James Brown	#27
1973	Nobody Wants You When You're Down and Out	Bobby Womack	#29
1973	The Message	Cymande	#48

SONGS WITH OSTINATOS (cont'd)			
1973	Sexy, Sexy, Sexy	James Brown	#50
1973	Woman to Woman	Joe Cocker w/The Chris Stainton Band	#56
1973	River	Joe Simon	#62
1973	Sixty Minute Man	Clarence Carter	#65
1973	Back for a Taste of Your Love	Syl Johnson	#72
1973	Black Byrd	Donald Byrd	#88
1973	If I Could Only Be Sure	Nolan Porter	#89
1974	Sweet Home Alabama	Lynyrd Skynyrd	#8
1974	I'm Coming Home	Spinners	#18
1974	Papa Don't Take No Mess (Part 1)	James Brown	#31
1974	Funky President (People It's Bad)	James Brown	#44
1974	There Will Never Be Any Peace (Until God Is Seated at the Conference Table)	The Chi-Lites	#63
1974	Most Likely You Go Your Way (And I'll Go Mine)	Bob Dylan/The Band	#66
1974	Goin' Down Slow	Bobby Blue Bland	#69
1974	Who Is He and What Is He to You	Creative Source	#69
1974	Do It, Fluid	The Blackbyrds	#69
1974	Pepper Box	The Peppers	#76
1974	Travelin' Prayer	Billy Joel	#77
1974	Quick, Fast, In a Hurry	New York City	#79
1974	(Everybody Wanna Get Rich) Rite Away	Dr. John	#92
1975	Low Rider	War	#7
1975	What Am I Gonna Do with You	Barry White	#8
1975	Do It Any Way You Wanna	People's Choice	#11
1975	Peace Pipe	B.T. Express	#31
1975	Trampled Under Foot	Led Zeppelin	#38
1975	Give It What You Got	B.T. Express	#40
1975	Caribbean Festival	Kool & The Gang	#55
1975	Free Man	South Shore Commission	#61
1975	King Kong – Pt. 1	Jimmy Castor Bunch	#69
1975	Action Speaks Louder Than Words	Chocolate Milk	#69
1975	Music in My Bones	Joe Simon	#92
1976	Play That Funky Music	Wild Cherry	#1
1976	Let 'Em In	Paul McCartney & Wings	#3
1976	Lowdown	Boz Scaggs	#3
1976	Takin' It to the Streets	The Doobie Brothers	#13
1976	Happy Music	The Blackbyrds	#19
1976	Livin' for the Weekend	The O'Jays	#20
1976	Last Child	Aerosmith	#21
1976	I Can't Hear You More	Helen Reddy	#29
1976	Like a Sad Song	John Denver	#36

SONGS WITH OSTINATOS (cont'd)

1976	Dance Wit Me	Rufus/Chaka Khan	#39
1976	Don't Stop It Now	Hot Chocolate	#42
1976	Get Up Offa That Thing	James Brown	#45
1976	Hot Stuff	The Rolling Stones	#49
1976	Roots, Rock, Reggae	Bob Marley	#51
1976	Harvest for the World	The Isley Brothers	#63
1976	Peter Gunn	Deodato	#84
1976	You Got the Magic	John Fogerty	#87
1976	You're Just the Right Size	Salsoul Orchestra	#88
1976	Nursery Rhymes (Part 1)	People's Choice	#93
1976	I Am Somebody	Jimmy James	#94
1976	Wow	Andre Gagnon	#95
1976	Tonight's the Night	S.S.O.	#99
1977	Lonely Boy	Andrew Gold	#7
1977	Ain't Gonna Bump No More (With No Big Fat Woman)	Joe Tex	#12
1977	Your Smiling Face	James Taylor	#20
1977	I Like to Do It	KC and The Sunshine Band	#37
1977	Disco Inferno	The Trammps	#53
1977	Theme from King Kong (Pt. 1)	Love Unlimited Orchestra	#68
1977	Darlin' Darlin' Baby (Sweet, Tender, Love)	O'Jays	#72
1977	Bodyheat (Part 1)	James Brown	#88
1977	While I'm Alone	Maze feat. Frankie Beverly	#89
1977	Let's Clean Up the Ghetto	Philadelphia International All Stars	#91
1978	Take a Chance on Me	ABBA	#3
1978	We Will Rock You/We are the Champions	Queen	#4
1978	Imaginary Lover	Atlanta Rhythm Section	#7
1978	You and I	Rick James	#13
1978	Werewolves of London	Warren Zevon	#21
1978	You Really Got Me	Van Halen	#36
1978	Bloat on Featuring the Bloaters	Cheech & Chong	#41
1978	Let Me Party with You (Party, Party, Party)(Part 1)	Bunny Sigler	#43
1978	Champagne Jam	Atlanta Rhythm Section	#43
1978	Wrap Your Arms Around Me	KC and The Sunshine Band	#48
1978	Your Love Is So Good for Me	Diana Ross	#49
1978	Reach for It	George Duke	#54
1978	Light the Sky on Fire	Jefferson Starship	#66
1978	Don't Cost You Nothing	Ashford & Simpson	#79
1978	Africanism/Gimme Some Lovin'	Kongas	#84
1978	Disco Rufus	Stargard	#88
1978	Louie, Louie	John Belushi	#89
1978	Miss Broadway	Belle Epoque	#92

	SONGS WITH OSTINATOS (cont'd)		
1979	My Sharona	The Knack	#1
1979	Good Times	Chic	#1
1979	Fire	Pointer Sisters	#2
1979	Shake Your Groove Thing	Peaches & Herb	#5
1979	Shake Your Body (Down to the Ground)	The Jacksons	#7
1979	Soul Man	Blues Brothers	#14
1979	Spooky	Atlanta Rhythm Section	#17
1979	I Got My Mind Made Up (You Can Get It Girl)	Instant Funk	#20
1979	Get Used to It	Roger Voudouris	#21
1979	Chase	Giorgio Moroder	#33
1979	Rubber Biscuit	Blues Brothers	#37
1979	Children of the Sun	Billy Thorpe	#41
1979	Dancer	Gino Soccio	#48
1979	Boogie Woogie Dancin' Shoes	Claudja Barry	#56
1979	Dancin'	Grey & Hanks	#83
1979	Whole Lotta Love	The Wonder Band	#87

SONGS WITH CALL AND RESPONSE

Call and response is when a vocalist sings a phrase (the call), and another singer or choir answers with a phrase (response). It is usually associated with a solo singer issuing the call, and a choir singing a response, but either part (or both parts) may be voiced with an instrument instead. Call and response is often used in gospel or blues music, and is used far less often in pop music. The songs in this list usually have just a section with call and response. Rarely will most (or all) of a pop song be call and response.

YEAR	SONG	ARTIST	HOT 100
1970	ABC	The Jackson 5	#1
1970	Be My Baby	Andy Kim	#17
1970	After Midnight	Eric Clapton	#18
1970	Cold Turkey	John Lennon	#30
1970	It's a New Day (Part 1 & 2)	James Brown	#32
1970	Mongoose	Elephant's Memory	#50
1971	If I Were Your Woman	Gladys Knight & The Pips	#9
1971	Get Up, Get Into It, Get Involved (Pt. 1)	James Brown	#34
1971	Think His Name	Johnny Rivers	#65
1971	My Sweet Lord	Billy Preston	#90
1971	Hymn 43	Jethro Tull	#91
1971	Chirpy Chirpy, Cheep Cheep	Lally Stott	#92
1971	Love's Made a Fool of You	Cochise	#96
1972	Black Dog	Led Zeppelin	#15

	SONGS WITH CALL AND RESPONSE (cont'd)		
1972	I Didn't Know I Loved You (Till I Saw You Rock and Roll)	Gary Glitter	#35
1972	Looking for a Love	J. Geils Band	#39
1972	Do the Funky Penguin (Part 1)	Rufus Thomas	#44
1972	Walk in the Night	Jr. Walker/The All Stars	#46
1972	Up in Heah	Ike & Tina Turner	#83
1972	You Really Got a Hold on Me	Gayle McCormick	#98
1973	Dueling Banjos	Eric Weissberg & Steve Mandell	#2
1973	Loves Me Like a Rock	Paul Simon w/The Dixie Hummingbirds	#2
1973	Could It Be I'm Falling in Love	Spinners	#4
1973	"Having a Party" Medley	The Ovations	#56
1973	Follow Your Daughter Home	The Guess Who	#61
1973	I Don't Know What It Is, But It Sure Is Funky	Ripple	#67
1973	One Last Time	Glen Campbell	#78
1973	Mother-In-Law	Clarence Carter	#80
1974	On and On	Gladys Knight & The Pips	#5
1974	Moonlight Special	Ray Stevens	#73
1975	Don't Let Go	Commander Cody	#56
1975	I'll Go to My Grave Loving You	The Statler Brothers	#93
1976	You'll Never Find Another Love Like Mine	Lou Rawls	#2
1976	Back to the Island	Leon Russell	#53
1977	Ma Baker	Boney M	#96
1978	Turn to Stone	Electric Light Orchestra	#13
1979	Heaven Knows	Donna Summer w/Brooklyn Dreams	#4
1979	Bustin' Loose Part 1	Chuck Brown & The Soul Searchers	#34
1979	California Dreamin'	America	#56
1979	Just the Same Way	Journey	#58
1979	Give Me an Inch	Ian Matthews	#67

SONGS WITH COUNTERMELODIES

A countermelody is when two different melodies are sung or played at the same time. One of the melodies will usually be more important, or featured, while the other melody is usually in the background. Another characteristic of countermelodies is that both of the melodies can be sung separately, and they'll sound just fine. If each part sounds boring or weird by itself, then it probably isn't a countermelody- it's most likely simply a harmony part.

Most countermelodies are vocal, but there are two on the list that are instruments and vocals- check out the songs with asterisks below.

One of the best examples of a song with a countermelody is "I Say a Little Prayer/By the Time I Get to Phoenix", by Glen Campbell and Anne Murray. If you're still unclear about what exactly a countermelody is, that song is a great place to start.

YEAR	SONG	ARTIST	HOT 100
1970	I'll Be There	The Jackson 5	#1
1970	One Less Bell to Answer	The 5th Dimension	#2
1970	No Time	The Guess Who	#5
1970	Share the Land	The Guess Who	#10
1970	Teach Your Children	Crosby, Stills, Nash & Young	#16
1970	Baby, I Need Your Loving	O.C. Smith	#52
1970	Think About Your Children	Mary Hopkin	#87
1971	Pin the Tail on the Donkey	The Newcomers	#74
1971	I Say a Little Prayer/By the Time I Get to Phoenix	Glen Campbell/Anne Murray	#81
1971	I Was Wondering*	The Poppy Family	#100
*An organ plays "I'll Be There" in the background.			
1972	I'd Like to Teach the World to Sing (In Perfect Harmony)	The New Seekers	#7
1972	I'd Like to Teach the World to Sing (In Perfect Harmony)	The Hillside Singers	#13
1972	Sing a Song/Make Your Own Kind of Music	Barbra Streisand	#94
1973	Playground in My Mind	Clint Holmes	#2
1973	Out of the Question*	Gilbert O'Sullivan	#17
*Instruments play verse melody while O'Sullivan sings outro melody at end of song.			
1973	Some Guys Have All the Luck	The Persuaders	#39
1973	He	Today's People	#90
1974	Mockingbird	Carly Simon & James Taylor	#5
1974	(Everybody Wanna Get Rich) Rite Away	Dr. John	#92
1976	Silly Love Songs	Paul McCartney & Wings	#1
1976	Tear the Roof off the Sucker (Give Up the Funk)	Parliament	#15
1976	Good Vibrations	Todd Rundgren	#34
1977	Blinded By the Night	Manfred Mann	#1
1978	Dance Across the Floor	Jimmy "Bo" Horne	#38
1978	Paradise By the Dashboard Light	Meat Loaf	#39
1979	Who Listens to the Radio	The Sports	#45

SONGS WITH DRONES

A drone is an unchanging pitch that is held for an extended number of beats or seconds. A note that is repeated over and over for an extended amount of time can also be considered a drone. Drones can be either low or high-pitched.

YEAR	SONG	ARTIST	HOT 100
1970	Ball of Confusion (That's What the World Is Today)	The Temptations	#3
1972	Footstompin' Music	Grand Funk Railroad	#29
1972	Rock and Roll	Led Zeppelin	#47
1972	Afro-Strut	The Nite-Liters	#49
1972	A Simple Man	Lobo	#56
1973	Summer (The First Time)	Bobby Goldsboro	#21
1975	Express	B.T. Express	#4
1975	Change with the Times	Van McCoy	#46
1975	What Can I Do for You?	LaBelle	#48
1976	The Rubberband Man	Spinners	#1
1976	Takin' It to the Streets	The Doobie Brothers	#13

TEMPO CHANGES

Tempo refers to the speed of the music. Most pop songs keep the same tempo throughout the entire song. The songs listed below, however, all have a clear shift in tempo.

YEAR	SONG	ARTIST	HOT 100
1970	Lookin' Out My Back Door	Creedence Clearwater Revival	#2
1970	Are You Ready?	Pacific Gas & Electric	#14
1970	A Song of Joy (Himno a la Elegria)	Miguel Ríos	#14
1970	Long Lonesome Highway	Michael Parks	#20
1970	Question	The Moody Blues	#21
1970	Our House	Crosby, Stills, Nash & Young	#30
1970	Breaking Up Is Hard to Do	Lenny Welch	#34
1970	Monster	Steppenwolf	#39
1970	Morning	Jim Ed Brown	#47
1970	Oh Well – Pt. 1	Fleetwood Mac	#55
1970	A Change is Gonna Come & People Gotta Be Free	The 5th Dimension	#60
1970	The Declaration	The 5th Dimension	#64
1970	Save the Country	Thelma Houston	#74

TEMPO CHANGES (cont'd)

1970	Buffalo Soldier	Flamingos	#86
1970	Thank God and Greyhound	Roy Clark	#90
1970	Rock Island Line	Johnny Cash	#93
1970	Move Me, O Wondrous Music	Ray Charles Singers	#99
1971	Uncle Albert/Admiral Halsey	Paul & Linda McCartney	#1
1971	Lonely Days	Bee Gees	#3
1971	Proud Mary	Ike & Tina Turner	#4
1971	If You Really Love Me	Stevie Wonder	#8
1971	What the World Needs Now Is Love/Abraham, Martin and John	Tom Clay	#8
1971	(I Know) I'm Losing You	Rod Stewart w/Faces	#24
1971	Behind Blue Eyes	The Who	#34
1971	Battle Hymn of Lt. Calley	C Company	#37
1971	Hot Pants	Salvage	#54
1971	Lonely Teardrops	Brian Hyland	#54
1971	Reason to Believe	Rod Stewart	#62
1971	Done Too Soon	Neil Diamond	#65
1971	When My Little Girl Is Smiling	Steve Alaimo	#72
1971	Suspicious Minds	Dee Dee Warwick	#80
1971	Handbags and Gladrags	Chase	#84
1972	American Pie (Parts 1 & 2)	Don McLean	#1
1972	Day by Day	Godspell	#13
1972	Walk on Water	Neil Diamond	#17
1972	American City Suite	Cashman & West	#27
1972	Sweet Inspiration/Where You Lead	Barbra Streisand	#37
1972	And You and I (Part 1)	Yes	#42
1972	Be My Lover	Alice Cooper	#49
1972	I Had It All the Time	Tyrone Davis	#61
1972	Since I Fell for You	Laura Lee	#76
1972	Runaway/Happy Together	Dawn featuring Tony Orlando	#79
1972	The Mosquito	The Doors	#85
1972	Get Out of Bed	Livingston Taylor	#97
1972	Suite: Man and Woman	Tony Cole	#97
1973	Live and Let Die	Paul McCartney & Wings	#2
1973	Say, Has Anybody Seen My Sweet Gypsy Rose	Dawn featuring Tony Orlando	#3
1973	Hi, Hi, Hi	Paul McCartney & Wings	#10
1973	Goin' Home	The Osmonds	#36
1973	Friends	Bette Midler	#40
1973	Music Everywhere	Tufano & Giammarese	#68
1973	Roll in My Sweet Baby's Arms	Hank Wilson (Leon Russell)	#78
1973	As Time Goes By	Nilsson	#86
1973	Sugar Magnolia	Grateful Dead	#91

TEMPO CHANGES (cont'd)

1974	I'm the Leader of the Gang	Brownsville Station	#48
1974	Moonlight Special	Ray Stevens	#73
1974	Teen Angel	Wednesday	#79
1975	Lucy in the Sky with Diamonds	Elton John	#1
1975	#9 Dream	John Lennon	#9
1975	Venus and Mars Rock Show	Paul McCartney & Wings	#12
1975	I Am Love (Parts I & II)	The Jackson 5	#15
1975	Free Bird	Lynyrd Skynyrd	#19
1975	Operator	The Manhattan Transfer	#22
1975	Brand New Love Affair (Part I & II)	Chicago	#61
1975	Turn Back the Pages	Stephen Stills	#84
1976	Love Hangover	Diana Ross	#1
1976	Bohemium Rhapsody	Queen	#9
1976	The White Knight	Cledus Maggard	#19
1976	Good Vibrations	Todd Rundgren	#34
1976	Silver Star	The Four Seasons	#38
1976	I'm Mandy Fly Me	10cc	#60
1976	Chain Gang Medley	Jim Croce	#63
1976	Kentucky Moonrunner	Cledus Maggard	#85
1976	Music	John Miles	#88
1977	Help Is on Its Way	Little River Band	#14
1977	My Way	Elvis Presley	#22
1977	The Killing of Georgie (Part 1 and 2)	Rod Stewart	#30
1977	Calling Occupants of Interplanetary Craft	Carpenters	#32
1978	MacArthur Park	Donna Summer	#1
1978	Last Dance	Donna Summer	#3
1978	Summer Nights	John Travolta & Olivia Newton-John	#5
1978	The Next Hundred Years	Al Martino	#49
1978	Portrait (He Knew)	Kansas	#64
1979	No More Tears (Enough Is Enough)	Barbra Streisand/Donna Summer	#1
1979	Come to Me	France Joli	#15
1979	Renegade	Styx	#16
1979	Happiness	Pointer Sisters	#30
1979	Rubber Biscuit	Blues Brothers	#37
1979	Remember (Walking in the Sand)	Louise Goffin	#43
1979	Light My Fire/137 Disco Heaven	Amii Stewart	#69
1979	Hey, St. Peter	Flash and The Pan	#76
1979	Don't Stop Me Now	Queen	#86

UNUSUAL TIME SIGNATURES/METERS

Every song has a time signature. The time signature indicates which kind of note gets the beat (for example, the quarter note), and it tells how many beats there will be in each measure. By far, the most common time signature used will indicate four beats per measure.

The songs below, however, used time signatures that sound and feel significantly different from the standard 4/4 time. Having five or seven beats per measure, as opposed to the standard four, creates significant challenges for both the musicians and listeners. It makes the music more interesting and much less predictable.

"Money" is one of the better-known pop songs with an unusual time signature. "Barracuda" is included because the alternating 3/4 and 4/4 time signatures make it feel like there are seven beats in a measure. It doesn't happen throughout the entire song, but when it occurs, it has a very distinct feel.

YEAR	SONG	ARTIST	HOT 100	NOTES
1973	Money	Pink Floyd	#13	Has 7/8, 7/4 sections, Gilmour has said both
1973	Dreidel	Don McLean	#21	Has triple meter section in middle of duple meter sections
1975	Send in the Clowns	Judy Collins	#36	Alternates between 12/8 and 9/8
1975	Nice, Nice, Very Nice	Ambrosia	#63	Some short sections of 5/4
1977	Barracuda	Heart	#11	Alternates between 3/4 and 4/4
1977	Solsbury Hill	Peter Gabriel	#68	Mostly in 7/4
1978	Point of Know Return	Kansas	#28	Alternates between 3/4, 4/4, and 7/4
1978	Fooling Yourself (The Angry Young Man)	Styx	#29	Has 4/4, 7/4, 5/8, and 6/8

VOICE

SONGS WITH AN A CAPPELLA SECTION

These songs all have at least a short section that can be described as "a cappella" (pronounced "ah-kah-pella"), that is, singing with no instruments.

"After the Goldrush" and "Da Doo Ron Ron (When He Walked Me Home)" are extremely unusual, because neither song has instruments at all ("Da Doo Ron Ron…" does have hand-claps). This is almost unheard of in pop songs on the Billboard Hot 100.

YEAR	SONG	ARTIST	HOT 100
1970	Share the Land	The Guess Who	#10
1970	Celebrate	Three Dog Night	#15
1970	Move Me, O Wondrous Music	Ray Charles Singers	#99
1971	Amazing Grace	Judy Collins	#15
1971	Nothing to Hide	Tommy James	#41
1971	Love's Made a Fool of You	Cochise	#96
1972	Once You Understand	Think	#23
1972	Ring the Living Bell	Melanie	#31
1972	A Piece of Paper	Gladstone	#45
1972	Delta Dawn	Tanya Tucker	#72
1972	Dance, Dance, Dance	The New Seekers	#84
1972	One Way Out	Allman Brothers Band	#86
1972	Deteriorata	National Lampoon	#91
1972	Da Doo Ron Ron (When He Walked Me Home)	Ian Matthews	#96
1973	Delta Dawn	Helen Reddy	#1
1974	Hooked on a Feeling	Blue Swede	#1
1974	After the Goldrush	Prelude	#22
1974	I'm a Train	Albert Hammond	#31
1975	Black Water	The Doobie Brothers	#1
1975	Thank God I'm a Country Boy	John Denver	#1
1975	Operator	The Manhattan Transfer	#22
1975	Don't Let Go	Commander Cody	#56
1976	Bohemium Rhapsody	Queen	#9
1976	Happy Music	The Blackbyrds	#19
1976	Street Singin'	Lady Flash	#27
1976	I.O.U.	Jimmy Dean	#35
1976	Rainbow in Your Eyes	Leon & Mary Russell	#52

\multicolumn{4}{c}{SONGS WITH AN A CAPPELLA SECTION (cont'd)}			
1976	Breaker – Breaker	Outlaws	#94
1977	Somebody to Love	Queen	#13
1977	Never My Love	Addrisi Brothers	#80
1978	Whenever I Call You "Friend"	Kenny Loggins & Stevie Nicks	#5
1978	Flash Light	Parliament	#16
1978	The Dream Never Dies	Cooper Brothers	#48
1978	Mary's Boy Child/Oh My Lord	Boney M	#85
1979	Renegade	Styx	#16
1979	Oh Well	Rockets	#30
1979	Rubber Biscuit	Blues Brothers	#37
1979	You Took the Words Right Out of My Mouth	Meat Loaf	#39

CHIPMUNK/WEIRD VOICES

YEAR	SONG	ARTIST	HOT 100
1971	Bridget the Midget (The Queen of the Blues)	Ray Stevens	#50
1976	Hey Shirley (This Is Squirrely)	Shirley & Squirrely	#48
1977	The Martian Boogie	Brownsville Station	#59

FALSETTO

Falsetto is a singing technique unique to the male singer that allows him to sing notes that sound impossibly high. Every song listed here has a section (if not the whole song) where a falsetto voice is featured. Songs that only have a falsetto voice for a few seconds are not included.

YEAR	SONG	ARTIST	HOT 100
1970	I'll Be There	The Jackson 5	#1
1970	Hey There Lonely Girl	Eddie Holman	#2
1970	Didn't I (Blow Your Mind This Time)	The Delfonics	#10
1970	5-10-15-20 (25-30 Years of Love)	The Presidents	#11
1970	Joanne	Michael Nesmith	#21
1970	If I Didn't Care	The Moments	#44
1970	Good Guys Only Win in the Movies	Mel and Tim	#45
1970	Don't Stop Now	Eddie Holman	#48
1970	Cryin' in the Streets (Part 1)	George Perkins	#61
1970	She Lets Her Hair Down (Early in the Morning)	The Tokens	#61
1970	I Love You	Otis Leavill	#63
1970	You've Been My Inspiration	The Main Ingredient	#64
1970	I Like Your Lovin' (Do You Like Mine)	The Chi-Lites	#72
1970	Groovin' (Out on Life)	The Newbeats	#82
1970	The Lights of Tucson	Jim Campbell	#93
1970	Don't Worry Baby	The Tokens	#95
1970	Can't Get Over Losing You	Donnie Elbert	#98
1970	(I Remember) Summer Morning	Vanity Fare	#98
1970	Message from a Black Man	The Whatnauts	#99
1971	Have You Seen Her	Chi-Lites	#3
1971	Baby I'm – A Want You	Bread	#3
1971	Inner City Blues (Make Me Wanna Holler)	Marvin Gaye	#9
1971	Stop, Look, Listen (To Your Heart)	The Stylistics	#39
1971	You're the Reasons Why	The Ebonys	#51
1971	Hey! Love	The Delfonics	#52
1971	All I Have	The Moments	#56
1971	Over and Over	The Delfonics	#58
1971	I'll Erase Away Your Pain	Whatnauts	#71
1971	You're a Big Girl Now	The Stylistics	#73
1971	Day by Day (Every Minute of the Hour)	The Continental 4	#84
1971	Lucky Me	Moments	#98
1971	We're Friends by Day (And Lovers by Night)	Whatnauts	#100

		FALSETTO (cont'd)		
1972	Papa Was a Rolling Stone		The Temptations	#1
1972	The Lion Sleeps Tonight		Robert John	#3
1972	I'm Stone in Love with You		The Stylistics	#10
1972	Little Bitty Pretty One		The Jackson 5	#13
1972	I Can't Help Myself (Sugar Pie, Honey Bunch)		Donnie Elbert	#22
1972	People Make the World Go Round		The Stylistics	#25
1972	I've Been Lonely for so Long		Frederick Knight	#27
1972	Take a Look Around		The Temptations	#30
1972	Toast to the Fool		Dramatics	#67
1972	Dedicated to the One I Love		The Temprees	#93
1972	Hushabye		Robert John	#99
1973	Break Up to Make Up		The Stylistics	#5
1973	Trouble Man		Marvin Gaye	#7
1973	My Maria		B.W. Stevenson	#9
1973	Rockin' Roll Baby		The Stylistics	#14
1973	Basketball Jones featuring Tyrone Shoelaces		Cheech & Chong	#15
1973	You'll Never Get to Heaven (If You Break My Heart)		The Stylistics	#23
1973	Future Shock		Curtis Mayfield	#39
1973	My Pretending Days Are Over		The Dells	#51
1973	It's Forever		The Ebonys	#68
1974	Bennie and the Jets		Elton John	#1
1974	You Make Me Feel Brand New		The Stylistics	#2
1974	Let's Put It All Together		The Stylistics	#18
1974	Dream On		The Righteous Brothers	#32
1974	Devotion		Earth, Wind & Fire	#33
1974	Sugar Baby Love		The Rubettes	#37
1974	Heavy Fallin' Out		The Stylistics	#41
1974	Tell Her Love Has Felt the Need		Eddie Kendricks	#50
1974	Keep Your Head to the Sky		Earth, Wind & Fire	#52
1974	Shoe Shoe Shine		Dynamic Superiors	#68
1974	Stop to Start		Blue Magic	#74
1975	One of These Nights		Eagles	#1
1975	Nights on Broadway		Bee Gees	#7
1975	Eighteen with a Bullet		Pete Wingfield	#15
1975	I Want to Be Free		Ohio Players	#44
1975	Get the Cream off the Top		Eddie Kendricks	#50
1975	My Little Lady		Bloodstone	#57
1975	Reconsider Me		Narvel Felts	#67
1975	Indian Love Call		Ray Stevens	#68
1975	I'm on Fire		Jim Gilstrap	#78
1975	It's Time for Love		The Chi-Lites	#94

	FALSETTO (cont'd)		
1976	December, 1963 (Oh, What a Night)	The Four Seasons	#1
1976	You Should Be Dancing	Bee Gees	#1
1976	Love So Right	Bee Gees	#3
1976	Fanny (Be Tender with My Love)	Bee Gees	#12
1976	You Are Beautiful	The Stylistics	#78
1976	I Can't Ask for Anymore Than You	Cliff Richard	#80
1977	Got to Give It Up (Pt. 1)	Marvin Gaye	#1
1977	Boogie Child	Bee Gees	#12
1977	Shake Your Rump to the Funk	The Bar-Kays	#23
1977	Dance Little Lady Dance	Danny White	#100
1978	Night Fever	Bee Gees	#1
1978	Shadow Dancing	Andy Gibb	#1
1978	Stayin' Alive	Bee Gees	#1
1978	Emotion	Samantha Sang	#3
1978	An Everlasting Love	Andy Gibb	#5
1978	Serpentine Fire	Earth, Wind & Fire	#13
1978	Turn to Stone	Electric Light Orchestra	#13
1978	Stay	Jackson Browne	#20
1978	Fantasy	Earth, Wind & Fire	#32
1978	There'll Never Be	Switch	#36
1978	When You Feel Love	Bob McGilpin	#91
1979	Too Much Heaven	Bee Gees	#1
1979	Tragedy	Bee Gees	#1
1979	What a Fool Believes	The Doobie Brothers	#1
1979	Don't Stop 'til You Get Enough	Michael Jackson	#1
1979	Love You Inside Out	Bee Gees	#1
1979	After the Love Has Gone	Earth, Wind & Fire	#2
1979	Lonesome Loser	Little River Band	#6
1979	September	Earth, Wind & Fire	#8
1979	Goodbye Stranger	Supertramp	#15
1979	I (Who Have Nothing)	Sylvester	#40
1979	Ghost Dancer	Addrisi Brothers	#45
1979	Animal House	Stephen Bishop	#73
1979	Walk on By	Average White Band	#92

SCAT

Scat, or scatting, is usually associated with vocal jazz. It is an improvised type of singing in which the singer imitates the sound of instruments with his/her voice.

YEAR	SONG	ARTIST	HOT 100
1975	I Am I Am	Smokey Robinson	#56
1976	This Masquerade	George Benson	#10
1976	Mr. Melody	Natalie Cole	#49
1976	Laid Back Love	Major Harris	#91
1978	On Broadway	George Benson	#7
1979	Love Ballad	George Benson	#18

SPOKEN WORD

The songs in this list all contain a fair amount of speaking. There might be some singing as well, but they all have a significant amount of speaking. Usually, the lead "singer" will be reciting a poem, describing his/her feelings, or telling a story.

YEAR	SONG	ARTIST	HOT 100
1970	What Is Truth	Johnny Cash	#19
1970	Welfare Cadilac	Guy Drake	#63
1970	Grover Henson Feels Forgotten	Bill Cosby	#70
1970	Where Have All Our Heroes Gone	Bill Anderson	#93
1971	Desiderata	Les Crane	#8
1971	Escape-ism (Part 1)	James Brown	#35
1971	Battle Hymn of Lt. Calley	C Company	#37
1971	Ajax Liquor Store	Hudson & Landry	#43
1971	The Court Room	Clarence Carter	#61
1972	Troglodyte (Cave Man)	Jimmy Castor Bunch	#6
1972	Hot Rod Lincoln	Commander Cody	#9
1972	King Heroin	James Brown	#40
1972	I Had It All the Time	Tyrone Davis	#61
1972	Another Puff	Jerry Reed	#65
1972	Ajax Airlines	Hudson & Landry	#68
1972	Your Precious Love	Linda Jones	#74
1972	Since I Fell for You	Laura Lee	#76
1972	Deteriorata	National Lampoon	#91

SPOKEN WORD (cont'd)			
1972	Buzzy Brown	Tim Davis	#91
1973	I'm Gonna Love You Just a Little More Baby	Barry White	#3
1973	Basketball Jones featuring Tyrone Shoelaces	Cheech & Chong	#15
1973	Love Jones	Brighter Side of Darkness	#16
1973	Doing It to Death	Fred Wesley/The J.B's	#22
1973	Super Fly Meets Shaft	John & Ernest	#31
1973	I've Got so Much to Give	Barry White	#32
1973	Swamp Witch	Jim Stafford	#39
1973	Baby I've Been Missing You	The Independents	#41
1973	I Wanna Know Your Name	The Intruders	#60
1973	Smoke! Smoke! Smoke! (That Cigarette)	Commander Cody	#94
1974	Americans	Byron MacGregor	#4
1974	Wildwood Weed	Jim Stafford	#7
1974	Earache My Eye	Cheech & Chong (Featuring Alice Bowie)	#9
1974	Are You Lonesome Tonight	Donny Osmond	#14
1974	Woman to Woman	Shirley Brown	#22
1974	Sister Mary Elephant (Shudd-Up!)	Cheech & Chong	#24
1974	The Americans (A Canadian's Opinion)	Gordon Sinclair	#24
1974	No Charge	Melba Montgomery	#39
1974	Old Home Filler-Up An' Keep On-A-Truckin' Café	C.W. McCall	#54
1974	Black Lassie (Featuring Johnny Stash)	Cheech & Chong	#55
1974	My Country	Jud Strunk	#59
1974	Makin' the Best of a Bad Situation	Dick Feller	#85
1974	Don't Eat the Yellow Snow	Frank Zappa	#86
1974	U.S. of A	Donna Fargo	#86
1974	There's Got to Be Rain in Your Life (To Appreciate the Sunshine)	Dorothy Norwood	#88
1974	The Americans (A Canadian's Opinion)	Tex Ritter	#90
1975	The Way We Were/Try to Remember	Gladys Knight & The Pips	#11
1975	The Bertha Butt Boogie (Part 1)	Jimmy Castor Bunch	#16
1975	From His Woman to You	Barbara Mason	#28
1975	Spirit of the Boogie	Kool & The Gang	#35
1975	Don't Take Your Love	Manhattans	#37
1975	Wolf Creek Pass	B.T. Express	#40
1975	(How I Spent My Summer Vacation) Or A Day at the Beach with Pedro & Man – Parts I & II	Cheech & Chong	#54
1975	Please, Mr. President	Paula Webb	#60
1975	Hoppy, Gene and Me	Roy Rogers	#65
1975	Cry to Me	Loleatta Holloway	#68
1975	King Kong – Pt. 1	Jimmy Castor Bunch	#69
1975	Leftovers	Millie Jackson	#87
1975	Let Me Start Tonite	Lamont Dozier	#87

SPOKEN WORD (cont'd)

1975	No Charge	Shirley Caesar	#91
1975	Chocolate City	Parliament	#94
1975	It Ain't No Fun	Shirley Brown	#94
1976	Convoy	C.W. McCall	#1
1976	Deep Purple	Donny & Marie Osmond	#14
1976	The White Knight	Cledus Maggard	#19
1976	One Piece at a Time	Johnny Cash	#29
1976	I.O.U.	Jimmy Dean	#35
1976	Hit the Road	Stampeders	#40
1976	Teddy Bear	Red Sovine	#40
1976	Framed	Cheech & Chong	#41
1976	Without Your Love (Mr. Jordan)	Charlie Ross	#42
1976	Yes, Yes, Yes	Bill Cosby	#46
1976	Hey Shirley (This Is Squirrely)	Shirley & Squirrely	#48
1976	Bigfoot	Bro Smith	#57
1976	Don't Touch Me There	The Tubes	#61
1976	Teddy Bear's Last Ride	Diana Williams	#66
1976	Eh! Cumpari	Gaylord & Holiday	#72
1976	There Won't Be No Country Music (There Won't Be No Rock 'N' Roll)	C.W. McCall	#73
1976	Kentucky Moonrunner	Cledus Maggard	#85
1976	I Don't Wanna Leave You	Debbie Taylor	#100
1977	Float On	The Floaters	#2
1977	The King Is Gone	Ronnie McDowell	#13
1977	The Martian Boogie	Brownsville Station	#59
1977	Dedication	Bay City Rollers	#60
1977	C.B. Savage	Rod Hart	#67
1977	Let's Clean Up the Ghetto	Philadelphia International All Stars	#91
1977	Up Your Nose	Gabriel Kaplan	#91
1978	Bloat on Featuring the Bloaters	Cheech & Chong	#41
1978	Reach for It	George Duke	#54
1978	I Love You, I Love You, I Love You	Ronnie McDowell	#81
1978	Woman to Woman	Barbara Mandrell	#92
1979	The Devil Went Down to Georgia	Charlie Daniels Band	#3
1979	Do You Think I'm Disco?	Steve Dahl	#58
1979	Cruel Shoes	Steve Martin	#91

TALK BOX/ROBOT VOICE

YEAR	SONG	ARTIST	HOT 100
1973	Rocky Mountain Way	Joe Walsh	#23
1974	Teenage Love Affair	Rick Derringer	#80
1975	Ain't That Peculiar	Diamond Reo	#44
1976	Show Me the Way	Peter Frampton	#6
1976	Do You Feel Like We Do	Peter Frampton	#10
1976	Wanna Make Love (Come Flick My BIC)	Sun	#76
1976	The Raven	Alan Parsons Project	#80
1977	Slowdown	John Miles	#34
1977	Everybody Be Dancin'	Starbuck	#38
1977	A Real Mother for Ya	Johnny Guitar Watson	#41
1978	Get Off	Foxy	#9
1978	Sweet Talkin' Woman	Electric Light Orchestra	#17
1978	Theme Song from "Which Way Is Up"	Stargard	#21
1978	Mr. Blue Sky	Electric Light Orchestra	#35
1978	Mind Bender	Stillwater	#46
1978	Flyin'	Prism	#53
1978	So Young, So Bad	Starz	#81
1979	Goodnight Tonight	Paul McCartney & Wings	#5
1979	Hot Number	Foxy	#21
1979	Wasn't It Good	Cher	#49
1979	Aqua Boogie (A Psychoalphadiscobetabioaquadoloop)	Parliament	#89

WHISTLING

YEAR	SONG	ARTIST	HOT 100
1970	Montego Bay	Bobby Bloom	#8
1970	Don't It Make You Want to Go Home	Brook Benton	#45
1970	Is Anybody Goin' to San Antone	Charley Pride	#70
1970	Simply Call It Love	Gene Chandler	#75
1971	Who Gets the Guy	Dionne Warwick	#57
1971	Ain't It a Sad Thing	R. Dean Taylor	#66
1972	Clair	Gilbert O'Sullivan	#2
1972	Good Time Charlie's Got the Blues	Danny O'Keefe	#9
1972	Me and Julio Down by the Schoolyard	Paul Simon	#22

WHISTLING (cont'd)			
1972	Butterfly	Danyel Gerard	#78
1972	Beat Me Daddy Eight to the Bar	Commander Cody	#81
1972	We're Together	The Hillside Singers	#100
1973	Hocus Pocus	Focus	#9
1973	Kissing My Love	Bill Withers	#31
1974	Billy – Don't Be a Hero	Paper Lace	#96
1975	School Boy Crush	Average White Band	#33
1976	Golden Years	David Bowie	#10
1976	Eh! Cumpari	Gaylord & Holiday	#72
1977	Dazz	Brick	#3
1977	The Killing of Georgie (Part 1 and 2)	Rod Stewart	#30
1977	Sunflower	Glen Campbell	#39
1979	Goodbye Stranger	Supertramp	#15

ADULT CHOIR

YEAR	SONG	ARTIST	HOT 100
1970	The Long and Winding Road	The Beatles	#1
1970	Midnight Cowboy	Ferrante & Teicher	#10
1970	Hi-De-Ho	Blood, Sweat & Tears	#14
1970	Oh Happy Day	Glen Campbell	#40
1970	Don't It Make You Want to Go Home	Brook Benton	#45
1970	America, Communicate with Me	Ray Stevens	#45
1970	I'm So Glad I Fell for You	David Ruffin	#53
1970	Together	The Illusion	#80
1970	Man of Constant Sorrow	Ginger Baker's Air Force (Denny Laine)	#85
1970	Father Come on Home	Pacific Gas & Electric	#93
1970	Move Me, O Wondrous Music	Ray Charles Singers	#99
1971	The Night They Drove Old Dixie Down	Joan Baez	#3
1971	Desiderata	Les Crane	#8
1971	Power to the People	John Lennon	#11
1971	Amazing Grace	Judy Collins	#15
1971	Friends with You	John Denver	#47
1971	Let It Be	Joan Baez	#49
1971	Think His Name	Johnny Rivers	#65
1972	The Candy Man	Sammy Davis, Jr. w/The Mike Curb Congregation	#1
1972	I'd Like to Teach the World to Sing (In Perfect Harmony)	The Hillside Singers	#13
1972	Every Day of My Life	Bobby Vinton	#24
1972	Softly Whispering I Love You	English Congregation	#29

ADULT CHOIR (cont'd)			
1972	Long Haired Lover from Liverpool	Little Jimmy Osmond w/The Mike Curb Congregation	#38
1972	Butterfly	Danyel Gerard	#78
1972	Wholy Holy	Aretha Franklin	#81
1972	Music from Across the Way	James Last	#84
1972	All His Children	Charley Pride w/Henry Mancini	#92
1972	The People Tree	Sammy Davis, Jr. w/The Mike Curb Congregation	#92
1972	Me and Jesus	Tom T. Hall	#98
1972	Don't Ever Take Away My Freedom	Peter Yarrow	#100
1973	Daytime Night-Time	Keith Hampshire	#51
1975	Ding Dong; Ding Dong	George Harrison	#36

CHILDREN'S CHOIR

YEAR	SONG	ARTIST	HOT 100
1970	Everything Is Beautiful	Ray Stevens	#1
1970	Mill Valley	Miss Abrams	#90
1971	Do You Know What Time It Is?	P-Nut Gallery	#62
1972	School's Out	Alice Cooper	#7
1972	Mary Had a Little Lamb	Paul McCartney & Wings	#28
1973	Playground in My Mind	Clint Holmes	#2
1973	Sing	Carpenters	#3
1973	I Like You	Donovan	#66
1973	My Merry-Go-Round	Johnny Nash	#77
1974	I Hate Hate	Razzy Bailey	#67
1974	Christmas Dream	Perry Como	#92
1975	(If You Add) All the Love in the World	Mac Davis	#54
1975	Shoes	Reparata	#92
1975	What Time of Day	Billy Thunderkloud	#92

FEMALE DUETS

YEAR	SONG	ARTIST	HOT 100
1976	Sixteen Reasons	LaVerne & Shirley	#65
1979	No More Tears (Enough Is Enough)	Barbra Streisand/Donna Summer	#1
1979	Since You've Been Gone	Cherie & Marie Currie	#95

MALE DUETS

YEAR	SONG	ARTIST	HOT 100
1970	Stand By Me	David & Jimmy Ruffin	#61
1971	You Just Can't Win (By Making the Same Mistake)	Gene Chandler & Jerry Butler	#94
1972	Starting All Over Again	Mel and Tim	#19
1972	War Song	Neil Young & Graham Nash	#61
1972	Men of Learning	Vigrass & Osborne	#65
1972	Ain't That Loving You (For More Reasons Than One)	Isaac Hayes & David Porter	#86
1972	Nobody But You	Loggins & Messina	#86
1972	I Received a Letter	Delbert & Glen	#90
1972	Southbound Train	Graham Nash & David Crosby	#99
1973	Your Mama Don't Dance	Loggins & Messina	#4
1973	Hummingbird	Seals & Crofts	#20
1973	Could You Ever Love Me Again	Gary & Dave	#92
1974	Dream On	The Righteous Brothers	#32
1974	What's Your Name	Andy & David Williams	#92
1975	I Dreamed Last Night	Justin Hayward & John Lodge	#47
1975	Carry Me	David Crosby/Graham Nash	#52
1975	Growin'	Loggins & Messina	#52
1975	I Like It Like That	Loggins & Messina	#84
1975	Changes	Loggins & Messina	#84
1975	Isn't It Lonely Together	Stark & McBrien	#85
1975	A Lover's Question	Loggins & Messina	#89
1976	Let Your Love Flow	Bellamy Brothers	#1
1976	Good Hearted Woman	Waylon Jennings & Willie Nelson	#25
1976	I Wanna Stay with You	Gallagher and Lyle	#49
1976	Heart on My Sleeve	Gallagher and Lyle	#67
1976	Hell Cat	Bellamy Brothers	#70
1976	Devil with a Blue Dress	Pratt & McClain	#71
1976	Satin Sheets	Bellamy Brothers	#73
1976	Out of the Darkness	David Crosby/Graham Nash	#89
1977	It's Sad to Belong	England Dan & John Ford Coley	#21
1977	Gone Too Far	England Dan & John Ford Coley	#23
1977	Back Together Again	Daryl Hall & John Oates	#28
1977	My Fair Share	Seals & Crofts	#28
1977	Something About You	LeBlanc & Carr	#48
1977	Why Do Lovers (Break Each Other's Heart?)	Daryl Hall & John Oates	#73

	MALE DUETS (cont'd)		
1978	We'll Never Have to Say Goodbye Again	England Dan & John Ford Coley	#9
1978	Falling	LeBlanc & Carr	#13
1978	You're the Love	Seals & Crofts	#18
1978	(You Got to Walk And) Don't Look Back	Peter Tosh w/Mick Jagger	#81
1978	Midnight Light	LeBlanc & Carr	#91
1979	Love Is the Answer	England Dan & John Ford Coley	#10
1979	Ain't No Stoppin' Us Now	McFadden & Whitehead	#13
1979	Livin' It Up (Friday Night)	Bell & James	#15
1979	What Can I Do with This Broken Heart	England Dan & John Ford Coley	#50
1979	Just the Same Way	Journey	#58

MALE AND FEMALE DUETS

YEAR	SONG	ARTIST	HOT 100
1970	(They Long to Be) Close to You	Carpenters	#1
1970	We've Only Just Begun	Carpenters	#2
1970	All I Have to do Is Dream	Bobbie Gentry & Glen Campbell	#27
1970	I Want to Take You Higher	Ike & Tina Turner	#34
1970	If I Were a Carpenter	Johnny Cash & June Carter	#36
1970	Soul Shake	Delaney & Bonnie & Friends	#43
1970	The Onion Song	Marvin Gaye & Tammi Terrell	#50
1970	Ticket to Ride	Carpenters	#54
1970	California Soul	Marvin Gaye & Tammi Terrell	#56
1970	Come Together	Ike & Tina Turner	#57
1970	Je T'Aime…Moi Non Plus	Jane Birkin & Serge Gainsbourg	#58
1970	Bold Soul Sister	Ike & Tina Turner	#59
1970	Where are You Going to My Love	Brotherhood of Man	#61
1970	Humphrey the Camel	Jack Blanchard & Misty Morgan	#78
1970	Comin' Home	Delaney & Bonnie w/Eric Clapton	#84
1971	Proud Mary	Ike & Tina Turner	#4
1971	Stay Awhile	The Bells	#7
1971	All I Ever Need Is You	Sonny & Cher	#7
1971	Never Ending Song of Love	Delaney & Bonnie	#13
1971	You've Got a Friend	Roberta Flack & Donny Hathaway	#29
1971	I Know I'm in Love	Chee-Chee & Peppy	#49
1971	After the Fire Is Gone	Conway Twitty & Loretta Lynn	#56
1971	I Love You Lady Dawn	The Bells	#64
1971	If It's Real What I Feel	Jerry Butler w/Brenda Lee Eager	#69
1971	What You See Is What You Get	Stoney & Meatloaf	#71

MALE AND FEMALE DUETS (cont'd)

1971	You've Lost That Lovin' Feelin'	Roberta Flack & Donny Hathaway	#71
1971	I Say a Little Prayer/By the Time I Get to Phoenix	Glen Campbell/Anne Murray	#81
1971	Fly Little White Dove Fly	The Bells	#95
1971	The Sound of Silence	Peaches & Herb	#100
1972	Hurting Each Other	Carpenters	#2
1972	Where Is the Love	Roberta Flack & Donny Hathaway	#5
1972	Goodbye to Love	Carpenters	#7
1972	How Do You Do?	Mouth & MacNeal	#8
1972	A Cowboy's Work Is Never Done	Sonny & Cher	#8
1972	It's Going to Take Some Time	Carpenters	#12
1972	Ain't Understanding Mellow	Jerry Butler & Brenda Lee Eager	#21
1972	When You Say Love	Sonny & Cher	#32
1972	Together Let's Find Love	The 5th Dimension	#37
1972	Those Were the Days	Carroll O'Connor & Jean Stapleton	#43
1972	Move 'Em Out	Delaney & Bonnie	#59
1972	Papa Was a Rolling Stone	The Undisputed Truth	#63
1972	We Can Make It Together	Steve & Eydie/The Osmonds	#68
1972	You Make Your Own Heaven and Hell Right Here on Earth	The Undisputed Truth	#72
1972	Hey, You Love	Mouth & MacNeal	#87
1972	(They Long to Be) Close to You	Jerry Butler w/Brenda Lee Eager	#91
1972	I Thank You	Donny Hathaway & June Conquest	#94
1972	Where There's a Will There's a Way	Delaney & Bonnie	#99
1973	Tie a Yellow Ribbon Round the Ole Oak Tree	Tony Orlando & Dawn	#1
1973	Top of the World	Carpenters	#1
1973	Yesterday Once More	Carpenters	#2
1973	You're a Special Part of Me	Diana Ross & Marvin Gaye	#12
1973	A Song I'd Like to Sing	Kris Kristofferson & Rita Coolidge	#49
1973	What My Baby Needs Now Is a Little More Lovin'	James Brown-Lyn Collins	#56
1973	Mama was a Rock and Roll Singer, Papa Used to Write All Her Songs (Part 1)	Sonny & Cher	#77
1974	(You're) Having My Baby	Paul Anka with Odia Coates	#1
1974	I'm Leaving It (All) Up to You	Donny & Marie Osmond	#4
1974	Mockingbird	Carly Simon & James Taylor	#5
1974	My Mistake (Was to Love You)	Diana Ross & Marvin Gaye	#19
1974	Don't Knock My Love	Diana Ross & Marvin Gaye	#46
1974	When the Morning Comes	Hoyt Axton	#54
1974	Sexy Ida (Part 1)	Ike & Tina Turner	#65
1974	Get Out of Denver	Bob Seger	#80
1974	Loving Arms	Kris Kristofferson & Rita Coolidge	#86
1974	(I'd Know You) Anywhere	Ashford & Simpson	#88

MALE AND FEMALE DUETS (cont'd)

Year	Title	Artist	Rank
1975	He Don't Love You (Like I Love You)	Tony Orlando & Dawn	#1
1975	Please Mr. Postman	Carpenters	#1
1975	Only Yesterday	Carpenters	#4
1975	The Way I Want to Touch You	Captain & Tennille	#4
1975	Run Joey Run	David Geddes	#4
1975	Swearin' to God	Frankie Valli	#6
1975	One Man Woman/One Woman Man	Paul Anka with Odia Coates	#7
1975	Morning Side of the Mountain	Donny & Marie Osmond	#8
1975	I Don't Like to Sleep Alone	Paul Anka with Odia Coates	#8
1975	Our Day Will Come	Frankie Valli	#11
1975	(I Believe) There's Nothing Stronger Than Our Love	Paul Anka with Odia Coates	#15
1975	Gone at Last	Paul Simon/Phoebe Snow	#23
1975	Hope That We Can Be Together Soon	Sharon Paige/Harold Melvin	#42
1975	Make the World Go Away	Donny & Marie Osmond	#44
1975	If I Could Only Win Your Love	Emmylou Harris	#58
1975	Fancy Lady	Billy Preston	#71
1975	Waterfall	Carly Simon w/James Taylor	#78
1975	Baby-Get It On	Ike & Tina Turner	#88
1976	Don't Go Breaking My Heart	Elton John & Kiki Dee	#1
1976	Fly Away	John Denver	#13
1976	Deep Purple	Donny & Marie Osmond	#14
1976	Paloma Blanca	George Baker Selection	#26
1976	Dance Wit Me	Rufus/Chaka Khan	#39
1976	Without Your Love (Mr. Jordan)	Charlie Ross	#42
1976	Rainbow in Your Eyes	Leon & Mary Russell	#52
1976	Don't Touch Me There	The Tubes	#61
1976	Don't Cry Joni	Conway Twitty w/Joni Lee	#63
1976	High Out of Time	Carole King	#76
1976	I'll Play the Fool	Dr. Buzzard's Original Savannah Band	#80
1976	Close to You	B.T. Express	#82
1976	I Hope We Get to Love in Time	Marilyn McCoo & Billy Davis, Jr.	#91
1976	Valentine Love	Norman Connors	#97
1977	You Don't Have to Be a Star (To Be in My Show)	Marilyn McCoo & Billy Davis, Jr.	#1
1977	Your Love	Marilyn McCoo & Billy Davis, Jr.	#15
1977	Ain't Nothing Like the Real Thing	Donny & Marie Osmond	#21
1977	Sometimes	Facts of Life	#31
1977	(Remember the Days of The) Old Schoolyard	Cat Stevens	#33
1977	It's in His Kiss (The Shoop Shoop Song)	Kate Taylor	#49
1977	Look What You've Done to My Heart	Marilyn McCoo & Billy Davis, Jr.	#51
1977	Heaven's Just a Sin Away	The Kendalls	#69
1977	Love Me One More Time (Just for Old Times Sake)	Karen Nelson & Billy T.	#79

MALE AND FEMALE DUETS (cont'd)

1978	You Don't Bring Me Flowers	Barbra Streisand & Neil Diamond	#1
1978	You're the One That I Want	John Travolta & Olivia Newton-John	#1
1978	Too Much, Too Little, Too Late	Johnny Mathis & Deniece Williams	#1
1978	The Closer I Get to You	Roberta Flack & Donny Hathaway	#2
1978	Whenever I Call You "Friend"	Kenny Loggins & Stevie Nicks	#5
1978	Summer Nights	John Travolta & Olivia Newton-John	#5
1978	Dance with Me	Peter Brown w/Betty Wright	#8
1978	Stay	Jackson Browne	#20
1978	You're a Part of Me	Gene Cotton w/Kim Carnes	#36
1978	Devoted to You	Carly Simon & James Taylor	#36
1978	(You're My) Soul and Inspiration	Donny & Marie Osmond	#38
1978	On the Shelf	Donny & Marie Osmond	#38
1978	Paradise by the Dashboard Light	Meat Loaf	#39
1978	Ease on Down the Road	Diana Ross & Michael Jackson	#41
1978	Sweet, Sweet Smile	Carpenters	#44
1978	You're All I Need to Get By	Johnny Mathis & Deniece Williams	#47
1978	Darlin'	Paul Davis w/Susan Collins	#51
1978	I Believe You	Carpenters	#68
1978	I'm on My Way	Captain & Tennille	#74
1978	Don't Cost You Nothing	Ashford & Simpson	#79
1978	Only You	Loleatta Holloway & Bunny Sigler	#87
1978	Take Me I'm Yours	Michael Henderson	#88
1979	Reunited	Peaches & Herb	#1
1979	Heaven Knows	Donna Summer w/Brooklyn Dreams	#4
1979	Stumblin' In	Suzi Quatro & Chris Norman	#4
1979	Shake Your Groove Thing	Peaches & Herb	#5
1979	Gold	John Stewart	#5
1979	Come to Me	France Joli	#15
1979	Found a Cure	Ashford & Simpson	#36
1979	We've Got Love	Peaches & Herb	#44
1979	Georgy Porgy	Toto w/Cheryl Lynn	#48
1979	A Little Lovin' (Keeps the Doctor Away)	The Raes	#61
1979	Four Strong Winds	Neil Young (w/Nicolette Larson)	#61
1979	Roller-Skatin' Mate (Part 1)	Peaches & Herb	#66
1979	Love and Desire (Part 1)	Arpeggio	#70
1979	You've Lost That Lovin' Feelin'	Long John Baldry & Kathi MacDonald	#89

MISCELLANEOUS

ONE-HIT WONDERS

The artists below all had only one song appear on the Hot 100 in their career. Seven artists barely made it, with their hit peaking at #100. While a handful of hits made the top ten, including a few #2 hits, no one-hit wonder made it all the way to #1.

YEAR	ARTIST	SONG	HOT 100
1970	Miss Abrams and The Strawberry Point School Third Grade Class	Mill Valley	#90
1974	Ace Spectrum	Don't Send Nobody Else	#57
1973	Afrique	Soul Makossa	#47
1978	Airwaves	So Hard Livin' Without You	#62
1976	American Flyer	Let Me Down Easy	#80
1974	Amesbury, Bill	Virginia (Touch Me Like You Do)	#74
1973	Anacostia	On and Off (Part 1)	#90
1972	Argent	Hold Your Head Up	#5
1979	Arpeggio	Love and Desire (Part 1)	#70
1978	Arvon, Bobby	Until Now	#72
1971	Ashton, Gardner & Dyke	Resurrection Shuffle	#40
1976	The Atlanta Disco Band	Bad Luck	#94
1976	Attitudes	Sweet Summer Music	#76
1971	Audience	Indian Summer	#74
1970	Brian Auger & The Trinity	Listen Here	#100
1977	Automatic Man	My Pearl	#97
1974	Axton, Hoyt	When the Morning Comes	#54
1974	Bailey, Razzy	I Hate Hate	#67
1970	Ginger Baker's Air Force	Man of Constant Sorrow	#85
1971	Ballin' Jack	Super Highway	#93
1979	Bama	Touch Me When We're Dancing	#86
1979	Bandit	One Way Love	#77
1976	The Band of the Black Watch	Scotch on the Rocks	#75
1972	Bang	Questions	#90
1975	Banzaii	Chinese Kung Fu	#98
1971	Barbara and The Uniques	There It Goes Again	#91
1979	Barnes, Cheryl	Easy to Be Hard	#64
1979	The Barron Knights	The Topical Song	#70
1975	Bazuka	Dynomite-Part 1	#10

ONE-HIT WONDERS (cont'd)

1979	Beckmeier Brothers	Rock and Roll Dancin'	#53
1971	The Beginning of the End	Funky Nassau-Part 1	#15
1975	Bell, Benny	Shaving Cream	#30
1974	Bell, Maggie	After Midnight	#97
1979	Bell & James	Livin' It Up (Friday Night)	#15
1978	Belle Epoque	Miss Broadway	#92
1978	Belushi, John	Louie, Louie	#89
1970	Berlin Philharmonic	Theme Music for the Film "2001" A Space Odyssey from Also Sprach Zarathustra	#90
1978	Plastic Bertrand	Ca Plane Pour Moi	#47
1975	Bimbo Jet	El Bimbo	#43
1970	Birkin, Jane, & Serge Gainsbourg	Je T'Aime…Moi Non Plus	#58
1979	Blackjack	Love Me Tonight	#62
1976	Blaze	Silver Heels	#95
1978	The Blend	I'm Gonna Make You Love Me	#91
1971	Bloodrock	D.O.A.	#36
1977	Blue	Capture Your Heart	#88
1973	Blue, David	Outlaw Man	#94
1973	Blue Haze	Smoke Gets in Your Eyes	#27
1970	Blue Mink	Our World	#64
1975	Bohannon, Hamilton	Foot Stompin' Music	#98
1972	Bones	Roberta	#94
1979	Taka Boom	Night Dancin'	#74
1979	Boyer, Bonnie	Got to Give in to Love	#43
1970	The Boys in the Band	(How 'Bout a Little Hand For) The Boys in the Band	#48
1976	Bradshaw, Terry	I'm So Lonesome I Could Cry	#91
1977	Brainstorm	Wake Up and Be Somebody	#86
1979	Tchaikovsky, Bram	Girl of My Dreams	#37
1978	Brandon, Bill	We Fell in Love While Dancing	#80
1975	The Brecker Brothers	Sneakin' Up Behind You	#58
1973	Brighter Side of Darkness	Love Jones	#16
1978	British Lions	Wild in the Streets	#87
1976	Broadway	You to Me Are Everything	#86
1979	Brood, Herman	Saturday Night	#35
1979	Brooks, Nancy	I'm Not Gonna Cry Anymore	#66
1974	Brother to Brother	In the Bottle	#46
1979	Brown, Chuck, & The Soul Searchers	Bustin' Loose Part 1	#34
1978	Brown, Don	Sitting in Limbo	#74
1970	Brown, Jim Ed	Morning	#47
1974	Brown, Oscar Jr.	The Lone Ranger	#69
1975	Brown, Polly	Up in a Puff of Smoke	#16
1979	Brown, Randy	You Says It All	#72

ONE-HIT WONDERS (cont'd)

1976	Brown Sugar	The Game Is Over (What's the Matter with You)	#76
1979	Buckeye	Where Will Your Heart Take You	#63
1972	Buckwheat	Simple Song of Freedom	#84
1976	Budd, Julie	One Fine Day	#93
1979	The Buggles	Video Killed the Radio Star	#40
1972	Bulldog	No	#44
1977	Bumble Bee Unlimited	Love Bug	#92
1970	Burrows, Tony	Melanie Makes Me Smile	#87
1973	Byrd, Donald	Black Byrd	#88
1970	The Caboose	Black Hands White Cotton	#79
1975	Caesar, Shirley	No Charge	#91
1976	Cain, Jonathan	'Til It's Time to Say Goodbye	#44
1975	Campbell, Debbie	Please Tell Him That I Said Hello	#84
1970	Campbell, Jim	The Lights of Tucson	#93
1975	Cantrell, Lana	Like a Sunday Morning	#63
1975	Canyon	Top of the World (Make My Reservation)	#98
1976	Carradine, Keith	I'm Easy	#17
1975	Carter, Ralph	When You're Young and in Love	#95
1970	Cash, Tommy	Six White Horses	#79
1976	Cashman, Terry	Baby, Baby I Love You	#79
1975	Castleman, Boomer	Judy Mae	#33
1978	Cazz	Let's Live Together	#70
1971	C Company Featuring Terry Nelson	Battle Hymn of Lt. Calley	#37
1971	C.C.S.	Whole Lotta Love	#58
1978	Celebration featuring Mike Love	Almost Summer	#28
1977	Bee, Celi, & The Buzzy Bunch	Superman	#41
1972	The Chakachas	Jungle Fever	#8
1977	Champagne	Rock and Roll Star	#83
1976	The Champs' Boys Orchestra	Tubular Bells	#98
1979	Chanson	Don't Hold Back	#21
1976	Chase, Ellison	Let's Rock	#92
1977	Chater, Kerry	Part Time Love	#97
1971	Chee-Chee & Peppy	I Know I'm in Love	#49
1978	Cheeks, Judy	Mellow Lovin'	#65
1972	Chicory	Son of My Father	#91
1975	Chocolate Milk	Action Speaks Louder Than Words	#69
1975	The Choice Four	When You're Young and in Love	#91
1973	Circus	Stop, Wait & Listen	#91
1977	Cisyk, Kasey	You Light Up My Life	#80
1978	City Boy	5.7.0.5.	#27
1971	Clay, Tom	What the World Needs Now Is Love/Abraham, Martin and John	#8

ONE-HIT WONDERS (cont'd)

1972	Clean Living	In Heaven There Is No Beer	#49
1978	Clout	Substitute	#67
1976	Cocciante, Richard	When Love Has Gone Away	#41
1971	Cochise	Love's Made a Fool of You	#96
1970	Cold Blood	You Got Me Hummin'	#52
1972	Cole, Tony	Suite: Man and Woman	#97
1971	Collins, Dave and Ansil	Double Barrel	#22
1972	Coltrane, Chi	Thunder and Lightning	#17
1975	Consumer Rapport	Ease on Down the Road	#42
1971	The Continental 4	Day By Day (Every Minute of the Hour)	#84
1974	Cooker	Try (Try to Fall in Love)	#88
1970	Cool Heat	Groovin' with Mr. Blue	#89
1977	Cory	Fire Sign	#89
1975	Cotton, Lloyd & Christian	I Go to Pieces	#66
1970	Country Coalition	Time to Get It Together	#96
1972	The Courtship	It's the Same Old Love	#93
1970	Crabby Appleton	Go Back	#36
1971	Crane, Les	Desiderata	#8
1977	Crawler	Stone Cold Sober	#65
1974	Creative Source	Who Is He and What Is He to You	#69
1973	Cross Country	In the Midnight Hour	#30
1974	Cunha, Rick	(I'm A) YoYo Man	#61
1977	Current	Theme from "Rocky" (Gonna Fly Now)	#94
1979	Currie, Cherie & Marie	Since You've Been Gone	#95
1979	Curry, Tim	I Do the Rock	#91
1973	Cymande	The Message	#48
1971	Daddy Dewdrop	Chick-A-Boom (Don't Ya Jes' Love It)	#9
1979	Dahl, Steve, and Teenage Radiation	Do You Think I'm Disco?	#58
1974	Dalton, Kathy	Boogie Bands and One Night Stands	#72
1971	Liz Damon's Orient Express	1900 Yesterday	#33
1979	Dash, Sarah	Sinner Man	#71
1979	Davis, John, and The Monster Orchestra	Ain't That Enough for You	#89
1972	Davis, Tim	Buzzy Brown	#91
1970	Daybreak	Good Morning Freedom	#94
1979	Daye, Cory	Pow Wow	#76
1976	The Deadly Nightshade	Mary Hartman, Mary Hartman	#79
1972	The Delegates	Convention '72	#8
1979	Delegation	Oh Honey	#45
1970	DeLory, Al	Song from M*A*S*H*	#70
1974	DeYoung, Cliff	My Sweet Lady	#17
1975	Diamond Reo	Ain't That Peculiar	#44

ONE-HIT WONDERS (cont'd)

1973	Dibango, Manu	Soul Makossa	#35
1971	The Dillards	It's About Time	#92
1976	Double Exposure	Ten Percent	#54
1978	Doucette	Mama Let Him Play	#72
1970	Drake, Guy	Welfare Cadilac	#63
1973	Drupi	Vado Via	#88
1970	Duke, Doris	To the Other Woman (I'm the Other Woman)	#50
1975	Duke & The Drivers	What You Got	#95
1977	Dundas, David	Jeans On	#17
1970	Dunn & McCashen	Alright in the City	#91
1974	Dynamic Superiors	Shoe Shoe Shine	#68
1975	East L.A. Car Pool	Like They Say in L.A.	#72
1976	Easy Street	I've Been Lovin' You	#81
1970	Eddie & Dutch	My Wife, The Dancer	#52
1975	Edelman, Randy	Everybody Wants to Find a Bluebird	#92
1972	Edwards, Jonathan	Sunshine	#4
1971	The Electric Express	It's the Real Thing – Pt. 1	#81
1970	Elephant's Memory	Mongoose	#50
1973	Emmerson, Les	Control of Me	#51
1972	The English Congregation	Softly Whispering I Love You	#29
1978	Eruption	I Can't Stand the Rain	#18
1979	Euclid Beach Band	I Need You	#81
1970	Fabulous Counts	Get Down People	#88
1979	Fabulous Poodles	Mirror Star	#81
1972	The Fabulous Rhinestones	What a Wonderful Thing We Have	#78
1977	Facts of Life	Sometimes	#31
1976	Fair, Yvonne	It Should Have Been Me	#85
1972	The Fantastics	(Love Me) Love the Life I Lead	#86
1970	Fantasy	Stoned Cowboy	#77
1979	The Faragher Bros.	Stay the Night	#50
1970	Feather	Friends	#79
1973	Fire and Rain	Hello Stranger	#100
1975	Firefly	Hey There Little Firefly Part 1	#67
1974	Fischoff, George	Georgia Porcupine	#93
1979	Five Special	Why Leave Us Alone	#55
1975	5000 Volts	I'm on Fire	#26
1970	The Flame	See the Light	#95
1972	Flash	Small Beginnings	#29
1979	Flash and The Pan	Hey, St. Peter	#76
1974	Fletcher, Louis	I Am What I Am	#64
1977	The Floaters	Float On	#2

ONE-HIT WONDERS (cont'd)

1979	Foley, Ellen	What's a Matter Baby	#92
1976	Fools Gold	Rain, Oh Rain	#76
1977	Foster, Bruce	Platinum Heroes	#63
1975	Fox	Only You Can	#53
1976	Franks, Michael	Popsicle Toes	#43
1979	Frehley, Ace	New York Groove	#13
1977	Friedman, Dean	Ariel	#26
1979	Funky Communication Committee	Baby I Want You	#47
1977	Funky Kings	Slow Dancing	#61
1979	Furay, Richie	I Still Have Dreams	#39
1978	Gabriel	Martha (Your Lovers Come and Go)	#73
1976	The Disco Sound of Andre Gagnon	Wow	#95
1972	Garcia, Jerry	Sugaree	#94
1976	Garrett, Lee	You're My Everything	#58
1973	Gary & Dave	Could You Ever Love Me Again	#92
1979	Gary's Gang	Keep on Dancin'	#41
1974	Gatlin, Larry, & The Gatlin Brothers	Delta Dirt	#84
1972	Gerard, Danyel	Butterfly	#78
1976	Gerrard, Donny	Words (Are Impossible)	#87
1976	Steve Gibbons Band	Johnny Cool	#72
1979	Gibson Brothers	Cuba	#81
1972	Gladstone	A Piece of Paper	#45
1976	The Glitter Band	Makes You Blind	#91
1972	Godspell	Day By Day	#13
1979	Goffin, Louise	Remember (Walking on the Sand)	#43
1979	Golde, Frannie	Here I Go (Fallin' in Love Again)	#76
1979	Gomm, Ian	Hold On	#18
1979	Gonzalez	Haven't Stopped Dancing Yet	#26
1975	The Goodies	The Funky Gibbon	#79
1973	Goodwin, Don	This Is Your Song	#86
1978	Goody Goody	#1 Dee Jay	#82
1972	Goose Creek Symphony	(Oh Lord Won't You Buy Me A) Mercedes Benz	#64
1974	Grand Canyon	Evil Boll-Weevil	#72
1976	Grecco, Cyndi	Making Our Dreams Come True	#25
1979	Grey & Hanks	Dancin'	#83
1972	Grin	White Lies	#75
1976	Groce, Larry	Junk Food Junkie	#9
1973	Gunhill Road	Back When My Hair was Short	#40
1974	Hamlisch, Marvin	The Entertainer	#3
1976	Handy, John	Hard Work	#46
1976	Hardy, Hagood	The Homecoming	#41

		ONE-HIT WONDERS (cont'd)	
1976	Harley, Steve, and Cockney Rebel	Make Me Smile (Come Up and See Me)	#96
1976	Don Harrison Band	Sixteen Tons	#47
1971	Hart, Freddie	Easy Loving	#17
1977	Hart, Rod	C.B. Savage	#67
1971	Havens, Richie	Here Comes the Sun	#16
1979	The Headboys	The Shape of Things to Come	#67
1977	The Heart and Soul Orchestra	Love in 'C' Minor	#46
1974	Heartsfield	Music Eyes	#95
1975	Hello People	Future Shock	#71
1978	Henderson, Michael	Take Me I'm Yours	#88
1977	Henhouse Five Plus Too (Ray Stevens)	In the Mood	#40
1979	Herman, Keith	She's Got a Whole Number	#87
1979	Hernandez, Patrick	Born to Be Alive	#16
1976	The Heyettes	The Fonz Song	#91
1972	Hodge, Chris	We're on Our Way	#44
1977	Hodges, James and Smith	Since I Fell for You/I'm Falling in Love	#96
1971	Hog Heaven	Happy	#98
1972	Holien, Danny	Colorado	#66
1973	Holland, Brian	Don't Leave Me Starvin' for Your Love (Part 1)	#52
1977	The Hollywood Stars	All the Kids on the Street	#94
1974	Holm, Michael	When a Child Is Born	#53
1973	Holmes, Clint	Playground in My Mind	#2
1970	Holmes, Jake	So Close	#49
1978	Horne, Jimmy "Bo"	Dance Across the Floor	#38
1972	Hot Butter	Popcorn	#9
1970	Hotlegs	Neanderthal Man	#22
1972	Hot Sauce	Bring It Home (And Give It to Me)	#96
1971	Houston, Cissy	Be My Baby	#92
1974	Howell, Reuben	Rings	#86
1971	Humphrey, Paul, & His Cool Aid Chemists	Cool Aid	#29
1970	I.A.P. CO. (The Italian Asphalt & Pavement Company)	Check Yourself	#97
1976	Impact	Happy Man (Pt. 1)	#94
1973	The Incredible Bongo Band	Bongo Rock	#57
1979	Instant Funk	I Got My Mind Made Up (You Can Get It Girl)	#20
1975	Jacks, Susan	You're a Part of Me	#90
1973	Jackson, Earnest	Love and Happiness	#58
1976	Ja-Kki	Sun…Sun…Sun…Pt. 1	#96
1974	James, Bob	I Feel Like Making Love	#88
1977	Jameson, Cody	Brooklyn	#74
1972	Jamestown Massacre	Summer Sun	#90
1970	Jamul	Tobacco Road	#93

	ONE-HIT WONDERS (cont'd)		
1973	John & Ernest	Super Fly Meets Shaft	#31
1974	Angel, Johnny T.	Tell Laura I Love Her	#94
1973	Johnson, Kevin	Rock 'N Roll (I Gave You the Best Years of My Life)	#73
1970	Johnson, Rozetta	A Woman's Way	#94
1972	Gunne, Jo Jo	Run Run Run	#27
1975	The Joneses	Sugar Pie Guy (Pt. 1)	#47
1979	The Jones Girls	You Gonna Make Me Love Somebody Else	#38
1971	Joy of Cooking	Brownsville	#66
1977	Kaplan, Gabriel	Up Your Nose	#91
1973	Karen, Kenny	That's Why You Remember	#82
1975	Katfish	Dear Prudence	#62
1972	Kay, John	I'm Movin' On	#52
1978	Kayak	I Want You to Be Mine	#55
1976	The Keane Brothers	Sherry	#84
1972	Kelly, Casey	Poor Boy	#52
1977	The Kendalls	Heaven's Just a Sin Away	#69
1972	Kennedy, Mike	Louisiana	#62
1970	King Crimson	The Court of the Crimson King – Part 1	#80
1979	Kinney, Fern	Groove Me	#54
1971	Kissoon, Mac and Katie	Chirpy Chirpy Cheep Cheep	#20
1977	Klaatu	Sub-Rosa Subway	#62
1970	The Klowns	Lady Love	#95
1972	Knight, Frederick	I've Been Lonely for So Long	#27
1970	Kolby, Diane	Holy Man	#67
1978	Kongas	Africanism/Gimme Some Lovin'	#84
1971	Kongos, John	He's Gonna Step on You Again	#70
1975	Kulis, Charlie	Runaway	#46
1978	LaBounty, Bill	This Night Won't Last Forever	#65
1978	Ladd, Cheryl	Think It Over	#34
1976	Lady Flash	Street Singin'	#27
1977	LaFlamme, David	White Bird	#89
1971	Lai, Francis, and His Orchestra	Theme from "Love Story"	#96
1977	L.A. Jets	Prisoner (Captured By Your Eyes)	#86
1977	Lake	Time Bomb	#83
1978	Lamb, Kevin	On the Wrong Track	#82
1976	LaRue, D.C.	Cathedrals	#94
1976	LaVerne & Shirley	Sixteen Reasons	#65
1979	Lazy Racer	Keep on Running Away	#81
1972	LeGrand, Michel	Brian's Song	#56
1977	Lemmons, Billy	Six Packs a Day	#93
1978	Le Pamplemousse	Le Spank	#58

		ONE-HIT WONDERS (cont'd)	
1979	Lia, Orsa	I Never Said I Love You	#84
1973	Limmie & Family Cookin'	You Can Do Magic	#84
1979	Liner	You and Me	#92
1970	Liquid Smoke	I Who Have Nothing	#82
1970	The Lost Generation	The Sly, Slick, and the Wicked	#30
1978	Love and Kisses	Thank God It's Friday	#22
1975	Love Childs Afro Cuban Blues Band	Life and Death in G&A	#90
1970	The Lovelites	How Can I Tell My Mom & Dad	#60
1977	The Lovers	Discomania	#100
1975	Low, Andy Fairweather	Spider Jiving	#87
1977	Lucas, Frank	Good Thing Man	#92
1972	Lunar Funk	Mr. Penguin – Pt. 1	#63
1975	Lundi, Pat	Party Music	#78
1979	M	Pop Muzik	#1
1973	Maceo and The Macks	Parrty – Part 1	#71
1974	MacGregor, Byron	Americans	#4
1979	Machine	There but for the Grace of God	#77
1972	Malo	Suavecito	#18
1972	Mark-Almond	One Way Sunday	#94
1976	Marley, Bob, & The Wailers	Roots, Rock, Reggae	#51
1979	Marshall Hain	Dancing in the City	#43
1971	Martine, Layng	Rub It In	#65
1979	Mas, Carolyne	Stillsane	#71
1970	Mashmakhan	As the Years Go By	#31
1970	McCann, Les	Compared to What	#85
1977	McCann, Peter	Do You Wanna Make Love	#5
1979	McClain, Alton & Destiny	It Must Be Love	#32
1975	McCrae, Gwen	Rockin' Chair	#9
1978	The McCrarys	You	#45
1977	McDaniel, Donna	Save Me	#90
1979	McFadden & Whitehead	Ain't No Stoppin' Us Now	#13
1977	McGee, Parker	I Just Can't Say No to You	#42
1978	McGilpin, Bob	When You Feel Love	#91
1979	McGuinn, Clark & Hillman	Don't You Write Her Off	#33
1971	Flint, McGuinness	When I'm Dead and Gone	#47
1976	McLean, Penny	Lady Bump	#48
1978	McNichol, Kristy & Jimmy	He's So Fine	#70
1974	Mead, Sister Janet	The Lord's Prayer	#4
1977	Mesa	Sailing Ships	#55
1976	Mighty Clouds of Joy	Mighty High	#69
1977	Mr. Big	Romeo	#87

		ONE-HIT WONDERS (cont'd)	
1979	Mistress	Mistrusted Love	#49
1971	The Mixtures	Pushbike Song	#44
1974	Mocedades	Eres Tu (Touch the Wind)	#9
1974	Montgomery, Melba	No Charge	#39
1976	Moonlion	The Little Drummer Boy	#95
1975	Moore, Bobby	(Call Me You) Anything Man	#99
1971	Morning Mist	California on My Mind	#96
1976	Most, Donny	All Roads (Lead Back to You)	#97
1972	The Move	Do Ya	#93
1977	Muhammad, Idris	Could Heaven Ever Be Like This (Part 1)	#76
1973	Mull, Martin, and Orchestra	Dueling Tubas	#92
1970	Mungo Jerry	In the Summertime	#3
1978	Musique	In the Bush	#58
1972	National Lampoon	Deteriorata	#91
1979	Nature's Divine	I Just Can't Control Myself	#65
1979	Naughton, David	Makin' It	#5
1970	Naylor, Jerry	But for Love	#69
1970	Nazz	Hello It's Me	#66
1970	The Neighborhood	Big Yellow Taxi	#29
1975	Nektar	Astral Man	#91
1977	Nelson, Karen, and Billy T	Love Me One More Time (Just for Old Times Sake)	#79
1971	Nero, Peter	Theme from "Summer of '42"	#21
1971	The Newcomers	Pin the Tail on the Donkey	#74
1970	The New Hope	Won't Find Better (Than Me)	#57
1972	New Riders of the Purple Sage	I Don't Need No Doctor	#81
1979	Niteflyte	If You Want It	#37
1971	Nix, Don	Olena	#94
1971	North, Freddie	She's All I Got	#39
1975	Northern Light	Minnesota	#88
1974	Norwood, Dorothy	There's Got To Be Rain in Your Life (To Appreciate the Sunshine)	#88
1974	NRBQ	Get That Gasoline Blues	#70
1970	Nyro, Laura	Up on the Roof	#92
1972	O'Connor, Carroll, and Jean Stapleton	Those Were the Days	#43
1971	Odds & Ends	Love Makes the World Go Round	#83
1972	O'Keefe, Danny	Good Time Charlie's Got the Blues	#9
1974	Oldfield, Mike	Tubular Bells	#7
1970	The Original Caste	One Tin Soldier	#34
1976	Oskar, Lee	BLT	#59
1970	Owen B.	Mississippi Mama	#97
1976	Ozo	Listen to the Buddha	#96
1973	Pagan, Ralfi	Soul Je T'Aime	#99

		ONE-HIT WONDERS (cont'd)	
1979	Pages	I Do Believe in You	#84
1973	Painter	West Coast Woman	#79
1970	Parks, Michael	Long Lonesome Highway	#20
1978	Patterson, Kellee	If It Don't Fit, Don't Force It	#75
1975	Paul, Christopher, and Shawn	For Your Love	#91
1971	Paycheck, Johnny	She's All I Got	#91
1979	Peek, Dan	All Things Are Possible	#78
1974	The Peppers	Pepper Box	#76
1970	Perkins, George, & The Silver Stars	Cryin' in the Streets (Part 1)	#61
1977	Philadelphia International All Stars	Let's Clean Up the Ghetto	#91
1977	The Philarmonics	For Elise	#100
1970	Phillips, John	Mississippi	#32
1979	Philly Cream	Motown Review	#67
1975	Philly Devotions	I Just Can't Say Goodbye	#95
1970	Pickettywitch	That Same Old Feeling	#67
1979	Pink Lady	Kiss in the Dark	#37
1970	The Pipkins	Gimme Dat Ding	#9
1976	Mary Kay Place	Baby Boy	#60
1971	P-Nut Gallery	Do You Know What Time It Is?	#62
1978	Pockets	Come Go with Me	#84
1971	Ponderosa Twins + One	You Send Me	#78
1972	Porter, David	Ain't That Loving You (For More Reasons Than One)	#86
1972	Potliquor	Cheer	#65
1979	Pousette-Dart Band	For Love	#83
1974	Powell, Cozy	Dance with the Devil	#49
1977	Powers, Tom	It Ain't Love	#92
1973	Pratt, Andy	Avenging Annie	#78
1975	Protheroe, Brian	Pinball	#60
1973	Pruett, Jeanne	Satin Sheets	#28
1975	Purple Reign	This Old Man	#48
1972	Jackson, Python Lee	In a Broken Dream	#56
1977	Q	Dancin' Man	#23
1973	Quateman, Bill	Only Love	#86
1979	The Raes	A Little Lovin' (Keeps the Doctor Away)	#61
1977	Ram Jam	Black Betty	#18
1970	The Rattles	The Witch	#79
1978	Ravan, Genya	Back in My Arms Again	#92
1978	Ray, Don	Got to Have Loving	#44
1971	Raye, Susan	L.A. International Airport	#54
1975	Read, John Dawson	A Friend of Mine Is Going Blind	#72
1976	The Real Thing	You to Me Are Everything	#64

ONE-HIT WONDERS (cont'd)

1979	The Records	Starry Eyes	#56
1974	Redding, Gene	This Heart	#24
1973	Redway, Michael	Good Morning	#85
1973	Reed, Lou	Walk on the Wild Side	#16
1974	Reeves, Martha	Power of Love	#76
1975	The Reflections	Three Steps from True Love	#94
1971	Reilly, Mike	1927 Kansas City	#88
1974	Reunion	Life Is a Rock (But the Radio Rolled Me)	#8
1976	Revelation	You to Me Are Everything, Part 1	#98
1971	Rhodes, Emitt	Fresh as a Daisy	#54
1972	Riley, Billy Lee	I Got a Thing About You Baby	#93
1970	Rios, Miguel	A Song of Joy (Himno a la Alegria)	#14
1971	Ríos, Waldo de los	Mozart Symphony No. 40 in G Minor K.550, 1st Movement	#67
1973	Ripple	I Don't Know What It Is, But It Sure Is Funky	#67
1976	The Road Apples	Let's Live Together	#35
1975	Roberts, Lea	All Right Now	#92
1970	Robinson, Freddy	Black Fox	#56
1972	Rock Flowers	Number Wonderful	#95
1976	Rogers, D.J.	Say You Love Me	#98
1975	Rogers, Roy	Hoppy, Gene and Me	#65
1970	Rotary Connection	Want You to Know	#96
1978	Roussos, Demis	That Once in a Lifetime	#47
1976	The Rowans	If I Only Could	#74
1971	Rowles, John	Cheryl Moana Marie	#64
1972	Royal Scots Dragoon Guards	Amazing Grace	#11
1974	The Rubettes	Sugar Baby Love	#37
1978	Rubicon	I'm Gonna Take Care of Everything	#28
1977	The Rubinoos	I Think We're Alone Now	#45
1972	Sailcat	Motorcycle Mama	#12
1979	Saint Tropez	One More Minute	#49
1971	Salvage	Hot Pants	#54
1977	The Sanford/Townsend Band	Smoke from a Distant Fire	#9
1971	Sans, Billie	Solo	#91
1976	Santos, Larry	We Can't Hide It Anymore	#36
1972	Savina, Carlo	Love Theme from "The Godfather"	#66
1976	Sawyer, Ray	(One More Year Of) Daddy's Little Girl	#81
1978	Scott, Marilyn	God Only Knows	#61
1976	Scott, Tom	Uptown & Country	#80
1978	Sea Level	That's Your Secret	#50
1971	Seatrain	13 Questions	#49
1974	Sellars, Marilyn	One Day at a Time	#37

ONE-HIT WONDERS (cont'd)

1975	Shelley, Peter	Gee Baby	#81
1973	Shepard, Jean	Slippin' Away	#81
1976	Shirley & Squirrely	Hey Shirley (This Is Squirrely)	#48
1979	Shoes	Too Late	#75
1976	Silver	Wham Bam (Shang-A-Lang)	#16
1975	Silverspoon, Dooley	Bump Me Baby Part 1	#80
1977	Silvetti	Spring Rain	#39
1979	Simmons, Gene	Radioactive	#47
1973	Simpson, Valerie	Silly Wasn't I	#63
1974	Sinclair, Gordon	The Americans (A Canadian's Opinion)	#24
1973	Skellern, Peter	You're a Lady	#50
1973	Skylark	Wildflower	#9
1976	Smith, Bro	Bigfoot	#57
1973	Smith, Cal	The Lord Knows I'm Drinking	#64
1978	Snail	The Joker	#93
1979	Sniff 'N' The Tears	Driver's Seat	#15
1979	Sober, Errol	Heart to Heart	#65
1979	Soccio, Gino	Dancer	#48
1970	Sommer, Bert	We're All Playing in the Same Band	#48
1971	Sounds of Sunshine	Love Means (You Never Have to Say You're Sorry)	#39
1974	Southcote	She's All I Got	#80
1974	The Souther, Hillman, Furay Band	Fallin' in Love	#27
1973	The South Side Movement	I' Been Watchin' You	#61
1979	Space	My Love Is Music	#60
1976	Special Delivery	The Lonely One	#75
1971	Spector, Ronnie	Try Some, Buy Some	#77
1978	Spellbound	Rumor at the Honky Tonk	#89
1977	Sperry, Steve	Flame	#91
1976	Spin	Grasshopper	#95
1975	Splinter	Costafine Town	#77
1979	The Sports	Who Listens to the Radio	#45
1971	Springwell	It's for You	#60
1976	S.S.O.	Tonight's the Night	#99
1977	Stallion	Old Fashioned Boy (You're the One)	#37
1973	Stampley, Joe	Soul Song	#37
1978	Stanley, Paul	Hold Me, Touch Me	#46
1970	Staples, Mavis	I Have Learned to Do Without You	#87
1975	Stark & McBrien	Isn't It Lonely Together	#85
1975	Starr, Kenny	The Blind Man in the Bleachers	#58
1975	Stewart, Baron	We Been Singin' Songs	#91
1978	Stillwater	Mind Bender	#46

ONE-HIT WONDERS (cont'd)

1971	Stookey, Paul	Wedding Song (There Is Love)	#24
1971	Stott, Lally	Chirpy Chirpy, Cheep Cheep	#92
1972	Sugar Bears	You Are the One	#51
1976	Sun	Wanna Make Love (Come Flick My BIC)	#76
1976	Sundown Company	Norma Jean Wants to Be a Movie Star	#84
1979	Sutton, Glenn	The Football Card	#46
1977	Suzy and The Red Stripes	Seaside Woman	#59
1971	Sweathog	Hallelujah	#33
1974	Sweet Dreams	Honey Honey	#68
1975	Sweet Sensation	Sad Sweet Dreamer	#14
1979	Tanner, Marc, Band	Elena	#45
1977	Taylor, Kate	It's in His Kiss (The Shoop Shoop Song)	#49
1972	The Temprees	Dedicated to the One I Love	#93
1970	Ten Wheel Drive with Genya Ravan	Morning Much Better	#74
1979	Third World	Now That We Found Love	#47
1974	Thomas, Ian	Painted Ladies	#34
1979	Thomas, Tasha	Shoot Me (With Your Love	#91
1979	Thorpe, Billy	Children of the Sun	#41
1975	Thunderkloud, Billy, & The Chieftones	What Time of Day	#92
1973	Today's People	He	#90
1970	Tolbert, Israel "Popper Stopper"	Big Leg Woman (With a Short Short Mini Skirt)	#61
1971	Travers, Mary	Follow Me	#56
1970	Travis, McKinley	Baby, Is There Something on Your Mind	#91
1978	Travolta, Joey	I Don't Wanna Go	#43
1978	Trooper	Raise a Little Hell	#59
1977	Trower, Robin	Caledonia	#82
1973	Tufano & Giammarese	Music Everywhere	#68
1978	Tuxedo Junction	Chattanooga Choo Choo	#32
1975	The 21st Century	Remember the Rain?	#100
1979	Tycoon	Such a Woman	#26
1979	Ultimate	Touch Me Baby	#82
1973	Uncle Dog	River Road	#86
1977	Universal Robot Band	Dance and Shake Your Tambourine	#93
1975	U.S. 1	Bye Bye Baby	#91
1972	Vigrass & Osborne	Men of Learning	#65
1970	The Village Soul Choir	The Cat Walk	#55
1979	Voudouris, Roger	Get Used to It	#21
1979	Voyage	Souvenirs	#41
1972	Wackers, The	Day and Night	#65
1971	Wadsworth Mansion	Sweet Mary	#7
1973	Wainwright, Loudon III	Dead Skunk	#16

	ONE-HIT WONDERS (cont'd)		
1975	Wakelin, Johnny & The Kinshasa Band	Black Superman – "Muhammad Ali"	#21
1978	Waldman, Wendy	Long Hot Summer Nights	#76
1975	Webb, Paula	Please, Mr. President	#60
1978	Weir, Bob	Bombs Away	#70
1978	Weisberg, Tim	The Power of Gold	#24
1973	Weissberg, Eric, & Steve Mandell	Dueling Banjos	#2
1976	Whirlwind	Full Time Thing (Between Dusk and Dawn)	#91
1977	White, Danny	Dance Little Lady Dance	#100
1975	Whittaker, Roger	The Last Farewell	#19
1975	Wier, Rusty	Don't It Make You Wanna Dance?	#82
1970	Wild, Jack	Some Beautiful	#92
1977	Wildfire	Here Comes Summer	#49
1977	Williams, Anson	Deeply	#93
1976	Williams, Diana	Teddy Bear's Last Ride	#66
1973	Williams, Johnny	Slow Motion (Part 1)	#78
1972	Williams, Paul	Waking Up Alone	#60
1977	Wilson, Meri	Telephone Man	#18
1979	Wilson Bros.	Another Night	#94
1977	Wilton Place Street Band	Disco Lucy (I Love Lucy Theme)	#24
1976	The Wing and a Prayer Fife and Drum Corps.	Baby Face	#14
1975	Wingfield, Pete	Eighteen with a Bullet	#15
1979	Witch Queen	Bang a Gong	#68
1974	The Wombles	Wombling Summer Party	#55
1979	The Wonder Band	Whole Lotta Love	#87
1979	Wood, Lauren	Please Don't Leave	#24
1979	Wray, Bill	Pinball, That's All	#96
1972	Yarrow, Peter	Don't Ever Take Away My Freedom	#100
1978	Young, Karen	Hot Shot	#67
1974	Zavaroni, Lena	Ma! (He's Making Eyes at Me)	#91

SHORT SONGS

You'd be hard-pressed to find a current hit that runs only two minutes. The 70s had quite a few of them. To make this list, a song could be no longer than two minutes and fifteen seconds long.

YEAR	SONG	ARTIST	HOT 100	LENGTH OF SONG
1973	Dueling Tubas	Martin Mull	#92	1:26
1972	Those Were the Days	Carroll O'Connor & Jean Stapleton	#43	1:27
1970	Theme Music for the Film "2001" A Space Odyssey from Also Sprach Zarathustra	Berlin Philharmonic	#90	1:38

	SHORT SONGS (cont'd)			
1970	Why Should I Cry	The Gentrys	#61	1:52
1971	My Heart Is Yours	Wilbert Harrison	#98	1:52
1970	Jennifer Tomkins	Street People	#36	1:53
1973	Queen of the Roller Derby	Leon Russell	#89	1:53
1971	That's the Way a Woman Is	Messengers	#62	1:54
1972	One Night Affair	Jerry Butler	#52	1:54
1978	Do You Wanna Dance	Ramones	#86	1:55
1970	Mississippi Mama	Owen B.	#97	1:56
1975	Sneaky Snake	Tom T. Hall	#55	1:57
1971	Grandma's Hands	Bill Withers	#42	1:58
1971	Valerie	Cymarron	#96	1:58
1977	Telephone Man	Meri Wilson	#18	1:58
1970	She	Tommy James & The Shondells	#23	2:00
1971	Waiting at the Bus Stop	Bobby Sherman	#54	2:00
1974	Mr. President	Dickie Goodman	#73	2:00
1975	Wonderful Baby	Don McLean	#93	2:00
1971	Are You Old Enough	Mark Lindsay	#87	2:01
1973	Country Sunshine	Dottie West	#49	2:01
1972	Kiss an Angel Good Mornin'	Charley Pride	#21	2:02
1972	Dance, Dance, Dance	The New Seekers	#84	2:02
1970	How Can I Forget	Marvin Gaye	#41	2:03
1970	Cinnamon Girl	The Gentrys	#52	2:03
1971	Me and My Arrow	Nilsson	#34	2:03
1971	I'm Comin' Home	Tommy James	#40	2:03
1971	Tell Me Why	Matthews' Southern Comfort	#98	2:03
1975	Mr. Jaws	Dickie Goodman	#4	2:03
1970	Rock Island Line	Johnny Cash	#93	2:04
1971	Ain't No Sunshine	Bill Withers	#3	2:04
1972	Motorcycle Mama	Sailcat	#12	2:04
1974	After the Goldrush	Prelude	#22	2:04
1970	Travelin' Band	Creedence Clearwater Revival	#2	2:05
1970	Long Lonesome Highway	Michael Parks	#20	2:05
1970	Chicken Strut	The Meters	#50	2:05
1970	Save Your Sugar for Me	Tony Joe White	#94	2:05
1972	He's an Indian Cowboy in the Rodeo	Buffy Sainte-Marie	#98	2:05
1973	Ridin' My Thumb to Mexico	Johnny Rodriguez	#70	2:05
1976	Hurt	Elvis Presley	#28	2:05
1973	Watergrate	Dickie Goodman	#42	2:06
1974	I Love	Tom T. Hall	#12	2:06
1975	When Will I Be Loved	Linda Ronstadt	#2	2:06
1978	Runaway Beach	Ramones	#66	2:06

	SHORT SONGS (cont'd)			
1970	Snowbird	Anne Murray	#8	2:08
1970	Going to the Country	Steve Miller Band	#69	2:08
1970	Mornin Mornin	Bobby Goldsboro	#78	2:08
1974	Rock Around the Clock	Bill Haley & His Comets	#39	2:08
1974	My Main Man	The Staple Singers	#76	2:08
1975	Who's Sorry Now	Marie Osmond	#40	2:08
1976	It's O.K.	The Beach Boys	#29	2:08
1970	Jesus Is Just Alright	The Byrds	#97	2:09
1971	Don't Knock My Love – Pt. 1	Wilson Pickett	#13	2:09
1971	Turn Your Radio On	Ray Stevens	#63	2:09
1971	Super Highway	Ballin' Jack	#93	2:09
1975	We May Never Love Like This Again	Maureen McGovern	#83	2:09
1978	Boogie Shoes	KC and The Sunshine Band	#35	2:09
1970	Gimme Dat Ding	The Pipkins	#9	2:10
1970	Is Anybody Goin' to San Antone	Charley Pride	#70	2:10
1970	I'm Gonna Love You	The Intrigues	#86	2:10
1971	I'm Girl Scoutin'	The Intruders	#88	2:10
1971	Soldier's Last Letter	Merle Haggard	#90	2:10
1973	Goin' Home	The Osmonds	#36	2:10
1973	Hearts of Stone	Blue Ridge Rangers	#37	2:10
1973	Silly Wasn't I	Valerie Simpson	#63	2:10
1973	They're Coming to Take Me Away, Ha-Haa!	Napoleon XIV	#87	2:10
1978	King Tut	Steve Martin and The Toot Uncommons	#17	2:10
1978	He's So Fine	Kristy & Jimmy McNichol	#70	2:10
1979	Good Timin'	The Beach Boys	#40	2:10
1974	Delta Dirt	Larry Gatlin	#84	2:11
1977	Just a Song Before I Go	Crosby, Stills & Nash	#7	2:11
1970	New World Coming	Mama Cass Elliot	#42	2:12
1970	Funky Chicken (Part 1)	Willie Henderson w/The Soul Explosions	#91	2:12
1970	The Lights of Tucson	Jim Campbell	#93	2:12
1971	A Long Time, A Long Way to Go	Todd Rundgren	#92	2:12
1972	Long Haired Lover from Liverpool	Little Jimmy Osmond w/The Mike Curb Congregation	#38	2:12
1973	Dueling Banjos	Eric Weissberg & Steve Mandell	#2	2:12
1973	That's Why You Remember	Kenny Karen	#82	2:12
1974	Rub It In	Billy "Crash" Craddock	#16	2:12
1974	I Don't See Me in Your Eyes Anymore	Charlie Rich	#47	2:12
1975	Every Day I Have to Cry Some	Arthur Alexander	#45	2:12
1977	Bless the Beasts and Children	Barry DeVorzon & Perry Botkin, Jr.	#82	2:12
1978	Stay Awhile	Continental Miniatures	#90	2:12
1970	My Wife, The Dancer	Eddie & Dutch	#52	2:13

		SHORT SONGS (cont'd)			
1972	I'd Like to Teach the World to Sing (In Perfect Harmony)	The Hillside Singers	#13	2:13
1973	Young Love	Donny Osmond	#25	2:13
1974	Don't Knock My Love	Diana Ross & Marvin Gaye	#46	2:13
1975	What a Man, My Man Is	Lynn Anderson	#93	2:13
1970	Thank You Girl	Street People	#96	2:14
1971	Ride a White Swan	Tyrannosaurus Rex	#76	2:14
1975	Tush	ZZ Top	#20	2:14
1975	Wooden Heart	Bobby Vinton	#58	2:14
1978	Peggy Sue	The Beach Boys	#59	2:14
1970	Big Yellow Taxi	The Neighborhood	#29	2:15
1970	Can't Help Falling in Love	Al Martino	#51	2:15
1970	Woodstock	The Assembled Multitude	#79	2:15
1970	A World Without Music	Archie Bell & The Drells	#90	2:15
1970	Sing Out the Love (In My Heart)	Arkade	#99	2:15
1970	Don't Let the Music Slip Away	Archie Bell & The Drells	#100	2:15
1971	Till	Tom Jones	#41	2:15
1972	Baby Won't You Let Me Rock 'N Roll You	Ten Years After	#61	2:15
1972	Da Doo Ron Ron (When He Walked Me Home)	Ian Matthews	#96	2:15
1973	Come Softly to Me	The New Seekers	#95	2:15
1974	Pepper Box	The Peppers	#76	2:15
1975	Main Title (Theme from "Jaws")	John Williams	#32	2:15
1975	I Fought the Law	Sam Neely	#54	2:15
1979	Different Worlds	Maureen McGovern	#18	2:15

LONG SONGS

Songs had to be at least five minutes long to make this list.

YEAR	SONG	ARTIST	HOT 100	LENGTH OF SONG
1976	Better Place to Be (Parts 1 & 2)	Harry Chapin	#86	9:30
1972	American Pie (Parts I & II)	Don McLean	#1	8:36
1978	Paradise By the Dashboard Light	Meat Loaf	#39	7:57
1975	I Am Love (Parts I & II)	The Jackson 5	#15	7:56
1972	American City Suite	Cashman & West	#27	7:44
1975	(How I Spent My Summer Vacation) Or a Day at the Beach with Pedro & Man – Parts I & II	Cheech & Chong	#54	7:24
1976	Do You Feel Like We Do	Peter Frampton	#10	7:18
1979	In the Midnight Hour	Samantha Sang	#88	7:17
1972	Layla	Derek & The Dominos	#10	7:10

	LONG SONGS (cont'd)			
1972	Papa Was a Rollin' Stone	The Temptations	#1	6:53
1971	They Can't Take Away Our Music	Eric Burdon & War	#50	6:50
1970	I Stand Accused	Isaac Hayes	#42	6:49
1975	Someone Saved My Life Tonight	Elton John	#4	6:45
1972	Taxi	Harry Chapin	#24	6:40
1978	Deacon Blues	Steely Dan	#19	6:40
1976	I Cheat the Hangman	The Doobie Brothers	#60	6:34
1977	The Killing of Georgie (Part I and II)	Rod Stewart	#30	6:31
1970	Heartbreaker	Grand Funk Railroad	#72	6:30
1974	Door to Your Heart	The Dramatics	#62	6:30
1972	Jubilation	Paul Anka	#65	6:29
1978	It's Late	Queen	#74	6:26
1972	A Lonely Man	The Chi-Lites	#57	6:23
1971	What the World Needs Now Is Love/Abraham, Martin and John	Tom Clay	#8	6:17
1972	Tiny Dancer	Elton John	#41	6:12
1977	Hotel California	Eagles	#1	6:08
1976	Queen of My Soul	Average White Band	#40	6:04
1972	Isn't Life Strange	The Moody Blues	#29	6:03
1972	Sweet Inspiration/Where You Lead	Barbra Streisand	#37	6:02
1976	Get the Funk Out Ma Face	The Brothers Johnson	#30	6:01
1979	Whole Lotta Love	The Wonder Band	#87	6:00
1978	Don't Look Back	Boston	#4	5:59
1976	The Wreck of the Edmund Fitzgerald	Gordon Lightfoot	#2	5:57
1976	I.O.U.	Jimmy Dean	#35	5:57
1979	Don't Stop 'Til You Get Enough	Michael Jackson	#1	5:56
1975	Lucy in the Sky with Diamonds	Elton John	#1	5:54
1976	Silly Love Songs	Paul McCartney & Wings	#1	5:54
1976	Music	John Miles	#88	5:52
1976	Bohemian Rhapsody	Queen	#9	5:50
1970	Are You Ready?	Pacific Gas & Electric	#14	5:49
1973	I Wanna Know Your Name	The Intruders	#60	5:49
1979	Sultans of Swing	Dire Straits	#4	5:49
1972	And You and I (Part 1)	Yes	#42	5:45
1975	Sex Machine (Part 1)	James Brown	#61	5:45
1977	Platinum Heroes	Bruce Foster	#63	5:45
1979	Goodbye Stranger	Supertramp	#15	5:45
1978	With a Little Luck	Paul McCartney & Wings	#1	5:42
1974	Newsy Neighbors	First Choice	#97	5:40
1977	I Feel Love	Donna Summer	#6	5:39
1971	Wild Horses	The Rolling Stones	#28	5:38
1975	Philadelphia Freedom	Elton John	#1	5:38

	LONG SONGS (cont'd)			
1975	Trampled Under Foot	Led Zeppelin	#38	5:38
1979	Children of the Sun	Billy Thorpe	#41	5:38
1972	Since I Fell for You	Laura Lee	#76	5:36
1977	Dazz	Brick	#3	5:35
1970	Whole Lotta Love	Led Zeppelin	#4	5:33
1974	Don't Let the Sun Go Down on Me	Elton John	#2	5:33
1978	Stone Blue	Foghat	#36	5:33
1970	A Change Is Gonna Come & People Gotta Be Free	The 5th Dimension	#60	5:32
1975	Tangled Up in Blue	Bob Dylan	#31	5:31
1970	Closer to Home (I'm Your Captain)	Grand Funk Railroad	#22	5:30
1976	I Don't Wanna Leave You	Debbie Taylor	#100	5:30
1979	I Want You Tonight	Pablo Cruise	#19	5:29
1976	Magic Man	Heart	#9	5:27
1978	Fooling Yourself (The Angry Young Man)	Styx	#29	5:27
1971	Don't Wanna Live Inside Myself	Bee Gees	#53	5:25
1979	Da Ya Think I'm Sexy?	Rod Stewart	#1	5:25
1974	Overnight Sensation (Hit Record)	Raspberries	#18	5:24
1978	So Long	Firefall	#48	5:24
1972	I Had It All the Time	Tyrone Davis	#61	5:23
1973	Gypsy Man	War	#8	5:22
1978	Mary's Boy Child/Oh My Lord	Boney M	#85	5:22
1976	Hot Stuff	The Rolling Stones	#49	5:21
1974	Bennie and the Jets	Elton John	#1	5:20
1975	It Ain't No Fun	Shirley Brown	#94	5:20
1973	Uneasy Rider	Charlie Daniels	#9	5:19
1977	Maybe I'm Amazed	Paul McCartney & Wings	#10	5:19
1976	Breezin'	George Benson	#63	5:18
1974	Earache My Eye (Featuring Alice Bowie)	Cheech & Chong	#9	5:17
1977	Another Star	Stevie Wonder	#32	5:17
1972	Woman Is the Nigger of the World	John Lennon	#57	5:15
1973	I've Got So Much to Give	Barry White	#32	5:15
1978	Cocomotion	El Coco	#44	5:15
1970	Susie-Q	José Feliciano	#84	5:14
1975	Hijack	Herbie Mann	#14	5:13
1973	Space Oddity	David Bowie	#15	5:12
1975	Feel Like Makin' Love	Bad Company	#10	5:12
1979	Boom Boom (Out Go the Lights)	Pat Travers	#56	5:12
1971	Maggie May	Rod Stewart	#1	5:11
1974	W*O*L*D*	Harry Chapin	#36	5:11
1970	Down in the Alley	Ronnie Hawkins	#75	5:10
1972	Honky Cat	Elton John	#8	5:10

	LONG SONGS (cont'd)			
1972	Colorado	Danny Holien	#66	5:10
1973	Palace Guard	Rick Nelson	#65	5:10
1974	Can You Handle It?	Graham Central Station	#49	5:10
1977	Burnin' Sky	Bad Company	#78	5:10
1978	On Broadway	George Benson	#7	5:10
1974	Band on the Run	Paul McCartney & Wings	#1	5:09
1971	Have You Seen Her	Chi-Lites	#3	5:08
1972	Levon	Elton John	#24	5:08
1976	Let 'Em In	Paul McCartney & Wings	#3	5:08
1979	Voulez-Vous	ABBA	#80	5:08
1972	Convention '72	The Delegates	#8	5:07
1972	Let It Rain	Eric Clapton	#48	5:07
1974	It's Only Rock 'N Roll (But I Like It)	The Rolling Stones	#16	5:07
1976	Touch and Go	Ecstasy, Passion & Pain	#98	5:07
1979	Take the Long Way Home	Supertramp	#10	5:07
1973	Doing It to Death	Fred Wesley/The J.B's	#22	5:05
1976	Eh! Cumpari	Gaylord & Holiday	#72	5:04
1973	Also Sprach Zarathustra (2001)	Deodato	#2	5:03
1975	Rockin' and Rollin' on the Streets of Hollywood	Buddy Miles	#91	5:03
1976	Fool to Cry	The Rolling Stones	#10	5:03
1976	Teddy Bear	Red Sovine	#40	5:03
1973	Bell Bottom Blues	Eric Clapton	#78	5:01
1974	Radar Love	Golden Earring	#13	5:01
1972	Dialogue (Part I & II)	Chicago	#24	5:00
1972	Don't Want to Say Goodbye	Raspberries	#86	5:00
1975	Hollywood Hot	The Eleventh Hour	#55	5:00
1975	The Little Drummer Boy	Moonlion	#95	5:00
1977	A Real Mother for Ya	Johnny Guitar Watson	#41	5:00
1978	We Will Rock You/We Are the Champions	Queen	#4	5:00
1978	Straight On	Heart	#15	5:00
1979	Tragedy	Bee Gees	#1	5:00
1979	You've Lost That Lovin' Feelin'	Long John Baldry & Kathi MacDonald	#89	5:00

SONGS WITH FAMOUS BACKUP MUSICIANS

YEAR	SONG	ARTIST	HOT 100	FAMOUS BACKUP MUSICIAN
1970	My Sweet Lord	George Harrison	#1	Billy Preston, Ringo Starr, Badfinger, Eric Clapton
1970	Candida	Dawn (Tony Orlando)	#3	Ellie Greenwich
1970	Fire and Rain	James Taylor	#3	Carole King (piano)
1970	Carolina in My Mind	James Taylor	#67	Carole King (piano)

SONGS WITH FAMOUS BACKUP MUSICIANS (cont'd)

1971	You've Got a Friend	James Taylor	#1	Joni Mitchell
1971	Theme from "Shaft"	Isaac Hayes	#1	Bar-Kays (various instruments)
1971	Knock Three Times	Dawn (Tony Orlando)	#1	Ellie Greenwich
1971	Maggie May	Rod Stewart	#1	Ron Wood (guitar), Pete Sears (of Jefferson Starship)(piano)
1971	It Don't Come Easy	Ringo Starr	#4	Badfinger
1971	So Far Away	Carole King	#14	James Taylor (guitar)
1971	Love the One You're With	Stephen Stills	#14	Rita Coolidge, David Crosby, Graham Nash, John Sebastian
1971	Long Ago and Far Away	James Taylor	#31	Joni Mitchell, Carole King (piano)
1971	Sit Yourself Down	Stephen Stills	#37	Rita Coolidge, David Crosby, Graham Nash, John Sebastian
1971	Marianne	Stephen Stills	#42	Nils Lofgren (of Grin)(guitar), Eric Clapton (guitar)
1971	Pin the Tail on the Donkey	The Newcomers	#74	Bar-Kays (various instruments)
1971	You've Got to Earn It	The Staple Singers	#97	Bar-Kays (backing band)
1972	I Can See Clearly Now	Johnny Nash	#1	Bob Marley's Wailers (backing band)
1972	Without You	Nilsson	#1	Gary Wright (piano)
1972	Heart of Gold	Neil Young	#1	Linda Ronstadt, James Taylor
1972	Bang a Gong (Get It On)	T. Rex	#10	Howard Kaylan & Mark Volman (of The Turtles)
1972	Walkin' in the Rain with the One I Love	Love Unlimited	#14	Barry White
1972	Rock and Roll Lullaby	B.J. Thomas	#15	Duane Eddy (guitar), The Blossoms, Dave Somerville (of the Diamonds)
1972	Spaceman	Nilsson	#23	Peter Frampton (guitar)
1972	All the Young Dudes	Mott the Hoople	#37	David Bowie (guitar and vocals)
1972	In a Broken Dream	Python Lee Jackson	#56	Rod Stewart
1972	That's What Friends Are For	B.J. Thomas	#74	Paul Williams
1972	Rock Me on the Water	Linda Ronstadt	#85	Glenn Frey, Don Henley, Randy Meisner of the Eagles
1972	Deteriorata	National Lampoon	#91	Melissa Manchester
1972	Happier Than the Morning Sun	B.J. Thomas	#100	Stevie Wonder (harmonica), The Blossoms
1973	You're So Vain	Carly Simon	#1	Mick Jagger
1973	Photograph	Ringo Starr	#1	George Harrison (vocals and 12-string guitar)
1973	You Are the Sunshine of My Life	Stevie Wonder	#1	Jim Gilstrap
1973	My Maria	B.W. Stevenson	#9	Larry Carlton (guitar)
1973	Daisy a Day	Jud Strunk	#14	Mike Curb Congregation
1973	You Turn Me on, I'm a Radio	Joni Mitchell	#25	Graham Nash (harmonica)
1973	You Can't Always Get What You Want	The Rolling Stones	#42	Al Kooper (of Blood, Sweat & Tears) (keyboards, French horn)
1973	As Time Goes By	Nilsson	#86	Gordon Jenkins (orchestra)
1974	You're Sixteen	Ringo Starr	#1	Nilsson, Paul McCartney (kazoo)
1974	You Haven't Done Nothin'	Stevie Wonder	#1	The Jackson 5
1974	Don't Let the Sun Go Down on Me	Elton John	#2	Carl Wilson & Bruce Johnston (of The Beach Boys), Toni Tennille (of Captain & Tenille)

SONGS WITH FAMOUS BACKUP MUSICIANS (cont'd)

1974	Jazzman	Carole King	#2	Tom Scott (sax)
1974	The Bitch Is Back	Elton John	#4	Dusty Springfield
1974	Oh My My	Ringo Starr	#5	Martha Reeves, Merry Clayton, Billy Preston (keyboards), Tom Scott (sax)
1974	Clap for the Wolfman	The Guess Who	#6	Wolfman Jack
1974	Daybreak	Nilsson	#39	Ringo Starr (drums), Peter Frampton (guitar), George Harrison (cowbell)
1975	Lucy in the Sky with Diamonds	Elton John	#1	John Lennon (guitar)
1975	You're No Good	Linda Ronstadt	#1	Andrew Gold (guitar)
1975	Bad Blood	Neil Sedaka	#1	Elton John
1975	No No Song	Ringo Starr	#3	Nilsson
1975	How Sweet It Is (To Be Loved By You)	James Taylor	#5	Carly Simon, David Sanborn (sax)
1975	Rockin' Chair	Gwen McCrae	#9	George McCrae
1975	Attitude Dancing	Carly Simon	#21	Carole King
1975	Help Me Rhonda	Johnny Rivers	#22	Brian Wilson of The Beach Boys
1975	It's All Down to Goodnight Vienna	Ringo Starr	#31	John Lennon (piano)
1975	Mexico	James Taylor	#49	David Crosby, Graham Nash
1975	As Long as He Takes Care of Home	Candi Staton	#51	RCR
1975	Anytime (I'll Be There)	Frank Sinatra	#75	RCR
1975	Costafine Town	Splinter	#77	George Harrison (bass guitar)
1975	Waterfall	Carly Simon	#78	James Taylor
1975	Turn to Stone	Joe Walsh	#93	Don Henley, Glenn Frey, Randy Meisner of the Eagles
1976	50 Ways to Leave Your Lover	Paul Simon	#1	Patti Austin, Phoebe Snow, Valerie Simpson
1976	Shower the People	James Taylor	#22	Carly Simon
1976	A Dose of Rock 'N' Roll	Ringo Starr	#26	Melissa Manchester, Peter Frampton (guitar)
1976	Steppin' Out	Neil Sedaka	#36	Elton John
1976	(The System Of) Doctor Tarr and Professor Fether	Alan Parsons Project	#37	John Miles
1976	It Keeps You Runnin'	Carly Simon	#46	The Doobie Brothers
1976	Back to the Island	Leon Russell	#53	The MG's (of Booker T. & The MG's)(backing band)
1977	Lonely Boy	Andrew Gold	#7	Linda Ronstadt
1977	Luckenbach, Texas (Back to the Basics of Love)	Waylon Jennings	#25	Willie Nelson
1977	Runaway	Bonnie Raitt	#57	Michael McDonald
1977	When Love Is New	Arthur Prysock	#64	John Davis & Monster Orchestra (backing band)
1978	Short People	Randy Newman	#2	Glenn Frey, J.D. Souther, Timothy B. Schmit
1978	Emotion	Samantha Sang	#3	Barry Gibb (of The Bee Gees)
1978	It's a Heartache	Bonnie Tyler	#3	Mike Gibbins of Badfinger (drums)
1978	Whenever I Call You "Friend"	Kenny Loggins	#5	Stevie Nicks
1978	Slip Slidin' Away	Paul Simon	#5	Oak Ridge Boys
1978	You Belong to Me	Carly Simon	#6	James Taylor

SONGS WITH FAMOUS BACKUP MUSICIANS (cont'd)

1978	Sentimental Lady	Bob Welch	#8	Christine McVie, Lindsey Buckingham
1978	Peg	Steely Dan	#11	Michael McDonald
1978	King Tut	Steve Martin	#17	The Dirt Band (backing band)
1978	Stuff Like That	Quincy Jones	#21	Ashford & Simpson, Chaka Khan
1978	Werewolves of London	Warren Zevon	#21	Mick Fleetwood (drums), John McVie (bass guitar) of Fleetwood Mac
1978	FM (No Static at All)	Steely Dan	#22	Timothy B. Schmit
1978	Paradise By the Dashboard Light	Meat Loaf	#39	Ellen Foley
1979	My Life	Billy Joel	#3	Peter Cetera
1979	Gold	John Stewart	#5	Stevie Nicks, Lindsey Buckingham (guitar)
1979	Ooh Baby Baby	Linda Ronstadt	#7	David Sanborn (sax)
1979	Please Don't Leave	Lauren Wood	#24	Michael McDonald
1979	Midnight Wind	John Stewart	#28	Stevie Nicks, Lindsey Buckingham (guitar)
1979	Georgy Porgy	Toto	#48	Cheryl Lynn
1979	Four Strong Winds	Neil Young	#61	Nicolette Larson
1979	(Sittin' On) The Dock of the Bay	Sammy Hagar	#65	Brad Delp & Barry Goudreau (of Boston)

SONGS THAT BORROW FROM OTHER CREATIVE WORKS

This section lists songs that sampled or borrowed lyrics or a melody from another work of art. Typically, the work of art was another song, but a few songs borrowed lyrics from a poem or some other source. This practice usually caused no problems. George Harrison, however, was ruled in court to have subconsciously plagiarized the melody from the Chiffons' 1963 hit, "He's So Fine", for "My Sweet Lord."

Songs that borrow from classical pieces of music, like those of Mozart and Beethoven, are listed in the section following this one.

YEAR	SONG	ARTIST	HOT 100 CHART	CREATIVE WORK BORROWED FROM
1970	My Sweet Lord	George Harrison	#1	The Chiffons' "He's So Fine"
1970	Everything Is Beautiful	Ray Stevens	#1	"Jesus Loves the Little Children"
1970	Travelin' Band	Creedence Clearwater Revival	#2	Little Richard's "Good Golly, Miss Molly"
1970	Montego Bay	Bobby Bloom	#8	Bloom sings part of "Oh, What a Beautiful Mornin'" at end
1970	El Condor Pasa	Simon & Garfunkel	#18	Peruvian folk melody from zarzuela composed by Daniel Alomía Robles
1970	The Declaration	The 5th Dimension	#64	Lyrics from the Declaration of Independence
1970	Free the People	Delaney & Bonnie & Friends	#75	Hymn "Rock of Ages"
1970	Cole, Cooke & Redding	Wilson Pickett	#91	Melody from Dion's "Abraham, Martin and John"
1971	Stagger Lee	Tommy Roe	#25	Folk song "Stack-O-Lee"
1972	Mary Had a Little Lamb	Paul McCartney & Wings	#28	Children's nursery rhyme

SONGS THAT BORROW FROM OTHER CREATIVE WORKS (cont'd)

1972	Baby Sitter	Betty Wright	#46	Children's song "Rock-A-Bye-Baby"
1972	The Young New Mexican Puppeteer	Tom Jones	#80	Score of 1940 Disney movie Pinocchio
1972	Simple Song of Freedom	Buckwheat	#84	"The Battle Hymn of the Republic"
1972	Jesus Was a Capricorn	Kris Kristofferson	#91	John Prine's "Grandpa Was a Carpenter"
1972	I Thank You	Donny Hathaway & June Conquest	#94	Uses lyrics from "Amazing Grace"
1973	With a Child's Heart	Michael Jackson	#50	"Ring Around the Rosy"
1974	My Melody of Love	Bobby Vinton	#3	German song by Henry Mayer: "Herzen haben keine Fenster"
1974	Americans	Byron MacGregor	#4	"America the Beautiful"
1974	The Americans (A Canadian's Opinion)	Gordon Sinclair	#24	"The Battle Hymn of the Republic"
1974	Surfin' U.S.A.	The Beach Boys	#36	Chuck Berry's "Sweet Little Sixteen"
1974	My Country	Jud Strunk	#59	Several American patriotic songs
1974	The Americans (A Canadian's Opinion)	Tex Ritter	#90	"America"
1975	#9 Dream	John Lennon	#9	Harry Nilsson's "Many Rivers to Cross"
1975	Don't Call Us, We'll Call You	Sugarloaf	#9	The Beatles' "I Feel Fine"
1975	The Little Drummer Boy	Moonlion	#95	"Jingle Bells", "Good King Wenceslas"
1976	Let 'Em In	Paul McCartney & Wings	#3	"Westminster Quarters"
1976	The Best Disco in Town	The Ritchie Family	#17	Several old pop hits
1976	Amazing Grace (Used to Be Her Favorite Song)	Amazing Rhythm Aces	#72	"Amazing Grace"
1976	Jukin'	Atlanta Rhythm Section	#82	"San Antonio Rose"
1976	Nursery Rhymes (Part 1)	People's Choice	#93	Several nursery rhymes
1976	Love Lifted Me	Kenny Rogers	#97	Hymn "Love Lifted Me"
1977	My Way	Elvis Presley	#18	French song "Comme d'Habitude"
1977	Dreamboat Annie	Heart	#42	Intro from "Crazy on You"
1977	Open Sesame – Part 1	Kool & The Gang	#55	Children's song known by several names: "The Streets of Cairo", "The Snake Charmer Song"
1977	Platinum Heroes	Bruce Foster	#63	Several musical "tributes" to the Beatles songs can be heard in this song.
1977	C.B. Savage	Rod Hart	#67	Children's songs played in background on barred instruments
1978	King Tut	Steve Martin and The Toot Uncommons	#17	Children's song known by several names: "The Streets of Cairo", "The Snake Charmer Song"
1978	Boats Against the Current	Eric Carmen	#88	"Row, Row, Row Your Boat"
1979	Do You Think I'm Disco?	Steve Dahl	#58	Parody of Rod Stewart's "Do You"
1979	The Topical Song	The Barron Knights	#70	Parody of Supertramp's "Logical Song"

SONGS THAT BORROW FROM CLASSICAL WORKS

A song will be listed below even if it only used a short snippet of a classical work. None of the names in the chart below should surprise, except perhaps, for Fučik's. You might not know his name, but you know his music. His melody from "Entrance of the Gladiators" was used in pop songs three times in the 70s, and is still instantly recognizable by almost everyone.

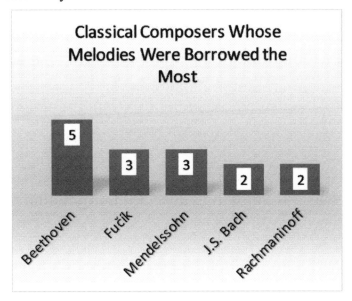

YEAR	SONG	ARTIST	HOT 100 CHART	CLASSIC WORK BORROWED FROM
1970	A Song of Joy (Himno a La Alegria)	Miguel Ríos	#14	Beethoven's Ninth Symphony
1970	When We Get Married	The Intruders	#45	Mendelssohn's "Wedding March"
1970	Whiter Shade of Pale	R.B. Greaves	#82	Bach's cantata "Sleepers Awake"
1970	Theme Music for the Film "2001" A Space Odyssey from "Also Sprach Zarathustra"	Berlin Philharmonic	#90	Strauss' "Also Sprach Zarathustra"
1971	When There's No You	Engelbert Humperdinck	#45	Leoncavallo's opera "Pagliacci"
1971	Mozart Symphony No. 40 in G Minor K.550, 1st Movement	Waldo de los Rios	#67	Mozart's 40th Symphony
1972	Joy	Apollo 100	#6	J.S. Bach's "Jesu, Joy of Man's Desiring"
1972	Nutrocker	Emerson, Lake & Palmer	#2	Tchaikovsky's "The Nutcracker Suite"
1972	Do the Funky Penguin (Part 1)	Rufus Thomas	#44	Mendelssohn's "Wedding March"
1972	Mendelssohn's 4th (Second Movement)	Apollo 100	#94	Mendelssohn's 4th symphony
1973	Also Sprach Zarathustra (2001)	Deodato	#2	Strauss' "Also Sprach Zarathustra"
1973	Rhapsody in Blue	Deodato	#41	Gershwin's work by same name
1973	Roll Over Beethoven	Electric Light Orchestra	#42	Beethoven's "Symphony #5"
1974	The Show Must Go On	Three Dog Night	#4	Fučik's "Entrance of the Gladiators"
1974	Sideshow	Blue Magic	#8	Fučik's "Entrance of the Gladiators"

SONGS THAT BORROW FROM CLASSICAL WORKS (cont'd)				
1974	American Tune	Paul Simon	#35	Hassler's "Mein G'müt ist mir verwirret,"
1975	Wildfire	Michael Murphey	#3	Scriabin's Prelude in D-flat, Opus 11 No. 15
1975	Could It Be Magic?	Barry Manilow	#6	Chopin's "Prelude in C Minor"
1975	I Believe in Father Christmas	Greg Lake	#95	Prokofiev's "Troika"
1976	A Fifth of Beethoven	Walter Murphy	#1	Beethoven's "Symphony #5"
1976	All By Myself	Eric Carmen	#2	Rachmaninoff's "Piano Concerto No. 2"
1976	Never Gonna Fall in Love Again	Eric Carmen	#11	Rachmaninoff's "Symphony #2" (3rd movement)
1976	It Should Have Been Me	Yvonne Fair	#85	Richard Wagner's opera "Lohengrin"
1977	I Caught Your Act	The Hues Corporation	#92	Fučík's "Entrance of the Gladiators"
1977	For Elise	The Philharmonics	#100	Beethoven's "Für Elise"

SONGS WITH FALSE ENDINGS

These are the songs that you think are over… but then they just keep going. Usually, these songs will just come to a sudden halt, only to continue a couple seconds later.

YEAR	SONG	ARTIST	HOT 100
1970	In the Summertime	Mungo Jerry	#3
1970	No Matter What	Badfinger	#8
1970	God, Love and Rock & Roll	Teegarden & Van Winkle	#22
1970	The Seeker	The Who	#44
1970	Country Preacher	Cannonball Adderley	#86
1971	Do You Know What I Mean	Lee Michaels	#6
1971	Whole Lotta Love	C.C.S.	#58
1971	Reason to Believe	Rod Stewart	#62
1971	We're All Goin' Home	Bobby Bloom	#93
1972	You're Still a Young Man	Tower of Power	#29
1972	I Love You More Than You'll Ever Know	Donny Hathaway	#60
1972	If We Only Have Love	Dionne Warwick	#84
1973	Only in Your Heart	America	#62
1974	I Can Help	Billy Swan	#1
1974	I've Got the Music in Me	The Kiki Dee Band	#12
1974	Overnight Sensation (Hit Record)	Raspberries	#18
1974	Travelin' Prayer	Billy Joel	#77
1974	Love Is the Message	MFSB/Three Degrees	#85
1975	The Rockford Files	Mike Post	#10
1975	Disco Queen	Hot Chocolate	#28

SONGS WITH FALSE ENDINGS (cont'd)			
1976	Let 'Em In	Paul McCartney & Wings	#3
1976	Make Me Smile (Come Up and See Me)	Steve Harley	#96
1978	Hot Love, Cold World	Bob Welch	#31
1978	Think It Over	Cheryl Ladd	#34
1978	I Believe You	Carpenters	#68
1978	Get Back	Billy Preston	#86
1979	Young Blood	Rickie Lee Jones	#40

SONGS WITH SOUND EFFECTS

YEAR	SONG	ARTIST	HOT 100	SOUND EFFECT
1970	In the Summertime	Mungo Jerry	#3	Motorcycle
1970	Rubber Duckie	Ernie (Jim Henson)	#16	Rubber Duck
1970	Grover Henson Feels Forgotten	Bill Cosby	#70	Rain
1970	Funky Chicken (Part 1)	Willie Henderson w/The Soul Explosions	#91	Chicken noises
1970	Monster Mash	Bobby (Boris) Pickett	#91	Laboratory noises
1970	Animal Zoo	Spirit	#97	Car horns
1971	Uncle Albert/Admiral Halsey	Paul & Linda McCartney	#1	Multiple
1971	What the World Needs Now Is Love/Abraham, Martin and John	Tom Clay	#8	Multiple
1971	Riders on the Storm	The Doors	#14	Thunderstorm
1971	I Play and Sing	Dawn	#25	Applause
1971	D.O.A.	Bloodrick	#36	Police siren
1971	Gotta See Jane	R. Dean Taylor	#67	Car noises
1971	Celia of the Seals	Donovan	#84	Animal noises
1972	In the Rain	Dramatics	#5	Thunderstorm
1972	School's Out	Alice Cooper	#7	School Bell
1972	Starting All Over Again	Mel and Tim	#19	Doorbell
1972	The Coldest Days of My Life (Part 1)	The Chi-Lites	#47	Seashore sounds
1972	I Had It All the Time	Tyrone Davis	#61	Airport, Telephone
1972	He's an Indian Cowboy in the Rodeo	Buffy Sainte-Marie	#98	Indian pow-wow
1973	Money	Pink Floyd	#13	Cash register
1973	Summer (The First Time)	Bobby Goldsboro	#21	Birds
1973	Keep on Singing	Austin Roberts	#50	Cheering crowd
1973	Gotta Find a Way	Moments	#68	Airport sounds
1974	The Streak	Ray Stevens	#1	Radio Interview
1974	Earache My Eye	Cheech & Chong (Featuring Alice Bowie)	#9	Buzzer, record scratch
1974	Wishing You Were Here	Chicago	#11	Ocean tide
1974	Train of Thought	Cher	#27	Train

SONGS WITH SOUND EFFECTS (cont'd)

1974	Tell Laura I Love Her	Johnny T. Angel	#94	Car race
1975	Lovin' You	Minnie Riperton	#1	Birds
1975	Fire	Ohio Players	#1	Siren
1975	Express	B.T. Express	#4	Train
1975	Don't Call Us, We'll Call You	Sugarloaf	#9	Phone sounds
1975	Doctor's Orders	Carol Douglas	#11	Phone call
1975	Bungle in the Jungle	Jethro Tull	#12	Animal noises
1975	Autobahn	Kraftwerk	#25	Cars
1975	Lizzie and the Rainman	Tanya Tucker	#37	Rain
1975	Alvin Stone (The Birth & Death of a Gangster)	Fantastic Four	#74	Gunfight
1976	Disco Duck (Part 1)	Rick Dees	#1	Duck noises
1976	Without Your Love (Mr. Jordan)	Charlie Ross	#42	Telephone
1976	Back to the Island	Leon Russell	#53	Animals
1976	Kentucky Moonrunner	Cledus Maggard	#85	Police siren
1976	The Fonz Song	The Heyettes	#91	Motorcycle
1976	We're on the Right Track	South Shore Commission	#94	Train
1976	Grasshopper	Spin	#95	Insects
1977	Star Wars Theme/Cantina Band	Meco	#1	Various Star Wars sound effects
1977	Telephone Man	Meri Wilson	#18	Telephone ring
1977	(Remember the Days of The) Old Schoolyard	Cat Stevens	#33	Kids playing
1977	In the Mood	Henhouse Five Plus Too (Ray Stevens)	#40	Chickens
1977	Bodyheat (Part 1)	James Brown	#88	Police siren
1978	5.7.0.5.	City Boy	#27	Dial tone
1978	Chattanooga Choo Choo	Tuxedo Junction	#32	Train
1978	Paradise by the Dashboard Light	Meat Loaf	#39	Baseball announcer
1978	Bloat on Featuring the Bloaters	Cheech & Chong	#41	Lots of burping
1978	Was Dog a Doughnut	Cat Stevens	#70	Dog bark
1978	Sgt. Pepper's Lonely Hearts Club Band/With a Little Help From My Friends	The Beatles	#70	Live audience sounds
1978	The Loneliest Man on the Moon	David Castle	#89	Wind
1979	Bicycle Race	Queen	#24	Bicycle bell
1979	Children of the Sun	Billy Thorpe	#41	Space ship sounds
1979	The Topical Song	The Barron Knights	#70	Car sounds

SONGS WITH MISTAKES

I stayed away from including songs where the error is simply someone coughing while they were recording, and other similar mistakes. I find the mistakes listed below far more interesting than those types of errors. What's interesting about War and the Police's entry on this list is that both mistakes occurred mere seconds into the recording. They could have easily stopped the tape and started over.

YEAR	SONG	ARTIST	HOT 100	MISTAKE
1974	Sweet Home Alabama	Lynyrd Skynyrd	#8	Lead singer tells sound engineer to "Turn it up" at the beginning. Also sounds like he talks about doughnuts around the 4:10 mark of the song.
1975	Why Can't We Be Friends?	War	#6	Just seconds in, the keyboardist flubs the intro.
1978	Just What I Needed	The Cars	#27	Drummer gets kick and snare drum mixed up on third verse.
1979	Roxanne	Police	#32	In first 10 seconds, Sting accidently bumps the piano, then laughs.

HITS WITH NO MUSIC AT ALL

These "songs" must be the rarest of all pop hits. They have no music at all. No singing or instruments. It's hard to imagine anything like this getting radio play today.

YEAR	SONG	ARTIST	HOT 100
1971	Ajax Liquor Store	Hudson & Landry	#43
1972	Ajax Airlines	Hudson & Landry	#68

SONGS WITH FOREIGN LANGUAGES

A song will be listed here even if it only has one word in a foreign language.

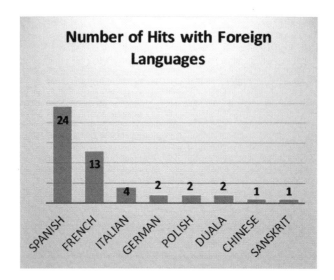

YEAR	SONG	ARTIST	HOT 100	LANGUAGE
1978	Bloat on Featuring the Bloaters	Cheech & Chong	#41	Chinese
1973	Soul Makossa	Manu Dibango	#35	Duala
1973	Soul Makossa	Afrique	#47	Duala
1970	Look What They've Done to My Song Ma	The New Seekers	#14	French
1970	A Song of Joy (Himno a la Elegria)	Miguel Ríos	#14	French
1970	Je T'Aime…Moi Non Plus	Jane Birkin & Serge Gainsbourg	#58	French
1972	Look What They've Done to My Song, Ma	Ray Charles	#65	French
1973	Soul Je T'Aime	Sylvia & Ralfi Pagan	#99	French
1975	Lady Marmalade	LaBelle	#1	French
1977	Whispering/Cherchez La Femme/Se Si Bon	Dr. Buzzard's Original Savannah Band	#27	French
1977	C'est La Vie	Greg Lake	#91	French
1977	My Cherie Amour	Soul Train Gang	#92	French
1978	Took the Last Train	David Gates	#30	French
1978	Ca Plane Pour Moi	Plastic Bertrand	#47	French
1978	Le Spank	Le Pamplemousse	#58	French
1978	Psycho Killer	Talking Heads	#92	French
1974	Christmas Dream	Perry Como	#92	German
1975	Autobahn	Kraftwerk	#25	German
1973	Vado Via	Drupi	#88	Italian
1975	To the Door of the Sun (Alle Porte Del Sole)	Al Martino	#17	Italian
1975	Volare	Al Martino	#33	Italian

	SONGS WITH FOREIGN LANGUAGES (cont'd)			
1976	Eh! Cumpari	Gaylord & Holiday	#72	Italian
1974	My Melody of Love	Bobby Vinton	#3	Polish
1975	Wooden Heart	Bobby Vinton	#58	Polish
1970	My Sweet Lord	George Harrison	#1	Sanskrit
1970	Spill the Wine*	Eric Burdon & War	#3	Spanish
	*Spoken by woman in the background			
1970	A Song of Joy (Himno a la Elegria)	Miguel Ríos	#14	Spanish
1970	Que Sera, Sera (Whatever Will Be, Will Be)	Mary Hopkin	#77	Spanish
1971	Oye Como Va	Santana	#13	Spanish
1972	Suavecito	Malo	#18	Spanish
1972	Brown Eyed Girl	El Chicano	#45	Spanish
1972	The Mosquito	The Doors	#85	Spanish
1972	Vaya con Dios	Dawn featuring Tony Orlando	#95	Spanish
1973	The Cisco Kid	War	#2	Spanish
1973	Corazon	Carole King	#37	Spanish
1974	Eres Tu (Touch the Wind)	Mocedades	#9	Spanish
1974	Don't You Worry 'Bout a Thing	Stevie Wonder	#16	Spanish
1974	Ballero	War	#33	Spanish
1975	Secret Love	Freddy Fender	#20	Spanish
1975	El Bimbo	Bimbo Jet	#43	Spanish
1975	Por Amor Viviremos	The Captain & Tennille	#49	Spanish
1975	Chico and the Man	José Feliciano	#96	Spanish
1976	Paloma Blanca	George Baker Selection	#26	Spanish
1976	Vaya Con Dios	Freddy Fender	#59	Spanish
1976	Living It Down	Freddy Fender	#72	Spanish
1976	You're Just the Right Size	Salsoul Orchestra	#88	Spanish
1977	Freddie	Charlene	#96	Spanish
1978	Manana	Jimmy Buffett	#84	Spanish
1979	Cuba	Gibson Brothers	#81	Spanish

ARTISTS WITH STRANGE NAMES

The Beginning of the End	Joy of Cooking
Bumble Bee Unlimited	Magic Lanterns
Chocolate Milk	Meat Loaf
Commander Cody and His Lost Planet Airmen	Mighty Clouds of Joy
Con Funk Shun	Peppermint Trolley Company
Continental Miniatures	Uncle Dog
Elephant's Memory	Universal Robot Band

ARTISTS FROM FOREIGN COUNTRIES

Artists are listed according to their birth place, not where they lived or grew up. For example, Brian Auger is listed as being from India, where he was born, instead of being from England, where he grew up.

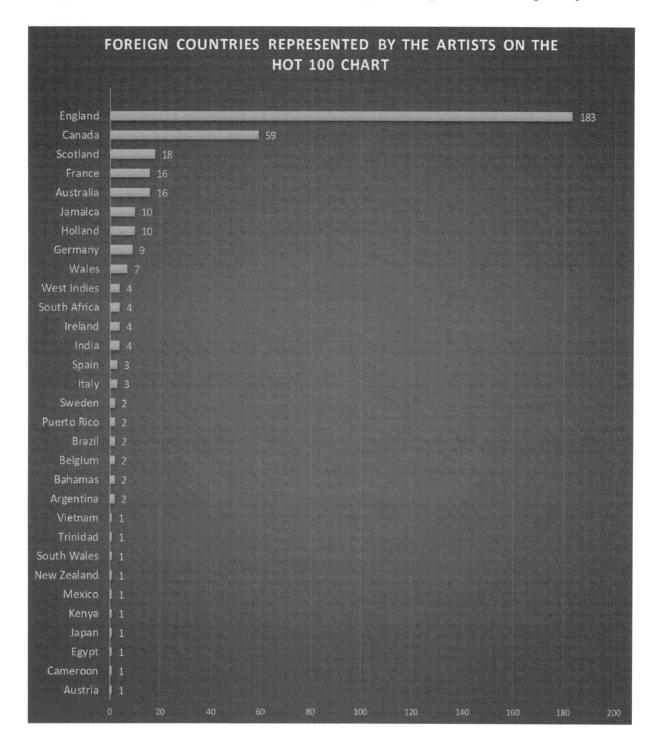

ARTISTS FROM ENGLAND

Ace	Fleetwood Mac	Robert Palmer
America	The Flying Machine	Paper Lace
Apollo 100	Foghat	Graham Parker
Argent	Fox	Alan Parsons Project
Ashton, Gardner & Dyke	Peter Frampton	The Philarmonics
Audience	Free	Pickettywitch
The Babys	Peter Gabriel	Pink Floyd
Bad Company	Genesis	The Pipkins
Ginger Baker's Air Force	Andy Gibb	The Police
Long John Baldry	Steve Gibbons Band	Cozy Powell
Bandit	Nick Gilder	Prelude
The Barron Knights	Gary Glitter	Procol Harum
The Beatles	Ian Gomm	Brian Protheroe
Bee Gees	Gonzalez	Queen
Jane Birkin (of Jane Birkin & Serge Gainsbourg)	The Goodies	Rainbow
Black Sabbath	Albert Hammond	John Dawson Read
Blue Haze	Keith Hampshire	The Real Thing
Blue Mink	Steve Harley and Cockney Rebel	The Records
Daniel Boone	George Harrison	Michael Redway
David Bowie	Murray Head	The Rolling Stones
Bram Tchaikovsky	Chris Hodge	Roxy Music
British Lions	The Hollies	The Rubettes
The Brotherhood of Man	Clint Holmes	Sad Café
Polly Brown	Rupert Holmes	Savoy Brown
The Buggles	Hot Chocolate	Leo Sayer
Eric Burdon (of Eric Burdon and War)	Hotlegs	The Searchers
Tony Burrows	Humble Pie	Peter Shelley
Bullet	Joe Jackson	Peter Skellern
Kate Bush	Mick Jackson	Slade
Jim Capaldi	Mick Jagger	Faces
C.C.S.	Jethro Tull	Hurricane Smith
Charlie	Jigsaw	Smokie
Chicory	Elton John	Sniff 'N' The Tears
Christie	Davy Jones	Splinter
City Boy	King Crimson	Dusty Springfield
Eric Clapton	The Kinks	Ringo Starr
Petula Clark	Kevin Lamb	Cat Stevens

ARTISTS FROM ENGLAND (cont'd)		
Climax Blues Band	Led Zeppelin	Rod Stewart
Cochise	John Lennon	Lally Stott
Joe Cocker	Lindisfarne	Supertramp
Tony Cole	Liquid Gold	Sutherland Brothers and Quiver
Crawler	Nick Lowe	Sweet
Tim Curry	M	Sweet Dreams
Roger Daltrey	Magic Lanterns	Sweet Sensation
Kiki Dee	Mark-Almond	10cc
Deep Purple	Marshal Hain	Ten Years After
Delegation	Dave Mason	Billy Thorpe
Dire Straits	Ian Matthews	Traffic
David Dundas	Paul McCartney/Wings	T. Rex
Easy Street	McGuinness Flint	Robin Trower
Edison Lighthouse	John Miles	Uncle Dog
Electric Light Orchestra	Mr. Big	Uriah Heep
Emerson, Lake & Palmer	The Moody Blues	Vanity Fare
The English Congregation	Mott The Hoople	Vigrass & Osborne
David Essex	Mungo Jerry	Johnny Wakelin & The Kinshasa Band
Fabulous Poodles	Graham Nash	White Plains
Fancy	Nektar	The Who
Don Fardon	Paul Nicholas	Jack Wild
Bryan Ferry	Maxine Nightingale	Pete Wingfield
First Class	Mike Oldfield	The Wombles
5000 Volts	Nigel Olsson	Yes
Flash		

ARTISTS FROM CANADA

Bill Amesbury	Dan Hill	Rush
Paul Anka	The Incredible Bongo Band	Buffy Sainte-Marie
April Wine	Johnny T. Angel	Gordon Sinclair
Bachman-Turner Overdrive	France Joli	Skylark
The Band of the Black Watch	Kenny Karen	Gino Soccio
The Bells	Andy Kim	Southcote
Terry Black	Klaatu	Stampeders
Chilliwack	Gordon Lightfoot	Stonebolt
Cooper Brothers	Lighthouse	Sweeney Todd
Burton Cummings	Byron MacGregor	Dean R. Taylor
Daybreak	Mashmakhan	Ian Thomas

ARTISTS FROM CANADA (cont'd)		
DeFranco Family featuring Tony DeFranco	Frank Mills	Billy Thunderkloud & The Chieftones
Doucette	Joni Mitchell	Pat Travers
Edward Bear	Anne Murray	Trooper
Maynard Ferguson	Olivia Newton-John	Gino Vannelli
Five Man Electrical Band	Painter	The Wackers
The Disco Sound of Andre Gagnon	The Poppy Family	Wednesday
Gary & Dave	Pousette-Dart Band	Neil Young
Carl Graves	Prism	Zwol
The Guess Who		

ARTISTS FROM SCOTLAND

AWB (Average White Band)	The Headboys	Gerry Rafferty
Bay City Rollers	Lulu	Royal Scots Dragoon Guards
Maggie Bell	The Marmalade	Stealers Wheel
Blue	Frankie Miller	Al Stewart
Donovan	Nazareth	John Paul Young
Gallagher and Lyle	Pilot	Lena Zavaroni

ARTISTS FROM AUSTRALIA

AC/DC	The Mixtures	The Sports
Lana Cantrell	Python Lee Jackson	Rick Springfield
Flash and The Pan	Helen Reddy	The Tarney/Spencer Band
Kevin Johnson	Samantha Sang	Tin Tin
Little River Band	Sherbs	T.M.G.
Sister Janet Mead		

ARTISTS FROM FRANCE

Banzaii	Danyel Gerard	The Peppers
Belle Opoque	Patrick Hernandez	Michel Polnareff
Bimbo Jet	Kongas	Space
Serge Gainsbourg (of Jane Birkin & Serge Gainsbourg)	Francis Lai and His Orchestra	Today's People
Cerrone	Michel LeGrand	Voyage
The Champs' Boys Orchestra		

ARTISTS FROM OTHER COUNTRIES

The New Seekers weren't put under any one country, as they had members from England and Sri Lanka. Likewise, Ozo had members from Hungary, Jamaica, Guyana, Sierra Leone, and Nigeria.

Argentina	Waldo de los Rios	Italy	Carlo Savina
Argentina	Silvetti	Jamaica	Claudja Barry
Austria	Penny McLean	Jamaica	Jimmy Cliff
Bahamas	The Beginning of the End	Jamaica	Dave & Ansil Collins
Bahamas	T-Connection	Jamaica	Carl Douglas
Belgium	Plastic Bertrand	Jamaica	Eruption
Belgium	The Chakachas	Jamaica	Jimmy James & The Vagabonds
Brazil	Morris Albert	Jamaica	Grace Jones
Brazil	Deodato	Jamaica	Bob Marley & The Wailers
Cameroon	Manu Dibango	Jamaica	Third World
Egypt	Demis Roussos	Jamaica	Peter Tosh
Germany	Heatwave	Japan	Pink Lady
Germany	Michael Holm	Kenya	Roger Whittaker
Germany	Mike Kennedy	Mexico	Santana
Germany	Kraftwerk	New Zealand	John Rowles
Germany	Lake	Puerto Rico	Celi Bee & The Buzzy Bunch
Germany	James Last	Puerto Rico	José Feliciano
Germany	The Rattles	South Africa	Clout
Germany	Don Ray	South Africa	The Flame
Germany	Silver Convention	South Africa	John Kongos
Holland	George Baker Selection	South Africa	Manfred Mann
Holland	Herman Brood	South Wales	Tom Jones
Holland	Champagne	Spain	Los Pop Tops
Holland	Focus	Spain	Mocedades
Holland	Golden Earring	Spain	Miguel Ríos
Holland	Kayak	Sweden	ABBA
Holland	Mouth & MacNeal	Sweden	Blue Swede
Holland	The Shocking Blue	Trinidad	Mac and Katie Kissoon
Holland	Spin	Vietnam	Richard Cocciante
Holland	The Tee Set	Wales	Airwaves
India	Cliff Richard	Wales	Badfinger
India	Brian Auger & The Trinity	Wales	Shirley Bassey
India	Biddu Orchestra	Wales	Dave Edmunds
India	Engelbert Humperdinck	Wales	Mary Hopkin
Ireland	Richard Harris	Wales	The Raes
Ireland	Van Morrison	Wales	Bonnie Tyler

ARTISTS FROM OTHER COUNTRIES (cont'd)			
Ireland	Gilbert O'Sullivan		West Indies	Boney M
Ireland	Thin Lizzy		West Indies	Cymande
Italy	Drupi		West Indies	Gibson Brothers
Italy	Giorgio Moroder		West Indies	Billy Ocean

ARTISTS WHO USED A STAGE NAME

STAGE NAME	REAL NAME		STAGE NAME	REAL NAME
Miss Abrams	Rita Abrams		Manfred Mann	Michael Lubowitz
"Cannonball" Adderley	Julian Edwin Adderley		Barry Manilow	Barry Pincus
Morris Albert	Morris Albert Kaisermann		Barry Mann	Barry Iberman
Bill Anderson	James William Anderson III		Herbie Mann	Herbert Solomon
Bobby Arvon	Robert Arvonio		Bobby Martin	Barbara Martin
Frankie Avalon	Francis Avallone		Moon Martin	John Martin
Razzy Bailey	Rasie Michael Bailey		Al Martino	Alfred Cini
George Baker Selection	Johannes Bouwens		Mac McAnally	Lyman McAnally
Ginger Baker's Air Force	Peter Baker		C.W. McCall	William Fries
Benny Bell	Benjamin Samberg		Paul McCartney	James McCartney
Vincent Bell	Vincent Gambella		Shamus M'Cool	Richard Doyle
William Bell	William Yarbrough		Meat Loaf	Marvin Aday
Brook Benton	Benjamin Peay		Meco	Domenico Monardo
Chuck Berry	Charles Berry		Melanie	Malanie Safka
Plastic Bertrand	Roger Jouret		Buddy Miles	George Miles
David Blue	Stuart David Cohen		Jody Miller	Myrna Brooks
Taka Boom	Yvonne Stevens		Joni Mitchell	Roberta Anderson
Daniel Boone	Peter Lee Stirling		Eddie Money	Edward Mahoney
David Bowie	David Robert Jones		Melba Moore	Melba Hill
Brown Sugar	Clydie King		Van Morrison	George Ivan
Peabo Bryson	Robert Bryson		Mouth & MacNeal	Willem Duyn and Maggie MacNeal
J.J. Cole	Jean Jacques Cale		Idris Muhammad	Leo Morris
Captain & Tennille	Daryl Dragon, Toni Tennille		Maria Muldaur	Maria D'Amato
Vikki Carr	Florencia Martinez Cardona		Anne Murray	Morna Murray
Cazz	Robert Lewis		Napoleon XIV	Jerry Samuels
Cerrone	Jean-Marc Cerrone		Ricky Nelson	Eric Nelson
Gene Chandler	Eugene Dixon		Peter Nero	Bernard Nierow
Charlene	Charlene D'Angelo		Mickey Newbury	Milton Newbury
Ray Charles	Ray Robinson		Juice Newton	Judy Newton
Ray Charles Singers	Charles Offenberg		Paul Nicholas	Paul Beuselinck
Cheech & Chong	Richard Marin, Thomas Chong		Nilsson	Harry Nelson

ARTISTS WHO USED A STAGE NAME (cont'd)

Chee-Chee & Peppy	Keith "Chee-Chee" Bolling, Dorothy "Peppy" Moore	Laura Nyro	Laura Nigro
Cher	Cherilyn Sarkisian	Billy Ocean	Leslie Charles
Desmond Child	John Barrett Jr.	Oliver	William Swofford
Lou Christie	Lugee Sacco	Tony Orlando	Michael Cassavitis
Eric Clapton	Eric Clapp	Marie Osmond	Olive Osmond
Tom Clay	Thomas Clague	Gilbert O'Sullivan	Raymond O'Sullivan
Merry Clayton	Mary Clayton	Robert Palmer	Alan Palmer
Jimmy Cliff	James Chambers	Billy Paul	Paul Williams
Joe Cocker	John Cocker	Johnny Paycheck	Donald Lytle
Natalie Cole	Stephanie Cole	Peaches & Herb	Francine Hurd & Herb Fame
Dave & Ansil Collins	Dave Barker and Ansil Collins	Esther Phillips	Esther Jones
Jessi Colter	Mirriam Johnson	Cozy Powell	Colin Powell
Perry Como	Pierino Como	Prince	Prince Nelson
Alice Cooper	Vincent Furnier	Jeanne Pruett	Norma Bowman
Cory	Cory Braverman	Eddie Rabbitt	Edward Rabbitt
Bill Cosby	William Cosby, Jr.	Jerry Reed	Jerry Hubbard
Daddy Dewdrop	Richard Monda	Lou Reed	Lewis Reed
Bobby Darin	Walden Cassotto	Cliff Richard	Harry Webb
James Darren	James Ercolani	Jeannie C. Riley	Jeanne Stephenson
Kiki Dee	Pauline Matthews	Tex Ritter	Maurice Ritter
Rick Dees	Rigdon Dees	Johnny Rivers	John Ramistella
Delaney & Bonnie	Delaney Bramlett, Bonnie Bramlett	Marty Robbins	Martin Robinson
John Denver	Henry Deutschendorf	Lea Roberts	Leatha Hicks
Deodato	Eumir Deodato	Smokey Robinson	William Robinson
Rick Derringer	Richard Zehringer	Johnny Rodriguez	Juan Rodriguez
Jackie DeShannon	Sharon Myers	D.J. Rogers	DeWayne Rogers
Dion	Dion DiMucci	Roy Rogers	Leonard Slye
Dr. John	Malcolm Rebennack	Diana Ross	Diane Ross
Donovan	Donovan Leitch	Brenda Russell	Brenda Gordon
Carol Douglas	Carol Strickland	Leon Russell	Claude Bridges
Drupi	Giampiero Anelli	Sami Jo	Sami Cole
Doris Duke	Doris Curry	Santana	Carlos Santana
Bob Dylan	Robert Zimmerman	Leo Sayer	Gerard Sayer
England Dan	Dan Seals	Boz Scaggs	William Scaggs
David Essex	David Cook	Peter Shelley	Peter Southworth
Don Fardon	Donald Maughn	Jean Shepard	Ollie Shepard
Narvel Felts	Albert Felts	T.G. Sheppard	William Browder
Crystal Gayle	Brenda Webb	Bunny Sigler	Walter Sigler
Gloria Gaynor	Gloria Fowles	Silvetti	Bebu Silvetti
Bobbie Gentry	Roberta Streeter	Nina Simone	Eunice Waymon

ARTISTS WHO USED A STAGE NAME (cont'd)

Daniel Gerard	Gerard Kherlakian	Frank Sinatra	Francis Sinatra
Andy Gibb	Andrew Gibb	Bro Smith	Alan Smith
Gary Glitter	Paul Gadd	Cal Smith	Calvin Shofner
Dickie Goodman	Richard Goodman	Hurricane Smith	Norman Smith
Dobie Gray	Lawrence Brown	O.C. Smith	Ocie Smith
R.B. Greaves	Ronald Greaves	Sammi Smith	Jewel Smith
Steve Harley	Steven Nice	David Soul	David Solberg
Freddie Hart	Fred Segrest	Joe South	Joe Souter
Joey Heatherton	Johanna Heatherton	J.D. Souther	John Souther
Michael Holm	Lothar Walter	Southside Johnny	John Lyon
Cissy Houston	Emily Houston	Red Sovine	Woodrow Sovine
Engelbert Humperdinck	Arnold Dorsey	Billie Jo Spears	Billie Jean Spears
Willie Hutch	Willie Hutchinson	Dusty Springfield	Mary O'Brien
Ian Janis	Janis Fink	Rick Springfield	Richard Springthorpe
Mick Jagger	Michael Jagger	Edwin Starr	Charles Hatcher
Etta James	Jamesetta Hawkins	Kenny Starr	Kenneth Trebbe
Rick James	James Johnson	Ringo Starr	Richard Starkey
Sonny James	James Loden	Candi Staton	Canzata Staton
Tommy James	Thomas Jackson	Cat Stevens	Steven Georgiou
Jefferson	Geoff Turton	Ray Stevens	Harold Ragsdale
Billy Joel	William Joel	B.W. Stevenson	Louis Stevenson
Elton John	Reginald Dwight	Rod Stewart	Roderick Stewart
Robert John	Robert Pedrick	Barbra Streisand	Barbra Streisand
Grace Jones	Grace Mendoza	Jud Strunk	Justin Strunk
Tamiko Jones	Barbara Ferguson	Donna Summer	LaDonna Gaines
Tom Jones	Thomas Woodward	Glenn Sutton	Royce Sutton
Julie	Julie Budd	Bettye Swann	Betty Champion
Casey Kelly	Daniel Cohen	Sylvester	Sylvester James
Mike Kennedy	Michael Kogel	Sylvia	Sylvia Vanderpool
Chaka Khan	Yvette Stevens	Little Johnny Taylor	Johnny Merrett
Andy Kim	Androwis Jovakim	Teegarden & Van Winkle	David Teegarden & Skip Knape
Albert King	Albert Nelson	Tammi Terrell	Thomasina Montgomery
B.B. King	Riley King	Joe Tex	Joseph Arrington Jr.
Ben E. King	Benjamin Nelson	B.J. Thomas	Billy Joe Thomas
Carole King	Carole Klein	Peter Tosh	Winston MacIntosh
King Curtis	Curtis Ousley	Tina Turner	Anna Bullock
Patti LaBelle	Patricia Holt	Conway Twitty	Harold Jenkins
Cheryl Ladd	Cheryl Stoppelmoor	Bonnie Tyler	Gaynor Hopkins
Denise LaSalle	Denise Craig	John Valenti	John LaVigni
Latimore	Benjamin Latimore	Frankie Valli	Francis Castellucio

ARTISTS WHO USED A STAGE NAME (cont'd)			
LaVerne & Shirley	Penny Marshall & Cindy Williams	Randy VanWarmer	Randall Van Wormer
Steve Lawrence	Sidney Leibowitz	Bobby Vee	Robert Velline
Eloise Laws	LaVern Laws	Bobby Vinton	Stanley Vinton
Otis Leavill	Otis Cobb	Narada Michael Walden	Michael Walden
Brenda Lee	Brenda Tarpley	Jerry Jeff Walker	Ronald Crosby
Dickey Lee	Dickey Lipscomb	Jr. Walker	Autry Walker
Laura Lee	Laura Rundless	Dionne Warwick	Marie Warwick
Little Milton	James Campbell	Dottie West	Dorothy Marsh
Little Richard	Richard Penniman	Andy Williams	Howard Williams
Lobo	Roland Lovoie	Anson Williams	Anson Heimlick
Lulu	Marie Laurie	Deniece Williams	Deniece Chandler
Loretta Lynn	Loretta Webb	Stevie Wonder	Steveland Morris
M	Robin Scott	O.V. Wright	Overton Wright
Byron MacGregor	Gary Mack	Tammy Wynette	Virginia Pugh
Cledus Maggard	Jay Huguely	Zwol	Walter Zwol
Mama Cass	Ellen Cohen		

1970s ARTISTS WHO ARE RELATED TO OTHER HOT 100 ARTISTS

1970s ARTIST	RELATIVE(S) WHO ALSO APPEARED ON THE HOT 100 CHART
AC/DC	Included bothers Angus & Malcolm Young
"Cannonball" Adderley	Brother Nat Adderley played cornet in his band
Steve Alaimo	Cousin of Jimmy Alaimo ("The Mojo Men")
Alive & Kicking	Organist Bruce Sudano married Donna Summer
The Allman Brothers Band	Included brothers Duane & Gregg Allman
Ashford & Simpson	Consisted of husband and wife: Nickolas Ashford & Valerie Simpson
Bachman-Turner Overdrive	Included brothers Randy & Robbie Bachman; Randy is Tal Bachman's father.
The Beach Boys	Included brothers Brian, Carl, and Dennis Wilson, and their cousin Mike Love.
Beckmeier Brothers	Brothers Freddie & Stevie Beckmeier
Bee Gees	Three brothers Barry, Maurice, and Robin Gibb; Their youngest brother Andy Gibb had ten hits. Maurice married Lulu.
The Beginning of the End	Included brothers Ray, Roy, & Frank Munnings
Bellamy Brothers	Brothers Howard & David Bellamy
Jack Blanchard & Misty Morgan	Husband and wife
Blue	Included brothers Hugh & David Nicholson
Blue Öyster Cult	Included brothers Joe & Albert Bouchard
Debby Boone	Daughter of Pat Boone
The Boys in the Band	Herman Griffin married Mary Wells
The Brecker Brothers	Brothers Randy & Michael Brecker
Brooklyn Dreams	Keyboardist Bruce Sudano married Donna Summer

1970s ARTISTS WHO ARE RELATED TO OTHER HOT 100 ARTISTS (cont'd)

The Brothers Johnson	Brothers George & Louis Johnson
B.T. Express	Included brothers Louis & Bill Risbrook
Jerry Butler	Brother of Billy Butler
Jonathan Cain	Married Tané Cain
Captain & Tennille	Husband and wife duo: Daryl Dragon & Toni Tennille
Carpenters	Brother and sister duo: Richard & Karen Carpenter
Clarence Carter	Married Candi Staton
Johnny Cash	Married June Carter, father of Rosanne Cash, step-father of Carlene Carter, and brother of Tommy Cash
Tommy Cash	Brother of Johnny Cash
David Cassidy	Half-brother of Shaun Cassidy
Shaun Cassidy	Half-brother of David Cassidy
Cate Bros.	Twin brothers Ernie & Earl Cate
The Chamber Brothers	Included brothers Willie, Joe, Lester, and George Chambers
Cher	Married Sonny Bono & Greg Allman
Eugene Record	Married Barbara Acklin
Christie	Mike Blakely brother of Alan Blakely (The Tremeloes)
Natalie Cole	Daughter of Nat "King" Cole
Jessi Colter	Married Duane Eddy & Waylon Jennings
Cooper Brothers	Included brothers Richard & Brian Cooper
Cornelius Brothers & Sister Rose	Family group: Edward, Carter, and Rose Cornelius
Creedence Clearwater Revival	Included brothers John & Tom Fogerty
Cherie & Marie Currie	Identical twins
DeFranco Family featuring Tony DeFranco	Family group: Tony, Merlina, Nino, Marisa, & Benny DeFranco
Delaney & Bonnie	Husband and wife duo: Delaney & Bonnie Bramlett
The Delfonics	Included brothers William & Wilbert Hart
Jackie DeShannon	Married Randy Edelman
Detroit Emeralds	Included brothers Abrim, Ivory, Cleophus, and Raymond Tilmon
Dire Straits	Included brothers Mark & David Knopfler
Dr. Buzzard's Original Savannah Band	Included brothers Stony & Thomas Browder
Carol Douglas	Cousin of Sam Cooke
Bob Dylan	Son Jakob Dylan (The Wallflowers)
Earth, Wind & Fire	Included brothers Maurice & Verdine White
Randy Edelman	Married Jackie DeShannon
The Emotions	Consisted of sisters Wanda, Shaila, and Jeanette Hutchinson
Eruption	Included brothers Gregory & Morgan Petrineau
Facts of Life	Jean Davis sister of Tyrone Davis
Yvonne Fair	Married to Sammy Strain (The O'Jays)
Fanny	Included sisters June & Jean Millington; Patti Quatro sister of Suzi Quatro
Fantastic Four	Included brothers Robert & Joseph Pruitt
The Faragher Bros.	Consisted of brothers Danny, Jimmy, Tommy, Davey, Marty, and Pammy Faragher

1970s ARTISTS WHO ARE RELATED TO OTHER HOT 100 ARTISTS (cont'd)	
The 5th Dimension	Marilyn McCoo married Billy Davis, Jr.
Five Man Electrical Band	Included brothers Rick & Mike Belanger
Five Special	Bryan Banks is brother of Ron Banks (The Dramatics)
The Five Stairsteps	Family group: Clarence, Jr., James, Kenneth, Dennis, Alohe, and Cubie Burke
The Flame	Included brothers Rikki, Steve, & Brother Fataar
The Flamingos	Included cousins Zeke & Jake Carey
Flash and the Pan	George Young is brother of Angus & Malcolm Young (AC/DC)
The Floaters	Included brothers Paul & Ralph Mitchell
Aretha Franklin	Sister of Erma Franklin
The Free Movement	Included brothers Adrian & Claude Jefferson
Marvin Gaye	Father of Nona Gaye
Crystal Gayle	Sister of Loretta Lynn
Bobbie Gentry	Married Jim Stafford
Andy Gibb	Brother of Barry, Robin, & Maurice Gibb (Bee Gees)
Gibson Brothers	Consisted of brothers Chris, Patrick, & Alex Gibson
Mickey Gilley	Cousin of Jerry Lee Lewis
The Glass House	Scherrie Payne is sister of Freda Payne
Louise Goffin	Daughter of Carole King
Eydie Gormé	Married Steve Lawrence
R.B. Greaves	Nephew of Sam Cooke
Heart	Included sisters Ann & Nancy Wilson, and brothers Roger & Mike Fisher; Ann & Nancy are sisters of Karl Wilson (Merrilee Rush and The Turnabouts)
Heatwave	Included brothers Johnnie & Keith Wilder
High Inergy	Included sisters Vernessa & Barbara Mitchell
The Hillside Singers	Bill & Joelle Marino are siblings; Mary Mayo is Lori Ham's mother; Rick & Ron Shaw are brothers
The Honey Cone	Edna Wright is sister of Darlene Love
Cissy Houston	Mother of Whitney Houston
Hudson Brothers	Consisted of brothers Bill, Brett, & Mark Hudson
The Impressions	Included brothers Arthur & Richard Brooks
Instant Funk	Included brothers Kim & Scotty Miller
Ironhorse	Randy Bachman is father of Tal Bachman
The Isley Brothers	Consisted of brothers O'Kelly, Ronald, & Rudolph Isley; Ronald married Angela Winbush
Jermaine Jackson	Brother of LaToya, Michael, Rebbie, & Janet Jackson
Michael Jackson	Brother of Latoya, Jermaine, Rebbie, & Janet Jackson
The Jackson 5	Consisted of brothers & sisters Michael, Jermaine, Marlon, Tito, Jackie, Rebbie, Latoya, & Janet Jackson; Sisters were backup singers; Not all were part of the group at the same time.
Waylon Jennings	Married Jessi Colter
Syl Johnson	Father of Syleena Johnson
Jo Jo Gunne	Included brothers Matthew & Mark Andes
The Jones Girls	Consisted of sisters Shirley, Brenda, and Valorie Jones
The Keane Brothers	Tom & John Keane

1970s ARTISTS WHO ARE RELATED TO OTHER HOT 100 ARTISTS (cont'd)

The Kendalls	Father-and-daughter duo: Royce & Jeannie Kendall
Chaka Khan	Sister of Taka Boom, mother of Milini Khan
The Kimberlys	Consisted of brothers Harold & Carl Kimberly and their spouses, sisters Verna & Vera Kimberly
Carole King	Mother of Louise Goffin
The Kinks	Included brothers Ray & Dave Davies
Mac and Katie Kissoon	Brother & sister duo
Gladys Knight & The Pips	Family groups consisting of siblings Gladys, Merald, & Brenda Knight, and cousins Williams & Eleanor Guest
Kool & The Gang	Included brothers Robert & Ronald Bell
Kris Kristofferson	Married Rita Coolidge
Steve Lawrence	Married Eydie Gorme
Vicki Lawrence	Married Bobby Russell
Eloise Laws	Sister of Debra Laws & Ronnie Laws
John Lennon	Father of Julian Lennon; married Yoko Ono
Jerry Lee Lewis	Cousin of Mickey Gilley
Limmie & Family Cookin'	Brother & sister group: Martha Stewart, Jimmy Thomas, & Limmie Snell
Liner	Included brothers Tom & Dave Farmer
Dave Loggins	Cousin of Kenny Loggins
Kenny Loggins	Cousin of Dave Loggins
The Lost Generation	Included brothers Lowrell & Fred Simon
The Lovelites	Included sisters Patti Hamilton & Ronzena Petty
Love Unlimited	Included sisters Glodean & Linda James; Glodean married Barry White
Nick Lowe	Married Carlene Carter
L.T.D.	Included brothers Jeffrey & Billy Osborne
Lulu	Married Maurice Gibb (Bee Gees)
Loretta Lynn	Sister of Crystal Gayle; cousin of Patty Loveless
Lynyrd Skynyrd	Included brother & sister Steve and Cassie Gaines
Malo	Jorge Santana is brother of Carlos Santana
Mama Cass	Sister of Leah Kunkel (The Coyote Sisters)
The Mamas & The Papas	John & Michelle Phillips were married; their daughter is Chynna Phillips (Wilson Phillips)
Henry Mancini	Married Ginny O'Connor (Mel Torme's Mel-Tones)
The Marshall Tucker Band	Included brothers Toy & Tommy Caldwell
Wings	Paul McCartney was married to Linda Eastman McCartney
Marilyn McCoo & Billy Davis, Jr.	Husband-and-wife duo
George McCrae	Married Gwen McCrae
Gwen McCrae	Married George McCrae
The McCrarys	Sibling group: Linda, Charity, Alfred, & Sam McCrary
Kristy & Jimmy McNichol	Brother-and-sister duo
Mel and Tim	Consisted of cousins Mel Hardin & Tim McPherson
The Meters	Arthur Neville is brother of Aaron Neville
Stephanie Mills	Married Jeffrey Daniels

1970s ARTISTS WHO ARE RELATED TO OTHER HOT 100 ARTISTS (cont'd)

The Miracles	Bobby Rogers married Wanda Young (The Marvelettes)
Mocedades	Included siblings Amaya, Izaskum, & Roberto Amezaga
Mother's Finest	Included married couple Glenn Murdoch & Joyce Kennedy
Ricky Nelson	Father of Gunnar & Matthew Nelson (Nelson)
The New Colony Six	Included Craig & Walter Kemp
Randy Newman	Nephew of Lionel Newman
NRBQ	Included brothers Terry & Donn Adams; Joey Spampinato married Skeeter Davis
Odyssey	Included sisters Lillian & Louise Lopez
100 Proof Aged in Soul	Joe Stubbs is brother of Levi Stubbs (Four Tops)
Donny Osmond	Member of the family group, The Osmonds; brother of Marie Osmond & Little Jimmy Osmond
Parliament/Funkadelic	Included brothers Phelps & William Collins
The Partridge Family	Included David Cassidy and his stepmother Shirley Jones
Christopher and Shawn Paul	Brother-and-sister duo; niece & nephew of Bob Engemann (The Lettermen)
Freda Payne	Sister of Scherrie Payne (The Supremes); married Gregory Abbott
The Peppermint Trolley Company	Included brothers Danny & Jimmy Faragher
Bonnie Pointer	Sister of Ruth, Anita, & June Pointer (Pointer Sisters)
Ponderosa Twins + One	Included two sets of twins: Alvin & Alfred Pelham, Keith & Kirk Gardner
The Poppy Family	Included married couple Susan & Terry Jacks
Prelude	Included married couple Irene & Brian Hume
Suzi Quatro	Sister of Patti Quatro (Fanny)
Quicksilver Messenger Service	John Cipollina was brother of Mario Cipollina (Huey Lewis & The News)
The Raes	Consisted of husband-and-wife duo Robbie & Cherrill Rae
Redbone	Included brothers Lolly & Pat Vegas
Smokey Robinson	Married Claudette Rogers (The Miracles)
The Ronettes	Consisted of Ronnie Spector, her sister Estelle Vann, & her cousin Nedra Ross
The Rowans	Consisted of brothers Peter, Lorin, & Chris Rowan
David Ruffin	Brother of Jimmy Ruffin
Jimmy Ruffin	Brother of David Ruffin
Merrilee Rush & The Turnabouts	Included brother & sister Merrilee & Neil Rush; Karl Wilson is brother of Ann & Nancy Wilson (Heart)
Carole Bayer Sager	Married Burt Bacharach
Seals & Crofts	Seals is brother of "England" Dan Seals, cousin of Troy Seals (Jo Ann & Troy) and Brady Seals (Little Texas)
Jean Shepard	Married Hawkshaw Hawkins
Shoes	Included brothers Jeff & John Murphy
Carly Simon	Sister of Lucy Simon (The Simon Sisters); married James Taylor
Paul Simon	Married Edie Brickell
Frank Sinatra	Father of Nancy Sinatra
Sister Sledge	Consisted of sisters Debra, Joni, Kim, & Kathy Sledge
Percy Sledge	Cousin of Jimmy Hughes

1970s ARTISTS WHO ARE RELATED TO OTHER HOT 100 ARTISTS (cont'd)

Sly & The Family Stone	Included Sylvester Stewart & brother Freddie Stone, sister Rosie Stone, & cousin Larry Graham
Rex Smith	Brother of Michael Smith (Starz)
Sonny & Cher	Husband-and-wife duo: Sonny Bono & Cher
Sounds of Sunshine	Consisted of brothers Walt, Warner, & George Wilder
Dusty Springfield	Sister of Tom Springfield (The Springfields)
Jim Stafford	Married Bobbie Gentry
The Staple Singers	Consisted of Roebuck Staples & son Pervis, & daughters Cleotha, Yvonne, & Mavis Staples
Starland Vocal Band	Included Bill and wife Taffy Danoff; John Carroll also married Margot Chapman
Starz	Michael Smith is brother of Rex Smith
The Statler Brothers	Included brothers Harold & Don Reid
Candi Staton	Married Clarence Carter
John Stewart	Brother of Mike Stewart (We Five)
Styx	Included brothers John & Chuck Panozzo
Donna Summer	Married Bruce Sudano (Alive and Kicking, Brooklyn Dreams)
Supertramp	Dougie Thomson is brother of Ali Thomson
The Supremes	Scherrie Payne is sister of Freda Payne
Sutherland Brothers and Quiver	Included brothers Iain & Gavin Sutherland
Glenn Sutton	Married Lynn Anderson
Switch	Included brothers Bobby & Tommy DeBarge; DeBarges are brothers to family group DeBarge
The Sylvers	Family group of nine brothers & sisters
Sylvia	Mother of Joey Robinson (West Street Mob)
Tavares	Consisted of brothers Ralph, Antone, Feliciano, Arthur, & Perry Tavares
James Taylor	Married Carly Simon, brother of Kate Taylor
Kate Taylor	Sister of James & Livingston Taylor
Livingston Taylor	Brother of James & Kate Taylor
T-Connection	Included brothers Theo & Kirk Coakley
Nino Tempo & April Stevens	Brother & sister duo
The Temptations	David Ruffin was cousin of Billy Stewart
Ian Thomas	Brother of Dave Thomas (Doug McKenzie)
Rufus Thomas	Father of Carla Thomas
The Tokens	Included brothers Phil & Mitch Margo
Toto	Joseph Williams is song of John Williams
The Trammps	Included brothers Harold & Stanley Wade
Joey Travolta	Brother of John Travolta
John Travolta	Brother of Joey Travolta
Ike & Tina Turner	Husband-and-wife duo
Van Halen	Included brothers Eddie & Alex Van Halen
Village People	Ray Simpson is brother of Valerie Simpson (Ashford & Simpson)
Wadsworth Mansion	Included brothers Steve & Mike Jablecki
Dee Dee Warwick	Sister of Dionne Warwick, cousin of Whitney Houston, niece of Cissy Houston

1970s ARTISTS WHO ARE RELATED TO OTHER HOT 100 ARTISTS (cont'd)	
Dionne Warwick	Sister of Dee Dee Warwick, cousin of Whitney Houston, niece of Cissy Houston
Wet Willie	Included brothers Jack & Jimmy Hall
Whirlwind	Family trio of brothers Charles & Eddie Ancrum and their sister Sandie Ancrum
The Whispers	Included brothers Walter & Wallace Scott
Andy Williams	Married Claudine Longet, uncle of Andrew & David Williams (The Williams Brothers)
John Williams	Father of Joseph Williams (Toto)
The Williams Brothers	Andrew & David Williams are nephews of Andy Williams
Jackie Wilson	Cousin of Hubert Johnson (The Contours)
Wilson Bros.	Consisted of brothers Steve & Kelly Wilson
Edgar Winter	Brother of Johnny Winter
Johnny Winter	Brother of Edgar Winter
Stevie Wonder	Married Syreeta Wright
Tammy Wynette	Married George Jones
Frank Zappa	Father of Dweezil & Moon Unit Zappa (Peace Choir)

ARTISTS WITH POSTHUMOUS HITS

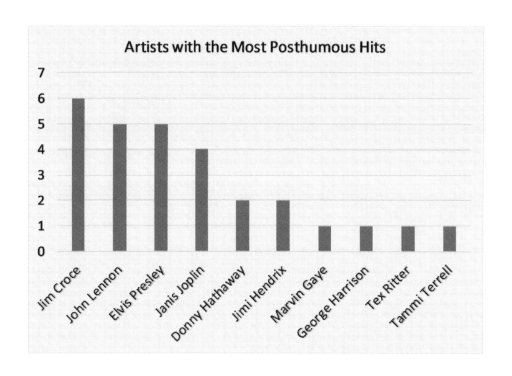

ARTISTS WITH THE MOST HITS ONLY IN THE 1970s

The artists in this chart didn't have a single hit in any other decade.

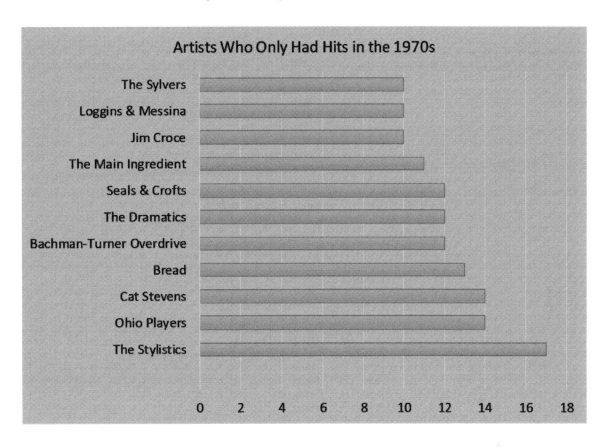

HONORABLE MENTION

These artists all had at least one hit in another decade.

ARTIST	60s HITS	70s HITS	80s HITS
Al Green	1	18	1
Eddie Kendricks		14	1
Gordon Lightfoot		10	1
Lobo		15	1
Harold Melvin and The Blue Notes	1	11	
Helen Reddy		20	1
Todd Rundgren		10	1
Ringo Starr		13	1

ARTISTS WHO SKIPPED THE 1970s

ARTIST	50s HITS	60s HITS	70s HITS	80s HITS	90s HITS	2000s HITS	2010s HITS
Louis Armstrong	3	4	0	1	1	0	0
The Animals	0	18	0	1	0	0	0
Gary (U.S.) Bonds	0	8	0	3	0	0	0
Chubby Checker	1	30	0	2	0	0	0
Nat "King" Cole	37	19	0	0	1	0	0
The Contours	0	8	0	1	0	0	0
Duane Eddy	10	17	0	1	0	0	0
The Everly Brothers	14	22	0	1	0	0	0
Sergio Mendes & Brasil '66	0	10	0	4	0	0	0
Roy Orbison	1	27	0	2	0	0	0
Billy Vera	0	3	0	3	0	0	0
Jeff Beck	0	1	0	1	0	1	0
The Five Satins	3	3	0	1	0	0	0
George Jones	2	3	0	0	0	1	1
Aaron Neville	0	2	0	1	6	0	0
Del Shannon	0	16	0	1	0	0	0
Belmonts	0	6	0	1	0	0	0
Sonny Charles	0	3	0	1	0	0	0
The Irish Rovers	0	3	0	1	0	0	0
Bill Medley	0	3	0	3	0	0	0
Mitch Ryder and The Detroit Wheels	0	11	0	1	0	0	0
Hank Williams Jr.	0	2	0	0	0	1	0

ARTISTS WHOSE HITS EACH CHARTED LOWER THAN THEIR PREVIOUS HITS

This section is kind of a downer. Each artist on this chart had a nice start, with either a #1 or a #3 hit, but things went south from there. Every single hit for Shaun Cassidy and The Knack peaked lower than their previous hit. Lynn Anderson's 2nd and 3rd hit both charted at #63, then they all went down. Must have been pretty depressing.

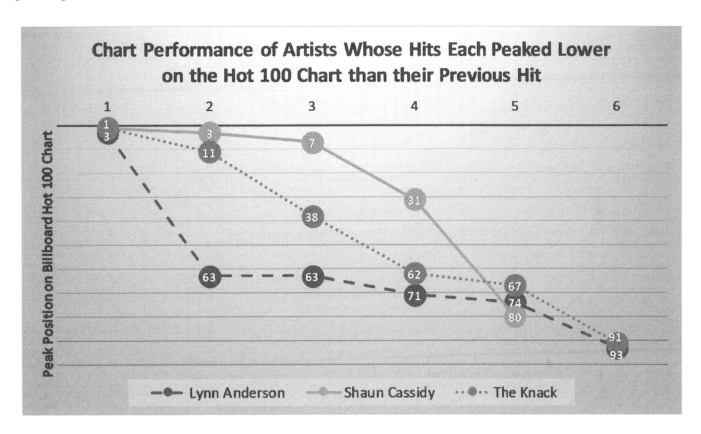

THE BEST DISCO SONGS OF THE 1970s

YEAR	SONG	ARTIST	HOT 100
1974	Jungle Boogie	Kool & The Gang	#4
1975	Who Loves You	Four Seasons	#3
1975	Get Dancin'	Disco Tex & His Sex-O-Lettes	#10
1975	Doctor's Orders	Carol Douglas	#11
1975	Forever Came Today	The Jackson 5	#60
1976	Love Hangover	Diana Ross	#1
1976	(Shake, Shake, Shake) Shake Your Booty	KC and The Sunshine Band	#1
1976	A Fifth of Beethoven	Walter Murphy	#1

	THE BEST DISCO SONGS OF THE 1970s (cont'd)		
1976	You Should Be Dancing	Bee Gees	#1
1976	Get Up and Boogie (That's Right)	Silver Convention	#2
1976	I Can't Hear You More	Helen Reddy	#29
1976	Flight '76	Walter Murphy	#44
1977	Keep It Comin' Love	KC and The Sunshine Band	#2
1977	Boogie Nights	Heatwave	#2
1977	I Feel Love	Donna Summer	#6
1977	Disco Inferno	The Trammps	#53
1977	Daddy Cool	Boney M	#65
1977	Welcome to Our World (Of Merry Music)	Mass Production	#68
1978	Night Fever	Bee Gees	#1
1978	Le Freak	Chic	#1
1978	Stayin' Alive	Bee Gees	#1
1978	Take a Chance on Me	ABBA	#3
1978	I Can't Stand the Rain	Eruption	#17
1978	Let's All Chant	Michael Zager Band	#36
1978	Supernature	Cerrone	#70
1978	Miss Broadway	Belle Epoque	#92
1979	I Will Survive	Gloria Gaynor	#1
1979	Tragedy	Bee Gees	#1
1979	Good Times	Chic	#1
1979	Heart of Glass	Blondie	#1
1979	Knock on Wood	Amii Stewart	#1
1979	Don't Stop 'til You Get Enough	Michael Jackson	#1
1979	Shake Your Groove Thing	Peaches & Herb	#5
1979	Boogie Wonderland	Earth, Wind & Fire/The Emotions	#6
1979	I Want Your Love	Chic	#7
1979	September	Earth, Wind & Fire	#8
1979	Hot Number	Foxy	#21
1979	At Midnight	T-Connection	#56
1979	Voulez-Vous	ABBA	#80

THE BEST INSTRUMENTAL SONGS OF THE 1970s

YEAR	SONG	ARTIST	HOT 100
1972	Mr. Penguin - Pt. 1	Lunar Funk	#63
1973	Dueling Banjos	Eric Weissberg & Steve Mandell	#2
1973	Also Sprach Zarathustra (2001)	Deodato	#2

	THE BEST INSTRUMENTAL SONGS OF THE 1970s (cont'd)		
1973	Bongo Rock	The Incredible Bongo Band	#57
1974	The Entertainer	Marvin Hamlisch	#3
1974	Tubular Bells	Mike Oldfield	#7
1974	Machine Gun	The Commodores	#22
1974	Jessica	Allman Brothers Band	#65
1975	Pick Up the Pieces	Average White Band	#1
1975	Main Title (Theme from "Jaws")	John Williams	#32
1975	Sexy	MFSB	#42
1975	Honey Trippin'	The Mystic Moods	#98
1976	A Fifth of Beethoven	Walter Murphy	#1
1976	The Homecoming	Hagood Hardy	#41
1976	Flight '76	Walter Murphy	#44
1976	My Sweet Summer Suite	The Love Unlimited Orchestra	#48
1976	Scotch on the Rocks	Band of the Black Watch	#75
1976	Peter Gunn	Deodato	#84
1977	Star Wars Theme/Cantina Band	Meco	#1
1977	Gonna Fly Now	Bill Conti	#1
1977	Star Wars Theme (Main Title)	John Williams	#10
1978	Let's All Chant	Michael Zager Band	#36
1979	Rise	Herb Alpert	#1
1979	Music Box Dancer	Frank Mills	#3
1979	Morning Dance	Spyro Gyra	#24
1979	Peter Piper	Frank Mills	#48

SONGS THAT DESERVED TO MAKE THE TOP 40

These are very good songs that I feel deserved a better fate on the charts. I'm not necessarily saying they are the best songs of the decade, just that they should've made the top 40. If you see a song you don't recognize or remember, go check it out! There are some great songs here, that generally don't get any airplay anymore.

YEAR	SONG	ARTIST	HOT 100
1970	Soul Shake	Delaney & Bonnie & Friends	#43
1970	Mighty Joe	Shocking Blue	#43
1970	Part Time Love	Ann Peebles	#45
1970	Chains and Things	B.B. King	#45
1970	We're All Playing in the Same Band	Bert Sommer	#48
1970	Mongoose	Elephant's Memory	#50
1970	On the Beach (In the Summertime)	The 5th Dimension	#54
1970	Rag Mama Rag	The Band	#56

	SONGS THAT DESERVED TO MAKE THE TOP 40 (cont'd)		
1970	Paranoid	Black Sabbath	#61
1970	Add Some Music to Your Day	The Beach Boys	#64
1970	Living Loving Maid (She's Just a Woman)	Led Zeppelin	#65
1970	If Walls Could Talk	Little Milton	#71
1970	I Like Your Lovin' (Do You Like Mine)	The Chi-Lites	#72
1970	Morning Much Better	Ten Wheel Drive	#74
1970	Them Changes	Buddy Miles	#81
1970	Lucifer	Bob Seger System	#84
1970	Dear Ann	George Baker Selection	#93
1970	Tobacco Road	Jamul	#93
1971	Pushbike Song	The Mixtures	#44
1971	When I'm Dead and Gone	McGuinness Flint	#47
1971	I'm a Believer	Neil Diamond	#51
1971	He Called Me Baby	Candi Staton	#52
1971	Angel Baby	Dusk	#57
1971	Don't Make Me Pay for Your Mistakes	Z.Z. Hill	#62
1971	Funky Music Sho Nuff Turns Me On	Edwin Starr	#64
1971	Rub It In	Layng Martine	#65
1971	Can You Get to That	Funkadelic	#93
1971	Banks of the Ohio	Olivia Newton-John	#94
1971	Love's Made a Fool of You	Cochise	#96
1971	I Been Moved	Andy Kim	#97
1971	Be Good to Me Baby	Luther Ingram	#97
1971	My Heart Is Yours	Wilbert Harrison	#98
1972	Tiny Dancer	Elton John	#41
1972	Lies	J.J. Cale	#42
1972	Chantilly Lace	Jerry Lee Lewis	#43
1972	Rock and Roll	Led Zeppelin	#47
1972	Heartbroken Bopper	The Guess Who	#47
1972	Iron Man	Black Sabbath	#52
1972	Way Back Home	Jr. Walker/The All Stars	#52
1972	Put It Where You Want It	The Crusaders	#52
1972	A Simple Man	Lobo	#56
1972	That's What Love Will Make You Do	Little Milton	#59
1972	Wedding Song (There Is Love)	Petula Clark	#61
1972	Guess Who	B.B. King	#61
1972	Cheer	Potliquor	#65
1972	Jubilation	Paul Anka	#65
1972	Jambalaya (On the Bayou)	Nitty Gritty Dirt Band	#84
1972	Hey, You Love	Mouth & MacNeal	#87
1972	Down By the River	Albert Hammond	#91

SONGS THAT DESERVED TO MAKE THE TOP 40 (cont'd)

1972	I Got a Thing About You Baby	Billy Lee Riley	#93
1972	Do Ya	The Move	#93
1972	Redwood Tree	Van Morrison	#98
1973	Drinking Wine Spo-Dee O'Dee	Jerry Lee Lewis	#41
1973	I Found Sunshine	The Chi-Lites	#47
1973	The Free Electric Band	Albert Hammond	#48
1973	Over the Hills and Far Away	Led Zeppelin	#51
1973	Dream On	Aerosmith	#59
1973	Finder's Keepers	Chairman of the Board	#59
1973	First Cut Is the Deepest	Keith Hampshire	#70
1973	Avenging Annie	Andy Pratt	#78
1973	Sail on Sailor	The Beach Boys	#79
1973	Am I Black Enough for You	Billy Paul	#79
1973	California Saga (On My Way to Sunny Californ-i-a)	The Beach Boys	#84
1973	Delta Queen	Don Fardon	#86
1973	I'm Sorry	Joey Heatherton	#87
1973	Sunshine	Mickey Newbury	#87
1973	Farewell Andromeda (Welcome to My Morning)	John Denver	#89
1973	He	Today's People	#90
1973	Stop, Wait & Listen	Circus	#91
1973	The Long Way Home	Neil Diamond	#91
1974	La Grange	ZZ Top	#41
1974	Can You Handle It?	Graham Central Station	#49
1974	Live It Up (Part 1)	Earth, Wind & Fire	#52
1974	Eyes of Silver	The Doobie Brothers	#52
1974	Old Home Filler-Up An' Keep On-A-Truckin' Café	C.W. McCall	#54
1974	Between Her Goodbye and My Hello	Gladys Knight & The Pips	#57
1974	Jolene	Dolly Parton	#60
1974	Jessica	Allman Brothers Band	#65
1974	Most Likely You Go Your Way (And I'll Go Mine)	Bob Dylan/The Band	#66
1974	Honey Honey	Sweet Dreams	#68
1974	Goin' Down Slow	Bobby Blue Bland	#69
1974	Beyond the Blue Horizon	Lou Christie	#80
1974	Get Out of Denver	Bob Seger	#80
1974	(Everybody Wanna Get Rich) Rite Away	Dr. John	#92
1975	Sexy	MFSB	#42
1975	Katmandu	Bob Seger	#43
1975	I Dreamed Last Night	Justin Hayward & John Lodge	#47
1975	Can't Give You Anything (But My Love)	The Stylistics	#51
1975	I Fought the Law	Sam Neely	#54
1975	Long Haired Country Boy	Charlie Daniels Band	#56

	SONGS THAT DESERVED TO MAKE THE TOP 40 (cont'd)		
1975	If I Could Only Win Your Love	Emmylou Harris	#58
1975	Forever Came Today	The Jackson 5	#60
1975	Love Is a Rose	Linda Ronstadt	#63
1975	(All I Have to Do Is) Dream	Nitty Gritty Dirt Band	#66
1975	Never Been Any Reason	Head East	#68
1975	Mamacita	The Grass Roots	#71
1975	Alvin Stone (The Birth & Death of a Gangster)	Fantastic Four	#74
1975	Blanket on the Ground	Billie Jo Spears	#78
1975	Leftovers	Millie Jackson	#87
1975	Shoes	Reparata	#92
1975	I'll Go to My Grave Loving You	The Statler Brothers	#93
1976	Falling Apart at the Seams	Marmalade	#49
1976	Ob-La-Di, Ob-La-Da	The Beatles	#49
1976	Free Ride	Tavares	#52
1976	Gotta Be the One	Maxine Nightingale	#53
1976	Back to the Island	Leon Russell	#53
1976	Ten Percent	Double Exposure	#54
1976	Ode to Billie Joe	Bobbie Gentry	#54
1976	If Not You	Dr. Hook	#55
1976	Honey I	George McCrae	#65
1976	Brand New Love Affair	Jigsaw	#66
1976	Baby, We Better Try to Get It Together	Barry White	#92
1976	Rose of Cimarron	Poco	#94
1977	Someone to Lay Down Beside Me	Linda Ronstadt	#42
1977	Dreamboat Annie	Heart	#42
1977	Money, Money, Money	ABBA	#56
1977	Daddy Cool	Boney M	#65
1977	Race Among the Runs	Gordon Lightfoot	#65
1977	Solsbury Hill	Peter Gabriel	#68
1977	Needles and Pins	Smokie	#68
1977	Welcome to Our World (Of Merry Music)	Mass Production	#68
1977	My Own Way to Rock	Burton Cummings	#74
1977	Light of a Clear Blue Morning	Dolly Parton	#87
1977	Moondance	Van Morrison	#92
1977	Ma Baker	Boney M	#96
1978	Sweet, Sweet Smile	Carpenters	#44
1978	Time for Me to Fly	REO Speedwagon	#56
1978	Wheel in the Sky	Journey	#57
1978	Substitute	Clout	#67
1978	Lights	Journey	#68
1978	Supernature	Cerrone	#70

	SONGS THAT DESERVED TO MAKE THE TOP 40 (cont'd)		
1978	Sgt. Pepper's Lonely Hearts Club Band/With a Little Help From My Friends	The Beatles	#70
1978	I'm on My Way	Captain & Tennille	#74
1978	(You Got to Walk And) Don't Look Back	Peter Tosh w/Mick Jagger	#81
1978	Anytime	Journey	#83
1978	Mary's Boy Child/Oh My Lord	Boney M	#85
1978	Miss Broadway	Belle Epoque	#92
1979	Good Times Roll	The Cars	#41
1979	It's All I Can Do	The Cars	#41
1979	If You Can't Give Me Love	Suzi Quatro	#45
1979	Slip Away	Ian Lloyd	#50
1979	Groove Me	Fern Kinney	#54
1979	At Midnight	T-Connection	#56
1979	Since You Been Gone	Rainbow	#57
1979	I'm Not Gonna Cry Anymore	Nancy Brooks	#66
1979	High on Your Love Suite	Rick James	#72
1979	Message in a Bottle	The Police	#74
1979	Voulez-Vous	ABBA	#80
1979	Cuba	Gibson Brothers	#81
1979	She's Got a Whole Number	Keith Herman	#87
1979	I Do the Rock	Tim Curry	#91
1979	Since You've Been Gone	Cherie & Marie Currie	#95

THE TOP 100 SONGS OF THE 1970s

Here it is. The best 100 songs of the 1970s. My favorite decade for music is actually the 80s, but I'll tell you what- The songs in this list stack up really well to any 100 songs from any other decade. These songs would make one heck of a playlist.

If you're about to burn this book because "Stairway to Heaven" isn't on this list, relax… Almost unbelievably, it never appeared on the Billboard Hot 100 chart. Therefore, it won't appear on any list in this book. The only appearance of "Stairway to Heaven" on the Billboard Hot 100 chart was Far Corporation's version in 1985.

RANK	YEAR	SONG	ARTIST	HOT 100
#1	1976	Bohemium Rhapsody	Queen	#9
#2	1972	American Pie (Parts 1 & 2)	Don McLean	#1
#3	1977	Hotel California	Eagles	#1
#4	1976	Crazy on You	Heart	#35
#5	1976	More Than a Feeling	Boston	#5
#6	1970	Bridge Over Troubled Waters	Simon & Garfunkel	#1
#7	1974	Already Gone	Eagles	#32

		THE TOP 100 SONGS OF THE 1970s (cont'd)		
#8	1970	The Tears of a Clown	Smokey Robinson & The Miracles	#1
#9	1974	You Haven't Done Nothin	Stevie Wonder	#1
#10	1979	Don't Stop 'til You Get Enough	Michael Jackson	#1
#11	1979	Sultans of Swing	Dire Straits	#4
#12	1972	Rock and Roll	Led Zeppelin	#47
#13	1973	Rocky Mountain High	John Denver	#9
#14	1970	Cecilia	Simon & Garfunkel	#4
#15	1979	What a Fool Believes	The Doobie Brothers	#1
#16	1977	Barracuda	Heart	#11
#17	1978	Roll with the Changes	REO Speedwagon	#58
#18	1974	Waterloo	ABBA	#6
#19	1972	Black Dog	Led Zeppelin	#15
#20	1972	Alone Again (Naturally)	Gilbert O'Sullivan	#1
#21	1975	Lyin' Eyes	The Eagles	#2
#22	1975	Killer Queen	Queen	#12
#23	1977	Peace of Mind	Boston	#38
#24	1976	(Don't Fear) The Reaper	Blue Öyster Cult	#12
#25	1972	Join Together	The Who	#17
#26	1970	ABC	The Jackson 5	#1
#27	1974	You Ain't Seen Nothing Yet	Bachman-Turner Overdrive	#1
#28	1972	I Gotcha	Joe Tex	#2
#29	1978	Take a Chance on Me	ABBA	#3
#30	1974	Sweet Home Alabama	Lynyrd Skynyrd	#8
#31	1976	December, 1963 (Oh, What a Night)	The Four Seasons	#1
#32	1973	Superstition	Stevie Wonder	#1
#33	1974	Piano Man	Billy Joel	#25
#34	1972	Layla	Derek & The Dominos	#10
#35	1975	Trampled Under Foot	Led Zeppelin	#38
#36	1973	D'yer Mak'er	Led Zeppelin	#20
#37	1976	Magic Man	Heart	#9
#38	1970	Let It Be	The Beatles	#1
#39	1974	Takin' Care of Business	Bachman-Turner Overdrive	#12
#40	1970	Instant Karma (We All Shine On)	John Lennon	#3
#41	1975	Sweet Emotion	Aerosmith	#36
#42	1974	Annie's Song	John Denver	#1
#43	1971	Me and Bobby McGee	Janis Joplin	#1
#44	1978	Wonderful Tonight	Eric Clapton	#16
#45	1973	Out of the Question	Gilbert O'Sullivan	#17
#46	1979	Tragedy	Bee Gees	#1
#47	1979	The Logical Song	Supertramp	#6
#48	1971	Imagine	John Lennon	#3

THE TOP 100 SONGS OF THE 1970s (cont'd)

#49	1975	Thank God I'm a Country Boy	John Denver	#1
#50	1977	Margaritaville	Jimmy Buffett	#8
#51	1971	Immigrant Song	Led Zeppelin	#16
#52	1979	Lovin', Touchin', Squeezin'	Journey	#16
#53	1977	(Your Love Has Lifted Me) Higher and Higher	Rita Coolidge	#2
#54	1972	Long Cool Woman (In a Black Dress)	The Hollies	#2
#55	1979	Tusk	Fleetwood Mac	#8
#56	1977	Somebody to Love	Queen	#13
#57	1973	China Grove	The Doobie Brothers	#15
#58	1973	Stuck in the Middle with You	Stealers Wheel	#6
#59	1973	Little Willy	The Sweet	#3
#60	1970	Little Green Bag	George Baker Selection	#21
#61	1979	I Will Survive	Gloria Gaynor	#1
#62	1976	Say You Love Me	Fleetwood Mac	#11
#63	1979	Goodbye Stranger	Supertramp	#15
#64	1975	Black Water	The Doobie Brothers	#1
#65	1977	Dreamboat Annie	Heart	#42
#66	1978	Don't Look Back	Boston	#4
#67	1978	Mary's Boy Child/Oh My Lord	Boney M	#85
#68	1974	Whatever Gets You Thru the Night	John Lennon	#1
#69	1979	Don't Bring Me Down	Electric Light Orchestra	#4
#70	1977	You Make Loving Fun	Fleetwood Mac	#9
#71	1975	Boogie on Reggae Woman	Stevie Wonder	#3
#72	1976	Squeeze Box	The Who	#16
#73	1976	The Wreck of the Edmund Fitzgerald	Gordon Lightfoot	#2
#74	1978	Werewolves of London	Warren Zevon	#21
#75	1977	Go Your Own Way	Fleetwood Mac	#10
#76	1978	My Best Friend's Girl	The Cars	#35
#77	1976	Looking for Space	John Denver	#29
#78	1977	Sir Duke	Stevie Wonder	#1
#79	1979	Renegade	Styx	#16
#80	1977	Long Time	Boston	#22
#81	1973	Live and Let Die	Paul McCartney & Wings	#2
#82	1973	Loves Me Like a Rock	Paul Simon w/The Dixie Hummingbirds	#2
#83	1972	Me and Julio Down by the Schoolyard	Paul Simon	#22
#84	1978	Hollywood Nights	Bob Seger	#12
#85	1970	Superstar	Murray Head w/The Trinidad Singers	#74
#86	1970	In the Summertime	Mungo Jerry	#3
#87	1970	I Want You Back	The Jackson 5	#1
#88	1976	I Do, I Do, I Do, I Do, I Do	ABBA	#15
#89	1970	Venus	The Shocking Blue	#1

		THE TOP 100 SONGS OF THE 1970s (cont'd)		
#90	1978	Fooling Yourself (The Angry Young Man)	Styx	#29
#91	1970	Evil Ways	Santana	#9
#92	1979	Pop Muzik	M	#1
#93	1976	Fox on the Run	Sweet	#5
#94	1978	Sgt. Pepper's Lonely Hearts Club Band/With a Little Help From My Friends	The Beatles	#70
#95	1976	Fernando	ABBA	#13
#96	1973	Over the Hills and Far Away	Led Zeppelin	#51
#97	1977	Maybe I'm Amazed	Paul McCartney & Wings	#10
#98	1970	Lola	The Kinks	#9
#99	1972	Listen to the Music	The Doobie Brothers	#11
#100	1973	Dueling Banjos	Eric Weissberg & Steve Mandell	#2

THE NEXT 138 BEST SONGS OF THE 1970s

These are good songs, but they didn't quite make the top 100. They are listed in alphabetical order.

YEAR	SONG	ARTIST	HOT 100
1970	25 or 6 to 4	Chicago	#4
1976	A Fifth of Beethoven	Walter Murphy	#1
1972	A Horse with No Name	America	#1
1970	After Midnight	Eric Clapton	#18
1973	Am I Black Enough for You	Billy Paul	#79
1970	American Woman	The Guess Who	#1
1979	Angeleyes	ABBA	#64
1979	At Midnight	T-Connection	#56
1978	Baby Hold On	Eddie Money	#11
1974	Band on the Run	Paul McCartney & Wings	#1
1972	Black & White	Three Dog Night	#1
1972	Burning Love	Elvis Presley	#2
1973	"Cherry Cherry" from Hot August Night	Neil Diamond	#31
1979	Cuba	Gibson Brothers	#81
1975	Dance with Me	Orleans	#6
1974	Dancing Machine	The Jackson 5	#2
1977	Dancing Queen	ABBA	#1
1975	Ding Dong; Ding Dong	George Harrison	#36
1979	Does Your Mother Know	ABBA	#19
1976	Don't Go Breaking My Heart	Elton John & Kiki Dee	#1
1974	Don't Let the Sun Go Down on Me	Elton John	#2
1977	Don't Stop	Fleetwood Mac	#3

THE NEXT 138 BEST SONGS OF THE 1970s (cont'd)

1979	Driver's Seat	Sniff 'N' The Tears	#15
1970	El Condor Pasa (If I Could)	Paul Simon	#18
1979	Escape (The Pina Colada Song)	Rupert Holmes	#1
1972	Feeling Alright	Joe Cocker	#33
1973	Finder's Keepers	Chairman of the Board	#59
1978	Follow You Follow Me	Genesis	#23
1973	Free Ride	Edgar Winter Group	#14
1976	Free Ride	Tavares	#52
1977	Give a Little Bit	Supertramp	#15
1974	Goin' Down Slow	Bobby Blue Bland	#69
1979	Good Times Roll	The Cars	#41
1976	Good Vibrations	Todd Rundgren	#34
1973	Goodbye Yellow Brick Road	Elton John	#2
1970	Green-Eyed Lady	Sugarloaf	#3
1977	Hard Luck Woman	Kiss	#15
1971	Have You Ever Seen the Rain	Creedence Clearwater Revival	#8
1979	Heart of Glass	Blondie	#1
1972	Heart of Gold	Neil Young	#1
1973	Here I Am (Come and Take Me)	Al Green	#10
1973	Higher Ground	Stevie Wonder	#4
1974	Honey, Honey	ABBA	#27
1972	Honky Cat	Elton John	#8
1979	Hot Number	Foxy	#21
1972	I Can See Clearly Now	Johnny Nash	#1
1976	I Can't Hear You More	Helen Reddy	#29
1975	I Wanna Dance Wit' Choo (Doo Dat Dance), Part 1	Disco Tex & His Sex-O-Lettes	#23
1975	I'm Not in Love	10cc	#2
1979	It's All I Can Do	The Cars	#41
1970	It's Only Make Believe	Glen Campbell	#10
1977	It's so Easy	Linda Ronstadt	#5
1973	Jambalaya (On the Bayou)	The Blue Ridge Rangers	#16
1973	Jesus Is Just Alright	The Doobie Brothers	#35
1974	Jolene	Dolly Parton	#60
1971	Joy to the World	Three Dog Night	#1
1974	Jungle Boogie	Kool & The Gang	#4
1978	Just What I Needed	The Cars	#27
1973	Kodachrome	Paul Simon	#2
1979	Lady	Little River Band	#10
1976	Let 'Em In	Paul McCartney & Wings	#3
1976	Let Your Love Flow	Bellamy Brothers	#1
1979	Let's Go	The Cars	#14

	THE NEXT 138 BEST SONGS OF THE 1970s (cont'd)		
1973	Long Train Runnin'	The Doobie Brothers	#8
1976	Love Hangover	Diana Ross	#1
1976	Love Hurts	Nazareth	#8
1976	Love Rollercoaster	Ohio Players	#1
1973	Love Train	O'Jays	#1
1975	Love Will Keep Us Together	The Captain & Tennille	#1
1975	Low Rider	War	#7
1971	Maggie May	Rod Stewart	#1
1970	Mama Told Me (Not to Come)	Three Dog Night	#1
1976	Mamma Mia	ABBA	#32
1979	Message in a Bottle	The Police	#74
1970	Montego Bay	Bobby Bloom	#8
1977	Moondance	Van Morrison	#92
1974	Most Likely You Go Your Way (And I'll Go Mine)	Bob Dylan/The Band	#66
1972	Mother and Child Reunion	Paul Simon	#4
1979	My Sharona	The Knack	#1
1975	Never Been Any Reason	Head East	#68
1977	Night Moves	Bob Seger	#4
1974	Nothing from Nothing	Billy Preston	#1
1976	Ob-La-Di, Ob-La-Da	The Beatles	#49
1976	Ode to Billie Joe	Bobbie Gentry	#54
1979	Old Time Rock & Roll	Bob Seger	#28
1979	One Way or Another	Blondie	#24
1976	Over My Head	Fleetwood Mac	#20
1979	Peter Piper	Frank Mills	#48
1973	Ramblin' Man	Allman Brothers Band	#2
1974	Rock and Roll, Hoochie Koo	Rick Derringer	#23
1972	Rocket Man	Elton John	#6
1979	Roxanne	Police	#32
1978	Running on Empty	Jackson Browne	#11
1973	Sail on Sailor	The Beach Boys	#79
1970	See Me, Feel Me	The Who	#12
1979	September	Earth, Wind & Fire	#8
1976	(Shake, Shake, Shake) Shake Your Booty	KC and The Sunshine Band	#1
1978	She's Always a Woman	Billy Joel	#17
1975	Sister Golden Hair	America	#1
1977	Solsbury Hill	Peter Gabriel	#68
1975	Someone Saved My Life Tonight	Elton John	#4
1975	SOS	ABBA	#15
1970	Spirit in the Sky	Norman Greenbaum	#3
1978	Stayin' Alive	Bee Gees	#1

	THE NEXT 138 BEST SONGS OF THE 1970s (cont'd)		
1974	Steppin' Out (Gonna Boogie Tonight)	Tony Orlando & Dawn	#7
1976	Still the One	Orleans	#5
1974	Sugar Baby Love	The Rubettes	#37
1974	Sundown	Gordon Lightfoot	#1
1974	Surfin' U.S.A.	The Beach Boys	#36
1971	Sweet City Woman	Stampeders	#8
1978	Sweet, Sweet Smile	Carpenters	#44
1971	Take Me Home, Country Roads	John Denver	#2
1979	Take the Long Way Home	Supertramp	#10
1975	That's the Way (I Like It)	KC and The Sunshine Band	#1
1972	That's What Love Will Make You Do	Little Milton	#59
1973	The Cover of "Rolling Stone"	Dr. Hook	#6
1979	The Gambler	Kenny Rogers	#16
1971	The Night They Drove Old Dixie Down	Joan Baez	#3
1974	The Streak	Ray Stevens	#1
1973	There It Is	Tyrone Davis	#32
1973	Top of the World	Carpenters	#1
1976	Turn the Beat Around	Vickie Sue Robinson	#10
1978	Turn to Stone	Electric Light Orchestra	#13
1978	Two Tickets to Paradise	Eddie Money	#22
1970	Up Around the Bend	Creedence Clearwater Revival	#4
1979	Video Killed the Radio Star	The Buggles	#40
1979	Voulez-Vous	ABBA	#80
1977	Walk This Way	Aerosmith	#10
1972	Way Back Home	Jr. Walker/The All Stars	#52
1977	We Just Disagree	Dave Mason	#12
1979	We've Got Tonite	Bob Seger	#13
1971	What Is Life	George Harrison	#10
1978	Wheel in the Sky	Journey	#57
1975	Who Loves You	Four Seasons	#3
1970	Whole Lotta Love	Led Zeppelin	#4
1973	Will It Go Round in Circles	Billy Preston	#1
1972	You Don't Mess Around with Jim	Jim Croce	#8
1978	You're the One That I Want	John Travolta & Olivia Newton-John	#1

THE WORST 40 SONGS OF THE 1970s

YEAR	SONG	ARTIST	HOT 100
1970	Cold Turkey	John Lennon	#30
1970	Ticket to Ride	Carpenters	#54
1970	Holy Man	Diane Kolby	#67
1970	Funky Man	Kool & The Gang	#87
1971	Don't Wanna Live Inside Myself	Bee Gees	#53
1971	You've Lost That Lovin' Feelin'	Roberta Flack & Donny Hathaway	#71
1971	Be My Baby	Cissy Houston	#92
1971	Stop! In the Name of Love	Margie Joseph	#96
1972	Troglodyte (Cave Man)	Jimmy Castor Bunch	#6
1972	Once You Understand	Think	#23
1972	Pretty as You Feel	Jefferson Airplane	#60
1972	Sing a Song/Make Your Own Kind of Music	Barbra Streisand	#94
1973	The Twelfth of Never	Donny Osmond	#8
1973	Living Together, Growing Together	The 5th Dimension	#32
1973	I Like You	Donovan	#66
1973	Please, Daddy	John Denver	#69
1973	Dueling Tubas	Martin Mull	#92
1974	(none)	(n/a)	(n/a)
1975	Lovin' You	Minnie Riperton	#1
1975	I Am Love (Parts I & II)	The Jackson 5	#15
1975	The Bertha Butt Boogie (Part 1)	Jimmy Castor Bunch	#16
1975	The Funky Gibbon	The Goodies	#79
1976	Disco Duck (Part 1)	Rick Dees	#1
1976	Hey Shirley (This Is Squirrely)	Shirley & Squirrely	#48
1976	Don't Touch Me There	The Tubes	#61
1977	Telephone Man	Meri Wilson	#18
1977	Dis-Gorilla (Part 1)	Rick Dees	#56
1977	Don't Turn the Light Out	Cliff Richard	#57
1977	Love Bug	Bumble Bee Unlimited	#92
1977	Discomania	The Lovers	#100
1978	Bloat on Featuring the Bloaters	Cheech & Chong	#41
1978	Wrap Your Arms Around Me	KC and The Sunshine Band	#48
1978	California	Debby Boone	#50
1978	#1 Dee Jay	Goody Goody	#82
1979	In the Navy	Village People	#3
1979	Here Comes the Night	The Beach Boys	#44

THE WORST 40 SONGS OF THE 1970s			
1979	One More Minute	Saint Tropez	#49
1979	Ready for the 80's	Village People	#52
1979	Love and Desire (Part 1)	Arpeggio	#70
1979	Animal House	Stephen Bishop	#73

NOTABLE SONGS

The songs listed here are interesting to me for one reason or another. Two bits of trivia wouldn't fit neatly into the list below, so I'll put them here. #1: Coven is interesting because they had three hits. Kind of. Each hit was a version, or a reissue of the same song: "One Tin Soldier (The Legend of Billy Jack)". #2: Trivia question: Which movie was so popular in 1977, that *four* different versions of its theme song made the Hot 100? The answer: "Rocky".

YEAR	SONG	ARTIST	HOT 100	NOTES
1970	My Sweet Lord	George Harrison	#1	Harrison was successfully sued for plagiarizing the 1963 Chiffons' hit, "He's So Fine" with this song.
1970	Make Me Smile	Chicago	#9	Has lengthy drum solo.
1970	A Song of Joy (Himno a la Elegria)	Miguel Ríos	#14	Spanish version of Beethoven's ninth symphony
1970	Rubber Duckie	Ernie (Jim Henson)	#16	Ernie, the muppet, had a hit.
1970	Gotta Hold on to This Feeling	Jr. Walker/The All Stars	#21	Starts with a 55 second saxophone solo. Also has four saxophone solos.
1970	Jennifer Tomkins	Street People	#36	Modulates repeatedly at the end
1970	Mongoose	Elephant's Memory	#50	Lyrics tell the story of a battle between a mongoose and a cobra.
1970	The Declaration	The 5th Dimension	#64	Lyrics are from the Declaration of Independence.
1970	Down in the Alley	Ronnie Hawkins	#75	Has lengthy harmonica, piano, and guitar solos
1971	Timothy	The Buoys	#17	Song about cannibalism
1971	Lowdown	Chicago	#35	Lengthy horn solos
1971	13 Questions	Seatrain	#49	Has lengthy electric violin solo
1972	Morning Has Broken	Cat Stevens	#6	Has 5 piano solos (They're all nearly identical)
1972	It's Going to Take Some Time	Carpenters	#12	Has a lengthy flute solo
1972	Looking for a Love	J. Geils Band	#39	Has middle section where multiple mini-solos are passed back and forth between harmonica, piano, organ, and guitar.
1973	Living in the Past	Jethro Tull	#11	Several lengthy flute solos
1974	Whatever Gets You Thru the Night	John Lennon	#1	Has four sax solos
1974	Life Is a Rock (But the Radio Rolled Me)	Reunion	#8	Mentions dozens of musicians, deejays, songs, etc.
1974	In the Bottle	Brother to Brother	#46	Song with most flute/sec.?
1974	Would You Lay with Me	Tanya Tucker	#46	Song has a round- very unusual in pop songs
1975	#9 Dream	John Lennon	#9	Lennon sings nonsense "words"
1975	From His Woman to You	Barbara Mason	#28	Answer song to Shirley Brown's "Woman to Woman"
1975	Hoppy, Gene and Me	Roy Rogers	#65	Rogers yodels at the end.
1975	Hang on Sloopy	Rick Derringer	#94	Has a steel drum solo section

	NOTABLE SONGS (cont'd)			
1976	Moonlight Feels Right	Starbuck	#3	Features lengthy marimba solo
1977	Year of the Cat	Al Stewart	#8	Features piano, guitar, and sax solo
1977	Dreamboat Annie	Heart	#42	The single version featured the intro to "Crazy on You" at beginning to lengthen the song.
1977	Man Smart, Woman Smarter	Robert Palmer	#63	Features steel drum solo
1977	C'est La Vie	Greg Lake	#91	Features lengthy accordion solo
1978	Fooling Yourself (The Angry Young Man)	Styx	#29	Song opens with 1:45 long intro.
1978	Rivers of Babylon	Boney M	#30	Pop hit with oldest lyrics? (From Psalm 137)
1978	In the Bush	Musique	#58	Was banned on many radio stations
1979	Tusk	Fleetwood Mac	#8	Recorded with USC marching band
1979	Rainbow Connection	Kermit (Jim Henson)	#25	Kermit the Frog had a hit.
1979	Video Killed the Radio Star	The Buggles	#40	Was first video ever shown on MTV
1979	Free Me from My Freedom/Tie Me to a Tree (Handcuff Me)	Bonnie Pointer	#58	Features banjo solo

QUOTE SOURCES

1 (n.d.). Retrieved from https://www.beegees-world.com/quotes.html

2 (n.d.). Retrieved from https://www.beegees-world.com/quotes.html

3 Daw, R. (2014, September 15). Beyonce Tributes Bee Gees Singer Robin Gibb. Retrieved from http://www.idolator.com/6513381/beyonce-tribute-bee-gees-robin-gibb?safari=1

4 (n.d.). Michael Jackson - Brett Ratner Interview (2004). Retrieved from https://prince.org/msg/8/178001

5 Samberg, J. (2013, February 4). Remembering Karen Carpenter, 30 Years Later. Retrieved from https://www.npr.org/2013/02/04/171080334/remembering-karen-carpenter-30-years-later

6 Rolling Stone. (2019, July 29). 100 Greatest Singers of All Time. Retrieved from https://www.rollingstone.com/music/music-lists/100-greatest-singers-of-all-time-147019/karen-carpenter-37100/

7 Rolling Stone. (2019, July 29). 100 Greatest Singers of All Time. Retrieved from https://www.rollingstone.com/music/music-lists/100-greatest-singers-of-all-time-147019/karen-carpenter-37100/

8 Schmidt, Randy (2010). Little Girl Blue: The Life Of Karen Carpenter. Chicago Review Press. ISBN 978-1-556-52976-4.

9 (n.d.). Lionel Richie. Retrieved from https://www.imdb.com/name/nm0005360/bio

10 Songfacts. (n.d.). Commodores Founder Thomas McClary : Songwriter Interviews. Retrieved from https://www.songfacts.com/blog/interviews/commodores-founder-thomas-mcclary

11 (2016, March 19). Commodores Member Revealed Long Standing Bitterness Toward Lionel Richie. Retrieved from https://www.iloveoldschoolmusic.com/commodores-member-revealed-long-standing-bitterness-toward-lionel-richie/

12 AllenCityTV. (2007, December 28). Exclusive Commodores Interview - June 2007 - Pt. 1 of 3. Retrieved from https://www.youtube.com/watch?v=htfHEZWDf8o

13 Bourne, J. (2013, November 29). John Denver Earthday Concert Tribute 2011 (Part 1). Retrieved from https://www.youtube.com/watch?v=Z_QIJ01l--4

14 Roberts, J. (2019, July 11). Chris Nole applauds masterful troubadour John Denver 20 years after his death. Retrieved from https://medium.com/@jeremylr/chris-nole-applauds-masterful-troubadour-john-denver-20-years-after-his-death-463d003fbdf3

15 https://www.telegraph.co.uk/culture/4707943/John-Denver-My-dark-night-of-the-soul.html

16 (2016, April 29). From Deutschendorf to Denver. Retrieved from https://www.goldminemag.com/articles/deutschendorf-denver

17 (2019, June 4). Neil Diamond. Retrieved from https://www.grammy.com/grammys/artists/neil-diamond

18 DJL. (2017, March 25). Neil Diamond Behind the Music 3 ND commercials and Cherry Cherry Video. Retrieved from https://www.youtube.com/watch?v=Klj573A8eTg

19 DJL. (2017, March 25). Neil Diamond Behind the Music 3 ND commercials and Cherry Cherry Video. Retrieved from https://www.youtube.com/watch?v=Klj573A8eTg

20 C, P. (2014, January 12). Kennedy Center Honours Neil Diamond Part 1. Retrieved from https://www.youtube.com/watch?v=gywKBKZcR7c

21 DaddySinister. (2011, January 31). 20/20 Michael Jackson Interview (1980). Retrieved from https://www.youtube.com/watch?v=O2hMPdexJRg

22 Sessions, C. E. (2012, August 8). Jermaine Jackson Interview From The 80's. Retrieved from https://www.youtube.com/watch?v=IdzjhY1UKVo

23 Burton, C. (2019, July 2). Inside the Jackson machine. Retrieved from https://www.gq-magazine.co.uk/article/jacksons-legacy-jackson-5

24 Msflower5552. (2012, August 20). Michael Jackson &The Jackson 5 Rock and Roll Hall of Fame 1997. Retrieved from https://www.youtube.com/watch?v=-2HgGwBUkkY

25 Ratican, K. (2014, July 2). "The great thing about rock and roll is that someone like me can be a star.". Retrieved from https://www.smoothradio.com/artists/elton-john/the-best-ever-quotes-from-elton-john/elton-john-rock-star/

26 Fussman, C. (2017, October 11). The Meaning of Life from a Musical Master of Words. Retrieved from https://www.esquire.com/entertainment/interviews/a11922/bernie-taupin-quotes-0112/

27 katar, tahir. (2016, September 19). ELTON JOHN HONOREE (COMPLETE) 27th KENNEDY CENTER HONORS, 2004 (135). Retrieved from https://www.youtube.com/watch?v=xxJnfd65epY

28 Ratican, K. (2014, July 2). "The great thing about rock and roll is that someone like me can be a star.". Retrieved from https://www.smoothradio.com/artists/elton-john/the-best-ever-quotes-from-elton-john/elton-john-rock-star/

29 Editors, R. D. (2016, April 16). 12 Magical Paul McCartney Quotes on Love, Optimism, and His Final Moments With George. Retrieved from https://www.rd.com/culture/paul-mccartney-quotes/

30 Wenner, J. S. (2018, June 25). Bob Dylan on Old America and 'Modern Times'. Retrieved from https://www.rollingstone.com/music/music-news/bob-dylan-on-old-america-and-modern-times-108284/

31 Cobas, C. (2012, November 8). PAUL McCARTNEY AT KENNEDY CENTER HONORS (Complete). Retrieved from https://www.youtube.com/watch?v=RL76v3qoEeI

32 Editors, R. D. (2016, April 16). 12 Magical Paul McCartney Quotes on Love, Optimism, and His Final Moments With George. Retrieved from https://www.rd.com/culture/paul-mccartney-quotes/

33 (n.d.). Linda Ronstadt. Retrieved from https://www.imdb.com/name/nm0740168/bio?ref_=nm_ql_1#quotes

34 Mattwardlawgmail-Com. (2014, April 11). The Full Text of Glenn Frey's Speech Inducting Linda Ronstadt into the Rock and Roll Hall of Fame. Retrieved from https://ultimateclassicrock.com/glenn-frey-linda-ronstadt-hall-of-fame-speech/

35 (n.d.). Linda Ronstadt. Retrieved from https://www.rockhall.com/inductees/linda-ronstadt

36 Linda Ronstadt. (n.d.). Retrieved September 30, 2019, from https://www.imdb.com/name/nm0740168/bio?ref_=nm_ql_1#quotes.

37 thewizboy. (2014, November 21). Diana Ross - Oprah Show 02-25-2011 (PART ONE). Retrieved from https://www.youtube.com/watch?v=kNW2x9i71Uc

38 Hamilton, J. (2018, June 25). Q&A: Diana Ross. Retrieved from https://www.rollingstone.com/music/music-news/qa-diana-ross-230900/

39 (2017, November 19). Diana Ross on longevity and life off the stage. Retrieved from https://www.latimes.com/entertainment/music/la-et-ms-diana-ross-interview-20171116-htmlstory.html

40 "Ross, D. (2019). Ross, Diana. Retrieved from https://www.encyclopedia.com/people/literature-and-arts/music-popular-and-jazz-biographies/diana-ross

41 MTV News Staff. (2012, May 18). Beyonce Says Goodbye To Donna Summer In Personal Note. Retrieved from http://www.mtv.com/news/2497990/beyonce-donna-summer-personal-note/

42 MTV News Staff. (2012, May 18). Beyonce Says Goodbye To Donna Summer In Personal Note. Retrieved from http://www.mtv.com/news/2497990/beyonce-donna-summer-personal-note/

43 Wikane, J. (2018, February 25). The Queen and Her Crayons: An Interview With Donna Summer. Retrieved from https://www.popmatters.com/the-queen-and-her-crayons-an-interview-with-donna-summer-2496152263.html

44 Macht, D. (2012, May 18). Stars Pay Tribute to Disco Queen Donna Summer. Retrieved from https://www.nbcconnecticut.com/entertainment/celebrity/Donna-Summer-Death-Celebrity-Reaction-151905345.html?amp=y

45 CNN. (2016, April 21). Prince Rogers Nelson's entire 1999 CNN interview (Larry King Live). Retrieved from https://www.youtube.com/watch?v=m8mg7CxAYUM

46 Reinhardt, D. (2017, October 13). STEVIE WONDER ""HONOREE"" - (COMPLETE) 22nd KENNEDY CENTER HONORS, 1999. Retrieved from https://www.youtube.com/watch?v=hHNfCn8LZro

47 screenocean. (2012, July 6). Stevie Wonder talks about visualizing instruments (Ear Say '84). Retrieved from https://www.youtube.com/watch?v=TVG0cEJCZm8&t=122s

48 (n.d.). Stevie Wonder on Keys of Life. Retrieved from https://blankonblank.org/interviews/stevie-wonder-on-keys-of-life-motown-singing-lyrics-racism-god-religion-detroit/

OTHER SOURCES

All 5,344 1970s hits were listened via YouTube, iTunes Streaming, and the author's personal music collection. All other information was gathered from the following sources:

"Record Reviews, Streaming Songs, Genres & Bands." *AllMusic*. N.p., n.d. Web. 13 Sept. 2019

"Movies, TV and Celebrities." IMDb.com, n.d. Web. 13 Sept. 2019

Whitburn, Joel. *Joel Whitburn's Top Pop Singles 1955-2002*. Menomonee Falls, Wisc.: Records Research, 2003. Print.

Whitburn, Joel. *Joel Whitburn's Pop Annual, 1955-2011*. Menomonee Falls, Wisc.: Records Research, 2012. Print.

Whitburn, Joel. *Joel Whitburn's Top Pop Singles, 1955-2015*. Menomonee Falls, Wisc.: Records Research, 2016. Print.